THE EVOLUTION OF
MEDIEVAL THOUGHT

The Evolution of Medieval Thought

David Knowles

Second Edition
Edited by D. E. Luscombe
and C. N. L. Brooke

Longman
London and New York

Longman Group UK Limited,
Longman House, Burnt Mill, Harlow,
Essex CM20 2JE, England
and Associated Companies throughout the world.

First Edition © Longman Group Limited 1962
Second Edition © Longman Group UK Limited 1988

First published 1962
Second edition 1988

British Library Cataloguing in Publication Data
Knowles, David
    The evolution of medieval thought. ——
    2nd ed.
    1. Philosophy, Medieval
    I. Title   II. Luscombe, D. E.
    III. Brooke, Christopher
    189   B721

ISBN 0-582-49426-5

Set in AM Comp-Set 10/12 Baskerville

Produced by Longman Group (FE) Limited
Printed in Hong Kong

Contents

Preface to the First Edition

This book is not an outline, still less a history, of medieval thought. It aims rather at showing some of the main currents of that thought and the channels through which they flowed. Many in the past have confined themselves to presenting the systems of the great scholastics or to tracing the intellectual life of the Middle Ages from its beginnings in the West or even from its origins in Christian antiquity; this book is an endeavour to present medieval or scholastic philosophy as a direct continuation of Greek thought, coloured though it may be by its surroundings, and impoverished by many losses, but also fertilized and enriched by Christian teaching.

All who have approached this subject are aware of their debt, not only to a host of scholars of France, Belgium and Germany, but to the great masters who have dominated the field in the past eighty years, eminent among whom are Franz Ehrle, Clemens Baeumker, Martin Grabmann and, above all, Etienne Gilson, who, in a scholar's life of more than fifty years, has illuminated by his touch almost every part of the age between St Augustine and Duns Scotus. The scope of the present book neither demands nor allows of reference to the multitude of specialists whose work has been used. A reader who is expert in the subject will see without difficulty when I am following a well-known authority, when I am using or criticizing a number of detached studies, and when in a few places the arguments and conclusions rest upon a re-assessment of the original sources. There are, however, three works to which all who study medieval philosophy owe an immense and particular debt: Grabmann's unfinished history of the scholastic method, B. Geyer's monumental survey of medieval thought, and Gilson's history of medieval philosophy in its various editions and forms.

In conclusion, I must thank my friends, Professor W. K. C. Guthrie, Master of Downing College, for reading the first two chapters, and Professor A. H. Armstrong, for reading the second and third. In each case I am indebted for many corrections and suggestions, but remain entirely responsible for such imperfections as remain.

DAVID KNOWLES

Preface to the Second Edition

David Knowles' *The Evolution of Medieval Thought* has given
sterling service as an introduction to the study of medieval thought
since it was first published in 1962. Dom David Knowles was a great
master of the history of medieval English monasteries and religious
orders; but he also made a seminal contribution in English circles to
the development of the study of medieval thought through his
teaching in the university of Cambridge. His book is the fruit of
lectures given especially in the late 1950s and early 1960s. It provides a
judicious and graceful introduction that draws upon the work of
earlier Continental scholars. In deciding to re-issue the book we have
of course recognized that the study of medieval thought has continued
to develop since 1962: subsequent impressions of the original volume
took account of some new publications down to the year 1972. Since
then there have appeared other surveys in English, including *The
Cambridge History of Later Medieval Philosophy ...*, ed. N.
Kretzmann and others (1982), as well as shorter introductions by
Michael Haren, *Medieval Thought* (1985), and by John Marenbon,
Early Medieval Philosophy (480-1150) (1983). European scholars too
have continued to make advances and to attempt syntheses. Among
them is F. van Steenberghen whose work is used and discussed by
Knowles on many pages and who has since published new works of
substantial scope. We may also mention L. M. de Rijk who has
recently capped his many original contributions to the history of
medieval logic with his book on *La Philosophie au Moyen Age*
(French translation from the Dutch by P. Swiggers, Leiden, 1985).

Our reason for republishing David Knowles' book is twofold. First,
it is still uniquely readable and helpful for the student who wishes to
have sketched for him the interests and the outlooks of great thinkers

from Plato to Ockham. Knowles' biographical portraits are often very fine; furthermore, his summaries of currents of thought and of important debates are appealing and helpful to both the historians and the general students of the Middle Ages who may not be, indeed who usually are not, trained philosophers. Secondly, we have judged that with suitable revision and updating *The Evolution of Medieval Thought* can continue to serve in the years to come as a reliable introduction. We have not sought to rewrite the text or the notes save where errors have been noticed or minor infelicities have occurred; in all essentials the book is as Knowles wrote it. But we have provided in an Introduction that follows this Preface a brief commentary and guide to the more recent study of medieval thought, making mention of historical revisions as they concern each of the parts of this book. We have also replaced the 'Suggestions for Further Reading'; these suggestions were not especially generous or evenly made and we have tried to amplify them as well as bring them up to date, without however seeking to be exhaustive. The serious student can use the references we give as a guide to a much wider range of texts and studies. We are grateful indeed to the publishers for the opportunity to give this book a new span of life.

Our work on it has been a modest tribute of thanks and affection to a great scholar, our teacher and our friend.

CHRISTOPHER BROOKE
DAVID LUSCOMBE
May 1987

Introduction to the Second Edition

Dom David Knowles was a great monastic historian; he was also a conservative Catholic theologian, to whom the thirteenth-century scholastics, and especially St Thomas Aquinas, represented the summit of medieval achievement. Much that followed was decline and confusion, the breakdown of the medieval synthesis. He had taken a classics degree at Cambridge and taught classics at Downside, and was widely read in Greek philosophy. From the early Middle Ages, in his eyes, there was indeed a process of growth and development, powerfully influenced by large infusions of Greek philosophy, especially in the twelfth and thirteenth centuries, which led to what he termed *The Evolution of Medieval Thought*. This helps to explain the form of the book: especially the large space allotted to the classical heritage, and the rapidity with which the book concludes after the death of Thomas.

Since 1962 there has been much new study in every region of this book, and in particular a marked shift of interest away from the study of medieval philosophy in its role as the handmaid or 'ancilla' of Christian theology. There has been much deeper study of the late scholastics, and especially William of Ockham and John Wyclif. Dom David lived to see the revival of Ockham, and clearly understood his interest and importance (see pp. 290-7); but he deplored the separation of theology from philosophy.

In this introduction we briefly survey the effects of modern study, and of changing perspectives, chapter by chapter, to help preserve this masterly introduction as a working tool of study. We refer on occasions to publications of which fuller details are given in the relevant section of the *Suggestions for Further Reading* on pp. 311-23.

PART ONE: THE LEGACY OF THE ANCIENT WORLD

Chapters 1–2: Plato and Aristotle; The Later Platonists and Plotinus

To Dom David medieval Christendom was a society of peoples deriving their discipline of thought from ancient Greece and Rome (pp. 3–4). Medieval thought was indeed deeply impregnated by Greek methods and notions, and almost all the leading ideas of medieval philosophers in the twelfth and thirteenth centuries were derived from Plato, Aristotle and a few other Greeks. Elements of continuity between ancient and medieval thought can certainly be found, but other historians have balanced this emphasis on the legacy of antiquity by pointing to original features in medieval philosophy, to discontinuities with antiquity.

Modern studies, which have transformed the approach to Plato and Aristotle and sketched anew the history of later Greek and early Christian thought, are noted in *'Suggestions for Further Reading'* (pp. 312–13). In particular, Knowles' Chapter 2 is covered by Parts I to IV of the much fuller *The Cambridge History of Later Greek and Early Medieval Philosophy*, edited by A. H. Armstrong (1967): here P. Merlan follows the history of Greek thought from Plato to Plotinus, H. Chadwick traces the beginnings of Christian thought, A. H. Armstrong studies Plotinus and A. C. Lloyd considers the later Neoplatonists, including Iamblichus (died *c.* 326). Above all, Plotinus was re-assessed by A. H. Armstrong, who shared with Dom David the wish to revive his fame as a great Platonist; but Knowles underestimated one great difference: Plotinus ignored Plato's politics and his concern for public affairs.

Chapters 3–5: St Augustine; Boethius and Dionysius; Education in the Ancient World

See pp. 313–14, and especially the recent literature on Augustine and Boethius.

Chapter 3. In this chapter Knowles shows how Augustine drew upon and adapted the legacy of antiquity, especially that of Plato and Plotinus, and how he provided subsequent medieval thinkers with a specifically Christian philosophy which became a system commonly known as Augustinianism. On page 34 Marius Victorinus is mentioned; Victorinus was like Augustine an African and a convert to Christianity and he provided a link between Greek philosophy and the Latin West in the fourth century. R. A. Markus (1967) has recently clarified this link: Augustine read Victorinus' translations of Neoplatonic works although he formulated independent teachings on God and the soul.[1] Knowles passes rapidly by other features of Augustine's teaching including his teaching on grace, evil and ethics and his vision of the two cities.

Chapter 4. One recurrent emphasis throughout this book is on the breadth and depth and persistence of the influence of the mystical thought of Dionysius or pseudo-Denis throughout the Middle Ages. Who the pseudo-Denis was remains unknown and quite a long list of possible identifications now exists. But there is general agreement that he wrote in the early sixth century and in a Syrian milieu. S. Gersh, *From Iamblichus to Eriugena. An Investigation of the Prehistory and Evolution of the Pseudo-Dionysian Tradition* (Leiden, 1978), has now examined the role of Dionysius' writings to the time of Erigena. Further general studies of their continuing role in later centuries would clarify a difficult but fundamental aspect of medieval thought. Much of the preliminary research on manuscripts, translators and commentators has been done, most brilliantly of all by H. F. Dondaine, *Le Corpus Dionysien de l'Université de Paris au XIIIe siècle* (Rome, 1953).

PART TWO: THE RENAISSANCE OF THE ELEVENTH AND TWELFTH CENTURIES

Chapter 6: The Rebirth of the Schools

Here Dom David briefly sketched the renaissance of thought and studies in the age of Charlemagne, and especially the development of the traditional study of the seven liberal arts and Carolingian policy towards the provision of education. He gave too little space to the encyclopedic works on which Carolingian educators drew for their knowledge of ancient education. Cassiodorus (*c.* 490–*c.* 583), through his *Institutions* and Isidore of Seville (560–636), in his *Etymologies.* made a particular contribution to the body of medieval learning fashioned out of classical sources. Knowles justly acclaimed the ideals set forth by the Carolingian reformers. J. Marenbon (1981) and other recent scholars have revealed how extensively the Carolingians

---

[1]References given by author and date may be found in full in the relevant section of *Suggestions for Further Reading*, pp. 311 ff.

developed the philosophical study of theology by glossing the works of Boethius and others. Of John the Scot Eriugena, or Erigena, Dom David wrote that he was the only original thinker between Boethius and Anselm (pp. 70-1) but that his thought, which is difficult and unorthodox, need not detain the reader. There are at least two reasons for varying this judgement: first, that John the Scot laid the foundations for the medieval study of Dionysius on which Knowles himself dwells at length in Chapter 4; second, that although John lacked direct imitators in later times, he had a very great influence on philosophy and on the tradition of glossing ancient texts in his own generation and the succeeding one, as Marenbon (1981) has now revealed.

Chapter 7: The Awakening of Western Europe

In the context of the renewal of study and teaching that gathered momentum in the eleventh and twelfth centuries, Dom David sketched the development of schools and the definition of 'scholasticism'.

On pages 79-84 Dom David defined, briefly but perceptively, the characteristics of medieval scholastic thought. On page 79 he pointed out that there are no good reasons for applying the term 'scholastic' to the content, as opposed to the method, of medieval philosophy – or of any other branch of medieval studies such as medicine or theology. The respect shown by medieval scholars for authority is correctly set in context on pp. 82-3. It is the body of teaching thought to be true that is held to be authoritative; in such a case the writer, be he Plato or Aristotle or another, becomes an authority. Medieval thinkers cited their authorities continually, not for ornament, but because they provided the evidence which led to judgement and 'sentence'. In discussing the Christian 'loading' of medieval philosophy, and the question whether philosophical enquiry was deflected by the primacy of belief in such Christian doctrines as creation out of nothing, the oneness of God, providence and personal immortality, Dom David fairly drew attention to the importance of social background. Christian theology provided an orientation to medieval Christian philosophers yet many medieval philosophers vigorously championed the autonomy of philosophy.

In recent years there has been much reappraisal of the social background, in particular of the importance of schools and their distinguishing features. Older ideas that certain schools became the recognized centres of particular studies – Paris for theology, Bologna for law and so on – have been modified in the light of further evidence of dispersed activities often pursued outside the schools in noble or episcopal households or the like. See S. Kuttner, 'The Revival of Jurisprudence' in R. L. Benson and G. Constable, *Renaissance and Renewal in the Twelfth Century* (1982) and P. Classen, *Studium und Gesellschaft im Mittelalter* (Stuttgart, 1983).

Knowles himself came to realize that the claims of twelfth-century Chartres to be a centre of humanistic philosophy had been badly shaken by historical criticism (see under Ch. 11). In twelfth-century England, to give other examples, the presumed link between a school in York and the teaching there of Master Vacarius has been dissolved (p. 78) and Northampton probably counted more than Oxford; for reading on this see the suggestions for further reading under *'The New Universities'* (pp. 318-19), especially Southern (1976) and Southern in Catto (1984).

Chapter 8: The Revival of Dialectic

The achievements of Berengar, Lanfranc and Anselm form the core of this chapter. As Knowles observed of the conflicts between dialecticians and traditional theologians, Lanfranc does not deserve to be treated as an obscurantist. His achievement was considerable as a teacher as well as an archbishop, and Gibson (1978) has consolidated the picture admirably. Important studies of the eucharistic question (on which Lanfranc engaged Berengar) are those of de Montclos (1971) and Macy (1984). Dom David concentrated also on Anselm and on his famous argument for the existence of God, which has been very variously interpreted before and since 1962; he did not discuss another striking demonstration in a matter of faith, that found in Anselm's *Cur Deus Homo* – why God became man – in which Anselm reasoned that the Incarnation was the *necessary* sequel to the Fall. On pages 88-9 Knowles considers Peter Damian and Manegold of Lautenbach as the foremost critics of the developing use of dialectic in the study of faith. More recent scholars have been inclined to diminish the reservations about philosophy to be found in Damian, and in particular to point out that his *De divina omnipotentia* does not maintain that God can realize contradictory things. Manegold's sceptical attitude to the human intellect should not conceal the fact that dialectic was a well-established part of the curriculum of learning.

On pages 85-6 he refers to Fulbert of Chartres and to his views of the relations of faith and reason. The source he cited is now thought to be by another Fulbert, not the bishop: see *The Letters and Poems of Fulbert of Chartres*, ed. and trans. F. Behrends (Oxford Medieval Texts, 1976), pp. lxii–lxiii; Behrends, 'Berengar of Tours, Fulbert of Chartres, and "Fulbertus exiguus" ', *Revue Bénédictine*, 85 (1975), 333 ff.

Chapters 9–10: The Question of Universals; Peter Abelard

Dom David correctly observed that the question of universals was not the only important issue arising from the revival of dialectic, but that none the less the debates on universals still merited special notice. On page 101 he briefly mentioned other subjects, such as the influence of the grammarians and the development of the logic of language, of *Sprachlogik*. More recently scholars have attached even greater importance to these other elements. The *Institutiones grammaticae* by Priscian (*fl.* A.D. 491–518), the time-honoured textbook for the study of the first of the liberal arts, attracted the attention of philosophers on account of the problems of language which it presented. Thus the study of the origins and significance of names, or the analysis of the verb 'to be', rests on the study of grammar. The grammatical masters of the eleventh and twelfth centuries developed the systematic study of syntax as well as grammatical speculation: and their originality was skilfully revealed by R. W. Hunt (1943–50, repr. 1980). In the eleventh century there can be detected signs of what might even be called a break away from Boethius and Aristotle as guides to the study of logic. Garland's *Dialectica* and Anselm of Bec's *De grammatico* show the development of logic as the study of argument which is expressed in language, a science of speech as well as of disputation. Abelard's own pre-occupation with the relationship between philosophy and language, together with the far-reaching implications of his extensive explorations, has been studied by Jolivet (1969).

The details of Abelard's life, and the chronology of his writings, have been the subject of extensive and sometimes heated debate. On the chronology of his writings, see Mews (1985). The main evidence for his life – the *Historia Calamitatum* or the *History of My Troubles* – has been subjected to severe criticism, most substantially by Benton in *Pierre Abélard, Pierre le Vénérable* (1975) and Silvestre (1985), who have argued that the whole correspondence between Héloise and Abelard is spurious; many other views have been held. There is a brief summary of much recent scholarship by Luscombe in Thomas and others (1980), and of the arguments in favour of the substantial authenticity of the correspondence in Luscombe (1979); Dronke (1976) has shown that the main lines of the story of Abelard and Héloise are confirmed by other early evidence. Although the controversies are still in full swing, many scholars would still find Knowles' account of Abelard's life acceptable in its main features. We have adjusted one sentence on page 108, because we believe that Abelard's marriage to Héloise was not canonically legal, as Knowles (following Gilson) had supposed. See on this C. Brooke, *Medieval Church and Society* (London, 1971), pp. 74–5n.

Characteristically, Dom David said of Abelard: 'The dogmas of the faith are not for him wells of infinite depth, the reflection in words of luminous supernatural truth. Rather, they are so many propositions or facts thrown, so to say, to the Christian philosopher, upon which he may exercise his ingenuity ...' (p. 113). This is true in so far as Abelard attempted to express the content of faith in ways that were both dialectically sound and intelligible to the critic and the non-believer. He did, however, have an inexhaustible concern with 'the interpretation of past ages', and tirelessly collected texts from the Judaeo-Christian and the pagan Graeco-Roman tradition which he sought to reconcile with Christian faith so far as he could. To do this he applied techniques of interpretation that were more than dialectical, for he believed that the words of philosophers as well as of saints did in fact often bear a deep and divine weight of meaning, which could be perceived once the veil or skein of language (*involucrum, integumentum*) has been removed from them and once their deeper meaning is grasped. Tullio Gregory (in *Peter Abelard*, ed. E. M. Buytaert, 1974) explains how Abelard so interprets Plato; the task of explaining how Abelard similarly explores the depths of Scripture remains a challenge, although a beginning has been made by E. Kearney (in *Petrus Abaelardus*, ed. R. Thomas, 1980).

Chapter 11: The School of Chartres and John of Salisbury

Sir Richard Southern's celebrated paper casting doubt on the existence of the 'School' of Chartres as Clerval and Poole and many others, including Knowles, had conceived it, was published in 1970, between the first edition of the book (1962) and the latest reprint; so Dom David was able himself to furnish the addendum on page 128. No one doubts that there was an episcopal school at Chartres; in what measure it was a major centre for the scholars previously thought to have been united in it has been debated by Southern and his critics (see p. 317). Some, indeed, of the common intellectual interests once discerned among the group, of men such as Adelard of Bath and Gilbert of Poitiers, appear to us to show only superficial similarities. In 1979 Southern examined the question whether the concept of a 'School of Chartres' characterized by Platonist convictions now 'helps or hinders our understanding of what was going on in the first half of the twelfth century'. The alleged 'pantheism of Chartres' was certainly over-emphasized by Knowles (pp. 123–4); recent scholars have countered this with broader investigations of science and poetry in this period. William of Conches, prominent among the supposed adherents of the 'School of Chartres' and of its Platonic tendencies, was as much a student of Priscian as of Plato. The contours of twelfth-century philosophy have now been redrawn by Peter Dronke who has, in presenting and editing *A History of Twelfth-Century Western Philosophy* (Cambridge, 1988), given less place to 'Schools' and more to 'new approaches' in science, grammar and logic. But in any account of innovation in the twelfth century the scholars discussed in this chapter retain their high importance; and the role of John of Salisbury himself as an erudite witness and observer of these figures remains secure (see especially Wilks, 1984).

Chapter 12: The School of St Victor and St Bernard

Here Dom David's summary stands scrutiny, though scholarship has not stood still: see page 318.

PART THREE: THE NEW UNIVERSITIES – THE REDISCOVERY OF ARISTOTLE

Chapters 13–14: The Origins of the Universities; Studies, Degrees and Text-books

These chapters contain a helpful account of the institutional and pedagogic changes that resulted in the birth of universities; but modern study is rapidly revising numerous details. On pages 140–8 Dom David surveys Bologna as the centre of studies in Roman and canon law. Bologna was indeed the main centre, but other centres also flourished; and the rediscovery of the *Digest*, on which Knowles rightly laid emphasis, linking it to the movement everywhere in progress to return to the authentic learning of the past, may have occurred in the great abbey library of Monte Cassino. As for Gratian, his designation as a monk of the order of Camaldoli now seems to be a legend: see Kuttner (1982) and J. T. Noonan, 'Gratian slept here . . .', *Traditio*, 35 (1979), pp. 145–72. The account on pages 151–2 of the origins of the university of Oxford, and of Vacarius' teaching there, has been overtaken by the chapters of Sir Richard Southern and others in Catto (1984).

Chapters 15–16: The Rediscovery of Aristotle; Arabian and Jewish Philosophy

It is now clear that no sort of 'school of translation' (p. 170) was established at Toledo by its archbishop, Raymund (1125–52). The translators out of Arabic worked widely in Spain; and Toledo only began to be one of the centres under Raymund's successor, John (1152–66): see d'Alverny (1982). We have corrected some of the dates originally given for translations into Latin of some of Aristotle's works in the light of Dod (1982).

Chapter 17: The Problems of the Soul and the Process of Cognition

The divergent interpretations put by Aristotle's commentators on his teaching on the philosophy of mind were explained by Knowles as the product of the excitement caused in the west in the thirteenth century after the translations, by William of Moerbeke and others, of certain key Arabic texts had been received. His account reflects the work of Gilson and others, and especially Gilson's influential article, 'Les sources gréco-arabes de l'augustinisme avicennisant', in the *Archives d'histoire doctrinale et littéraire du moyen âge*, 4 (1929–30), pp. 5–149. Gilson returned to the topic in his 'Avicenne en Occident au Moyen Age', *Archives*, 36 (1969), pp. 89–121. Impressive advances in knowledge have recently been made in Belgium, especially by G. Verbeke. In 1957 Verbeke introduced and edited Themistius (see below, p. 194): *Themistius, Commentaire sur le traité de l'âme d'Aristote. Traduction de Guillaume de Moerbeke* (Louvain & Paris, 1957). In 1966 Verbeke did the same for John Philoponus: *Jean Philopon. Commentaire sur le De Anima d'Aristote. Traduction de Guillaume de Moerbeke* (Louvain & Paris). In 1968–72 Verbeke published introductions to Avicenna's psychological teaching in the first two volumes of S. van Riet (ed.), *Avicenna Latinus: Liber de Anima seu Sextus de Naturalibus* (Louvain & Leiden): 1972, pp. 1*–90*; 1968, pp. 1*–73*.

PART FOUR: THE ACHIEVEMENT OF THE THIRTEENTH CENTURY

Chapter 18: The Philosophical Revolution of the Thirteenth Century

On pages 201-3 Dom David presents the basic ingredients of the philosophical 'revolution' of the thirteenth century, and summarizes the view of it taken by van Steenberghen; and this is the view on which Knowles based his account and with which he wrestles on later pages. But he concentrated mainly – though not exclusively – on the infiltration of Aristotle's philosophy into theology, and tended to neglect the immense efforts also made to assimilate Aristotle's philosophy with the current philosophies. Aristotle's thought on the physical universe, which included the theory of the four elements and the theory of celestial spheres, was deeply influential in the interpretation of physical, biological and psychological phenomena. Since 1962, furthermore, van Steenberghen himself has continued to publish and to advance his interpretations with a monumental series of studies: see van Steenberghen (1966, 1970, 1974, 1977, 1980).

Chapters 19-22: The Franciscan School at Paris; Albert the Great; St Thomas Aquinas; Siger of Brabant and the Faculty of Arts

Bonaventure, Albert and above all Aquinas receive glowing praise from Dom David; and no one would reasonably deny their towering stature. Allowance must be made for the fact that the great mendicant doctors wrote in a crowded milieu: they were surrounded by numerous other masters who were themselves formulating opinions and marshalling the materials of thought on which scholars might freely draw. Dom David's characteristic portraits of Bonaventure, Albert and Aquinas are sympathetic, revealing and poignant. But his accounts of Siger of Brabant and Boethius of Dacia should be read with caution. He was inclined to support Gilson in his antipathy to Siger and other leading members of the Faculty of Arts at Paris at the height of the troubles which led to the ecclesiastical condemnations of 1270 and 1277; and here he selected ground which has proved to be far from firm. Knowles tried to check and qualify the views of van Steenberghen, who has, however, continued to advance and to elaborate his position, most notably in his new study of Siger (1977). Dom David recognized (p. 245) that a definitive assessment of Siger and of his circle of colleagues and followers would depend on further historical discoveries, especially since this is 'a matter where the climate of opinion needs to be analysed'. That is to say, the motives and doctrines of Siger cannot be fairly evaluated until his writings and those of other contemporary artists are better known. Some editions of texts which were previously unknown or inadequately appreciated have recently appeared. In 1966 J. Vennebusch edited 'Die Questiones metaphysice tres des Siger von Brabant' in *Archiv für Geschichte der Philosophie*, 48, pp. 163–89. In 1972 A. Marlasca edited *Les Quaestiones super Librum de Causis de Siger de Brabant* (Philosophes médiévaux, 12, Louvain & Paris), and B. Bazán the *Quaestiones in Tertium de Anima, De Anima Intellectiva, De Aeternitate Mundi* (Philosophes médiévaux, 13, Louvain & Paris). In 1974 Bazán published *Siger de Brabant, Ecrits de Logique, de Morale et de Physique* (Philosophes médiévaux, 14, Louvain & Paris). To call the teaching of the artists 'obnoxious' (p. 247) seems one-sided, for Knowles based the word on the condemnation of Siger's critics, not on his own writings – but the passage is ambiguous and he may have meant only to give the theologians' view. Yet his sympathy is clear.

Meanwhile in Denmark, the homeland of Boethius of Dacia, the late Jan Pinborg started the publication of the *Opera omnia* of Boethius in 1969 in the series called Corpus Philosophorum Danicorum Medii Aevi; and in 1964 G. Sajó had published the *editio altera* of *Boetii de Dacia tractatus de aeternitate mundi* (Quellen und Studien zur Geschichte der Philosophie, 4, Berlin). One can no longer say, as Knowles did (p. 248), that Boethius' particular field was ethics; he ranged more widely than this in the arts. As for the condemnation of 219 propositions in 1277, this has been subjected to thorough and searching analysis by R. Hissette (1977) who has shown, *inter alia*, that only one of them – and not several (as Knowles implied, pp. 249, 270 – has any certain connection with Aquinas's teaching.

None the less, even when account has been taken of welcome advances in scholarship, Dom David rendered a genuine service by bringing to life the great academic controversies of the thirteenth century, and by skilfully evaluating them in the light of the knowledge available to him. He did not belittle Siger: he acknowledged that he enjoyed a high reputation among his contemporaries (pp. 249–50), as Berengar had done two centuries earlier. On one fundamental point Knowles made a positive contribution to scholarly debate. The issue was whether Siger and his associates were Averroists or pure Aristotelians; or more precisely, whether they were committed to Averroës' interpretations of Aristotle or objectively trying to establish Aristotle's own teaching without thereby challenging Christian revelation. One difficulty is that there were some artists who – irrespective of the consequences for Christian doctrine – concluded that the correct interpretation of some of Aristotle's doctrines was the interpretation given by Averroës. Knowles defended the view that in the thirteenth century Averroës did have some influence on the radical or out-and-out Aristotelians (pp. 250-1). He did not yield to all van Steenberghen's arguments against the existence of a Latin Averroist movement before the fourteenth century. He suggested too that Siger might have moderated his teachings under pressure (p. 270). More recently, Professor E. P. Mahoney has written of Siger's 'abandonment' of Averroës and of the 'heavy blow' to Averroism of the condemnation of 1277. (*The Cambridge History of Later Medieval Philosophy* ..., 1982, pp. 602-22).

Dom David gave preference to religious thinkers and showed little tolerance of those in the thirteenth century who did not mingle religion with their philosophy. In this he represents an influential tradition of historical writing upon the scholastics. Other historians, especially those writing in the later twentieth century, have wished to study medieval philosophers for the sake of their contributions to semantics, linguistic theory and formal logic, to epistemology, psychology, ethics and natural philosophy, without feeling the need to evaluate the religious or other quality of the works they study. Such scholars are less likely than Knowles to be concerned with the problems implicitly posed by a Siger or a Boethius of Dacia to thirteenth-century Christianity.

Chapter 23: England in the Thirteenth Century

Dom David's comments on the special character of England's part in the evolution of medieval thought, especially the interest shown by English scholars in mathematics and the natural sciences, would certainly be endorsed by later historians. However, we do not today think it helpful to link this scientific bent with the Oxford schools and university, nor to compare Oxford with the school at Chartres, since Oxford had no particular scientific inclination in the thirteenth century and the school at Chartres played little part in the development of medieval science. The nature and early progress of Oxford have been greatly illuminated by *The History of the University of Oxford*, i (1984), ed. J. Catto.

The career and writings of Robert Grosseteste are richly

documented, yet full of problems; many of these have been clarified by Sir Richard Southern in his *Robert Grosseteste* (1986), but much remains to be elucidated. We have revised the details of his career with Southern's help; and it is now clear that Knowles' original judgement (which we have revised on page 255) that Grosseteste was a theologian 'of the older school, of Peter Comestor and Stephen Langton', will not stand. He was *sui generis*, a man of vast learning, yet eclectic in his use of sources, ignoring his immediate predecessors. His learning, and especially the infusion of mathematical and scientific learning, and some knowledge of Greek, into his biblical commentaries and theological treatises, make him a phenomenon even in the world of the thirteenth-century scholastics. More eccentric, and much less influential, Roger Bacon remains, as Dom David portrayed him, a many-sided as well as a strange genius. He had no certain connection with Oxford before 1257: his early career is wholly unclear. But to the picture of his philosophical and scientific interests developed by Knowles should be added his efforts to revive an interest in the knowledge of the Greek and Hebrew languages with a view to confounding the creed of Islam, his deep interest in the Bible as the foremost text for the study of the Christian faith, and his fascination with the work of Greek theologians.

PART FIVE: THE BREAKDOWN OF THE MEDIEVAL SYNTHESIS

Chapters 24–28: The Aftermath of Aristotle; Henry of Ghent and Duns Scotus; The Breakdown of the Synthesis; William of Ockham; The Harvest of Nominalism

In 1274 both St Bonaventure and St Thomas Aquinas died, and with them passed the era of achievement which Dom David had characterized, following a well-worn tradition, as the synthesis of Christian and Greek thought. He endeavoured to present scholastic philosophy as a direct continuation of Greek thought, fertilized and enriched by Christian teaching. Thus he was describing the *evolution* of medieval thought as he understood it. This led Dom David to portray the subsequent history of medieval thought as a Christian retreat from rationality, as the breakdown of former achievement.

This approach raises at least two problems of perspective. First, even in the thirteenth century, the constant infusion of Greek and Arabic philosophy confuses the pattern of continuity, so that the conflicts and ecclesiastical condemnations which followed can be seen either as tensions arising between Christian understanding and reviving paganism, or simply as the fruit of different modes of interpreting Aristotle. Secondly, in the fourteenth century, as most historians now think, we move into a world not just of extravagance and dissolution but of great and varied new achievement. Dom David acknowledged the fertility of fourteenth-century thought and culture: 'We may indeed well consider the fourteenth century more prolific than the thirteenth in those *idées-forces* that were to determine the course of European intellectual life' (p. 304) – by which he meant the extreme statements of papal and anti-papal positions, sharpened discussions of predestination, and scientific advance. He properly included accounts of Duns Scotus and William of Ockham, as well as of English scientists and natural philosophers; but he was unsympathetic to 'mere logic', found nominalism to be corrosive of theology, and took little interest in linguistic theory and the philosophy of science. He would have been surprised to witness the recent discussions of the development of logic – which show that already in the twelfth and thirteenth centuries successive attempts were made to create new logic and new science: L. M. de Rijk has established the existence of a modern logic in the twelfth century; and others have studied the *modistae* who appear first in late thirteenth-century Paris and who developed new interests in the theory of logic and grammar.

William of Ockham is central to an understanding of fourteenth-century thought, and the historical context of his originality, the parentage of his doctrines and the character of their effects continue to be vigorously explored by scholars. Of Ockham's flight from papal Avignon to imperial Munich it must be said that not all would now represent these events as a switch to support of the empire against the papacy. Rather Ockham found protection and asylum in Bavaria and from there wrote about the nature and limits of papal power. As regards Ockham's philosophy and theology, Knowles was unsympathetic to what he and many others saw as Ockham's use, following Duns Scotus, of the conception of God's absolute power (*potentia absoluta*) as a means of destroying earlier and particularly Thomist conceptions of divine order and of natural law (p. 295). Other scholars disagree and deny that Ockham's God is an arbitrary tyrant who renders the working of the universe unpredictable; God has absolute power but in choosing to realize only certain possibilities imposes a plan upon creation which is not necessary but contingent.

Knowles was unsympathetic also to nominalist criticism of earlier metaphysics, not least because it removed the basis of a demonstrable theology. Other scholars would, however, reject his use of the term 'agnosticism' (p. 297) to describe the aftermath of Ockham. As physics became released from metaphysics, and as the laws of nature were explored through the study of this world, rational and scientific investigation and experimentation were able to develop – and God's freedom was revalued when the older framework of necessary laws of nature had been loosened by criticism. The struggles in the fourteenth century between the *via antiqua* of realism and the *via moderna* of nominalism, together with all their implications in logic, epistemology, metaphysics, ethics, theology and politics, have cast long shadows reaching down to the present – and disagreements can be expected to continue into the future. Much excellent recent enquiry has tended to support sympathies and interpretations very different from those shown in this book. We have in mind the work of, among many scholars, M. Clagett, W. J. Courtenay, J. E. Murdoch and H. O. Oberman. Yet it is still not possible to recommend a single available general history of the 'evolution' of medieval thought after Duns Scotus and William of Ockham. Attempts at a synthesis are, however, particularly needed as a great deal of the knowledge now available on such topics as the mathematics and physics of the Oxford Calculators (or Mertonians) or on individual thinkers including (among many others) Jean Buridan and Walter Burley would greatly benefit from being made more widely known.

We ourselves would draw attention to one fruitful example of recent advances in scholarship. It is now known (*pace* p. 300) that Ockhamism was not as unified or entrenched a force in the mid-fourteenth century, at least in England, as was previously supposed. Certainly Ockham's teachings had a stimulating effect, especially among the Mertonians, but even Robert Holcot (p. 300) was not a thorough-going Ockhamist and a more conservative atmosphere emerged in Oxford in the 1360s and 1370s.

One of the central figures of the realist revival was John Wyclif, whose reputation as a philosopher has enjoyed a remarkable renewal. So far from being the extravagant and extreme realist he has sometimes been thought, a group of philosophers with Anthony Kenny – who can count Wyclif as one of his most famous predecessors as Master of Balliol – at their centre have shown him to be a moderate realist and a more constructive philosopher than had once been thought; but he remains obscure and difficult on many points. In 1961 J. A. Robson showed (*Wyclif and the Oxford Schools*) that there was a clear link between Wyclif's metaphysics and his eucharistic theology; and a similar link has been discerned between Wyclif's realist doctrines and his belief in the unity and indissolubility of scripture, and its literal truth. Dom David had supposed that the growing tendency in the fourteenth century to dispense with tradition and to appeal to scripture was part of the 'harvest of nominalism', along with the tendency to dispense with natural theology. But in Wyclif's case the opposite seems to be true: there is a natural link between realist philosophy and his approach to scripture.

A discussion has developed, however, whether the 'heretical' ideas of Wyclif's last years owed more to deduction from his realism or to the evangelical fervour with which he studied the scriptures (M. Keen in A. Kenny, ed., *Wyclif in his Times*, Oxford, 1986, Ch. 1). What is clear is that one of the largest gaps in Dom David's final chapters is the absence of any extended study of the history of the Bible. The study of the Bible was always in principle of equal importance to the study of the *Sentences* of Peter Lombard in the late medieval schools of theology: and it is now clear that the development of the view that divine revelation was contained in the letter of scripture was a fundamental fact in the history of medieval thought between the twelfth and the fourteenth centuries. It was a complex development, and is by no means to be equated with the growth of religious dissent or theological scepticism – and the vernacular Bibles promulgated by Wyclif's disciples were so enormously popular that it is likely that many of their owners were not Lollards. C. Lindberg has listed 230 manuscripts of part or whole of the Wycliffite bibles (*Neophilologica*, xlii (1970), 333–47); and Anne Hudson points out that 'the translation is ... entirely uncontroversial, entirely lacking in any Wycliffite slant or polemical twisting' (*Wyclif in his Times*, p. 94). There is much still to learn about the study of the Bible in the late Middle Ages in both orthodox and unorthodox settings; meanwhile Beryl Smalley's final version of her *The Study of the Bible in the Middle Ages* (3rd edn, Oxford, 1983) remains a secure guide, broadly based.

PART ONE
The Legacy of the Ancient World

CHAPTER ONE
Plato and Aristotle

Philosophy has been defined as the study of ultimate reality and of the general causes and principles of things, with a particular reference to the human being, and to the principles and ends of human conduct. More briefly, we may prefer to consider it as a criticism and elucidation of assumptions and ways of thought that are the common property of mankind. However we define or regard it, there will be general agreement that, for men of what may still be called the Mediterranean tradition of civilization, philosophy as we know it took its rise in ancient Greece, and rose swiftly to maturity in Asia Minor, Magna Graecia, and, finally, in Athens. Christianity, in its origins and pre-history, had little kinship with Greece, but what we call Christendom, for more than a thousand years from the conversion of the emperor Constantine, was almost exclusively a society of peoples deriving their intellectual discipline and the habits of reasoning directly or indirectly from the Greco-Roman culture of the ancient world. It would consequently be scarcely an exaggeration to say that the philosophy of Christendom in those centuries is so deeply impregnated with the methods and ideas of Greek thought, and with the doctrines of non-Christian and more particularly of pre-Christian philosophers, as to be in a very real sense a direct extension or prolongation of ancient philosophy. This is above all true of the central portion of the so-called medieval period of European history, upon which in this book we shall be concentrating our attention. Indeed, if we have in mind only the twelfth and thirteenth centuries, it is possible to say that almost all the leading ideas of medieval philosophy, with the partial exception of that branch of it later known as natural theology, were identical with, or were directly derived from, ideas put into currency at Athens between 450 and 300 B.C. by a handful of Greek thinkers, among whom two, Plato and Aristotle, stand supreme.

The Greek genius was many-sided, and no other small racial group in Western history has ever produced so many monuments and masterpieces of thought, literature and art in so brief a space of time as the Greeks, but there would be general agreement that a characteristic note of the Greek genius, which distinguishes the Greek mind from, let us say, the Roman or the Anglo-Saxon mind, is its tendency and ability to intellectualize and to rationalize every object that it touches; to see reality in terms of reason and order; to analyse, to criticize, to clarify and to define. It is therefore natural that the Greek genius should have shone most brightly in the realms of mathematics and philosophy. But by no calculation of likelihood could it have been reckoned that within the brief space of fifty years there should have emerged, one immediately after the other, two thinkers of the supreme eminence of Plato and Aristotle.

These two great men, of whom the second was both pupil and critic of the first, have been considered ever since their day as the leaders of two schools, and even of two contrasted approaches to the chief problems, of thought. Gilbert's meditative sentry noted with amused interest that each of his fellow-citizens of either sex was born with what traditional scholastics might have called a *ratio seminalis,* or inborn tendency, to Liberalism or Conservatism. There is still more truth in Coleridge's dictum that each of us is from birth a Platonist or an Aristotelian. Already in the ancient world, and, as we shall see, later, in the medieval world, numerous attempts were made to produce a harmony or a synthesis of their systems, and contemporaries and modern writers alike have castigated these attempts as futile, and compared them to the endeavour in everyday life to mix water and oil. The characteristic elements of the two may be juxtaposed; they cannot be fused. To many, Plato, with his exquisite style, perhaps the most flexible and melodious vehicle of thought the world has ever known – Plato, with his unforgettable picture of Socrates, with his deep moral earnestness and lofty idealism, with his unshakable faith in the beautiful and in the good, with his vision of the godlike soul and its immortal destiny, with his soaring flight from what is temporal and visible to what is unseen and eternal – to many Plato will always seem to mirror so faithfully all the nobler intuitions of the human mind that his supremacy will remain unassailable and even unchallenged. Yet to others the majestic fabric of Aristotle's thought, massive even when shorn of the vast substructure of biology and physics – Aristotle, with his cool and limpid sanity, with his knowledge, which never becomes cynical, of the common man, with his inspired common sense and the sudden vistas that he opens upon the steep-down gulfs of metaphysics – Aristotle, with his insistence upon the value of observation and action in the visible world, with his unwavering assertion that our powers and faculties can of their nature attain to truth and reality each in its own sphere and measure, with his unrivalled precision of terminology and his sureness of touch in analysis and combination – to many Aristotle will seem to have reached the limits of the human mind's achievement here below. That immortal rivalry, overt or unperceived, will vex the greatest minds throughout the Middle Ages.

The differences between the two, alike of temperament, tastes, treatment and topics treated are indeed very great. Plato has become to all subsequent generations the source and exemplar for all those who would find the ultimate reality, to which all appearance can be reduced, in thought, and who regard the universe presented to our senses and all that has 'material' shape as an image or reflection only, while Aristotle is the philosopher of common experience, who in the last resort aims only at expressing accurately and in set terms what is the normal unreflective impression of all men. Seen from another angle, Plato is the idealist moulding this life and its institutions upon the model of a city not made with hands 'yonder in the heavens', and leading the individual up a ladder of perfection to another life in which his highest powers will be enlarged and find their true object, while Aristotle the realist, with his feet firm upon the earth in a Greek city-state, a man among men, lays down the lines of a fruitful and happy life on earth. Finally, Plato is one of the most religious of thinkers. Many of his most eloquent passages deal with the pursuit of virtue and with the soul's destiny of suffering or enlightenment, and in more than one passage he outlines what might seem to be a mystical approach to the problems of knowledge and action. Life for him is a strife of good and evil, and he would have agreed, as a philosopher, that the man who gained the world and lost his soul had made no bargain. Aristotle, on the other hand, has little religion in the modern sense of the term. The soul is no more than the form of the body, and probably has no individual life when separated from it. God is little more than a metaphysical postulate, with no personal knowledge or care of men. Aristotle's *Ethics*, so many would say, makes clear by its title a moderation of aim and effort that contrasts with Plato's all-but-Christian struggle for virtue and love.

All this, stripped of its rhetorical colour, has in it much of truth, and it is also true that by no merely mechanical, ingenious, logical manœuvring can a single coherent system be built out of an amalgamation of Platonic and Aristotelian elements. On certain

5

crucial points of metaphysics and epistemology the opposition between the two is irreducible.

Yet the contrast must not be exaggerated. When the two systems are compared with those of almost all other philosophers, ancient and modern, the resemblances between the two seem greater than their differences. Thus both are the opponents of materialism and scepticism; for both a real knowledge of a real universe is possible, and for both the act of cognition is a spiritual process, the highest activity of man. For both the universe has a design and a purpose, for both the good is equated with the real, with the true and with the beautiful, and the good life is the goal of all rightly ordered human endeavour. For both the human soul differs in kind and in excellence from any other living being of which we have knowledge; it does not owe its existence to any material agency and the principle of its highest activity, at least, is deathless. Finally, in contrast to many, if not most, great philosophers of the medieval and modern worlds both are, as philosophers, keenly interested in the social and political life of their times, and assume as a frame of reference the characteristic political unit of contemporary Greece, the small city-state.

Indeed, though a complete concordance or synthesis of the two systems at the same 'power' or level, so to say, is manifestly impossible, the sequel was to prove that important elements from both might be used, at certain points or at different levels, in systems wider and more inclusive than either. This may be seen very clearly where it is least expected. Plotinus, if anyone, desired and believed himself to be a Platonist, and in many ways he did indeed extend or produce the thought of Plato in a truly authentic fashion. Yet there is much of Aristotle in Plotinus, and it is the Aristotelian element that supplies the sinewy, elastic network that binds the Plotinian universe into a single whole. Thus the Aristotelian doctrines of matter and form, of potency and act, are used most effectively throughout, and the Aristotelian epistemology is applied to the cognition of the mind while still tied to the material world. At the other end of the scale of thought St Thomas Aquinas, if any other, is an Aristotelian, but what helps to make his system something new and more comprehensive than Aristotle's is his use of Platonic and Neoplatonic elements. It is true that these are chiefly (though not exclusively) to be found in the parts of his work that are concerned with speculative theology, but they are not themselves part of the revealed truth; they are rational explanations or elucidations of it, as the use made of the Platonic Ideas by later Platonists, who transformed them into exemplars of created things in the 'mind' of God.

It is no part of our purpose to give even the briefest outline of Plato's system of thought. In view of what has to be said later, however, a few words upon two or three of his most influential and characteristic doctrines will not be out of place. When Plato was a young man, the atmosphere in all circles of discussion and debate, at Athens in particular, was one of intellectual and ethical scepticism. Plato was therefore driven, as a philosopher, to decide what, if any, abiding reality existed behind the unceasing flux and often deceitful appearance of the world of visible things, as he also was constrained to explain, in the realm of ethics, what abiding reality lay behind all the many actions and motives that were or could be described as good or just. His answer was the celebrated doctrine of Ideas or Forms, which asserted that the individuals and their qualities in the visible world were only appearances, reflections of or approximations to the real exemplar or Form (one had almost said Thought) in the realm of reality, which Form was comprehensible only by a perfected intelligence. In other words: 'besides pluralities of phenomena, transient, mutable, imperfect, which become and are objects of opinion, there are unities, eternal, immutable, perfect, which really exist, and are objects of knowledge'.[1] This doctrine, in its essential lines, Plato maintained to the end of his life against arguments which others, and he himself, brought against it, but he never formulated clearly and finally his answers to three most important questions, viz., to what things or classes of things were there Forms to correspond; what was the relationship of the Form to the individual things perceived by the senses; and what was the relationship of the Forms to the Idea of Good that occupied the highest place in Plato's hierarchy of being. To the first question he returned different answers at different moments of his life. Thus in the *Republic,* while seeming to admit ideal counterparts of every object and quality, he devoted particular attention to the Forms of abstract qualities and made of the Idea of Good the monarch and in some sense the source and divine cause of the world of Forms. Later, when his attention was being given more to metaphysics and to physics, the Forms that received most frequent mention were those of mathematical figures and symbols, which seem at times to be considered as the exemplars and constituents of the perceptible world. Moreover, Plato never, in the matter of the Forms, made clear the distinction (if any) between Forms of the visible world and Forms of the æsthetic and moral perceptions of the mind and soul. As for the relationship of

[1] Henry Jackson in *Companion to Greek Studies*, ed. L. Whibley (Cambridge, 1916), p. 202.

individuals to the Forms, he speaks now of the thing sharing, reflecting, or embodying the Forms, and now of it as striving after or approximating to, the Form; the former explanation is clearly more applicable to material things, the latter to all forms of volition and exertion. As to the relationship of the Forms among themselves, no answer is given save for the isolated exaltation of the Form of Good in a single passage of the *Republic*,[2] and an inconclusive discussion of the 'overlapping' or 'interpenetration' of Forms in the *Sophist*, but in practice the Form is in some of the later dialogues handled very much as if it were a subsistent, metaphysical counterpart to the intellectual concept, while elsewhere the only Forms mentioned are those of mathematics, to which all reality conforms. Indeed it would seem that Plato never clearly drew the line of demarcation between the logical, epistemological and metaphysical implications of the Form-theory, while on the other hand he failed to make clear the distinction between extra-mental reality and intra-mental processes. Such, in brief, is the Platonic doctrine of Forms or Ideas, but this summary can give no impression of the depths and riches of Plato's thought and in particular takes no account of another and a very important aspect in which an emotional, one had almost said a mystical, value is found in the striving of the human soul towards an attainment of the perfection seen in the Form, such as that of Beauty. This is the Platonic Eros, which is an essential and characteristic factor governing all mental and ethical activity, and of which an Aristotelian echo can be heard in the motive of love which the Philosopher attributes to the whole universe in relation to God.[3]

Aristotle, as is well known, after a youthful period of discipleship, abandoned many of the cardinal doctrines of Plato, and in particular the theory of Forms. His principal argument, indeed, that the Form must be either individual or universal; that if individual, it would itself need a Form; and if universal, could not be present in any conceivable sense in the individual, has never been adequately answered, though the more we spiritualize the Form as Thought, the more nearly does the difficulty disappear. This and other obscurities in Plato's system have given endless scope for the labours of commentators and later philosophers, both in ancient and in modern times. It is not likely that agreement will ever be reached, and few have been found willing to follow Plato in all his attempts to formulate his doctrine, but even the most casual reader of his dialogues, and in

[2] *Republic* 509 B ff.
[3] See the essay on the Platonic Eros in F. M. Cornford, *The Unwritten Philosophy*, ed. W. K. C. Guthrie (Cambridge, 1950), pp. 68–80.

particular of the *Republic,* can grasp and to a certain degree feel intellectual sympathy with the basic contention which Plato maintained with such eloquence and tenacity; that the sensible and 'material' universe is in some way the expression or extension of invisible mind or spirit, and that man, by striving towards an ideal of moral and æsthetic perfection, is in some way entering into harmony with the spirit of goodness and beauty that gives reality to whatever exists and dominates its every activity.

In Plato's early presentation of the Forms he was concerned with them simply as the real, unchanging counterpart to their shifting corruptible reflections in the world of sense. In his later dialogues, and particularly in the *Timaeus,* he passed beyond them to an account, in part physical, in part theological, of the whole universe. Here again there are obscurities and inconsistencies, and the reader's quest is rendered still more confusing by the presence in the dialogue of the most elaborate of all Plato's myths, in which the 'divine' Artificer forms the material world, using as his exemplar the world of Forms. Even when he is not using the language of myth Plato seems to hold that a 'divine' Mind or Soul is the ultimate ruler of the universe, while the heavenly bodies and the earth itself are informed in some way by soul. In this matter the ever-present difficulties of interpretation that beset the reader of Plato's dialogues as a whole are increased by the further difficulty, experienced by all nurtured in the Hebraic or Christian tradition, of grasping the Hellenic conception of the divine. The God of the Old and New Testaments is not only essentially personal, but the conception of His unity, omnipotence and omniscience, of His immanence and transcendence, of His possessing, or rather of His having within His being, all created perfections to an eminent degree, is so much a part of our religious thought that it is very hard for us to grasp the conception of a partial and limited divinity. Nor is the difficulty lessened by Plato's intense warmth of religious feeling, both ethical and mystical, which would seem to us possible only in one who held the existence of a personal, all-loving God. In fact, so far as his philosophical thought is concerned, Plato would seem to have avoided precision or clarity as to the nature of God, the eternal Living Being. He was more concerned to show that Mind or Soul was the ultimate reality, and, though there is much in his language and speculation that anticipates or adumbrates the elaborate theological systems of later Platonists, the Master's own teaching may perhaps be best formulated in the statement that 'what we call mind, and what we call matter, can both ... be expressed in terms of the thought of one universal intelligence[4]'. Indeed, Plato's latest presentation of the 'material' universe is that of a universe of thought 'economized', so to say, to human capacity in terms of space and mathematical abstractions such as number.

Yet if Plato, in one department of his system, seems to eliminate 'matter' from consideration as an evil, he remains throughout as a moralist conscious of the struggle between higher and lower elements within the human soul. He remains also convinced of the soul's immortality, of its existence, that is, both before and after its passage through this mortal life. To presenting that conviction he devotes not only some of his most eloquent writing, but also some of his most profound thinking. Here, indeed, he approaches at times very nearly to the outlook on life and on human destiny and endeavour of the Hebrew psalmist and the Christian ascetic, and it is not surprising that his arguments for the soul's immortality should have become classical among Christian apologists and that he himself should have been considered by some of the early Fathers as a Christian *avant le mot*, or even as one who had learnt part of his theology from the Old Testament.

Indeed, Plato is a thinker of such breadth and depth that he can be seen as having sown the seeds of many of the most influential ideas of later centuries. He is the father of all those who have held that Soul or Spirit or Mind is the only reality, of those who regard all movements and activity as ultimately intellectual, of those who find the true life of the human spirit in an upward striving towards the divine. In his doctrine of the divine Mind he seemed to some to adumbrate the Christian doctrine of the Logos or Word of God, and in his account of the part played by the Forms in the Creation of the world he seems to hint at the Neoplatonic teaching, later Christianized by St Augustine, of the forms or ideas as exemplary in the 'mind of God'. On the other hand, by his own explanation of the universe (possibly owing something to Eastern religious thought) in the terms of the deification of the world and of the heavenly bodies, he pointed the way to the hierarchy of emanations and descents of being from the One to the Many that formed part of so many later systems. In more than one of his dialogues he outlines the ascent of the mind and soul through the levels of being up to God which became the mystic's ascent of Neoplatonism and Dionysius, and in a few places, where he insists upon the pure rationality of mind or soul, he supplies a hint for another doctrine, which was to find fortune in the Middle Ages,

[4]Jackson in *Companion to Greek Studies*, p. 205.

that of the highest or deepest part of the soul which remains untouched by evil.

Aristotle, at least in his mature thought, was confessedly a reagent against Platonism. He is one of the earliest, as he is one of the most illustrious, instances of that dialectic of human tastes and opinions which takes place in all speculative and æsthetic pursuits, but would seem to occur with a more rapid rhythm in philosophy than in any other field. Whereas Plato had found the objects of true science in the 'beyond' of a supra-sensible, intellectual world, for Aristotle the individual, perceptible thing was fully real, and the whole process of cognition took place within the ambit of mundane experience. Objects outside the mind impinged upon the senses, and from the sense-impression, after a process of sorting and cataloguing, the light of reason enabled the mind to extract the essence, that which made the thing what it was; this essence formed the basis of all scientific knowledge, and by this process the external thing became an inmate of the mind, not as it existed with bulk and qualities, but according to the mode and manner of an intellectual comprehension. As for the perceptible object itself, whereas for Plato it was the space-conditioned reflection of its unseen constitutive form or idea, for Aristotle the metaphysical analysis of being took effect within the visible thing or substance and nowhere else.

Substance, in fact, is the key word in Aristotle's metaphysic, and what is an Aristotelian term of art and new coinage must not be overlaid in our minds by modern physical or colloquial associations. A substance is the individual thing regarding which assertions can be made, but which cannot itself be asserted of a subject. Such a definition immediately demands elucidation in face of the problem which had driven Plato to formulate his doctrine of forms: the necessity, that is, of explaining the apparent multiplicity and mutability of things. This explanation Aristotle found in his complementary doctrines of matter and form, potentiality and actuality, of which the former pair represent the static and the latter the dynamic aspects of the analysis of substance.

All being, then, that can be perceived by the senses and adequately known by the mind can be analysed into matter and form. Matter is the unknowable substratum carrying the qualities of a substance, and surviving all, even substantial, change; in all 'material' or composite things it is the constitutive element of individuality. Form, or essence, is the universal, cognoscible element which specifies the individual and can be abstracted by the mind. If things are regarded not as being but as becoming or changing, then matter is the potential element, susceptible of a multiplicity of forms in succession, whereas form is the actuality; the relationship of matter and form, potentiality and actuality, therefore, extends over the whole range of being from prime or pure matter, which cannot be perceived and which has no independent existence, to pure form which is the last and rarest being to come within grasp of the mind at the other end of the scale; as for the other pair, the actual and the potential, they are bound together by the striving towards actuality of all that is potential; though an individual is in potency before it is in act, the actual is prior both logically and chronologically to the potential, for it exists as the goal and aim of the potency before the process of actualization begins.

To Aristotle therefore the whole cosmos is seen on every analysis as an ordered hierarchy of being from the 'pure' matter to the 'pure' form, from unity to multiplicity and again back to unity, and, within the ambit of Nature, from the inorganic and inanimate, through the vegetable and animal kingdoms, to the highest species, mankind.

Aristotle, like Plato, recognized the unique and supreme character of the human reason and soul among all the other beings of the world, but his mature definition of the soul and his conception of its nature differs greatly from that of Plato.[5] While for Plato the soul is, almost as it is in Christian teaching, at once a richly endowed, autonomous entity, and the theatre of striving and contest and achievement, to Aristotle it is, in the last analysis, a metaphysical abstraction, the form or perfective element of the body. Moreover, since soul and body make up a single individual human being, and as the soul is the form of the living body, it cannot be considered as separable or as able to exist apart from the body. Yet in spite of this the highest part, at least, of the soul in Aristotle's opinion, does not derive from the potentiality of matter, like the souls of animals, but from 'outside', and this highest part is not subject to corruption, but he does not make it clear, and would seem not greatly to have cared, whether it lives on individually or whether it is absorbed as a drop of water into a larger soul.

God is for Aristotle at once more essential to the universe as its crown and mainspring, and less significant to the individual, than he is for Plato. He is at once the summit of the scale of being, pure form, uncaused, and the cause of all movement, development and change within the cosmos. It is he who, as first unmoved mover, gives energy and change, but as his own being is the only fit object for his contemplation he has no knowledge of, or care for, the individual,

[5] For a fuller discussion of Aristotle's theory of the soul, see below Chapter 17, pp. 188 ff.

and the whole machinery of the world is set and kept in motion by the love and desire that all being, consciously or unconsciously, has for God.

For Aristotle as for Plato the good life is the supreme aim for man, and, like Plato, he finds the supreme good in happiness, and while there is in the *Ethics* none of the passion and urgency of some of Plato's most moving pleading, and though the virtuous man is primarily a good 'member of society' – one had almost said 'of a club' – yet Aristotle has a strict hierarchy of virtues and recognizes the danger of unruly desires and man's proneness to evil. At the summit, too, he is at one with Plato though, so to say, the charge is at a lower voltage. The highest and final activity for man is the contemplation of truth. But whereas with Plato it is the ardour, or at least the brilliance, of a contemplation that hopes for a fuller, purer light in the beyond, with Aristotle it is the calm gaze at knowledge attained, and at the causes and essences of things.

Like Plato, Aristotle attributed life and soul to the visible heavenly bodies, at least in the form of some directive intelligence, inferior to the Prime Mover, and, as is well known, he presented in considerable elaboration an astronomical and planetary system in which the heavenly bodies, composed of a fifth element unknown to this world, were carried round in concentric spheres, and were sharply distinguished in composition from the sublunary region which was composed of the same elements – earth, air, fire and water – as is our world. At the centre of the whole system was the earth. But we are not concerned here with a detailed view of Aristotle's physics.

As will have been realized, Aristotle's whole system, physical and metaphysical, is a herculean endeavour to explain what we perceive as existing outside ourselves. The two last words, indeed, beg a fundamental question of philosophy, but Aristotle assumes, what indeed all men assume for most of their lives, and most men assume without question for the whole of their lives, that the universe presented to our senses is real, that we ourselves are real, if minute, parts of a great whole, and that we have faculties, limited but adequate, enabling us to perceive and comprehend the reality outside ourselves. Aristotle's philosophy is, in consequence, the philosophy of common-sense; it expresses in technical language what most men had always thought before they began to philosophize. Whereas, when we read Plato, we seem to be 'voyaging in strange seas of thought', whence, through the darkness and fog we see, or think we see, the outlines of a whole new continent of glowing reality, when we read Aristotle and break through the crust of unfamiliar terminology, we attain suddenly to 'dazzling glimpses of the obvious'. Aristotle is, besides, pre-eminently the philosopher of order and of purpose. Every being within the universe strives, and is fitted, to attain its end, which is also its perfection. There is therefore no illusion, no futility, no random form or faculty, just as there is, on the other hand, no veil for the magician or mystic to pierce, no city in the heavens, no other world where this world's wrongs are righted. Though the use of the term Nature, in its senses of a regular law or order, and of an originating and moving power, is found occasionally before Aristotle, it is he who gave these senses the currency and the weight of meaning that they have ever since possessed, and which they possess today. It was he who, first and most characteristically, used as coordinates the terms God and Nature, as in his well-known axiom 'God and Nature make nothing that does not fulfil a purpose',[6] and it is perhaps the last fragment of Aristotle's great legacy to scientific thought that Nature has remained, in many sciences at least, as a quasi-personified, quasi-deified power imagined, if not conceived, as a power external to the beings that compose her 'kingdom'.

[6]*De caelo*, 1.4.6.

CHAPTER TWO
The Later Platonists and Plotinus

It may at first surprise those who follow the course of later Greek thought that the two great systems of Plato and Aristotle had comparatively little influence on the generations immediately following their inception, and that it was not till after several centuries that the development and partial fusion of the two took place. Nothing, however, is more striking in the history of thought than the immediate transience, and the final permanence, of genial philosophical ideas. It is as if the human mind, stimulated and exercised in a genial period of prolific excellence, returns always to criticize what it has been given to feed upon, but that when, after a time of slumber, a new age begins, new minds seize once again upon one or more of the limited patterns of ideas in which men can express their comprehension of the universe. In this, thought differs from science, which is ever advancing to a fuller grasp, and from art, where the old vision is expressed in a new idiom.

Be that as it may, the great creative period of Greek philosophy continued for half-a-century after the death of Aristotle, and within that half-century were born the two new systems of thought which continued, till the end of the Western Empire, to rival the Academy and the Lyceum. These were Stoicism, founded at Athens by the Cypriot Zeno (335–263), and Epicureanism, which took its name from its founder Epicurus, an Athenian by race (341–270). Though both these systems, and especially the former, had a long and lasting influence, first in the Hellenistic world, and then in the Roman Empire, they did little to fashion the shape of Christian and medieval thought, save for the Stoic element in the Roman legacy of law and political thought, and the Stoic vein of moral exhortation.

The reasons for this are to be found in the character of these two philosophies. Neither school produced speculative or metaphysical doctrines of any importance; each rested upon a dogmatic cosmology and psychology which were entirely materialistic; what attracted followers of both was the ethical teaching which aimed, in very different ways, at an escape from the ills of life and of society, and in the case of the Stoics had often a religious warmth. Their materialism was as repellent to the surviving Platonists as it was to Christian thinkers, while on the other hand the extremely theocentric and dynamic Christian moral teaching, with its twofold assumption of human depravity and divine aid, had no common ground with the self-sufficient and aristocratic endurance of the Stoic or with the escapist quietism of the Epicurean. It was only when the Christian church had to apply its principles to politics and law and the amelioration of society that many of the Stoic formulae seemed capable of adaptation.

While Stoicism and Epicureanism commanded wide attention among the educated classes of Greece, Asia Minor, Alexandria and Rome, and Stoicism passed through many stages of development, the doctrines of Plato and Aristotle had fallen almost out of sight. The Academy at Athens, indeed, remained as a school with a series of masters who maintained a kind of apostolic succession from Plato, but within a century of Plato's death the teachers had become interested chiefly in the critical and polemical discussion of rival schools of thought; while wholly successful in exposing the metaphysical weakness of the Stoics and Epicureans, they themselves adopted a position of intellectual scepticism, or rather of philosophical 'agnosticism'. This became characteristic of the early or Old Academy. There was even less continuity of doctrine in the peripatetic school, but the corpus of Aristotelian writing remained, and although the metaphysical parts were commonly neglected, the scientific treatises became part of the heritage of the educated world, while the logic was adopted as a technique or tool-box by all those engaged in higher education.

A revival of true Platonic thought took place shortly before A.D. 100 and issued in a movement known as Middle Platonism. Metaphysics once more became a principal interest, and a specifically religious or at least deistic interest, in sympathy with the needs of the age, helped to direct attention to the religious element that had always been present in Plato's thought. A feature of this period was a readiness to admit into the philosophical synthesis that was being constructed elements from other schools of thought, particularly from Aristotle and the Neopythagoreans, but although many of the thinkers who encouraged this have been called eclectics, they did not select favourite doctrines from this or that system which might prove incompatible with Platonism; rather, they took genial and fruitful ideas from outside to complete or enrich the system of Plato. They also amplified or prolonged suggestions or hints that Plato had thrown out in the form of myth or *obiter dictum,* and then perhaps had dropped, whether from accident or design. As a result of this, a series of notable, but not remarkably original, thinkers converted the rich but often undigested and unsystematic mass of Platonic thought into something that resembled a coherent system and one which was, at least in its theological aspects, more susceptible of a monotheistic interpretation.

The most important of these developments was the establishment of a supreme principle (sometimes called 'god') at the head of the hierarchy of being, transcending all inferior degrees. This gave an essential position to an entity that Plato had only mentioned transiently and without emphasis. The place that he had attributed in one and only one important passage to the Form of Good was now given to the Supreme Mind, with the great advantage that this latter, transcending all other forms of being, could be regarded as their author, and not merely as *primus inter pares.* When this step had been taken, the Forms could become the 'thoughts' of the Supreme Mind which was also, under Neopythagorean influence, identified with the One existing above all multiplicity. Yet another step was made; the Supreme Mind, the One, was identified with Aristotle's remote transcendent Mind that kept the universe of being in motion. The object of the philosophical life now became to purify oneself by reflection and contemplation of truth for an existence without the body and for the vision of the Supreme Being.

All this, to one looking back upon it with the main outlines of Christian teaching in his mind, represents a very great advance towards what was to become orthodox natural theology. It had, however, some important limitations. The first was that the supreme being, although transcendent, was yet still within the hierarchy of universal being. Direct contact, therefore, and control of the universe by him, either as immanent in all being or as external to it, was impossible. Consequently a series of one or more intermediaries was inserted to gear down, so to say, the Supreme Mind to the level of human intelligence and the visible world. Here again the hints and myths of Plato, and especially the great myth of the *Timaeus,* and suggestions in Aristotle's cosmology, were given a firm philosophical base, and a Second Mind and a World-Soul were interposed between

17

the Supreme Mind and the human soul. This indeed was the achievement of the eminent thinkers of the Middle Academy in their academic teaching; it will readily be understood that in a world where there was no general doctrine of monotheism there was opportunity at the infra-philosophical level for the insertion of gods and daemons and astrological influences at all stages of the hierarchy of being.

In the countries of the Hellenic world bordering the eastern Mediterranean, and in the Roman Empire which was gradually absorbing them into itself, there was no single dominant system of philosophy, and no thinker of the first rank had arisen since the end of the fourth century before Christ. While Stoicism and Epicureanism had been carried westwards, in the Greek-speaking countries Platonism was still current in the cities where higher education was given, and in particular at Alexandria. Among the Jews of the dispersion, as among the early Christians, there was in general an aversion from philosophy, and St Paul could contrast the lofty-sounding but empty debates of the wise with the simplicity and truth of the gospel. When, as at Alexandria in the days of Philo and later in the days of Origen, Jewish or Christian theologians or apologists made use of philosophy, it was to Plato and the later Platonists that they turned to find, as Christian thinkers have found again and again, the lofty idealism and otherworldliness that seemed a divinely ordained preparation for the gospel. The great Fathers of the eastern Church, some of whom had had a philosophical training at Athens, made extensive use of Platonic modes of thought and technical terms. In the history of Western thought, however, the decisive influence was that of Plotinus (A.D. 205–270).

Of all the great thinkers of the West Plotinus has in modern times been the most neglected, and if justice has been tardily done to him in recent years by scholars in France, Italy, Germany and England he still remains, for the general reader and even for the majority of classicists and historians, an unfamiliar if not positively distasteful figure.

The reasons for this eclipse are many. First, there is the educational tradition of the past five centuries. When western Europe turned to a study of the ancient world, an arbitrary line was drawn, mainly by those interested in language and literature, at a point after which neither the writings, nor the history, nor the thought of the Greco-Roman world was studied. For Greek literature and thought, this line was drawn several centuries before Plotinus, and for Latin literature at the end of the age of Tacitus and Juvenal. Even in more recent times, when a classical education in all countries became a study of the whole of ancient civilization, this study ended, where Gibbon had marked the beginning of the decline of the Roman Empire, with the end of the age of the Antonines (A.D. 180). When modern historical studies, in their turn, began to move backwards into the middle ages, they too ceased to look beyond the sixth or fifth centuries. Plotinus, therefore, lay for most scholars, even those highly qualified to interpret him, in what was a no-man's land, an interlunary period.

Next, there was the matter and the style to reckon with. Plato, as all agree, was one of the greatest masters of a flexible, fully articulated prose style that the West has known. He wrote not only as a philosopher, but as a man among men in a highly refined and supremely intelligent society. Even to one uninterested in the thought, many of the dialogues can read as pure literature and as repositories of lofty ethical teaching and humane ideals.[1] Similarly Aristotle, though his appeal as a stylist is less, remained till our own day the master of European logic, and the great encyclopedist and scientist until the seventeenth century; moreover, the *Ethics* and *Politics* and *Poetics* have never ceased to interest large numbers who have little taste for metaphysics or cosmology, and in these works at least, the style is clear and the sense in general simple of comprehension. Plotinus, on the other hand, is by common consent difficult to read and hard to understand, and though he is certainly often concerned with human conduct and psychology he makes none of the concessions to human nature, in the way of vivid dialogues and touches of characterization, that Plato in all save a few of his later works makes as it were unconsciously. Plotinus never deviates from his purely philosophical purpose, which he pursues without any reference to the persons of his own acquaintance or the surroundings of his own life. Nor does he throw off, as do both Plato and Aristotle, innumerable thoughts and hints about the pursuits and difficulties and foibles and interests of the common man. Plotinus constructs a system more complete and logically knit together than anything in the work of his predecessors; it is in many ways a more profound and satisfying answer to the great problems of thought than is given by any other ancient philosopher; but to one who is not greatly concerned to learn and to live his teaching from start to finish Plotinus may well appear too intense, too rarified a thinker, perhaps even unsympathetic and distasteful. Indeed, the philosophy of Plotinus is a religion, both intellectual and ethical, and as such he suffers from all disabilities that the advocate of a religious system

[1] Lord Macaulay, who had no interest in or understanding of speculative philosophy, read and re-read Plato constantly throughout his life.

must always suffer: Christians are suspicious if not positively hostile, while to those who are not convinced Christians Plotinus makes little appeal, save perhaps to a rare individual or to a group of devoted Platonists.

Yet Plotinus is a figure of crucial importance, both in his own right as a thinker and in the influence which his thought has had on succeeding ages. His supreme achievement was to take up and prolong the various essential strands of Plato's metaphysical thought, discarding the unsuitable and the errant, strengthening and extending the significant, and to bind them all into a complete and self-contained system, using for this purpose all that was most valuable and firm in the metaphysical and psychological armoury of Aristotle.[2]

Plotinus, throughout his writings,[3] which are the content of his public teaching during the latter years of his life, considered himself always a faithful follower of Plato, from whose doctrine he always professed himself unwilling to depart. The Plotinian system is indeed essentially Platonic in character and inspiration, and many of the features in it which are not to be found in Plato's writings may be thought to be justifiable, or even logical, extensions of the master's thought, but it is with systems of philosophy as with styles in art and literature, the imitation of the past in the hands of genius is always something wholly different from what has gone before. The thought of Plotinus is not only praeter-Platonic in its structure and emphasis, but it also contains many doctrines which are either original or are taken from post-Platonic philosophers. In its way, the Plotinian system stands to Plato as the Thomist system stands to Aristotle.

The most noticeable difference is the logical completeness of the system of Plotinus. Whereas Plato starts again and again from different points in his endeavour to rise above the visible and the changeable to permanent reality, and seizes one problem after another to discuss, without ever successfully presenting a complete statement of the universe of being, Plotinus describes from various angles and starting-points a single picture of the hierarchy of being, with an explanation and analysis of all its degrees and kinds and activities, all linked together and held at the summit by the One that is above all being. Within this universe is a rhythm of outgoing and

[2]This judgment leaves out of account Plato's political and aesthetical teaching.

[3]His teaching in the *Enneads*, in the order and final literary form in which it has come down to us, is due to the editorial care of his disciple Porphyry, but the language is substantially the Master's own.

reflux, emanation and return, and a vast richness and scale of values, intellectual and ethical.

A second important development and advance upon Plato has already been mentioned in passing: the recognition of an Absolute, the One from which all being has its origin and to which all being aspires. This recognition, as has been seen, was the achievement of the school of Middle Platonism, but for these thinkers the Supreme Mind was the head of the hierarchy of being and therefore metaphysically and practically separated from all lower orders. Plotinus took the further and most important step of removing the One beyond and outside all categories and orders of being, though he did not render it capable of exercising immediate, immanent and direct influence upon all that is.

A third advance upon Plato is seen in the end proposed to human endeavour and activity. Plato had been concerned to prepare and purify the soul and mind, by moral and intellectual discipline, for a knowledge of the Forms, that is, of essential reality, dimly in this life and more fully in another. With Aristotle, beatitude consisted in the contemplation of metaphysical and physical reality, perhaps in this life only, though later followers of his school made this contemplation in some sense the employment of immortal intelligences. Plotinus, on the other hand, sees the final activity of the soul in a union of knowledge and love with the One beyond being, which can be attained partially and fleetingly even in this life. There is therefore a religious, a mystical character in the thought of Plotinus. Traces or adumbrations of this are certainly present in Plato, and in greater measure than some commentators would allow, for there are deep undertones in many a phrase and rejoinder in the dialogues that elude inclusion in any scheme of Plato's thought, and room must somehow be found for the *Symposium* in any summary of Platonic doctrine. Nevertheless, Plato in his magisterial passages speaks only of an intellectual employment for the philosopher, and of a plurality of Forms for him to contemplate; Plotinus finds employment for what we should call the whole personality in a union of knowledge and love with One ineffably present to the soul.

The universe of Plotinus is wholly spiritual. Here again he is an original thinker, and he is the first philosopher to recognize and state clearly the distinction between the spiritual as opposed to the material – not as they exist, for he would have denied the existence in any real sense of the material, but as the material is supposed to exist by the ordinary man and still more by the Stoic or Epicurean philosopher. Whereas for Plato the non-spiritual had at least a quasi-reality, a shadow existence, while for Aristotle the division between what common-sense would call physical and spiritual being was taken for granted, for Plotinus all reality is spiritual reality, mind and its thought. This is not to say that for Plotinus what we call the physical or material world is either illusory, or the unreal creation of our mind, or something existent outside our mind which we cannot comprehend in its true form. For him all reality, even that apprehended by our senses, is spiritual reality: that is, either mind or its thought. These two in fact are not separable; they are, so to say, metaphysical correlatives; just as the object of thought cannot exist without the thinking mind, so the mind cannot exist without its object of spiritual reality. Both are equally real and equally spiritual. This whole position is a blending and elevation of the Platonic account of the nature of reality as intellectual truth with the Aristotelian doctrine of the essential presence of the thing known in the mind of the knower.

Plotinus, however, transcends both Plato and Aristotle in his explicit recognition of the degrees of spiritual existence and knowledge, both in the universe of being and in the individual man. Within man are Spirit, Soul and Body: in the category of divine principles are the One, the wholly transcendent Absolute; Spirit; and the Universal Soul. All these must be considered a little more carefully.

At the summit of all is the One or the Good, that which in modern terminology would be called the Absolute. As the One it is the first cause, as the Good it is the last end, of all that is. The One is absolutely transcendent; nothing can be predicated of it, not even being or existence, not because it lacks any excellence but because it surpasses all categories. It is its own cause and the object of its love is itself; it does not know itself, for this would imply duality of knower and known, but it has awareness of itself. The One of Plotinus is, as has been said, nearer to the God of Christian natural theology than is any other first principle in Greek philosophy. From the One proceeds all being as a by-product of self-contemplation. For Plotinus contemplation always has this reflex, which in another aspect is the self-diffusiveness of good, and in every case something less than the producer issues from contemplation, while the producer remains without any loss or diminution. In the case of the One there is no beginning and no time in this production; all is eternal with the One. Nevertheless the One is the cause of the beginning, the fountain of all, and Plotinus explains the cause of this outflowing as the need there is in all good of diffusing itself.

The second hypostasis in the spiritual world is the Divine Mind or Spirit. This, together with its correlative, the whole spiritual nature, is the product of the One. The Spirit is the highest form of being, but unlike the One, it can be analysed, and the subject-object antithesis can be found in it, though it must be remembered that the Spirit and the spiritual world cannot exist in separation. The object of the contemplation of the Divine Mind is the totality of the Forms. It is at this point that Platonic territory is entered, but the land has been surveyed more completely than in Plato's day, if the metaphor may be allowed. There are Forms of all the thoughts of the Spirit, and these forms are the archetypes of all things that have present or future existence. Human individuals also have Forms, but not, so it would seem, human artefacts. However enunciated or understood, the doctrine of Forms and Archetypes is at best a difficult one. Not only the common-sense man of Plato's dialogue, but the physicist and the biologist who is nowadays half-awake in most of us, will always try to pull the argument down from the metaphysical to the physical level, but it may be fairly said that the Platonic doctrine of Forms received from Plotinus a more persuasive and logical statement than ever before. Not only does he give it, in the One, a cause and a control, but by regarding it *a parte Dei* so to say, and not, with Plato, *a parte nostra,* he gives it a completeness and a unity which it never had before. Moreover the Forms, united as they are so closely with the Divine Mind, are themselves living intelligences that interpenetrate with one another and exist as a totality in the Divine Mind. In a sense, therefore, the One and the Divine Mind, if conflated, would seem at first sight to make up the God of Christian natural theology, and it is certain that Christian speculation makes use, in the treatise *De Deo,* of elements of Plotinian thought taken from both these Divine Hypostases. We may indeed feel a lack of clear distinction between God and all else. That is, however, largely a consequence of the absence in Plotinus of the clear line drawn by Jew and Christian between creature and Creator, and also of the lack in all ancient thought of an adequate definition of personality. Though Plotinus is certainly not a pantheist, his doctrine of procession and return down and up the ladder of being from the transcendent One is not fully theist.

Below Mind in the hierarchy of being is Soul, which is the radiation or contemplation-product of Mind. Soul is the framer and guide and life of the universe, which it informs and penetrates; it has affinities with the One and yet reaches down to the lowest levels of being. Even in what we call Matter there is soul, which we call

Nature, but it is a soul asleep, as it were, or on the very edge of disappearance. Plotinus is no monopsychist. For him individual human souls exist as truly as the Universal Soul; both derive from Mind, and both are 'twofold', with a higher and lower phase of being, the one 'in the heavens', the other 'combined with body'.[4] Yet in a very real way all souls can interpenetrate and each has, or can have, direct intercourse with the universal soul. Plotinus has his own explanation of the relationship of soul and body. While Plato had made soul the reality, a part of universal soul, and the body a mere shadow of reality, and while Aristotle had reduced soul to the complete expression or 'form' of the body, with little existence in its own right, Plotinus regards individual souls as immortal spirits informing visible bodies. For him as for all Greek philosophers, immortality stretches backwards as well as forwards; he has therefore to explain, as have all Platonists, how soul came to be embodied. Here he has no settled doctrine. Regarding the body as in some sense an imprisonment and a danger, he attempts to solve the problem sometimes by attributing embodiment (with Plato) to overruling necessity, sometimes to choice. With Plato he makes this life in some ways a punishment for evil conduct in another existence, or the result of a 'fall', he regards the 'coming down' of the soul as in some sense a misfortune;[5] it may be the result of a rash choice. Yet at other times he suggests that souls come down out of a desire to diffuse some sort of good even upon the lowest form of being.

Beneath Soul is 'matter'. Matter for Plotinus is never 'material'; it is the Aristotelian matter,[6] a receptacle of Form, pure potentiality, the principle of want and negation, the last reflection of Soul. 'Material' things stand to the senses as concepts stand to the reason and as Forms stand to the Spirit. They are the least real, not because they are more 'subjective', but because the faculty that apprehends them is the furthest removed from reality and therefore its objects are the least real.

Matter, however is one of the points of tension in the Plotinian system. Is it merely the least real, or has it something active in it, something evil? With Plotinus, as with Plato, we can see the luminous clarity of Greek thought brought up against the inescapable conviction of every honest mind viewing itself and others that there is something positively inimical to good in the world: it is the philosophical problem of evil. His answer, the answer that had

[4]Plotinus, *Enneads*, II 3.9.
[5]Plotinus, *Enneads*, III 2; IV 3.16; IV 8.4.
[6]Perhaps even the Platonic, if the ὑποδοχή of the *Timaeus* is equated with the ὕλη of Aristotle.

been given by others before him and which is perhaps the only answer that pure philosophy can give, is that what we call evil is a lack of good, a lack of the positive, a 'silence implying sound'. Yet at times there are traces in Plotinus of the Orphic and Pythagorean and Platonic concept of the human body, as something resisting the right functioning of soul.

Plotinus, again like Plato and Aristotle, is intensely concerned with human life and conduct. Not only the good life in this world, but the ascent of the soul from the lower to the higher levels of being, is the centre of his interest. Just as there is a radiation, a procession, from higher to lower, so there is a yearning and a striving and an invitation to the lower to mount upward. Life is a discipline and a purification, and we owe to Plotinus and his followers, as an addition to the cardinal virtues and the physical, moral and intellectual discipline of Plato, the three classical stages of incipient, proficient and perfect – purgative, illuminative and unitive – with the various virtues practised in three moods of increasing perfection. Plotinus is nowhere more profound and more subtle than in his psychology, and on two points his teaching has found its way into Christian tradition: the one, that the human soul is present everywhere in the human organism as informing and uniting the whole, and nowhere locally; the other, that in the disembodied spirit the functions directly depending upon the body, such as reasoning and memory, will be in abeyance. For Plotinus, even more truly than for Plato, the hereafter or rather, as both prefer to call it, the 'yonder' is more real than the now and the here. Each soul has its archetype in the ideal world – the Nûs, the 'real man' – and as long as this exists (and it is eternal), so long does the individual soul exist. Plotinus throughout insists on the interpenetrability or communion of spirit with spirit, and he probably means no more than this when he seems sometimes to think of individual spirits merged into a greater unity.

Plotinus admits three mental processes of cognition, corresponding to the human 'trinity' of Body, Soul and Spirit, and employing respectively the senses, the reason, and spiritual perception or intuition. The senses furnish 'images' of greater and lesser trustworthiness; with these the reason can reflect and define. It is capable of the latter function because it has within it the Forms of things which are illuminated by the Spirit above it. Finally, there is spiritual knowledge, the exercise of a faculty 'which all possess and few use', when we are in union with the Spirit. The goal of all abstention and discipline is the peace and self-control that make possible spiritual contemplation, by which Plotinus understood the intuition of spiritual truth in all its aspects, with the corresponding by-product of action. Above this again was the mystical experience, the union with the One, which was the rare, perhaps even the uncovenanted and God-given result of utter abstraction from all things, but which was nevertheless unique in its value. While the mystical element in Plotinus's system has often been exaggerated, as if it were the normal and distinctive feature of Neoplatonism, it must not on that account be slurred over or tacitly ignored. Nor on the other hand must it be forgotten that the Plotinian union with the One is not a union between persons, the one human, the other divine. The One, in Plotinus's thought, stands outside personality.

In this brief sketch attention has necessarily been directed towards the Platonic elements and characteristics of the thought of Plotinus, for it is these that give it the ideal, spiritual quality that distinguishes it from every other construction of ancient thought, and Plotinus himself desired no more than to be a disciple of Plato. No reader, however, who is at all conversant with Greek philosophy, can fail to be aware of the great debt which he owes to Aristotle. He differed, indeed, from his predecessors in rejecting the fusion of Plato's Idea of Good with Aristotle's First Mover, which was essential if a crown, a summit, were to be given to the hierarchy of being, but Aristotle's two great metaphysical relationships, that of Form to Matter and Potency to Act, are an integral cement of the Plotinian system from the base to summit; it is they that give the continuity, the escape from barriers and gulfs, throughout the range of being from highest to lowest. Similarly, Aristotle's doctrine of intellectual cognition makes it possible for Plotinus to explain his doctrine of the interpenetrability of subject and object, self and other, in the realm of spirit.

The historian of philosophy is not as such concerned with the truth or the value of a system, but since the high idealism and the logical strength of Plotinus's thought has been noted, it may be well to draw attention to some characteristics that make it less attractive to many minds. Three may be mentioned, all of them found in greater or less degree in all Greek thought. The first is the heavy demand it makes upon the intellectual powers of its adepts. While of necessity a philosophical system is an intellectual construction, one which is also a way of life, a religion, must, if it is to be of wide acceptance, be readily comprehensible in its broad lines by the many. Neoplatonism is a religion for philosophers only; in its pure state it could only appeal to trained thinkers, and it is perhaps significant that when it aimed at becoming a religion and supporting a cause it degenerated into theurgy and daemonology and magic.

A second disability is almost a corollary of its logical completeness. The universe, and human life, must always remain mysterious to finite minds that are adapted, as regards their natural powers in this life, to the reception of only a small part of the information that the universe of being has to give. Any elaborate metaphysical construction, therefore, which does not remain very closely tied to all other forms of knowledge and experience, is bound to seem vulnerable as a purely intellectual construction made by a single mind. Here again Neoplatonism in its Plotinian simplicity soon proliferated into greater and more improbable complexity. Thirdly, like so much of human speculation, it is too simple. It does not fully accept or explain the inescapable facts of life – sin, suffering, ignorance – and it therefore fails to give the answer or the help precisely where it is most needed.

Thus far we have spoken of Plotinian Neoplatonism as a system of thought. If, looking forward, we regard this last and fullest flower of the Greek genius as a theodicy that could rival, or alternatively assist, Christian theology, two observations will at once be felt necessary. The first is, that the opposition between creator and creature is never made. Plotinus is not a pantheist, but on the other hand, there is no absolute barrier between the degrees of being. While he secures an Absolute as the cause and origin of all being, he does this at the cost of setting that Absolute outside the realm of being, and beyond personality or existence. The second is, that the Plotinian system has no place for the supernatural, in the technical theological sense of that word. The human soul is, potentially at least, akin to all that is highest in the universe of being: it cannot be raised to a true communion with the One that is beyond being. Christianity, on the other hand, is a religion of rebirth, of a grace that surpasses nature, and of a real, though supernatural, union of the human and the divine.

Plotinus has been discussed, not indeed at length and not adequately, but at least without haste, partly because his greatness and his importance as a thinker, and the reasons for this, are even now not widely understood, and partly because his significance in the history of Christian thought is certainly not even now grasped except by a few specialists. As we shall see, the legacy of what is loosely called Neoplatonism to later medieval thought has been widely recognized, and the value of this legacy has been often debated. What has not been so fully grasped is the influence of the thought of Plotinus himself upon those who were to be the sources of Western philosophy. No doubt it is true that Plotinus was the vehicle by which Plato's thought passed down to Christian thinkers, and the truly Platonic nature of Plotinus's genius must not be obscured by the un-Platonic character of much, though by no means all, in later Neoplatonism, but the destiny of Plato has always been to inspire, leading the thinkers of the world into the light and up to the heights. Plotinus did something else; he created a system and an order which could be adopted and transformed; and the history of medieval philosophy is in part a history of that transformation.

Neoplatonism, indeed, appears throughout late antiquity and the Middle Ages as the principal ingredient of Christian philosophical thought and theological speculation. The Platonism of Plato himself was all but unknown, and Aristotle was long familiar only as a logician. Neoplatonism was alone in the field as a treasure house of philosophical ideas, and its influence was felt in recurring waves, from Augustine, from Dionysius, from John Scotus Erigena, from the Arabs and Jews, and from the rediscovered Neoplatonic texts in the thirteenth century. Fortified by the authority now of Augustine, now of Boethius, now of the supposedly apostolic Dionysius, it had an easy entry among theologians who might well have recoiled from Plotinus and Iamblichus and Proclus. In its purest form it helped to give theological expression to Christian dogma regarding the Godhead; in a more dubious shape it helped to systematize angelology and psychology. At second hand in the writings of the Areopagite it provided a theological formulation of mysticism. In its deeply religious tone, its tendency to emanationism and pantheism, and its negation of the supernatural gift of God it is an ambivalent influence, now good now dubious, in the history of Christian theology. Without it, Thomism would be poorer, but the history of Christian mysticism might well have been simpler.

CHAPTER THREE
St Augustine

St Augustine, it would be generally agreed, has had a greater
influence upon the history of dogma and upon religious thought and
sentiment in Western Christendom than any other writer outside the
canon of Scripture. It is easy to find at least one reason for this in the
circumstances of the age during which his life was passed. From
about A.D. 350 till about A.D. 500 the vital powers of the ancient
civilization were steadily declining, while at the same time the
Church was coming to social maturity with a number of insistent
needs and demands which had not made themselves felt until full
freedom of action had been attained. This period was followed by
another, some five hundred years in length, in which intellectual life
at the higher levels was all but extinct in the West, and this epoch in
its turn by one in which an adolescent Europe turned avidly for
mental food to the masters nearest to hand and latest in time, the
Latin writers of the imperial decline, who alone were available in the
libraries of the age. These circumstances gave great importance and a
new significance to a scattered group of teachers who had been the last
to absorb the message of the ancient world while it was still to be
heard, and who had therefore been the last to hand on the legacy of the
past; some of them had indeed been conscious of their responsibilities
in the matter. Many of these writers thus came to hold a position in
the history of Western thought which was greater than their intrinsic
merit might seem to deserve. Among them were the names of men,
some of whom we shall meet later, such as Boethius, Cassiodorus,
John Cassian, St Benedict, St Isidore of Seville and St Gregory the
Great. Above all, in their influence on religious and philosophical
speculation, were St Augustine and the pseudo-Denis. It can certainly
be allowed that a part, at least, of the commanding position held by St
Augustine was due to his place in the ancient West at the moment of
its dissolution and to the survival and wide distribution of his

voluminous writings, which could be pondered and imitated for centuries by generations of monastic writers.

This, however, is far from being a sufficient explanation of the unique authority of St Augustine. He was in his own right a star of the first magnitude. Only thus can his unique position be accounted for. In the medieval and modern worlds half-a-dozen great religious orders have looked to him as their law-giver and patron, and many lesser ones have based their code upon his teaching. He has given his name to a succession of schools of theology. For a thousand years after his death all theologians and spiritual writers turned to him as to a court from which there was no appeal, and in the modern world of the last five centuries the output of editions and translations and commentaries and discussions of every aspect of his work and thought has far exceeded that devoted to any other theological writer, St Thomas not excluded, while his book of *Confessions* remains the only composition of a Father of the early Church that has become one of the world's classics.

Yet, strangely enough, there is an obverse to this brilliant medallion. If Augustine was a second Bible to the dark and middle ages, he was all but the gospel of the three great heresies, Lutheranism, Calvinism and Jansenism, that absorbed so much of the mental activity of the sixteenth and seventeenth centuries, while during much of this period even orthodox Catholics were in violent collision over the interpretation of some of his writings. Not only has his teaching on grace, free-will and predestination been pressed into service against orthodox belief, but his teaching on the Eucharist has been interpreted in a non-Catholic sense. Similarly, even in the Catholic schools there has been, since the mid-thirteenth century, more than one movement of retreat from the Augustinian presentation of metaphysics and epistemology. Indeed, almost all the theories and speculations of Augustine, including his views on the historical and political processes, the nature of his own conversion, his conception of human knowledge and of mystical contemplation, have proved peculiarly hard to seize with precision when subjected to minute criticism. All this has led those standing outside the arena to hint that after all the genius and significance of Augustine may have been exaggerated. He was not, they say, a great and original thinker, but the transmitter of Plotinus; as a theologian he was overborne by his own inner experiences; as a writer he was only the greatest of a decadent rhetorical school. So they may say, and yet those who know Augustine – and more than any other great thinker Augustine has seemed a personal friend, 'their' Augustine, to many – will never agree with this verdict. The range, the depth, the power, the originality with which that great mind and soul handle and interpret the whole of Christian revelation and tradition, the innumerable intuitions and flashes of light that abound, above all, the sense of personal contact with uncreated light, the Incarnate Word of God, that pervades the whole body of his writings – these characteristics will always defeat those who attempt to belittle or to antiquate Augustine. It is that marvellous personality, penitent and saint, at once a type and yet intensely individual, that illuminates every page and seems so often to be as it were our own mind and soul alone with God. *Noverim Te, noverim Me.*

In what follows we are concerned, not with a saint or a theologian, but with Augustine as an agent in the creation of a system of Christian thought. It has indeed been questioned whether Augustine can be called a philosopher, or be said to have had a system. Save in a few of his early dialogues he is never a 'pure' philosopher. The Christian faith and a Christian's wisdom are his topics. He would not have allowed that a philosophy that was not divine wisdom could have any meaning for a mature believer. The division, classical and axiomatic to all who look to Aquinas as master, between natural, rational wisdom and supernatural wisdom, between reason and Christian revelation, between philosophy, in fact, and theology, has no place in Augustine, partly because the theology of grace and the supernatural life had not yet been elaborated; partly because in actual life – in the Christian life of the individual – the divine action, whether of the immanent creator and sustainer, or of the divine Redeemer and grace-giver, flow from one divine source and are not in fact divisible; partly because Augustine has at no time any interest in analysing or describing either the universe or the microcosm of man in philosophical terms.

Moreover, it would be an anachronism to think of any philosopher of the ancient world (and Augustine, with all his modernity, is an ancient) as constructing a system of pure philosophy as distinct from theology. In the first place, the conception of man as sharing a higher, supernatural life, bestowed by an omnipotent creator, was utterly foreign to the mental furniture of a non-Christian philosopher. We must not confuse myth or magic or legend with the full and accurately defined plenitude of revealed truth. On the other hand, the three great Greek philosophers whom we have been considering extended the purview of their thought far beyond the bounds of 'natural' philosophy. A Christian thinker of to-day may seem to accept much of the idealistic doctrine of Plato and Plotinus, and still more of the Aristotelian analysis of reality, but he does not in fact accept their presentation of ultimate reality, the unseen world. An Inge may seem at first sight to be both a Christian and a Neoplatonist, but it is clear on inspection that, whether or not he may be an integral Christian, he is certainly not an integral Neoplatonist: he holds, for example, the redemptive sacrifice of an incarnate divine Person, which in itself, apart from its consequences for man, could not possibly find a place in a Platonic scheme of things. Similarly, a Thomist may seem to use Aristotle as a framework for his theology, but close inspection shows that he can do so only by silently changing or misinterpreting Aristotle at half-a-dozen crucial points, such as the immortality of the individual soul and the nature of the Prime Mover. To expect Augustine, therefore, to 'isolate' from the system of Plotinus a viable 'natural philosophy' on which to superimpose a Christian theology would be to demand the unthinkable. He did not even perform the feat which Aquinas attributed to him, of 'taking from the Platonists what seemed right in their thought and changing what seemed to be wrong'. That was, in general, what St Thomas himself did with Aristotle. Rather, St Augustine, in his search for truth, had found what he believed to be a true presentation of reality in what he had read of Plato, Plotinus and Porphyry. Though he was quite clear, at least when he had had time to acquire a knowledge of Christian theology, as to what had been revealed in Scripture and Tradition, he had no clear and formulated judgment on the extent to which the greatest and noblest non-Christian philosophers might (either by natural genius or divine illumination) have arrived at an adumbration or partial realization of revealed truth, nor had he the guidance of any Christian predecessors in determining what, if any, errors lay in the sublime, and to Christian minds often very attractive, speculations of Plato and Plotinus. In consequence, on almost all points where Scripture gave no lead, Augustine accepted from the *Timaeus* and *Meno* of Plato and the *Enneads* of Plotinus the explanations they gave of the intellectual problems that engaged his attention, and if a reader of Augustine is in doubt as to the origin of a particular philosophical idea, he will usually find the answer in Plotinus. But Augustine was never one to take words and propositions from another without re-thinking them for himself; he was moreover, himself an original thinker of great power, and when Scripture gave him a clear lead, as in the first chapters of Genesis, in the third chapter of Exodus, and in the first chapter of St John, he did not fail to enunciate ideas that were to influence all subsequent Christian thought. Thus by making Being, rather than Unity and

Goodness, the basis of his account of God, he supplemented the Aristotelian and Plotinian traditions, with their many inadequacies, and wrote of a God, at once immanent and transcendent, supereminent in Being, but the Creator of a universe that reflected His perfections, and the provident and loving ruler and Father of His children. Similarly, in the matter of grace and predestination, where he had a living opponent who contradicted what Augustine felt to be both Christian tradition and his own experience, and where the Platonists gave no help, Augustine took St Paul as his master and based on the Apostle's teaching a new fabric of theology. But where Scripture gave no lead, and the Neoplatonists were available, he used their doctrines to the full to depict what was the main interest of his own life, the journey of the Christian mind to God, the finding of the perfect wisdom which bestowed beatitude. This interest, this aim, has been that of generations of Augustinians in century after century, and it is the reason why Augustinism, however we define it, cannot, like Aristotelianism, be an article of export for Christian thinkers. While the Aristotelian Thomist, by a decision of the will and a distinction of the mind, can separate absolutely, for the purposes of discussion, the realms of nature and grace, the Augustinian seizes all at once upon the rich, existing mass of human consciousness and Christian experience as he knows it in his own mind and life.

Augustine is not primarily a philosopher, still less a 'pure' philosopher. He is a profound, and a profoundly religious, thinker, who is concerned, not with framing a system or criticizing the endeavours of others, but with knowing and presenting to others his knowledge of the two immediate realities of life, God and the human soul. All his aim and interests are contained in the two celebrated aphorisms uttered when he was still of no long standing as a Christian. 'I desire', he says, 'to have knowledge of God and the soul. Of nothing else? No, of nothing else whatsoever.'[1] And again: 'O God, always one and the same, if I know myself, I shall know Thee.'[2] As a consequence, he makes no attempt to build up a system of many parts, or to prove the capability of the human mind to attain to a true knowledge of what lies outside itself. Rather, he desires to explain and interpret the nature of God and of the soul with all the means at his command, whether he finds help in philosophers of the past, and in the Scriptures and teaching of the Church, or whether he presents the result of his own reasoning and religious experience. He regarded

[1]Soliloquies, I. 2, n.7.
[2]Soliloquies, II. i, n.1.

philosophy very much in the same way that we regard the elements of science; as a body of ascertained knowledge on which one could draw for illustration and explanation, not as a bundle of questions to discuss or opinions to criticize. When he needs a philosophical argument or explanation he takes it from thinkers of the past of whom he has knowledge and whom he recognizes as having attained to truth. Rarely or never does he treat any philosophical question 'in the void' or merely theoretically, nor, when writing in a philosophical context, does he make the distinction, later to become classical among Christian thinkers, between the powers and activities of a regenerate, Christian soul in a 'state of grace', and a human soul as such without any gratuitous aid. He is discussing always the only soul in which he is interested, the Christian soul, as it were his own soul. Though so trenchant as a theologian when 'nature' and 'grace' are discussed as states of mankind, he does not, when the powers of the soul are in question, consider its 'natural' and 'supernatural' capabilities; he does not, to use M. Jacques Maritain's familiar phrase, distinguish with a view to uniting. He begins, and he ceases, to speak as a philosopher when he chooses and without warning, and it is not always possible to catch the moment when he does so: we become suddenly aware that he has 'lifted his sights'.

Augustine as a young man had no training in philosophy, and at no time in his life did he acquire any kind of adequate knowledge of Greek philosophy as a whole. The extent of his knowledge of Greek is still a controversial issue, but it has never been maintained that he had any wide acquaintance with the Platonic corpus, or any knowledge of the metaphysical and epistemological teaching of Aristotle. He was a trained and professional rhetorician, and his style and treatment of all topics throughout his life reflect this; it accounts for the extraordinary fluency which at times becomes fluidity. His first encounter with Greek thought was the sceptical New Academy as seen in Cicero's writings, but his sole important debt was to Plotinus and to Porphyry; he certainly read, and knew well perhaps even in Greek, but later certainly also in the translation of Victorinus, parts at least of the *Enneads.* This was before his conversion, and he owed to Plotinus the realization that true reality (and therefore God) is spiritual, not corporeal, substance, as also the doctrine that evil is merely lack of good. He did not pursue his study of philosophy; he therefore never had a complete view even of the system of Plotinus, and it has been held that he seriously misunderstood important parts of it, but he remained convinced of its excellence as a description of reality, and on several important points his thought always remained true to Platonism, (i.e. Neoplatonism), or what he took to be such. But although he was intellectually capable of being a great thinker, and did in fact put into currency a number of profound ideas, some of which still influence thought, he never became a philosopher to the extent that St Thomas might be called a philosopher, as distinct from a theologian. Augustine was always potentially, and for much of his life actually, the Christian priest and bishop concerned with the interpretation of the Scriptures and Catholic doctrine and the Christian life, and it is as such that he has been throughout the ages a doctor of the Church and a guide to individuals. His works were read in centuries which neither knew nor cared about philosophy, and but for the historical circumstances of the thirteenth century at Paris his followers might never have been called upon to discover and to defend his philosophical teaching. Challenged they were, however, and it is therefore incumbent upon any student of medieval thought to understand Augustine's teaching, at least in so far as it influenced subsequent schools.

Augustine never attempted to construct a system. Certain important topics never came within his purview at all. Thus, not being fully acquainted with Plato and Aristotle, and still less with the pre-Socratics, he was never exercised by the problem of the one and the many, substance and change, universals and particulars, and thus a great tract of metaphysical territory lay altogether out of his sight. Its place was taken by the Christian doctrine of God and creation and the individual soul, and the intellectual universe of Plotinus was accepted as the adequate human commentary on the universe as displayed for the believer by scriptural revelation. Moreover, difficulties on both sides were avoided or ignored by Augustine's apparent acceptance of the Plotinian emanation as the equivalent of creation, by his lack of a full realization of the utter transcendence of the Plotinian One, and by his acceptance of the three divine Hypostases as a pagan prevision of the Trinity. He was thus able to apply to the Second Person of the Christian Trinity, the Word, what Plotinus attributed to the Divine Mind.

Augustine based all his thought on the Scriptural presentation of God as pure, omnipotent, eternal, infinite Being. He may be said thereby to have initiated a specifically Christian philosophy. To this Being, known by Christian faith as Three in One, Augustine applied the Plotinian doctrine of the Three Hypostases, the Word, as we have seen, being taken to correspond to the Divine Mind of Plotinus. For Plotinus, the object of contemplation for the Divine Mind was the (Platonic) world of Ideas or Forms; Augustine was able therefore to place the Ideas in the Word Who, like the Divine Mind, was the intellectual light of human souls. In this way the Forms of Plato placed in the Mind of God by the Middle Academy, and set by Plotinus in the Divine Mind as exemplary and creative agencies for the universe of sensible being, passed into Christian theology and became the common property of all schools.

A second basic position of originality and great significance in the thought of Augustine was his assertion of the self-knowledge possessed by each individual human being. By this he knows that he exists and knows; knowledge, moreover, is of its essence the knowledge of something existent, something real, therefore, of something true; truth is immutable and eternal, it therefore possesses divine attributes; indeed, ultimately truth is God. Thus for Augustine the certain knowledge of God arises directly from the realization of the soul's own existence and knowledge; the soul, as we know from Scripture, is the image of God Himself, and its knowledge is a reflection of the divine light.

This process of argument brings us into the presence of the crucial and difficult matter of Augustine's epistemology. As we have seen, the only epistemological dialogue of Plato with which he was familiar was the *Meno*, where knowing is presented as remembering the ideas of a previous existence. Of Aristotle's doctrine he knew nothing. In all considerations of Augustine's psychology and epistemology, we must bear in mind that for him, as for Plato, the soul is a complete spiritual entity 'using' a body. A consequence of this is that all perception and knowledge arises within the soul; the soul is not acted upon directly by the external world, nor does it 'abstract' anything from that world in the process of cognition. Being in a body it realizes that the body has physical sensations and feelings, and this awareness is what we call sensory perception. Moreover, as the mind cannot receive within itself anything from without, its thoughts and judgements about the universe around it must originate from within, stimulated by its awareness of what the body feels and perceives. Augustine, however, in agreement with Plato, is neither a sceptic nor an agnostic nor a nominalist; the ideas of things in the soul are as real as the things themselves, for the soul can find reflected within itself the ideas that are, in the mind of God, the exemplary causes of the physical and spiritual beings in the universe. Such, at first sight and at a first reading of certain passages in his writings, would seem to be Augustine's scheme of knowledge and reality. But elsewhere, and more frequently, we are introduced to his explanation of the process of cognition by the 'divine illumination of the intellect' and this was to become in the Middle Ages such a shibboleth of authentic Augustinian thought that we must look at it more closely.

No point in Augustine's teaching has proved harder of comprehension and explanation than his theory of the divine illumination of the intellect. When even the most competent and sympathetic exponents of Augustine's thought, including minds of such outstanding clarity as Portalié and Gilson, both admit the difficulty of explaining the doctrine and differ widely from each other in the explanations they give, and when a succession of 'Augustinian' thinkers have confidently but vainly propounded what were claimed to be clear and convincing expositions, there would seem to be grounds for thinking that the difficulty is a real one, and that either Augustine's thought must be unformed and ill-expressed, or else his outlook must differ so widely from that of any medieval or modern philosopher as to make it very hard for us to grasp the context and atmosphere in which he lived and speculated.

But if no agreement has been attained in explaining the doctrine, at least some difficulties and disagreements of the past have been cleared away. It is, for example, universally recognized that the 'divine illumination' is not in essence, and on all levels of cognition, either supernatural or mystical; that is to say, it does not imply the presence in the subject of either faith or sanctifying grace, nor does it imply in the mind of the recipient an experimental or existential recognition of its presence. Augustine is peremptory on the point; the divine illumination, at least on its lowest levels, is the way of knowledge for all men. It is also commonly agreed that Augustine in his maturity held neither the Platonic doctrine of knowledge from memory (*anamnesis*) nor that of innate ideas, and there is a fair unanimity among recent scholars against the opinion that he supposed the ideas to be seen in God by the human mind (the so-called 'ontologism'), or that he supposed the divine illumination to be a divine actuation within the process of cognition, an adaptation of the Aristotelian agent intellect as an essential component of the intellective process. There would seem to be no trace in Augustine's writings of a division of the intellect along Aristotelian lines.

Within the past few decades determined efforts have been made to consider Augustine's epistemology by means of a careful collation of all the passages in his writings where he touches upon the subject. From these it would seem clear that Augustine applied to all degrees of knowledge the concept that light of one kind or another is both the formal and efficient cause of the cognitive process, and that therefore in all degrees and kinds of knowledge there is an activity analogous to that by which visual perception attains its object by means of physical light: the light strikes upon the external, 'material' objects of sight and renders them capable of reception by the organ of sight which is itself either light-giving by participation, or at least perfectly disposed to receive the light from those objects.[3] What are the elements of the analogous process of intellection? The subject is the human understanding. The intelligible, immaterial objects are, on the lowest level of scientific knowledge, 'numbers' beginning with unity, which Augustine consistently regarded as the basic type of intellectual knowledge; numbers are not as such perceptible to the senses, but are certain, immutable, incorruptible ingredients of all judgments upon physical things; they are grasped and maintained, whether implicitly or explicitly, by every sane intelligence. In Augustine's system 'numbers' took something of the place occupied by 'first Principles' in Aristotelian thought; both have, ultimately, Platonic overtones. On the higher level of sapiential knowledge the object is wisdom itself, evident to compulsion to every healthy mind as the 'truth' in which the highest good is seen (*cernitur*) and grasped (*videtur*), and which implies and can be broken down into the great axioms such as the recognition that the eternal is superior to the temporary, and that truth itself is unchangeable. These objects are not innate in the soul, nor are they formed from sense-perceptions by the activity of any abstractive faculty. They are 'irradiated into' the soul, 'participated' by created beings, and 'illuminated' for the mind's perception by a divine light. What is that light? It is neither mystical nor supernatural in the later, technical sense of the word, since all men possess it, at least in a rudimentary form. Nor is it, like physical light on the one hand and uncreated light on the other, consciously experienced as given and withdrawn. It is something of which the presence is demanded by the analysis of reason. It has indeed been suggested that it is no more than what was later called by theologians the 'natural co-operation' (*concursus naturalis*) of God, that unexperienced influence of the First Cause giving actuality to all natural created activities. To Augustine, however, it is certainly more than this. It is in some sense 'truth' itself, the intelligible aspect of what we call reality, shining from eternal truth and illuminating in our minds the first principles of knowledge and the prime values of ethics and æsthetics. And what are the objects 'participated' and 'illuminated'? Augustine calls them indifferently forms, ideas, reasons (*rationes*) and rules (*regulae*), and sometimes more

---

[3]This analogy between light and the intellective process derives from Neoplatonism which in turn found it in both Aristotle and Plato.

specifically numbers, judgments of value and obligation, or more comprehensively 'truths', all of which derive their being from transcendent, divine truth. This, then, is the process of which so many explanations have been given.

There is a practical rule which rarely fails the commentator on Augustine's philosophy; it is that when a source for his thought is wanting the *Enneads* of Plotinus should be searched. The rule is valid here. Both the thought and the expression of Augustine in this matter would seem to rest upon the teaching of Plotinus; a comparison of Augustine's scheme with the relevant passages from the *Enneads* leaves little room for doubt. Plotinus had posited a triple process of cognition; first and lowest, that by ratiocination based on sense perceptions; secondly, that by the illumination in the individual human soul of the ideas or forms of things present in the world soul, and hence by emanation in the human soul also;[4] thirdly, by the intuition which had as its object the Divine Mind (Nûs) or Intellectual Principle. Above all these lay the mystical union of love and knowledge with the ineffable One. A parallel scheme can be traced in Augustine, as has already been outlined. He constantly speaks of a *science*: of the things perceptible by sense, of a *wisdom* of higher knowledge, and (occasionally) of the attainment of a (non-mystical) glimpse of Truth itself. Above all these is the specifically mystical experience of God. For the moment we are concerned with the second kind of knowledge, that of wisdom, which is the true process of the intellectual cognition of truth by the human mind. Let us first consider Plotinus. Plotinus does not explicitly and formally take over the Aristotelian distinction of the Active and Passive Intellect, but his noetic is unquestionably influenced by Aristotle, not only on the level of sense perception, but on this higher level also. For Plotinus therefore Mind (Nûs) takes the place of the Active Intellect of Aristotle, while Soul (Psyche) corresponds to the passive intellect.[5] Mind is spoken of as 'in act' and 'impassible', while Soul is potential

---

[4]Plotinus, *Enneads*, V 3.3. 'Sensation has seen a man and furnished the image (τυπόν) of him to reason. And what does reason say? It may say nothing yet, but takes knowledge of him and there stops. But if reason reflects with itself, "who is this?", and having met him before, calls in the help of memory, it says, "It is Socrates." If it develops the form of Socrates, it divides what the imagination gave it. If it adds that Socrates is good, it speaks still of things known by the senses, but what it affirms – "goodness" – it takes from itself, because it has within it the standard of the good (κανόνα τοῦ ἀγαθοῦ). But how can it have the good in itself? Because it has the form of good (ἀγαθοειδής) and therefore is strengthened for the perception of goodness by the spirit which shines upon it; for this pure power of Soul receives the prints of Spirit which is just above it.'

[5]*Enneads* V 9. 4. Cf. V 3. 8.

and passive; soul acts as 'matter' to mind, and mind confers a 'form' on soul. This is pure Aristotelian technique. Moreover, it is illumination by Mind that makes Soul intelligent, and Mind is compared to the sun, some of whose light is retained by the soul.[6] Since in Plotinus, Mind and the (Platonic) Forms are identical, this is equivalent to saying that the soul is illuminated or irradiated (the phrase is that of Plotinus) by the Forms.

Augustine has even less trace than Plotinus of any division of the intellect into active and passive, but all the Plotinian constituents of the intellective process are present in his scheme. The Plotinian Mind' is replaced by the divine Word, and the human soul is the recipient of Its illumination; Its light irradiates into the soul the immaterial intelligible objects – forms, ideas, reasons, rules – and illuminates them for its perception. Such, it would seem, is the origin and explanation of the divine illumination of the intellect which later 'Augustinian' thinkers were to interpret so differently.

Augustine, however, met with more than one difficulty in transposing the Plotinian epistemology into a Christian framework. In the first place, since he lacked a thorough first-hand knowledge of Plato's own writings, he was without an adequate knowledge of the Platonic doctrine of Forms, which even to modern scholars, after centuries of comment, presents great difficulties of interpretation. Hence he is neither clear nor (so it would seem) consistent in his definition of the objects of cognition. Secondly, while Plotinus, with his eternal and necessary procession from the One and the Good, had no philosophical difficulty in explaining the presence or the reflection of the divine ideas in the soul of man under the influence of a divine light, Augustine as a creationist had a more difficult task; for to him the soul was created without an inflowing of divinity. He escaped the difficulty, of which he was perhaps not fully aware, partly by understanding Plotinus in a sense not very different from that of a creationist, partly by resting his teaching on the words of the Gospel: 'That was the true light, which enlighteneth every man that cometh into this world.' The use of this text, however, is precisely the cause of the embarrassment felt by most modern critics. Quite apart from the purely exegetical controversy as to the true reading and the exact meaning of the evangelist's words,[7] it is difficult to see how the phrase

[6]*Enneads*, V 3. 8.

[7]With a single change in punctuation from the normal Vulgate text, John 1:9 would read: 'That was the true light coming into the world, which enlighteneth every man.' Exegetically, the 'true light' is probably the Word Himself, not a light proceeding from Him.

can be taken as an explanation of the machinery, so to say, of cognition on the level of purely natural knowledge. Even if we are agreed that it does not describe a gratuitous, supernatural enlightenment, we shall probably feel that the evangelist is not giving an account of the way in which man understands, but an assertion that all truth and knowledge, natural as well as supernatural, have the Word of God as their ultimate source. To Augustine, however, writing as a Christian for Christians, and regarding the explanation of Plotinus as a kind of prevision of Christianity, the difficulty did not present itself – rather, he regarded the description of the Platonists as a divinely appointed foreshadowing of the truth proclaimed by the Evangelist.

Intimately connected with the doctrine of divine illumination of the intellect is Augustine's proof of the existence of God. At different points in his writings he makes use of the more general proofs which had become current among Christian writers, containing elements drawn both from Greek philosophy and from Scripture: the argument from order and design; the argument leading from the imperfect creation to the perfect creator; the argument from the beauty of the universe, the movement and the change of created things, the degrees of perfection, and the universal desire for beatitude. These, however, he mentions in passing. To a further, more rigorous proof, based on his own system of thought, he devotes particular care. The argument runs thus. If there is a being higher than, and superior to, the human soul, that being is God. Now by our intellectual process of thought we attain to, and know that we attain to, truth. But this truth is not 'our' truth, since all may have it and recognize it, both those who have gone before us and those who will come after. It is in itself permanent and immutable, whereas what we see is only partial and changeable. There is therefore 'above' us a Truth perfect and unchangeable. This Truth, which can be shown to be also the Good and the Beautiful, is God. In this argument, as always, the interest of Augustine lies with God, the eternal truth, on the one hand, and with the soul and its marvellous potentialities on the other.

Augustine, indeed, is always more occupied with God and with the soul than with metaphysics and a knowledge of the universe. His analysis of the process and degrees of knowledge is little more than a clearing of the ground for his main structure, the road by which the soul goes to God. Before his days as priest and bishop, he had been by profession an educator, and throughout his life the psychological process of instruction and the relationship of master to pupil were very near the surface of his consciousness. Yet to say that Augustine has a theory or a doctrine of education is only partially true. His writings which deal professedly with education are elementary and unoriginal; they treat only of the early stages; he is not, like Plato, possessed of the divine fire of the great educationist who sees in education the instrument for changing the world into something nobler, and the foundation of eternal life. When once he has laid the basis of grammar Augustine turns to another aim – his real aim – which is to lead the Christian, his mind, his heart and his soul, upwards to God. Here again the Plotinian source is obvious. For Plotinus also life was an ascent of mind and soul, in which there were three degrees; that on which the reason dealt with the universe of sense, that on which the soul, now possessed of wisdom, saw the reflection of the divine ideas in itself, and that on which it had intuitional knowledge of God. Above this was the ecstatic union with the One above all differentiation. Augustine has a parallel ascent; the knowledge of creatures by science; the knowledge of Scripture and theology by wisdom; and the knowledge of the supreme, immutable Truth by intuition. Above all this is the mystical, ineffable union with God. In this ascent, however, he parts company with both Plato and Plotinus: with Plato, because Augustine's eye is from the beginning fixed on the journey to God, not on the formation of a citizen or a philosopher; with Plotinus, because Augustine relies from the beginning, and with growing insistence, upon a help and a light to which the human powers of the individual cannot attain, and to which they have no claim.

By giving this spiritual, supernatural end and means to his teaching, Augustine was to influence both educational and spiritual teaching in the West for centuries. His influence was not immediately felt, but when the ancient framework of society had wholly disappeared, and his works were read throughout Western Europe *in vacuo*, so to say, and without context, they became the only guide. In his scheme the religious and intellectual elements, mental and moral forces, natural and supernatural assistance, were blended and enfolded; they were not, as has often been alleged, confused. Rather, they were considered and assumed to be, as they are in the concrete Christian individual and, for all we know, in others besides, mingled inextricably in the individual mind and soul, separable only by a process of external and even quasi-subjective analysis. It was this being, the individual Christian, Augustine himself if you will, that the Doctor of Grace had before him as the unique object of his concern. For knowledge as an end in itself, or as a means for controlling physical forces, he had no interest. Nor did he take notice as a thinker of the sorts and kinds of Christians existing round him, or of the diversity of gifts and graces and vocations. He is considering the abstract, 'ideal' Christian, very much as St John of the Cross considers steadfastly the 'perfect' contemplative; and, we may add, in each case the saint concerned is in fact, without a touch of egoism or self-consciousness, 'the great sublime he draws'.

In addition to the doctrine of the divine illumination of the intellect, there are a number of points in the Augustinian scheme of metaphysics, not of any great importance in themselves, but noteworthy either as idiosyncratic, or on account of their adoption in later centuries by the whole medieval phalanx of Augustinians.

One of these is his doctrine of 'seminal principles' (*rationes seminales*). According to this, God at the creation implanted in matter formative principles comparable to seeds which ultimately germinated into the material organisms with which we are familiar. This must not be considered as an adumbration of transformation or evolution; it is not a continuous, unending process, nor the change of one distinct species into another, but the gradual emergence of the species and individuals, past, present and future, of which we have, or future ages will have, knowledge. The doctrine derives from the materialistic Stoics, who held that there were seeds of the Divine Fire implanted in matter, resulting in the development of individual beings. Plotinus took up the conception, but transferred it, giving it an ideal sense, and made of it a seminal reason present in the matter that formed the potentiality of the sensible world. Augustine transferred the idea still further into the process of creation, to explain that God created all things, even those that did not arrive at once at their fullness of being; secondary causes had therefore only an apparent causality in the matter.

Another conception present in Augustine's system, that was to have a great fortune in the distant future, was that of 'spiritual matter'. For Aristotle matter and form were the meta-physical constituents of all substance, i.e., of the whole visible universe, but he did not apply the doctrine consistently to spirit or soul; for him soul was of itself the form of the human body. For Plotinus, to whom as an idealist matter did not exist as a correlative to spirit, the Aristotelian terminology implied simply the opposition of potency and act, and matter was, so to say, the last trace of spirit on the verge of nonentity. Since for him the question of creation did not arise, and individual human souls were regarded as emanations of Universal Soul, he was able to consider as 'matter' the potential, limiting element in the human soul, and to apply the doctrine of form and matter to it, thus adumbrating what later schools were to call 'spiritual matter'. Augustine adopted it into his scheme of creation, though without emphasis, as an explanation of the potentiality to change that existed in every soul, but he explicitly refused to explain it further.

Yet another strange Plotinian influence can be seen in Augustine's repeated inclination to toy with the Platonic and Neoplatonic conception of a World Soul, which in modern times has seemed not unattractive to Leibniz and even to Inge. Similarly, Augustine took from the Neoplatonists that interest in numbers, which to the ordinary reader of his works seems an idiosyncrasy. We have seen that Plato, influenced by the Pythagoreans, tended towards the end of his life to see the ideal world – reality – as made up of mathematical concepts and symbols, which were therefore the metaphysical constituents of the visible universe. Plotinus adopted the conception, probably from the Neopythagoreans, and Augustine in turn took it from the Neoplatonists. For him number is the intelligible formula which describes the qualities of being and the manner of change, so that all change throughout the universe, which presents so much philosophical difficulty, can in a sense be 'controlled' by numbers, just as an algebraic formula might express an electrical transformation or an engineering stress. Numbers are, in fact, a rationalization of the seminal reason of things. Numbers as used by Augustine had, of course, no scientific or mathematical basis, and it was easy, as Augustine found, to allegorize them, but the rational, or at least the pseudo-rational, foundation for what seems to many to be a strange aberration of a great genius can be seen to be one more legacy from Neoplatonism.

Finally, there is in Augustine at least a suggestion, a foothold, for the medieval metaphysic of light. For him, with Plotinus and St John as guides, light is the one intellectualizing element in the whole of creation, reflecting the uncreated light of God. In man it is the illumination of the Word; in the sensible world (which Augustine would never call the *material* world) it is the created light of the sun, and in things inanimate it is the number which is, as it were, a light immanent in things.

Augustine wrote and spoke for a small circle in a single province, which was soon to be engulfed in a sea of barbarism, and ultimately absorbed into the vast empire of Islam. He ruled no order; he founded no school; his immediate influence upon the Church, save in the matter of the Pelagian controversy, cannot have been great, and all traces of his presence upon earth soon disappeared. It was not so with his writings. They remained to spread like oil in the centuries to come, and his many ideas germinated and blossomed far and wide like seeds from some famed garden of Europe broadcast upon the primeval virgin prairie.

CHAPTER FOUR
Boethius and Dionysius

The influence of Augustine on the thought, as distinguished from the theology, of Western Christendom, was slow in making itself apparent. The province of Africa, where he had been born and educated, and where his life and work as a bishop and doctor of the Catholic church had come to fulfilment, and which for more than two centuries had been one of the brightest centres of Christian life and letters, was lost to the Church shortly after the death of its most eminent son, and has remained to this day remote from the main stream of Western culture. Augustine had no organized school of disciples, and his peculiar and most characteristic contribution to philosophical method, the psychological approach to all the problems of human life and destiny, met with little sympathy or understanding in the last age of the ancient civilization in Italy and Gaul.

The last great thinker of the Roman world, the 'last of the Romans' as he has been called, though born fifty years after the death of Augustine, might seem to one ignorant of their respective chronology to belong to an earlier age. Boethius (c. 480–525/6) was born into one of the noblest and most distinguished of Roman families at that moment of rapid change in the West in which the name and pattern of the Western Empire had gone for good, while the administrative machinery and intellectual activity was still in great part untouched, and sections of the higher ranks of society in Italy and Gaul were prolonging the cultural life of the past. Indeed, there was a revival, a last flare-up, of ancient thought and letters more intense, and in some ways more authentic in spirit, than the pagan reaction of Augustine's day. By a strange, and at first sight paradoxical, twist of sentiment and fashion, the cultivated society of Rome and Gaul, though wholly Christian in its allegiance, showed in the outward forms of its life and monuments little resemblance to the specifically Christian and otherworldly outlook of the Church of the apologists and early fathers. The cultivated, literary bishops, such as Germanus of Capua, and the scholarly Roman senators of the fifth century, seem at first sight to be in reaction against the Christian way of life, as they had certainly, a few decades before, showed themselves hostile to the life of the early monks and ascetics.

Boethius was born at the moment when the line of western emperors had ceased for ever, and he was an eminent member of the Roman senatorial aristocracy which was used by Theodoric to administer Italy under his oversight with the old imperial technique of government. The young senator rose rapidly with precocious talent, becoming consul in 510, and attracted the notice of Theodoric who set him in 522, as Master of the Offices, in charge of the domestic administration and foreign policy of his kingdom. A year later, for causes that have not yet been fully elucidated, he was condemned on a charge of treason and other crimes, and, after almost a year's imprisonment, was executed. It was during his imprisonment that he wrote the book that has immortalized his name, *The Consolation of Philosophy*.

Boethius, though a man of great practical ability, was by education and predilection a philosopher. He had assimilated not only the ruling Neoplatonism but also the authentic teaching of both Plato and Aristotle in its original Greek linguistic dress. He was himself an eclectic, and cherished hopes of blending or harmonizing the doctrine of the two great masters; meanwhile he took his logic and natural science from Aristotle, his metaphysics and cosmology largely from Plato, and added to these something at least of the teaching and interpretation of the Neoplatonists. Before he was thirty, he had decided to devote his life to making a Latin translation, with a philosophical commentary, of the complete works of Plato and Aristotle. This stupendous task, which would in any case have demanded a long lifetime of application, was first thrown out of gear by the claims of public service and then abruptly ended by the confinement and death of the author when little more than forty years old. Boethius in fact succeeded in translating only the *Categories* and *De interpretatione* with commentaries, together with the *Introduction* of Porphyry and two commentaries, and several other treatises on formal logic which have survived. In addition he translated the works of Euclid, Ptolemy and others on music, arithmetic and geometry. In another field, there are several short treatises on theological subjects, chiefly the Trinity and Incarnation, now universally recognized as his. Finally, there is *The Consolation of Philosophy*.

The reputation of Boethius, whose influence upon the literature, the thought and the method of the eleventh and twelfth centuries, and indeed upon that of the great scholastics down to, and including, St Thomas, was second only to that of Augustine, has not endured into the modern world. His *Consolation* has made little appeal to Christian sentiment since the Reformation, and still less to the rationalist or materialist philosopher, while his legacy of method and technique, adopted and improved by the schools, became part of the system of scholasticism, and passed out of fashion when new disciplines were introduced. Nevertheless, the historian of medieval thought cannot neglect Boethius, for the thinkers of that age owed to him a great and manifold debt.

This debt was felt at every level of teaching. His surviving educational treatises did much to stereotype the programme of the *quadrivium,* and the very term was of his coinage. The schools of the eleventh and early twelfth centuries owed to him almost all they had, not only of the authentic works of Aristotle but also of their knowledge of his doctrines. We shall see later how dynamic this knowledge was to prove in a crucial issue of epistemology, the question of universals. Next, the thinkers of that age, and of the School of Chartres in particular, owed to his commentaries and to the general tendency of his writings such information as they possessed of the spirit and doctrines of Plato, tinged with Neoplatonism; this was none the less valuable through the accident of its transmission by a mind less powerful and original than that of Augustine, and with interests other than his. Beyond this, the early scholastics took from him their method, for he was an adept in all parts of the Aristotelian logic, and had himself much of the Aristotelian rationality and clarity of thought and expression that are not found in Augustine. Boethius was the first to apply Aristotelian methods to theological problems and to the elucidation of dogmatic statements. His conception of the functions of philosophy in analysing, defining and explaining doctrine approaches very nearly to that of the scholastics, who in fact were building upon his foundations, while on the purely linguistic level Boethius was second only to Cicero, if indeed he was second to any man, in coining Latin forms of technical Greek terms. As for definitions of terms and concepts that had become, and were to remain, the materials of theological analysis and speculation, many of the most familiar can claim Boethius as their author. Those of 'person', 'nature', 'eternity', 'providence', 'wisdom' and many others which are used in his treatises, became classic in the schools and were adopted by St Thomas with specific acknowledgment of their paternity.[1] His programmatic wedding of faith and reason, while owing much to Augustine, is expressed in a philosophical idiom more comprehensible, because more Aristotelian, than that of the earlier doctor. Finally, in the *Consolation* and elsewhere, Boethius, resting upon Plato and Aristotle, but adapting their principles to a universe governed by a personal God, the Creator and providential Governor of his creatures, put into currency ideas and formulae on eternal life, on the reconciliation of God's foreknowledge with man's free will, on the purely negative character of evil, and on the true freedom and beatitude of the just man unjustly condemned to suffer, which have ever since become part of the Christian heritage, while such familiar features as the argument for the existence of God drawn from the necessity of a perfect being as presupposed by any realization of the imperfection of beings in common experience, and in metaphysics, the difference between form and substance, found their first clear expression in his writings.

Many readers in modern times have been perplexed by the total absence of any allusion to specifically Christian doctrine or sentiment in the *Consolation*. If, however, we reflect that it was precisely in the centuries which we call the 'ages of faith' that the appeal of Boethius's work was felt most strongly, we may be led to think that the apparent problem may be rather one of sentiment than of essentials. In any case, a fuller knowledge than we possess both of the intellectual climate of Roman society at the time, and of the personality of Boethius himself, would probably do much to remove any difficulties that may be felt. Meanwhile, the reflection that the work was a spiritual classic precisely during the millennium when the Christian revelation was accepted integrally and without hesitation by all, would seem to show that it cannot be precisely our finer religious sense that is shocked. The explanation may well lie in the changed attitude towards philosophy since the later Middle Ages. Between the days of Augustine and those of Siger of Brabant it was the universal conviction among those who thought seriously that there was a single true rational account of man and the universe and of an omnipotent and provident God, as valid in its degree as the revealed truths of Christianity. The great men of old, pagan though they might have been, had attained and expressed this truth in their philosophy could one but reproduce their teaching faithfully, and with their aid a true

[1] *'Persona* est naturae rationalis individua substantia.' *'Aeternitas* est interminabilis vitae tota simul et perfecta possessio.' *'Providentia* est ipsa divina ratio in summo omnium principe constituta quae cuncta disponit.' These three definitions, among others, were accepted by Aquinas.

and sufficient answer could be given to the problems of human life and destiny. It was with these answers that the philosophical mind could meet the world and all the disasters of life. Behind the rational arguments, no doubt, in the unseen realm of the soul, an individual could meet the personal love and grace of Christ.

This was assuredly a very different way of thinking from that of Augustine, but Augustine was an African, a psychologist, and a saint; Boethius was a Roman and a scholar. To each of these great men the medieval thinkers were deeply indebted, and if the influence of Augustine was more profound in the realms of pure thought, Boethius, more than any other man, was the direct ancestor of the scholastic method.

While Boethius, in Rome and at Pavia, was sowing for posterity the seeds that were to provide matter and a method for a whole epoch of intellectual life, an unknown contemporary in Syria or Asia Minor was putting into circulation works that were to have an even greater and more durable influence upon the thought of the West. This writer, probably a Syrian monk, whose literary activity seems to have taken place around the beginning of the sixth century, effectually concealed his identity under the name of St Paul's convert, Dionysius the Areopagite, and by his references to Timothy and other personages connected with the Apostle, and to the Dormition of the Blessed Virgin, created the belief, at least in readers at a distance in space and time, that he was a witness to the teaching and way of thinking of the primitive Church. It is possible that no large-scale imposition was ever intended, and that the writer adopted, as a literary device, to suit his principal theme, the name of one who had worshipped the Unknown God, in Whom we live and move and have our being, and had added, as corroborative literary detail, a few topical references to his exposition of theology. However that may be, the unknown writer not only concealed his identity very effectually from posterity, but also ensured for his writings, for more than a thousand years, a respect and an authority which they would certainly not otherwise have acquired, and in consequence, through a misapprehension without parallel in either sacred or profane literature, much of his teaching has become embedded in the theological tradition of the West.

No serious doubt was raised as to the primitive character of the works of Denis until the fifteenth century, by which time all the forces of conservatism were ranged against those who, with inadequate proofs, attempted to expose the unauthenticity of the claim to apostolic authority, and it was not till the last decade of the nineteenth century, when two scholars, working independently, proved beyond a doubt that the pseudo-Denis derived some of his doctrine from Proclus (410–485), that general agreement was reached as to the true date and climate of ideas of the anonymous author.[2] As so often happens in such cases, the pendulum of critical opinion swung too far in the general feeling of disillusion. The undoubtedly Neoplatonic character of some of the sources of Denis led to assertions that his whole system was a version of Neoplatonism, and that the Christian inspiration and orthodoxy of his works were questionable. More recent study has led to a more balanced judgment. It has been convincingly shown that the principal debt of Denis is to St Gregory of Nyssa, and through him to Clement of Alexandria and Origen; in other words, Denis was an adept of the Christian Platonism that existed before and had developed independently of the thought of Plotinus and his school, and that the direct borrowings from the later Neoplatonism and Proclus were such as might have been made by any Syrian or Greek writer of the time. Denis, in fact, brought as his main contribution to the West the thought, deeply impregnated with Platonic and Plotinian elements, of the later patristic age in the Eastern Church. This, to one accustomed to the way of thinking in the Western Church, whether in the Middle Ages or today, might seem unfamiliar and even distasteful, but certainly not necessarily unorthodox, and the additional dosage of Neoplatonism received from Proclus intensified rather than constituted its leading tendencies.

Denis, therefore, in common with a large section of Greek patristic thought, accepted (as did St Augustine) many of the characteristic doctrines of Neoplatonism. God is above all attributes and qualities, even above Being itself, and to attain to a true expression of what He is we have to pass through assertion and denial to a re-assertion at a level above all that we can know or comprehend. God is ineffably unique, the One, in Whom all that exists participates without Himself participating in anything. Denis expounds the Plotinian circle in which all derives (Plotinus would have said emanates) from God and flows back to Him, but he also uses a mixture of Christian and Neoplatonic conceptions to make of the universe of spirit a vast hierarchy of laymen, monks, priests and bishops on earth, and in heaven of the orders of angelic beings, each order in heaven and on earth having its function, and each receiving from above the illumination, sacramental or intellectual as the case may be, that it passes on to those in the degree beneath itself.

[2]The two scholars were J. Stiglmayr and H. Koch, who both published in 1895.

The principal parts of the Dionysian legacy to the West were the negative and superlative theology, the strongly hierarchic conception of being, an elaborate angelology, and the doctrine of mediated illumination and spiritual knowledge conferred by the sacraments and by angelic ministration. This teaching was contained in the three larger writings, *On Divine Names, On Celestial Hierarchy,* and *On Ecclesiastical Hierarchy.* In addition to these, his small treatise on *Mystical Theology* was destined to have an even greater influence. Here, treating of the soul as an individual and not as the member of a hierarchy, Denis escapes from the economy of mediated illumination, and uses the degrees of being and spirit as so many degrees in the ladder of abnegation and ascent to be scaled by the soul in its progress Godward. From the beauties of creation it rises to the orders of spiritual beings and thence to a God-given contemplation of the divine names or the things of God. Above this, rarely and briefly, comes the ecstatic leap to the divine darkness, and union in that darkness with God. We can here recognize the Plotinian ecstasy, which we have met elsewhere translated into the terms of Augustine's experience, and which here reappears in an ambiguous form which could be, and was, accepted as the summit of the Christian mystic's attainment, but only after it had been subtly and perhaps even unwittingly changed from a primarily intellectual to a primarily volitional achievement, and from the brief immersion of the spirit in darkness and cloud to the consummation of union with the Word, the Spouse of the soul.

The Dionysian writings did not penetrate to the West for more than three centuries, and their full influence was not felt till another four hundred years had passed. Part of the original corpus of the Areopagite, indeed, failed to survive both in the East and in the West. Nevertheless, we cannot pass by the sixth century, so fruitful in writers and thinkers and leaders who were to mould the whole pattern of medieval life – the century of Boethius, of Cassiodorus, of Benedict of Nursia and of Gregory the Great – without remembering that it is also the century of a more elusive figure who, among the inheritors of the long Platonic tradition that was to be broken, it may be, even while he was writing, was the last in time but not the least in power to take his place among those who framed the pattern of Christian thought in the West.

CHAPTER FIVE
Education in the Ancient World

The system of education in the early Middle Ages, that is, from the time of Gregory the Great (*c.* 600) to the intellectual revival of the eleventh century (*c.* 1050), was a lineal descendant of the education that had been brought to perfection in the ancient classical civilization. As with so much that was of value in the realm of ideas and in the training of the mind and character, it had come to maturity in the century that elapsed between the ascendancy of Pericles at Athens and the death of Alexander the Great – between the birth of Plato and the death of Aristotle – and in the subsequent millennium, although its sphere of influence had broadened immeasurably and its technique had been perfected, it had gradually but steadily lost much of its original rich content and dynamic force. Even when the western world had become the theatre of human activities of a very different kind from those of the Athenian or even of the Alexandrian, the aims and practices of education had acquired very little that was new.

Greek education, as it first appeared in history, was essentially aristocratic in character. It was the culture of the few, the sons and daughters of men of rank and wealth, and was directed neither to the acquisition of a skill, trade or profession, nor to the cultivation of science, art, or philosophy, but to the formation of a full personality adapted to a particular way of life. So far as it consisted of instruction, as opposed to imitation and admiring recognition, it comprised athletics and music, both vocal and instrumental, but its core was literary tradition, with the Homeric poems as the text-books alike of letters and of life. This education, which in intention was ethical and psychological rather than technical or economically helpful, was that which came to be regarded by conservatives of the golden age of Athens, such as Aristophanes and at least one facet of Plato's mind, as the training that had produced the great men of old, the pristine honour and simplicity of the city.

This unprofessional and untechnical education was finally challenged and ousted, towards the end of the fifth century B.C., by a class of teachers, representatives of the new spirit of discussion, enquiry and criticism, known as the sophists, a term ambiguous even in its Greek form, and quite untranslatable into any single word of a modern European language. Both in their own day and since the sophists have come in for a great deal of criticism and abuse, some of it no doubt justified, but when we remember that Socrates was considered by many of his contemporaries to belong to the class, that Thucydides and Euripides were among the early pupils of the new masters, and that Isocrates, one of the greatest educationalists of history, was a sophist *par excellence*, we may hesitate before framing a sweeping judgement upon them.

The aim of the sophists was frankly practical: to fit a young man of brains (and few Athenians lacked mental agility) to take a leading part in the struggle for power and influence that was going on in every city-state of Greece and Magna Græcia. They were often opportunists and sceptics with regard to metaphysical and moral problems, and their enthusiasm for rhetoric and dialectic, the arts of debate and persuasion, led them to pay attention to what was useful rather than to what was virtuous, and to what was currently accepted rather than to what was true, but many of them were men of worth as well as talent, and their cult of versatility and urbanity was a characteristic, not of themselves alone, but of the genius of the Greek race throughout its history. Their abiding achievement was, in general, to make education primarily a training of the intellect, and, more particularly, to put rhetoric, the art of speaking well and persuasively, at the very heart of Greek education, and thus at the heart of all subsequent higher education until the rise of the medieval university.

At the time, however, it was not clear that the victory was to lie with Isocrates and his friends. His exact contemporary, Plato, had a very different ideal of education, which he elaborated in his masterpiece, the *Republic*, and put into practice in part at least, in his foundation, the Academy at Athens. In Plato's scheme education not only took on a moral and a civic aspect, to make it the nursing mother of good men and wise statesmen, but had also a transcendental value as an essential instrument in the acquisition of knowledge and wisdom and as a preparation of the soul for its immortal destiny. According to Plato's design, the literary and musical training of childhood was followed by a testing time of physical endurance; this in its turn was succeeded by the mental discipline of mathematics (i.e., geometry) and finally, after a space devoted to the practical life of government, by the dialectic of philosophical enquiry. The *Republic* is indeed a textbook for the establishment of a good society and for the ordering of a man's whole life; but in the sphere of education it marked an epoch, for Plato's scheme, and his own practice, made a clear distinction for the first time between primary and secondary education, and between education as a preparation for an active, practical life, and the higher education of philosophy, the attainment of moral and intellectual truth.

The scheme of Isocrates was less ambitious and more directly practical. With him the literary and mathematical stages were both preparatory; they were followed by a training in 'eristic' or the technique of disputation and argument, and this led on to what was the crown of all, the art of speaking well and persuasively. The two short generations (390–320 B.C.) in which Plato, Isocrates, and Aristotle were, either together or in succession, teaching and writing in Athens were perhaps the most genial and influential in all the history of education. In them Western mental training in all its essentials came to maturity both in theory and in practice. It is significant and fitting that the material buildings in which Plato and Aristotle taught, the Academy and the Lyceum, should have given their names in almost all Western languages to institutes of higher education.

Great and permanent, even in this field, as was the influence of the two philosophers, the victory and the future lay with Isocrates. His aims and precepts, though less profound and less sublime, were more practical and more comprehensible. When the age of Greece changed, after the conquests of Alexander, into the Hellenistic age, and the cities in all the countries bordering upon the eastern Mediterranean developed a Greek culture and Greek institutions, their education was a more schematized version of that of Isocrates. It is a mistake to think of him as a sophist in the pejorative sense of the word. While he considered that neither philosophy nor the higher mathematical studies were very valuable pursuits for a lifetime, he was equally intolerant of rhetoric as a purely utilitarian accomplishment. He conceived of it as the noblest of sciences, to be acquired by long and careful study, and as leading not only to practical wisdom, but to the formation of a sane, broad and virtuous mind: it was indeed the humanistic ideal that has been put forward at intervals ever since the Renaissance as the aim and end of a literary, classical education.

The Hellenistic education, as has been said, was a more schematized version of that of Isocrates. The three grades, primary, secondary and superior, now became universal: in the first the child learnt to read, to write and to cipher; in the second the boy absorbed the Greek classics, which now comprised a selection from the Athenian theatre and some other poetry, such as Hesiod, in addition to the Homeric corpus. At this stage a fuller technique had been evolved; Homer was now the object of systematic exegesis, in grammar, vocabulary and general meaning, completed often by an allegorical or ethical interpretation. In the third grade the youth studied geometry (i.e., Euclid), arithmetic, that is, not practical or applied arithmetic, but the study of number and its proportions, and harmony, which considered sound in all its relationships. This curriculum was a descendant of the original Pythagorean 'quadrivium' or fourfold exercise of arithmetic, geometry, astronomy and acoustic, from which astronomy had fallen out to become the province of scientific experts. It was enlarged or supported by courses of information on every kind of current knowledge, then known as 'encyclopedic' training; the original meaning of the term 'encyclopedia' was education in the information that 'lay around' to be known; the modern sense of comprehensive or complete information dates only from the sixteenth century. When supported, as it was in the great cities of Egypt, Syria and Asia Minor, by large collections of books, and facilities for research such as were supplied by the Museum of Alexandria, it was perhaps the finest system of general education that was ever to be found widespread in the ancient world. It must however be noted that it was not a university education in the modern sense of the word. Neither science nor philosophy formed part of the curriculum. These disciplines, which had come together for a brief space in the works and system of Aristotle, parted company almost at once. Science, both in its applied branches and in its mathematical and astronomical specializations, proceeded to develop in the hands of experts outside and above the ordinary educational profession, while philosophy became, and remained, a separate pursuit in the schools of Athens. Two further parts of what has been the pattern of academic discipline in the medieval and modern worlds, the medical and the legal education, remained the professional care of the practitioners in what was more like a guild than a part of university teaching.

Meanwhile, the literary elements steadily gained ground at the expense of the scientific and the mathematical, and by the middle of the third century B.C. rhetoric had conquered as the sole pursuit of the higher education, and philosophy was beginning to take on the aspect of a way of life, almost a religion, to which the individual turned by a species of conversion, and which he studied in a personal relationship with a distinguished teacher and guide.

In the early Roman republic there was no education of the intellect. The son grew up under the tutelage of his father, learning how to follow his example and the conventions and ideals of the golden age in the past. It was not until after the conquest of Achaea, when the wars with Carthage were over, that Greek culture began to influence the higher ranks of Roman society, and Greek education was introduced at the middle of the second century B.C. Thenceforward for almost a century the full Greek system was applied. This was the happiest age of Roman education. Restricted in practice to the senatorial class and the great families, it was rhetorical, in the sense that it aimed at making a man a fluent and persuasive speaker, but it was without any taint of 'sophistry' and was fully in touch with the demands of Roman life. The Roman noble had indeed to make his way by speaking – as an advocate in the forum, as a candidate to the people in the campus, as a counsellor or consul in the Senate, and even as a general in the camp – but his career was not that of a demagogue or a barrister or a parliamentarian. He held civil and military office; he judged; he administered; he commanded an army and he ruled a province. In consequence 'oratory' included a knowledge of all arts and knowledge that a leader of men should possess – history, law, literature – and all that might enable him to be a man among men, humane and just as well as capable and versatile. The education of which Cicero gives such a full and brilliant picture in the *De oratore* was indeed both a literary and a practical one; the sciences, mathematics and geometry, and philosophy are not parts of it; but it must not be confused or condemned along with the rhetorical education of the post-Augustan age. The education which produced a Cicero and a Cæsar, the one able to guide the State with distinction as consul, and to govern a province and lead troops without a long apprenticeship to arms, and the other able to speak as brilliantly as the greatest advocate, to show himself a gifted literary critic, and to be an authority on Latin grammar as well as to appear as the Cæsar of Gaul and the great dictator, cannot be pronounced either unpractical or bookish.

A great change came over education, as over all else, within a decade or two of the deaths of Cæsar (44 B.C.) and Cicero (43 B.C.) The change was twofold. On the one hand, under the Principate of Augustus all reality finally disappeared from the republican institutions. Careers were now either strictly professional and carefully graded in the army and civil administration, or directed by the choice of the *princeps* who controlled domestic and foreign policy, and to some extent even the judiciary. Oratory was no longer a prime necessity for public life, and open debate was no longer a preliminary to all decision. The change was not completed at once, but its progress was inevitable. The only use in practical life for the set speech was in the law-court, and there the speaker was no longer the orator, young or old, making his career or revisiting the forum as a man of reputation to aid a friend or client, but the professional barrister (*causidicus*) or persuasive pleader (*rhetor*). Eloquence moved from the forum and the senate to the lecture-hall and the private *salon*; the set declamation took the place of the speech or the political debate.

Concurrently, another great change was coming about. Cicero and his contemporaries had been nurtured on Greek literature and trained in Greek schools of rhetoric and philosophy. But within the fifty years following Cicero's entrance into public life (70–20 B.C.) a great flowering of genius had given Rome a native literature, if not as copious and as sublime, at least sufficiently notable to form a substitute for Greek in a consciously patriotic age. There was, within a generation, an almost complete change-over of language, literature and teachers. Cicero replaced the Greek orators and philosophers, Virgil stood for Homer, Livy and Sallust for Herodotus and Thucydides, Horace and Ovid for the Greek lyric poets and dramatists, until Seneca supplied a further need, and the list of school textbooks was augmented by every new arrival of acknowledged merit in the Silver Age. As a result, higher education lost throughout in vigour and life. Its product was the fluent speaker rather than the cultivated and humane man of action, the good critic rather than the good man. It is the distance between the *De oratore* of Cicero and the *Institutio oratoria* of Quintilian. Rhetoric was all in all. Law was the province of the professional, philosophy the pursuit of the few. The literary education became less and less a study of life, and more and more a pedantic and minutely erudite commentary. In the West Rome alone had teachers of law and philosophy.

From the middle of the second century of our era Roman education, while remaining unchanged in kind, became progressively more bookish and artificial. No new subjects, methods or text-books were introduced, and the rhetoric that was taught had less and less relevance to the political or social life of the times. Whether this lack of educational initiative should be regarded as a consequence of the general decadence of social and official enterprise, or whether it was itself a principal cause of that decadence, may be doubtful, but the conservatism of all concerned with education, in an age which witnessed a reorganization of the Empire, the triumph of Christianity, and a series of great calamities, is very remarkable. The revival of speculative thought with Plotinus and his disciples had no effect on higher education; the Neoplatonists, in the first century of their existence, were less an intellectual force than a sect; their influence might be compared to that of the Quakers or the Cambridge Platonists of the seventeenth century rather than to that of Hobbes or Locke, save that Neoplatonism came to have its greatest influence in aristocratic circles and to join forces with the conservative, anti-Christian cult of the old Roman religion. We are not concerned here with the Eastern half of the Empire, which in the event was to have so little influence on the West, but it may be noted in passing that the great Greek Fathers were almost without exception familiar with philosophy from study at Athens, Antioch or Alexandria, and that this philosophy was Platonic in character.

The Christian Church in the West was for long recruited principally from the lower, unleisured strata of society. When in the fourth century it began to win the educated classes there was no opposition or rival system to the old Roman primary education based on grammar and the classics. Christian children attended the schools of non-Christian masters, while Christian masters taught all comers according to the old curriculum. There was, however, a prejudice against a devotion to an adult, intensive study of pagan literature, and it need not be said that no Christian at this time would have become, so to say, a 'practising' Neoplatonist philosopher.

The view has often been put forward in the past that the early and patristic Church was consistently hostile to secular literature, including the Greek and Roman classics. As a broad and sweeping statement this cannot be maintained; one must distinguish between regions and periods. Christianity grew to adolescence in a world in which Greek and Latin literature were both classical and living, and when Greeks and Romans of education became Christians they used all the resources of those literatures in their own thought and writings. The Greek Fathers in particular adopted more or less consistently the view that ancient philosophy and literature were in a way a fore-shadowing of, an avenue leading to, Christian theology, and we have seen something of this outlook in St Augustine.

A change came when the Church, freed from restraint, mingled freely and even victoriously with the pagan world. On the one hand,

59

the new monastic movement tended to be strongly puritan in its attitude to culture, while on the other hand the Church was now on an equality with, or in a superior position to, the old mythological religion and ethic, and to the philosophical sects of Stoics or Neoplatonists. Consequently, some (though not all) of the most eminent Christian writers, especially in the West, came to regard the literature of Greece and Rome as pagan and immoral, and its charms as a sinful temptation. The two most celebrated examples of this tendency were themselves consummate masters of style who, secure in possession of all that the education of the day could give, reacted to what they felt to be their own excessive love of worldly beauty. Jerome's account of his appearance at the Judgment-seat, and his condemnation for his love of Plautus and Cicero – 'Thou art a Ciceronian, not a Christian; for where thy treasure is, there shall thy heart be also' – has been quoted in a hundred manuals. It is not so often recorded that long after his dream Jerome wrote the purest idiomatic Latin, with many quotations from Cicero, and composed letters in the best vein of a Juvenal. Similarly, Augustine's regret in his *Confessions*, that he had once been moved to tears by Virgil's Dido, must not be allowed to obscure the fact that to the end of his days Augustine used all the devices of rhetoric. Nevertheless, these two, and others besides, did sincerely condemn the study of ancient literature as un-Christian and reprehensible. A century later, as we have seen, Boethius and Cassiodorus were doing all they could to salve and to propagate ancient thought and letters, while a century later still Gregory the Great declared it unworthy to subject the inspired word of God to the rules of Donatus, and reproved literary bishops for letting the name of Jove pass their Christian lips, while professing himself careless of grammatical subtleties.

It was perhaps natural to attack a literature which was the principal attraction of a rival religion and philosophy, and fairly safe to do so while one could still enjoy, without effort, many of the amenities with which that culture had adorned life. But when Christianity was left alone to fight the battle of civilization in the west under the gloom of a leaden sky in a savage age, it was natural to look with other eyes upon the civilization of the past, and from A.D. 600 to 1000 the cultural history of Western Europe is a series of attempts, far separated in time and space, to recreate the glories of past ages by amassing and imitating their learning and literature. Nothing in literary history is more strange than these attempts, now in Ireland, now in Wessex, now in Northumbria, now in Touraine, now in Germany, to copy exactly the expressions, the metres and the vocabulary of ancient Rome under conditions so widely different. The literary monuments of those attempts are as exotic flowers or fruit appearing on the grafted branches of woodland trees; in Virgil's phrase, they marvel at their unfamiliar leaves and fruit that belongs to another;[1] and, like grafted trunks, they tend always to return to the wild.

The leaders of these revivals had a very different attitude to ancient literature from that of Jerome and Augustine. To them the ancients are a marvel; all knowledge comes from them; they are the only models; to imitate and reproduce them is the only hope. Alcuin and his Anglo-Saxon masters went a stage further: the liberal arts are not the work of man, but of God, who has created them as a part of nature for men to find and develop. The ancients did this, how much more eagerly and successfully should a Christian do so! And Alcuin in a well-known passage enunciates the functions of Christian humanism. In the morning of his life he had sown in Britain; in the evening of that life he ceased not to sow in France. His one desire was to build a new Athens in France, or rather, an Athens better than the old, for the old had only the science of the seven arts, but the new has in addition the seven Gifts of the Holy Ghost. Alcuin without knowing it was an Aristotelian in his view of nature, and all but a Thomist *avant le mot* in his account of the relationship between grace and nature. And in yet another way Alcuin reverses Jerome. Jerome turned to the monastic life as a flight from letters; Alcuin exhorts his monks to abandon the spade for the pen: *Fodere quam vites melius est scribere libros.*[2]

---

[1]*Georgics*, II. 82.
[2]*Carmina*, 94. 'Tis better to write books than plant vines' in E. Duemmler (ed.) *Monumenta Germaniae Historica. Poetae Latini Aevi Carolini* (Berlin, 1881), I, p. 320.

PART TWO
The Renaissance of the Eleventh and Twelfth Centuries

CHAPTER SIX
The Rebirth of the Schools

According to the Oxford Dictionary, the term 'dark ages' was originally applied to the Middle Ages, to denote the intellectual darkness of the times. Generations of historians have long ago pushed the dawn back from 1450 to 1050 or even to 800, and neither the age of Bede in Northumbria nor that of Isidore in Spain deserves the epithet of gloom, but both these areas of light were in fact eclipsed before long and if we look only at the area bounded by the Pyrenees, the Alps, the Rhine and the western sea there is little of educational and literary activity in the seventh and eighth centuries save in a few monasteries. Public schools had long since ceased to be, and the study of letters was preserved only in monasteries and a few bishops' households; the enlightened bishops were in most cases themselves monks. Gregory of Tours (538–94), though a voluminous historian, is frequently ungrammatical and uncouth, and apologizes for his lapses, and the language of St Benedict, the contemporary of Cassiodorus (*c*. 490–*c*. 583), shows equally the breakdown of classical grammar. Elementary education, where it existed at all, was almost entirely personal – that of the gifted priest teaching his clerk or a forward boy of his parish. In consequence, the legislation of King Charles the Great was epoch-making in this respect as in so many others. He announced his policy in general terms in a capitulary of uncertain date (*c*. 780–800):

> It has seemed to us and our faithful counsellors that it would be of great
> profit and sovereign utility that the bishoprics and monasteries of
> which Christ has deigned to entrust to us the government should not
> be content with leading a regular and devout life, but should undertake
> the task of teaching those who have received from God the capacity to
> learn, each according to his abilities .... Doubtless [he continues] good

works are better than great knowledge, but without knowledge it is impossible to do good.[1]

A celebrated capitulary of 789 is more precise:

> In every bishop's see, and in every monastery, instruction shall be given in the psalms, musical notation, chant, the computation of years and seasons, and in grammar; and all books used shall be carefully corrected.[2]

This was reiterated by the Council of Chalon in 813:

> As our emperor Charles ... commanded, bishops shall set up schools where letters and the science of the Scriptures shall be taught; in these schools [the fathers add, somewhat sententiously] shall be brought up those to whom the Saviour says with justice: 'Ye are the salt of the earth.'[3]

We can see these instructions being passed down to a lower level by Alcuin's friend and successor Theodulf, bishop of Orleans and abbot of Fleury:

> In the villages and townships the priests shall open schools. If any of the faithful entrust their children to them to learn letters, let them not refuse to instruct these children in all charity ... when the priests undertake this task, let them ask no payment, and if they receive anything, let it be only the small gifts offered by the parents.[4]

These decrees have been cited at some length, in order to show the simplicity of the educational system of the empire, and thus to show also how impossible it was that anything that could be called higher education should come into being in the Europe of the Carolingian epoch. This simple framework was all that existed – and that only when wars, invasions and human inertia permitted – from 800 till well after A.D. 1000. Monks received what their elders in the monastery had to give; children, whether children sent by their parents to the priest, or oblates taught by their master in the cloister, learnt grammar and psalmody; the fortunate might receive instruction in letters and elementary calculation in the schools of a monastery or a cathedral city; theology was the only 'advanced' study, either in the monastery or in the bishop's *familia*. There was no higher education north of the Alps, nor any professional class of teachers whether lay or clerical. Clearly, any kind of philosophical activity was out of the question.

[1]*Capitularia regum francorum*, i, ed. A. Boretius, *Mon. Germ. Hist.* (1883), 29.
[2]*Capitularia*, i, 22, c. 72.
[3]*Concilia aevi karolini*, ed. A. Werminghoff, *Mon. Germ. Hist.* (1906), pp. 274–5.
[4]*Capitula ad presbiteros*, 20 (Migne, *P. L.* cv. 196).

Nevertheless, it was from the Carolingian schools that the intellectual life of the middle ages developed, and it may be well to look for a moment at the pattern of education as they saw it, a ghost of the curriculum of the ancient world, yet a ghost which was in time to be a true *revenant*, a 'come-back' from the great days of Athens.

In the last century of the Roman Republic Varro (116–27 B.C.), 'the most learned of the Romans', had written a lengthy description of the 'nine liberal arts' – grammar, logic, rhetoric, geometry, arithmetic, astronomy, music, medicine and architecture. These were to be the basis of the medieval education, but under the Roman Empire all save the first three fell out of the educational programme. Varro's classification was taken up, in the last century of the Empire, by Martianus Capella, who wrote, *c.* 410–39, an encyclopedia of education destined to be the principal text-book of schools in the early Middle Ages. He has only seven liberal arts, i.e., Varro's nine less medicine and architecture, which had become professional subjects, and this new arrangement became classic, forming in later centuries the two groups of the *trivium* and *quadrivium*. Capella had sweetened his doctrine by presenting it in the form of an allegory, the marriage of Philosophy with Mercury, in which the bride was accompanied by seven maidens, the nurses of the liberal arts, each replete with symbolic attributes. His book was popular throughout the Middle Ages, and lent itself to illustration; the liberal arts soon passed into art, where they had a distinguished career in manuscript illuminations, in stone on the porches of Chartres and Laon, in stained glass and, finally, in Botticelli's frescoes at the Villa Lemmi. Alcuin, taking things seriously, endeavoured in his dialogues on Grammar, Rhetoric and Dialectic to de-allegorize and make practical the traditional scheme. He was followed by Theodulf of Orleans who, while remaining allegorical, simplified Capella, and by Hrabanus Maurus who, in his work on the Instruction of Clerks, gave a short practical instruction for those who wished to cover all the ground. For all the various parts of the scheme time-honoured text-books were classic. Thus for Grammar Priscian and Donatus were learnt, and their instructions applied to reading and composition in Latin prose and verse. For Rhetoric the text-books were the *De oratore* of Cicero and the *Institutio Oratoria* of Quintilian. For Dialectic were used the *Isagoge* or *Introduction* of Porphyry, the *Categories* and *De interpretatione* of Aristotle, with the commentary of Boethius. Arithmetic began with simple multiplication and division, which included in their higher reaches the manipulation of the *abacus* or counting-board, rendered necessary by the impracticability of the

Greek and Roman numerals; it continued with chronology, of which a large part consisted in the computation of the indictions and of the date of Easter; finally the allegorical interpretation of numbers, highly developed by Augustine and others, had a part here. The text-books were Bede's *Liber de temporibus* and *Liber de ratione temporum*. Geometry consisted of a certain amount of Euclid, eked out by Gerbert of Aurillac, and for Astronomy Pliny augmented by Bede. Finally came Music which, we must remember, was *musica* as opposed to *cantus*. Plainchant and its neums, when they developed, were taught until the eleventh century, when the stave and written music became more common, almost entirely by practice and memory to the choir or *schola cantorum* by the *cantor* or *precentor*. Music as a part of education consisted in a study of the relation of the notes of the scale to numbers and arithmetic, and ultimately to the harmony of the universe, the music of the spheres, a distant legacy from Pythagoras. Here the text-books were Boethius and Bede. In addition to all these parts of the *trivium* and *quadrivium* there was the parallel encyclopedic literature, reaching back by way of Varro to Alexandria. Here the text-books were Isidore of Seville in the more recent editions of Bede, Alcuin and others.

All this apparatus of learning was intended to lead up to the crown of all, the study of Scripture and the greater Latin Fathers. Actually, however, between 600 and 1000 the *quadrivium* was in eclipse as an educational syllabus, and was either omitted altogether or treated simply in a brief, factual way. Of the *trivium* likewise one element, dialectic, was omitted or treated rather as a piece of memory work than as an intellectual discipline. This left Grammar and Rhetoric – that is, a purely literary education – in possession of the field, and consequently we find that most of the notable writers and teachers of the dark ages devoted all their talents to history or versifying or grammatical writing, and that those who wrote theological works did so in a literary way. It is also possible to see in the current treatment of the *trivium* and *quadrivium* how and whence the principal trends of the eleventh and twelfth centuries developed from this curriculum. The literary background of the historians, poets and humanists comes from the fully developed grammar and rhetoric; philosophy and speculative theology rose in due time from revived dialectic; and medieval science was in a development of the encyclopedic learning of Isidore and Bede and their continuators, later augmented by Arabic and Aristotelian treatises. Finally we may note that in the Carolingian age dialectic was so little prized that it was transposed from its true place to a position between grammar and rhetoric, as something to be got over quickly. In the revival of the eleventh century it was restored to its rightful place, developed enormously, and then augmented by the whole Aristotelian corpus of philosophy and its accompanying commentaries. The change from rhetoric to logic as the *pièce de résistance* of the curriculum is the index of a cultural revolution.

Seen from a distance in the perspective of history, the Carolingian revival is only one of the many revivals, Irish, English, continental, that occurred during the early Middle Ages; a patch of sunlight rather brighter than the others which in its turn disappeared in a swirl of mist. Historically, however, it is more important and had more permanent results than any of its predecessors for a number of reasons.

In the first place, the legislation of Charles and his immediate successors was something new. Even if it rested in part on practice or ancient decrees, it was novel in its crisp precision and universal application. Though soon neglected in practice it remained, like much else in Carolingian legislation, as a memory, a precedent and a basis for future action and law. Secondly, and in this unlike the previous insular or German centres of light, the Carolingian revival did not wholly vanish from Europe. Like a fire in dry grass it passed here and there, always alive at this monastic centre or that. And finally, the teaching and example of Alcuin,[5] who insisted on the necessity of good copies of all the best models in the field of text-books, and who had himself set up excellent *scriptoria* in many places, had given a new impetus and technique to the copying of manuscripts; this continued without abatement at very many monasteries, more methodically and with a wider scope than before; and in the so-called Carolingian minuscule, which actually owed much to the script of Ireland and Northumbria, it had an instrument of great power. With Alcuin began the great age of the copying of Latin manuscripts, both patristic and classical, and this gradual accumulation of clearly (and more correctly) written books was of inestimable value when the more comprehensive revival came two centuries later.

From the time of Alcuin onwards there were in north-western continental Europe two types of school, in accordance with Charlemagne's legislation, viz., the cathedral or episcopal school and the monastic school. The cathedral school, theoretically existent in every bishopric, but in fact by no means common, was conducted either by the bishop himself or (more frequently) by a school master

[5]For Alcuin see Eleanor Duckett, *Alcuin* (New York, 1952).

known as the *scholarius, capiscola* or *magister scholarum*. His pupils were boys and young clerks of every age, destined for the priesthood and often living with the canons, at cathedrals where the chapter followed a rule, very much on the same terms as the children of the cloister lived with the monks. The monastic school was, in the intention of both Charlemagne and Alcuin, made up of two branches, the one consisting of the children and young monks of the house, including those sent from less well-equipped monasteries, and the other an extern school for clerks conducted by the monks. Outside the two classes of clerks and monks few at this period would have received any schooling in letters.

Of these three schools only one was permanent and ubiquitous, the internal monastic school, which was a *sine qua non* for a community's prosperous existence. Of the other two, the bishop's school often disappears, and in the monasteries either a lack of pupils or motives of reform often led to the suspension of the extern school. For the two centuries after Charlemagne, therefore, the monasteries and the monks were the chief seats and agents of culture on the Continent, and these are the centuries known with some justice as the monastic or Benedictine centuries. Famous among a host of abbeys were Tours, the home of Alcuin, Fulda, where Hrabanus Maurus, the pupil of Alcuin, became 'the schoolmaster of Germany', and Reichenau, home of Walafrid Strabo. Hrabanus Maurus, encylopedist and theologian, Lupus of Ferrières, the indefatigable borrower and copier of manuscripts and humanist writer of letters, Walafrid the poet, who describes in detail the plants in the garden at Reichenau – these are, with Einhard, the biographer of Charlemagne, the greatest figures of the generation after Alcuin. All are, in their way, literary humanists; lovers, that is, of ancient poetry and learning for its own sake; nor can we wholly despise the muse of those who have given us some of the finest of the Latin hymns, the *Gloria, Laus* of Palm Sunday, the majestic *Ut queant laxis* of the Baptist, and the incomparable *Veni Creator*. None of them was, however, an original thinker. Indeed, the only writer to deserve such a title between Boethius and Anselm was John the Scot (i.e., the Irishman, as his surname, Erigena, implies), who lived from *c.* 810 to *c.* 877. Erigena is a voice in the wilderness; he knew Greek, and in this respect was superior to any of the Carolingian scholars, he had read many of the Greek Fathers, including Origen, and he had translated the pseudo-Denis into Latin and developed a whole system of theology based on later Neoplatonism. He was the head of the palace school under Charles the Bald (*c.* 852) and disappears from history *c.* 877, to reappear later both in myth and as a wandering star of thought. Erigena's system is a difficult one to grasp and is certainly unorthodox in implication, though not in intention, but it had so little direct influence on the scholastics that it need not detain us here.

Soon after the end of Erigena's career the Carolingian renaissance foundered under the stress of dynastic and feudal wars and invasions of the Northmen, and a century (880–980) began which, save in England under Alfred, Athelstan and Dunstan, was as dark as any that had gone before it. 'A century of iron, lead, and darkness', was the severe judgement of the unsympathetic Italian historian Baronius in the sixteenth century, and Mabillon, while pointing to the birth of Cluny, did not do much to lighten the picture. It was indeed a dark time, save for England, yet in a number of monasteries in inland districts untouched by war or by the Northmen the fire of learning smouldered on under the ashes. The tide turned about 970, though so little material is as yet available for the history of education, especially in Italy, that it is not possible to say when or by what agency the decisive change began. In north Italy the urban schools of grammar and perhaps also of law had never wholly ceased to function, and it is notable that the great figures born in the early part of the eleventh century – Peter Damian, Lanfranc, Cardinal Humbert – whatever their views on literature and learning, show themselves to be possessed either of a wide and accurate literary culture, or of a technical knowledge of law, Roman or Canon, or of all these accomplishments. Henceforth, and especially after the first decade of the eleventh century, there is a real change, slow at first but unmistakable. Henceforward, there is such a thing as European education and thought, and though technique and framework change, there is a steady passage from one phase to another, and, generally speaking, from the superficial to the deeper, and from the narrow to the broader. Now, though both in thought and literature the ancients remain authorities to be imitated or followed, until 1200 at least in literature and for a century after that in thought, yet the writers, and above all the thinkers, consciously criticize and innovate and, what is more significant, move boldly forward on uncharted seas of metaphysics and theology. Henceforward, therefore, both thought and its technique, and the institutions which harboured it, become topics susceptible of detailed examination and criticism.

71

CHAPTER SEVEN
The Awakening of Western Europe

Although the myth of a Christendom awaiting imminent dissolution in the year 999, and surging forward in relief in 1001, has been effectively banished from serious historical writing, the millenary year, coinciding as it did with part of the brief pontificate of Silvester II, the most learned man of his day in Europe, is an easy and convenient date to mark the opening of a new epoch. The great revival of the eleventh century, which gathered amplitude and momentum in the twelfth century, and reached its highest and most characteristic, though not perhaps its most universal, achievement in the thirteenth century, was manifest in all contemporary mental activities and affected theology, philosophy, religious reform, both public and private, literature as well in poetry as in prose, architecture, sculpture, illumination, law both canon and civil, mathematics and the natural sciences. Here we are not concerned with art, and can consider mathematics and science only incidentally; our principal concern is with thought, and more superficially with literature and law in so far as they reflect thought.

In all the departments of mental activity that have been mentioned there was a simultaneous renaissance and a parallel, though not in every case an equally swift or extensive, advance. Thus the period 1000–1150 was distinguished primarily by a literary renaissance, culminating in the age of the great historians, humanists, preachers and letter-writers of the age of St Bernard, William of Malmesbury and John of Salisbury. Thenceforward, Latin letters declined. Philosophy and theology, on the other hand, developed slowly but steadily from 1050 onwards, reaching their fullest expansion only between 1220 and 1350, after which a rapid decline began. Law, for its part, grew steadily in importance during the eleventh century, made its most spectacular advances in the middle decades of the twelfth century, and continued as an influential discipline, though without striking developments and changes, until the end of the Middle Ages and beyond.

This great European revival had certain leading characteristics which help the historian to describe its course.

It was in origin confined to the regions covered by the modern countries of France and Belgium and the northern Italian district of Lombardy; it subsequently spread to and absorbed Great Britain south of the Firth of Forth, southern and western Germany, central and south Italy and Sicily, and part of northern Spain. It is, however, remarkable that there was no national or political focus, and for more than a century it was officially fostered by neither pope nor emperor, and patronized neither by a monarch nor by an aristocracy. It was in every sense of the word a supra-national movement, forming a republic of teachers, thinkers and writers. It had the characteristic, peculiar to itself in the history of Western Europe, of becoming in its final development a supra-racial, yet wholly homogeneous, culture. For three hundred years, from 1050 to 1350, and above all in the century between 1070 and 1170, the whole of educated Western Europe formed a single undifferentiated cultural unit. In the lands between Edinburgh and Palermo, Mainz or Lund and Toledo, a man of any city or village might go for education to any school, and become a prelate or an official in any church, court or university (when these existed) from north to south, from east to west. It is the age of Lanfranc of Pavia, Bec and Canterbury, of Anselm of Aosta, Bec and Canterbury, of Vacarius of Lombardy, Canterbury, Northampton and York, of Hugh of Avalon, Witham and Lincoln, of John of Salisbury, Paris, Rheims, Canterbury and Chartres, of Nicholas Brakespeare of St Albans, France, Scandinavia and Rome, of Thomas of Aquino, Cologne, Paris and Naples, of Duns Scotus of Dumfries, Oxford, Paris and Cologne, of William of Ockham, Oxford, Avignon and Munich. In this period a high proportion of the most celebrated writers, thinkers and administrators gained greatest fame and accomplished the most significant part of their life's work far from the land of their birth and boyhood. Moreover, in the writings of all those who have just been named, there is not a single characteristic of language, style or thought to tell us whence they sprang. True, we are speaking only of a small educated minority, to which the land-owning aristocracy in general, many monarchs, and even some bishops, did not belong. The world of Church and State was often rent by schisms and wars, while the bulk of the population, fast rooted in the soil, knew nothing beyond the fields and woods of their small corner. But on the level of literature and thought there was one stock of words, forms and thoughts from which all drew and in which all shared on an equality. If we possessed the written works without their authors' names we should not be able to assign them to any country or people. If we contrast the group of writers mentioned above with half-a-dozen eminent contemporaries of the unusually stable European culture of the eighteenth century – with such men as Kant, Hume, Johnson, Voltaire, Goethe, John Wesley and St Alfonso de' Liguori – we shall immediately feel the difference. Each of the former group is intellectually 'stateless'; each of the latter group has something regional about him.

Yet within the ring-fence of this common culture, movements, institutions and pursuits varied and developed from place to place and from time to time. Thus, speaking very generally, and excluding the largely homeless and rootless group of the Roman curia, the highest mental activity south of the Alps was urban and largely lay, and found its most typical expression in medicine and law. This, the north Italian culture, had an important spill-over into Provence. North and west of the Alps, on the other hand, the revival in the first century was wholly clerical and monastic; it had its centres in the monasteries and cathedral cities, and found its highest and most typical expression in philosophy and theology.

Speaking still more generally, and regarding the dynamics of the revival, we can see a steady shift northward of the centre of gravity. In the middle decades of the eleventh century Salerno, Monte Cassino and the Roman curia were in the van of the advance. Fifty years later the leadership had shifted to Bologna, and before the end of the century France was becoming the schoolmistress of Europe. At the end of the next century Paris was firmly established as the intellectual centre of Europe, and if she remained in pride of place for a century more, other schools, such as Cologne and Oxford, drew level, and for a few decades in the middle of the fourteenth century the two English universities between them perhaps surpassed Paris in their galaxy of talent. Yet if the centre of gravity shifted, men of the most diverse provenance would be constantly found at every point of importance. At the beginning of the fourteenth century both Duns the Scotsman and Marsilio the Paduan left their mark on Paris.

There is a comparable shift in balance if we consider the institutions, the practitioners and the disciplines of this culture. As regards institutions, the organs or instruments of education were: the monastery from 1000 to *c.* 1150; the cathedral school from 1000 to 1200; the individual master from 1050 to 1150; and the university from 1150 onwards in Italy, and from 1200 onwards in France. These various types of education were reflected in the classes who frequented them. The eleventh century was still primarily the age of the monks, though the secular clerks were growing in numbers at the cathedral schools; the twelfth century was the age of the secular masters and clerks and of the lawyers; in the thirteenth and early fourteenth centuries these classes were still very numerous, but in many of the most celebrated universities the class that gave distinction and set the tone in all matters of philosophy and theology was a new one, that of the friars. As regards the disciplines in fashion, the mental atmosphere of the eleventh century was predominantly literary and humanistic; humanism reached its finest point early in the following century, but already dialectic and speculative theology had become more and more attractive and absorbing and universal in their appeal. From about 1175 they had completely ousted the old literary culture; in the thirteenth century philosophy in all its branches began for the first time to find for itself a curriculum and a discipline that made it an alternative to, and not merely a preparation for theology, and henceforward the two drifted more and more apart.

No adequate cause can be assigned for this great reawakening. Those which have been proposed, such as the return of peace to Western Europe, with a consequent growth of ordered government, wealth and leisure, are certainly not the originating causes of such a widespread, permanent and dynamic change; they are scarcely even necessary conditions. The revival can best be described by a simile: it was the psychological and intellectual adolescence of the new races in Europe. Just as the awakening of the powers of criticism, and a new potentiality of emotion, come in the life of the normal individual, though not always at precisely the same age, so here something analogous occurred in a group of peoples. If we leave the realm of simile, we may say that about A.D. 1000 in north-western Europe, just as in the peoples around the Aegean sea *c.* 1000 B.C., the elements that combine to produce the mental and psychological qualities of man began to group and blend in a peculiarly harmonious way. The parallel with ancient Greece is indeed very striking. There, as in medieval Europe, the intellectual rebirth cannot be tied down to a single moment or assigned to a single cradle, it appears everywhere within a very wide area; in Greece, as in Europe, a principal part was ultimately taken by dialectic and speculative thought, and there sprang up everywhere men of the most acute mental perception; in

Greece also, before and during the lifetime of Socrates and Plato, the weapons of logic and dialectic were turned against venerable institutions and doctrines, as they were in medieval France; there, as here, a great body of logic, metaphysics and ethics was built up; there, as here, a sceptical and opportunist school of thought succeeded in breaking the fabric of thought constructed by the great creative masters, in Greece, Plato and Aristotle, in Europe, St Bonaventure and St Thomas.

Further than this, however, the parallel between ancient and medieval must not be pressed. A principal difference lies in the scope of the revival. The Greeks were the masters of every department of thought and of all the arts; they were, besides, framers of a political and legal system that was both original and admirable, and they excelled in all the mental qualities that civilize and adorn civic and private social life. The men of the middle ages rivalled the golden age of Greece in powers of speculation, in architecture and even perhaps in the plastic arts, but in literature in all its branches they cannot compare with Greece, nor did they create a fully developed polity of their own. Nevertheless, the parallel between the three ages of Greek thought – the pre-Socratic, the sophistic, and the mature thought of the Academy and the Lyceum – and the three stages of scholasticism – that of the cathedral schools of the eleventh century, that of the great dialectical masters such as Abelard and Gilbert de la Porrée, and that of the epoch of the universities of Paris and Oxford – is within limits both valid and valuable. And to complete the picture, there is the perennial rivalry, in medieval France as in Hellenistic thought, between those who claim to follow the doctrines of Plato and those who choose the system of Aristotle.

Before passing in review the principal masters of the eleventh century it may be well to consider the educational resources of the age and to attempt some kind of definition of what we so readily label as 'scholasticism'.

In the century before the outlines of the university began to crystallize there were four types of *foci* of higher education: the monastery, the cathedral school, the urban school and the individual and often peripatetic master.

The monastic school at this time was almost exclusively domestic, that is, it existed for the benefit of monks alone. Nevertheless, since the monastic body was large and influential, and counted among its members a majority of the thinkers and writers of all kinds prior to *c.* 1150, the schools of the cloister were still of significance. In general, they continued throughout this period to give the traditional literary education, and they were *ex hypothesi* impervious to the direct influence of the great secular masters, whether attached to a cathedral school or peripatetic, though indirectly, through the writings of these teachers, or through their old pupils who had become monks, there was a certain infiltration into the monasteries from the schools. On the whole, the chief significance of the monasteries continued to lie in their possession of rich libraries, and their facilities for the multiplication of texts, and their principal literary pursuits were the writing of history and the continuation of the unsystematic, meditative treatment of theology. Two houses, however, stand out from the rest and compel us to make some modification of the broad general statements just given.

These two monasteries were, in their different ways, so eminently important in the intellectual history of their age that they have often been regarded by historians as typical, rather than as exceptions to a general practice. We are speaking, of course, of the abbeys of Monte Cassino in central Italy, and of Bec in Normandy. The former, with its magnificent library, its connections with the Byzantine world, and its series of distinguished abbots, greatly assisted, and was itself affected by, the revival of medicine and letters in central and southern Italy. Monte Cassino was at its apogee *c.* 1050–90, when abbot Desiderius, later Pope Victor III, was supervising the multiplication of the classical poets and prose writers, and the African monk Constantine was translating Hippocrates and Galen into Latin. At almost the same time, *c.* 1045–90, Bec was winning renown all over Europe as the home of the two greatest writers and theologians of the age. Lanfranc, already famous as a teacher before he became a monk, lectured to all comers in the abbey's early days in order to obtain for it the means of existence; Anselm, so far as we know, taught only in the cloister, but monks from other monasteries came to Bec to attend his lectures. It must also be remembered that many of the ablest and most celebrated bishops of the time were monks, and were thus in a position to influence, directly or indirectly, their own cathedral schools as well as individual pupils.

The cathedral school was at once the most universal and the most stable centre of enlightenment. In law and theory, as we have seen, each cathedral possessed a school, and in the period 1050–1200 most of the important sees in central, northern and north-eastern France did in fact have such a school, as did also Lorraine, the Rhineland and, later, England, though there was never a time when the practice was universal. These schools had a fixed point, so to say, in the official chancellor who had, under the bishop, the duties of organization and teaching, and in fact the most celebrated masters and ways of thought were for long based upon cathedral schools such as Chartres, Laon, Orleans and Paris. Later, and especially after *c.* 1100, when a number of individual teachers came to eminence and drew pupils from all over Europe, individual cathedral schools waxed and waned, but *c.* 1150 York could be visited by the great Italian lawyer Vacarius, while fifty years later Lincoln and Exeter were still celebrated enough to attract Gerald of Wales and Thomas of Marlborough, later chronicler and abbot of Evesham.

During the first great phase of medieval thought the most celebrated cathedral schools lay in a relatively small region of France between Orleans and Rheims, with its centre in the Ile de France. Here lay Orleans, Chartres, Paris, Laon and Rheims. Further north, on the confines of modern Belgium, lay another group including Liège and Tournai. Among the French schools Orleans and its neighbours on the Loire were distinguished for their cult of classical literature and poetry; Chartres stood supreme with its rich humanistic library, leading from letters through mathematics to Platonic philosophy; Laon enjoyed a brief but brilliant epoch of theological teaching; and Paris early became celebrated as a centre of dialectic and speculative theology. Below the level of these schools there existed, in ever-increasing number, schools of grammar and literature. How efficient these could be, whether conducted by a secular master or a religious house, may be seen from the achievements of 'old boys' of local schools otherwise unknown, such as those that formed the mind and style of Bernard of Clairvaux and Ailred of Rievaulx.

Urban schools were in the eleventh century restricted to northern Italy, where in large part they took the place of the cathedral school of the north. Here again unknown schools produced an Anselm of Aosta and a Damian of Ravenna, while on a higher level the chief towns had schools of Lombard law, such as that attended by Lanfranc, perhaps at Pavia.

Finally, the eleventh century saw the rise of a new class of teacher, the professional master who moved from school to school or from place to place, carrying with him or attracting a numerous following by virtue of his purely personal qualities. One of the first examples of this type was Anselm of Besate, an Italian who called himself the Peripatetic and who passed through Burgundy to Germany by slow stages. This class, by their acceptance or assumption of the title of 'sophist', themselves recognized their affinity with the Greek sophists of the age of Socrates. The very fact of mobility was something new, and it argued an enterprise, if also a restlessness, of mind, and alike in their concentration upon dialectical methods, in their critical and showy behaviour, in their appeal to youth and in their acceptance of fees, they recalled their Hellenic prototype. They were, as may be imagined, *bêtes noires* for the traditional masters.

With the masters of logic of the mid-eleventh century the age of scholasticism may be said to begin; it lasted for roughly three hundred years, that is, from 1050 to 1350, from Berengar to Wyclif. How then are we to define scholasticism?

For a century and more historians have agreed to use the term as a synonym of 'medieval' when treating of systems of thought. Scholastic philosophy or 'scholasticism' has consequently become a current and unavoidable label. This has created a difficulty for more recent scholars, for when regarded more closely 'scholasticism' proved unsusceptible of formal definition or description. It is indeed, formally speaking, a meaningless term. A 'scholastic' was originally one who learnt or who taught in a school, specifically in a school of the middle ages, and scholastic philosophy is the kind of philosophy taught in those schools. Thus the term of itself tells us no more than that medieval thought was beaten out and handed down in the daily give-and-take of the public schools. This is indeed a characteristic of medieval thought, by which it is distinguished from ancient thought, such as that of Socrates or Plotinus, and even much of that of Plato, as it is also from most modern thought, which makes its first appearance in printed books, but it tells us little or nothing of the essence and character of the thought itself. Indeed, the term 'scholastic' cannot rightly be applied to the content, as opposed to the method, of medieval philosophy; it is essentially a term of method. If by a scholastic method we understand a method of discovering and illustrating philosophical truth by means of a dialectic based on Aristotelian logic, then 'scholastic' is a useful and significant term. This medieval dialectic, whether, as in an early phase, it is based on Boethian precepts, or whether, as in its mature phase, it rests upon the whole corpus of Aristotelian logic, or whether, in its phase of disintegration, it is a criticism or a supposedly new and truer interpretation of Aristotle, follows throughout a basic pattern of question (*quaestio*), argument (*disputatio*) and conclusion (*sententia*), and it is recognizable throughout the range of forms in which medieval thought finds expression, whether it be the dialogues of St Anselm, the *Sentences* of the Lombard, or the *Commentaries on the Sentences*, the *Summae* and the *Quæstiones disputatae* of the thirteenth century, or the *De causa Dei* of Bradwardine. Thus understood as a methodical process, 'scholasticism' is almost, though not quite, coextensive with medieval thought. Certain works stand apart, which are certainly a part of medieval intellectual achievement and yet are scarcely scholastic in method, such as the theological writings of St Bernard, the *Itinerarium mentis ad Deum* of St Bonaventure, and the vernacular sermons of Eckhart; the first is quite untouched by Aristotelian dialectic, and in the two latter the 'scholastic' element is only occasional and accidental. On the other hand, the writings of Siger of Brabant, and of some of the followers of William of Ockham, are fully 'scholastic' in form, but in content have few or none of the specific characteristics of medieval thought.

What are these characteristics? Many attempts at isolating them have been made within the past sixty or seventy years, but it has been with medieval thought as with such descriptive terms as 'liberal' and 'romantic': we all feel that we know very well what they imply, and do not hesitate to say that this or that falls within their definition, but when it comes to a formal classification, we are all to seek. Maurice de Wulf, the earliest of the qualified historians of medieval thought of our own day, proposed as notes of scholasticism the acceptance by all thinkers of a wide range of philosophic postulates, such as the existence of God and His creative action, the worth of human personality, the existence of a supernatural order of being, and the objectivity of human knowledge. This would indeed distinguish scholastic philosophy from Arabian and from much modern thought, though it would also exclude the Parisian 'integral' Aristotelians, who were certainly 'scholastics', but it would scarcely differentiate it from any truly Christian system, such as that of Augustine, or indeed from any form of orthodox Christian Platonism.

Martin Grabmann, criticizing de Wulf, saw the essence of medieval thought in the Anselmian *credo ut intelligam*, the employment of the human reason in penetrating and explaining the truths of revelation, the supernatural truths of religion, and in the philosophical approach which such an attempt demanded. It was, however, pointed out by de Wulf and others that while this might be adequate as a description of medieval thought when applied to theological truths, it did not satisfy as a definition of medieval philosophy as such, which was from the first, and became more and more as time went on, an autonomous discipline to which some very acute minds devoted themselves without any reference to theology.

The truth is that the progress of research and criticism has shown that medieval philosophy is far from being a monolithic system.

Though more homogeneous than either ancient or modern thought, it is nevertheless a tapestry whose design varies both vertically and horizontally. On the one hand Platonism and Neoplatonism, and later, and to a less extent, Averroism and Avicennism, existed side by side with Christian Aristotelianism of varied strength; on the other hand, the teachers of 'mere' or 'pure' philosophy, who in the early days had been restricted to elementary logic, came gradually to inherit the whole corpus of Aristotelian and Arabian doctrine, and were able to erect a system of thought covering the whole of human experience without reference to the truths of faith, and this development was greatly assisted by the contemporary tendency amongst theologians to separate the spheres of nature and grace, of reason and revelation. In other words, there was in the medieval world, as in the modern, a variety (if only a limited variety) of systems of thought, as also a steady disintegration or rather delimitation of the spheres of theology and philosophy which resulted in the emergence of the latter as an autonomous, self-sufficient, if also very self-critical discipline.

Yet when all has been said, medieval thought, taken in gross and in its most widely diffused and typical forms, has a colour of its own that distinguishes it, when seen in bulk, alike from all ancient philosophy and from all modern schools that are not its direct descendants. It may be described, though it can scarcely be defined, by the following three characteristics, the first connected with its purpose and goal, the second with its form and appearance, and the third with its manner of presentation and development. First, then, there is the close connection of philosophy with religion. Originally regarded as no more than an instrument or means of understanding or 'extending' revealed truth, it came later to be regarded as a discipline of the reason with adequate objects of its own, but these were long considered in their relationship to divine truth and Christian ethics, and never until the decline of the schools did it cease to be regarded by most of its adepts as primarily a necessary preparation for and approach to theology, as also an explanatory and apologetic agent. Secondly, there is throughout a close dependence upon ancient philosophy, especially as presented by Aristotle, and this philosophy is regarded as a corpus of rational, natural truths which are as ascertainable and valid in their degree as is the body of revelation. Even at the end, with Ockham and his school, the greatest reverence, so far as words go, is still shown to Aristotle, and the logic of the *moderni* is, in word at least, a more faithful interpretation of the Philosopher. Thirdly, on the level of technique, there is the method of *quaestio* and *disputatio* which is used throughout, not only for purposes of exposition, but also for those of research.

Finally, a few words must be said of two further general characteristics of medieval philosophy: its adaptability as a school-subject, and its Christian content.

Greek philosophy in the pre-Socratic era and as understood by Socrates himself, and by Plato and Aristotle after him, was the search for truth unfettered by dogma, authority or convention; it was the following of reason whithersoever reason might lead. Yet already in the lifetime of Plato, and still more in that of Aristotle, the adoption of philosophy as the queen and crown of higher education, together with the immense prestige of the two great masters, brought about a change from the discipline of debate and interrogation to that of learning and imitation, and in the Hellenistic world philosophy came to be taught like any other subject. The concept of philosophy as a search or a pursuit did, indeed, never wholly vanish so long as anything of the spirit and traditions of ancient Greece remained, but again and again the original work of a great mind was accepted and taught in the school that derived from him.

A new attitude was adopted by some of the early Fathers, and later by Augustine. Holding, as they did, that there was only one true God, and one true revelation of the divine economy, and that the God of revelation was also the source and guarantee of all being and truth, they accepted as a consequence of this that 'natural' truth, including metaphysical and ethical truth, was something ascertainable and permanent. In other words, there was a body of natural truth or philosophy, containing, among its other data, a natural theodicy and psychology and ethic, which could be ascertained with certainty and which could be used as a foundation for, and aid to the understanding of, Christian theology. And to Augustine, as to the Greek and Alexandrian Fathers, there was no doubt that Aristotle's logic, and the system of Plato in general, represented the true findings of the human mind unassisted by divine grace and revelation. In consequence, Augustine and several of the Greek Fathers took Plato (or Plotinus) for granted, so to say, and looked to him as the authority to be quoted and followed in all questions of philosophy.

The early Middle Ages paid even more deference to the classical past, and when they came, in the eleventh century, to face for the first time some of the great problems of metaphysics and epistemology, they naturally turned to what they knew of the heritage of Greek thought, their ruling authority. For more than two hundred years the little that was known of Plato, and the ever-increasing heritage of

Aristotle were accepted by and large as a body of philosophical truth, an 'authority', that could be used and handed down to others. No medieval thinker started, like Descartes or Kant, to build up a great system from the postulates of his own mental experience; philosophy could be received from others and taught like any other subject. This attitude of mind was fully in keeping with the spirit of Aristotelian logic. If that, in its totality, is learnt, accepted and practised, a whole great system of thought becomes available. It is at once the strength and the weakness of Aristotelian thought, both in the Middle Ages and in more modern times, that a tightly bound network of syllogisms radiates from a single great axiom, and that within that network every part appears, logically speaking, to be the inevitable consequence of its neighbour. Such a system, it is clear, can be memorized and taught in the same way as grammar or mathematics, and for many pupils in the ages of scholasticism and neo-scholasticism, philosophy has been no more than an exercise of memory.

The second characteristic is its Christian 'loading'. Much has been written on the theme of Christian philosophy. At first sight the phrase must seem a contradiction in terms. Thought, the working of the natural reason of man and its attainment of truth, can be neither Christian nor Islamic nor heathen. Truth is truth, and cannot be coloured by the non-rational or supra-rational beliefs of the thinker. M. Etienne Gilson, in his series of Gifford Lectures that threw so much light upon the nature of medieval thought, helped to answer the difficulty by pointing out that every group or school of thinkers has a social or cultural or confessional background, and that this leads it to focus its attention upon certain fields of the great area of thought available for development. A group of Christians, working in a fully Christian society and for purposes that are largely theological, will naturally direct its attention to subjects, such as the existence of God, the immortality of the soul, human free will, and the like, which come inevitably into the forefront of its interests. An isolated philosopher who is also a Christian might conceivably devote all his attention to Logical Positivism, but one could scarcely imagine the whole Faculty of Philosophy at the university of Louvain doing so. It was natural therefore for medieval thinkers, like St Augustine before them, to investigate before all others those fields of thought that touched most nearly upon the truths of religion. But beyond this, in the case of a thinker who is not only a Christian, but who has never been accustomed to separate, even in his mind, man in the 'state of nature' from man as he is, the actual or potential recipient

of divine grace, and man, moreover, who is tainted with original sin –
such a one will, with St Augustine and his many medieval disciples,
make use of philosophy only by the way, to explain or to illustrate
topics, such as the powers of the soul or the processes of cognition and
volition, which are also theological topics. In this sense the medieval
Augustinians were 'Christian philosophers', but they, unlike the
Christian Aristotelians, never attempted to construct a whole system
of thought side by side with their system of theology.

CHAPTER EIGHT
The Revival of Dialectic: Berengar, Lanfranc and Anselm

The most remarkable feature of the mental awakening of the eleventh century is the revival of dialectic. No symptom of the new power that had come to the minds of Western Europe could be more striking than the rapid emergence of dialectic as a critical agent and the centre of a programme of education and debate, nor could any evidence be found of the importance of this moment for Western thought more impressive than the rise of dialectic from a perfunctory memory-technique to the principal place in education. This change was not occasioned by any discovery of ancient texts. The works of Boethius and the fragments of Aristotle had always been available, but whereas in the past they had evoked no response in the minds of their readers, they were now appreciated in all their dynamic force. In the mental growth of many an individual a moment comes when the power of words and arguments is suddenly realized, when logic seems an irresistible weapon, and verbal ingenuity and dexterity an intoxicating pursuit. So now all over north-western Europe the forms of logic sprang into life, and the clarity of the Gallic genius was displayed in all its brilliance.

The first great name in the history of medieval thought is that of Gerbert of Aurillac, who was master of the school of Rheims *c.* 972 and ended his life as Pope Silvester II (999–1003). In his writing on logic, and still more in his mathematical interests and his use of Arabian sources, he was the harbinger of many new things. It was during his life as a teacher that one of his disciples, Fulbert, developed a school at Chartres (*c.* 990), of which city he was bishop from 1006 to 1028, and Fulbert is significant as having laid down the programme of a wide literary and philosophical culture in which supreme respect was paid to the mysteries of the faith as presented by the authority of the Scriptures and the traditions of the Fathers. While making use of dialectic, he never tired of asserting that the human mind, when unable of its own powers to discuss the causes of the divine arrangement of things, should close its eyes in reverence before what it could not understand and should abandon all attempts at argument.[1]

Very soon, however, the growing self-confidence of the schools found expression in controversy and assertions of the supremacy of the reason. There seemed no limits to the field which the human mind could master, and all arguments that were not strictly logical and formal seemed worthless. Rationalism in the modern sense made its appearance, with its accompaniments in individuals of scepticism and pessimism. For the first time since the patristic age major controversies of all kinds broke out, the symptoms and consequences of the adolescence of Western Europe. Men were creating the technique of thought and argument, and were anxious to use it. Yet the age was also one of moral and religious earnestness, with a consequent zeal for reform, and thus a tension was set up which gave its character to the intellectual life of the later part of the century, the tension between dialectic and traditional theology in the realm of thought and that between art and the ancient culture and monastic severity in the realm of Christian action. In the former of these two tensions, with which alone we are concerned, two main problems can be discerned. Has dialectic a true place in Christian thought? And, if so, can any limit be assigned to separate the provinces of reason and faith?

The first unmistakable sign of the coming conflict was given by Berengar of Tours (*d.* 1088), originally a pupil of Fulbert of Chartres. Theological preoccupations of modern times led for long to a totally unhistorical treatment of Berengar, who was looked upon as the medieval protagonist of reform in the age-old Eucharistic controversy and as the predecessor (along with the English Aelfric) of Wyclif, Luther and Zwingli. Historically speaking, the significance of Berengar does not lie in his precise views, which in any case were quite different from those of later controversialists, but in his resolute attempt to submit the mysteries of faith to treatment by dialectic. He is ready to state positively that reason, and not authority, is mistress and judge. Dialectic is the art of arts, and it is the sign of an eminent mind that it turns in all things to dialectic. Anyone who does not do so abandons his principal glory, for it is by his reason that man resembles God. He intends, therefore, to have resort to dialectic in all

[1]Epistle 5 in Migne, *PL* cxli col. 196–7.

things, because dialectic is the exercise of reason, and reason is incomparably superior to authority when it is a question of ascertaining the truth.[2] It is not easy to decide whether Berengar's theorizing came from a fundamental neglect of revelation and spiritual truth, or from an honest conviction that reason of itself could attain to a knowledge and explanation of the mysteries of religion. On the whole, the former interpretation would seem to be the more correct, in the sense that Berengar was essentially a logician, and that his interests lay wholly in dialectic; consequently, doctrines were regarded as verbal forms and thus as food for the logician. Lanfranc, who should have known, certainly thought that this was his aim, to settle everything by reason – *rationibus omnia velle comprehendere* – abandoning all tradition – *relictis sacris auctoritatibus*.[3]

More recently, a sympathetic and acute critic[4] has seen in Berengar, as others have seen in Abelard and Gilbert de la Porrée, an exponent of *Sprachlogik*, an instance of that attribution of reality to words as not only the symbols, but as the perfect expression, the translation of things into another mode of existence. On this view, things and words would have a real, not merely a conventional correspondence; the pronoun 'this', in the words of Eucharistic consecration, would exactly represent its noun, and the substance 'bread' would remain present.

It has been suggested in the past that Berengar was the father of the scholastic method of dialectic and disputation. Such an opinion could only be held by those who were unaware of the mental climate of France at the time, and indeed long before Berengar appeared. He has nevertheless an important position in the history of scholastic thought. He was the first to stir up a major theological controversy in which all parties used the dialectical method, thus contributing greatly to its extension. He also played a part in the formation of a technical philosophical language with additions unknown to Boethius; thus 'substance', 'accident' and 'transubstantiation' crystallized as technical terms with a fixed meaning in the stress of the Eucharistic controversy. Finally, his example initiated a whole series of theological monographs in which the writings of the Fathers and the pronouncements of authority were treated in a dialectical fashion, though not necessarily in the extreme and provocative form of Berengar's own treatise.

[2] Berengarius, *De sacra coena* (ed. Vischer), 100, 101.
[3] Lanfranc, *De corpore et sanguine Domini, c.* 17, 7 (Migne, *PL* cl, 427, 416).
[4] R. W. Southern, 'Lanfranc of Bec and Berengar of Tours', in *Studies in Medieval History presented to F. M. Powicke* (Oxford, 1948), 27–48.

His writings had also another result. Berengar was a very considerable figure, with a reputation as a person and as a teacher which was not seriously shaken by his condemnation. He was consequently the foe, not only of traditional theologians in the Eucharistic controversy, but of conservatives and obscurantists in general. Among these the most eminent and in some ways the most typical figure was that of St Peter Damian, master in the schools of Ravenna, hermit, and for a time cardinal bishop of Ostia (1007–72). Celebrated also as a theologian who upheld the traditional doctrine on the question of the re-ordination of simoniacs, as the most representative figure among the monastic and moral reformers, and as the supporter of a moderate view in the contest between papacy and empire, Damian, who had himself taught school before his conversion, and throughout his career used all the arts of rhetoric against the study of letters and philosophy, was naturally on the extreme right wing against dialectic and rationalism. Yet, rhetorical and impulsive as he is, he is not always logical or consistent in his expressions, and different opinions have been held as to his considered judgement on the value of philosophy. Grabmann maintained that Damian, though in a well-known passage he proclaimed the rôle of philosophy to be that of a mere handmaid of theology – *velut ancilla dominae quodam famulatus obsequio* – had no intention of denying its competence in this menial position. This, however, is to ignore the most crucial phrases in Damian's argument. He is discussing the divine omnipotence, and asks whether God can make the past not to have been, or can make contraries (e.g., being and not-being) true at one and the same time and aspect; he answers that such things, though impossible in nature and to man's reason, are not impossible to God. 'This impossibility', he says, 'may rightly be asserted, if we are talking about natural impotence, but God forbid that we should apply this way of speaking to the divine omnipotence.'[5]

Others went even further than Damian. Thus Manegold of Lautenbach (*d.* 1103/19), himself also, like Damian, a leading publicist in the papal-imperial controversy, repeatedly speaks of philosophy as useless (*superfluum*) to the theologian, and regards the mysteries of the faith, such as the Virgin Birth and the Resurrection, as upsetting and annihilating philosophical wisdom and human reason. Here, as elsewhere at this time, we see clearly that the apparent extravagance of language arises not precisely from a distrust of reason as a process of knowledge, but from a failure to perceive different

[5] Peter Damian, *De divina omnipotentia* xi, ed. A. Cantin, *Sources chrétiennes* (Paris, 1972), p. 448.

levels or spheres of divine operations, and to distinguish between God as the author of the supernatural order and God the author of the natural order of things.

Compared with such men as Damian and Manegold, Berengar's adversary, Lanfranc, appears to be as indeed he was in fact, a man of moderate and carefully pondered opinions. Regarded during his lifetime as the greatest master and theologian of his age, Lanfranc has suffered in more recent times through comparison with his greater pupil, Anselm, with Abelard, and with later thinkers, while his contemporary reputation for holiness of life and for wise spiritual and temporal administration has suffered equally from the disclosure of his supposedly close association with some of the harsher measures of William the Conqueror. In the latter field his action has been largely vindicated by more recent historians, and as a great archbishop and monastic reformer his position is now secure. As a thinker and scholastic teacher, however, the praises of his contemporaries, who wrote before the developments of the twelfth and thirteenth centuries had altered all scales and proportions, cannot now be accepted as absolutely valid. Though undoubtedly he was in person the most influential teacher of his day, in the history of method and ideas he has nothing of the significance of either Anselm or Abelard. On the other hand, he does not deserve the neglect into which he has fallen, still less the contempt with which, as a supposed obscurantist, he has been treated by liberal historians and by those whose sympathies in the Eucharistic question lie with Berengar.

Lanfranc, born of good family *c.* 1010, and probably at Pavia, began his studies in arts and law in Lombardy but he crossed the Alps *c.* 1030 and taught the arts for a time at Avranches. Then, seeking a strict monastic life, he joined the infant community of Bec, where he soon opened a school to acquire funds for the monastery. As to his influence all are agreed. His pupil Guitmund of Aversa wrote that through him the arts had been reborn gloriously in France, and eighty years later William of Malmesbury refers to Bec in his day as 'a great and celebrated school of letters'. It was during his period at Bec that he was bidden to take up the cause of orthodoxy against Berengar, and though here again he fared hardly at the hands of the old school of historians, candid examination in recent years agrees with the unanimous opinion of contemporaries that he had the better of the argument. Though admittedly preferring tradition and Scripture in theological matters, Lanfranc made use of dialectic also against Berengar, so as not to appear unable to meet him on his own ground. As he said elsewhere, in his commentary on St Paul's

Epistles, 'dialectic is no enemy of the mysteries of God, rather it confirms them, if rightly used, when the matter demands it'.[6] Appointed founding abbot of the Conqueror's monastery at Caen in 1063, he was chosen by William as archbishop of Canterbury in 1070. He died in 1089.

The relationship of mutual affection and esteem that existed between Lanfranc and his pupil Anselm is one more proof that he was no enemy to philosophy and dialectic. It was to him that Anselm owed the tools of his argument and submitted his great treatise, the *Monologion*. Lanfranc, indeed, though not an original or epoch-making thinker, stood in the mean way between dialectic and the phobias of extreme conservatives.

With Lanfranc's great pupil Anselm we meet the highest achievement of what may be called the medieval Augustinian use of dialectic, the summit of the early scholastic genius and the ripest fruit of the monastic schools. We meet indeed with more than this, for Anselm, both as a thinker and as a personality, is one of the rare significant figures who belong to all time, one to whom philosophers and historians and innumerable readers will turn for enlightenment and counsel irrespective of any attempt to fit him into his place in the history of thought. Among all the host of medieval philosophers and theologians perhaps only Aquinas and Bonaventure are in his company as thinkers who have put into currency, so to say, ideas which may again and again provoke controversy and meet with contradiction, but which cannot with impunity be despised, for they will again and again make their appeal to another generation in the future. In addition to this, Anselm, surpassing in this respect his two rivals of the later century, succeeded in putting into all his writings, and so in transmitting to us, that charm of personality, that supremely winning and compelling charm, which, as he himself tells us, none of his contemporaries could resist save through conscious hostility. In this he is among the small band of saints throughout the ages, that band in which are Augustine, Francis of Assisi, Thomas More, Teresa of Avila and François de Sales, who all embody the same moral and spiritual appeal in a variety of outward forms, and who instantaneously win our affection before they have won our admiration.

Born of noble family at Aosta in 1033, he went north in search of learning and entered Bec, drawn by the fame of Lanfranc, in 1060; when Lanfranc went to Caen in 1063 he succeeded him as prior, and at the death of Herluin in 1078 he became abbot, perhaps the nearest

[6]Lanfranc, in *I Corinth.* i (Migne, *PL* cl 157).

approach to the ideal abbot that the Benedictine centuries ever saw. Fifteen years later he was summoned against his will to Canterbury by William Rufus, and after a stormy episcopate died there in 1109.

Though, as has been said, he acknowledged with sincerity and modesty his debt to Lanfranc, his genius far exceeded that of his master not only in degree but in kind. There is nothing in Anselm's greatest work that derives from his own age or from his teacher; in this he is more original than Abelard or Aquinas. If we fix our eyes only on his own century, he is a sudden emergence, a Melchisedech without father or mother or genealogy. It is his achievement to stand forth as absolutely great in an age when others were only feeling their way towards thought and expression.

So much having been said, it may seem contradictory to emphasize at once Anselm's immense debt to Augustine, though Augustine had of course in no sense a contemporary or a personal influence upon him. However derived, the debt is there beyond a moment's question. Every page of Anselm recalls, not only by its verbal cadences and vocabulary, but by the writer's intellectual and emotional approach to every subject he discusses and to God Himself, the Augustine of the *Confessions* and the *Soliloquies*. If any doubt there were, Anselm himself is ready to dispel it. Nothing is to be found in his work, so he tells us in the preface to the *Monologion*, which is not in absolute harmony with the writings of Augustine. Yet Anselm is far from being a mere imitator or the continuator of a school. His more important writings could never be mistaken for those of Augustine and, what is more important, he is not an Augustinian in the technical sense of the word. He shows no trace of that reliance upon Neoplatonism that meant so much to Augustine; he does not rest upon the Platonic theory of forms and the theory of the divine illumination of the intellect that bulk so large in Augustine himself and in Bonaventure and his later disciples. Anselm, in fact, has the philosophical background of his time; he is of the Boethian age, with no awareness of Neoplatonic thought and with no real awareness of metaphysics or epistemology at all. It is indeed one of the secrets of Anselm's universal appeal that he approaches all problems with a mind not committed to any system of the past; it is this that allows us to retain our first impression that he is following the guidance of pure reason alone as he proceeds on his way. If the hands are the hands of Augustine, the voice is the voice of Anselm. It is not in philosophy, but in speculative theology, that Anselm had a share in handing down the tradition of the past.

Anselm's characteristic and original trait lies in the strong and serene confidence with which he explores the great mysteries of the faith – the nature of God, the Trinity, the Incarnation and Redemption, Predestination and Freewill – with the aid of reason, that is, of dialectic. Here he resumed, almost unconsciously, and as if it had been scarcely interrupted, the theological task that had been abandoned soon after Augustine's death by the divines of the West. His motto, enunciated as the original title of the *Proslogion*, was the celebrated *Fides quaerens intellectum*, 'faith seeking to understand', and he explains it himself. 'I desire,' he says, addressing God after his usual manner, 'to understand in some measure thy truth, which my heart already believes and loves. And indeed I do believe it, for unless I believe, I shall not understand.' Here again Anselm is echoing Augustine, who had quoted Isaiah VII:9 from the Septuagint: 'unless ye believe, ye shall not understand', but the implication he sees in the words goes far beyond Augustine's thought.

As a basis, he presupposes an unshakable faith in the revealed doctrines as expressed in precise and familiar traditional terms. His dialectic, therefore, is directed neither towards establishing revealed truth nor towards criticizing it; his primary aim is to penetrate with dialectic the truth held by faith. His *credo ut intelligam*, 'I believe in order to understand', does not mean either that faith is a condition of all knowledge as a kind of epistemological medium, or that the truths of faith can be fully understood, though of these two extreme opinions Anselm's words, if not his thought, approach more nearly to the latter. He did in fact hold that the mind could arrive at a real, if inadequate, understanding of the mysteries of the faith. As he writes in a well-known passage: 'that which we hold by faith [he is speaking of the Holy Trinity] can be proved by formal arguments'.[7] By this phrase, in which the word *necessarius* bears a technical meaning, he certainly did not mean that all the truths of faith could be established by demonstrative arguments that would be irresistible to any who used their reason aright, in the manner of a proposition of Euclid. The adjective *necessarius* means 'formally admissible', 'probable', rather than 'compelling'. Anselm does, however, seem to have held that the believer, meditating upon the truths of the faith, could come to see, not only their appropriateness but also their inevitability, given the nature and purpose of God as presented in Christian teaching. In this he was not followed by the scholastics of the golden age, who restricted (with Aquinas) the function of reason to showing the suitability of revealed truth, and that it implied no logical contradiction. Anselm in fact, so some may think, failed as did all

[7]Anselm, *Epistola de Incarnatione Verbi* c. 6 (ed. Schmitt ii 20).

before Aquinas to distinguish clearly between the natural powers of
the reason, present in all men even if unbelievers or sinners, and the
supernatural powers of the reason enlightened by God which can
search His hidden things. Here, as elsewhere, he did but echo the
thought of Augustine, and like him, he speaks of his own experience,
the experience of a deeply spiritual personality, rather than of that of
men in general or of the 'natural' intelligence. Moreover, though
much of the expression of his thought hovers on the borderline of
mystical knowledge, he echoes Augustine in speaking of intellectual
processes without making the distinction, classical among later
theologians, between natural, communicable knowledge and that
which is supernatural, obscure, and incommunicable. Finally, he
probably failed also, in the confidence of the fresh spring sunlight of
newly discovered dialectic, to appreciate the limits of the human
reason as an instrument of precision. It is conditioned, like the senses,
though in a different way, by the medium in which it acts. Pure
being and pure matter alike elude its grasp, as does also pure
spiritual truth.

Anselm never attacked the problems that lie at the roots of
philosophical thought, for the simple historical reason that they had
not yet come into focus as problems that must be dealt with. He was
not concerned with metaphysics in the technical sense, nor with
epistemology. He would have thought of himself as primarily one
pondering upon theology, and for all save professional theologians,
his celebrity rests chiefly upon his argument – the so-called
'ontological argument' – for the existence of God. The name is
modern, deriving from the terminology of Kant, for whom an
ontological proof was any proof independent of experience and based
upon a simple analysis of concepts. To give this name to Anselm's
argument is to beg the question of its nature, but the phrase is
familiar and as such permissible.

Anselm himself describes the genesis of this argument.[8] He had, in
the *Monologion*, given three traditional proofs of the existence of
God drawn from a consideration of the visible universe. What is seen
to be good is also seen to be more or less good; that is to say, it
participates to a greater or lesser degree in absolute goodness. But the
goodness which is absolute is good in itself, that is, by a further
process of argument, God. Similarly, it can be shown that everything
has a cause, and by a process of elimination of causes all must
ultimately be referred to a single cause which exists of itself, that is,

---

[8]Anselm, *Proslogion*, prooemium, and cc. 2–3, ed. Schmitt i 93–4, 101–3. Eadmer,
Life of St. Anselm, ed. R. W. Southern. Nelson's Medieval Texts (1962) pp. 29–31.

God. Finally, the relative degrees of perfection in the universe argue a being more perfect than all the rest; this is, in the last resort, God.

After having proceeded thus Anselm, so he tells us, under pressure from his disciples, began to question with himself, whether there might not be found a single argument 'which would be self-sufficient and all-sufficient', and after long cogitation the answer came to him suddenly, in the so-called 'ontological' proof, which runs in outline as follows.

The definition of God, in Whom all Christians believe, contains the statement that God is a Being than which no greater can exist. Even the Fool in the Psalm (Ps. 14:1), who said that there was no God, understood what was meant by God when he heard the word, and the object thus defined existed in his mind, even if he did not understand that it exists also in reality. But if this being has solely an intra-mental existence, then another can be thought of as having real existence also, that is, it is greater (by existence) than the one than which no greater can exist. But this is a contradiction in terms. Therefore the Being than which no greater can be conceived exists both in the mind and in reality.

The short passage in which this celebrated argument is propounded has been pored over and commented upon more than any other text of equal brevity in medieval philosophy. Though the language of each clause is pellucid and the meaning of the words perfectly clear, very few readers will succeed in mastering the argument at a glance, and many will have an uneasy feeling that a logical sleight of hand has been brought off at their expense. They need not be ashamed of their bewilderment. A glance at the voluminous literature debating this argument, with the various explanations of it that have been given, together with the contrary judgements that have been passed upon it, and the consequent mutual charges between scholars of misunderstanding and misrepresenting Anselm, would seem at least to show that the layman's sense of frustration is not due solely to lack of intelligence. When such a one as M. Gilson can write 'when everyone disagrees, a lone individual has very little chance of hitting upon the truth',[9] and then proceeds to give his own interpretation, which has certainly not silenced all contradiction, the ordinary reader may take heart of grace and frankly admit that he is gravelled. When we find even M. Gilson confessing that his only reason for adding yet another explanation to

[9]E. Gilson, 'Sens et nature de l'argument de saint Anselme', in *Archives d'histoire doctrinale et littéraire du moyen âge*, 9 (1934), 5–51.

those already in existence is that he cannot resist the temptation to do so, we may be excused if we ourselves feel unable to see what Anselm meant.

His argument was in fact denounced at birth as a fallacy, and Gaunilo, a contemporary monk of Marmoutier, defended the Fool with a *reductio ad absurdum*, that is, 'it proves too much'. By the same process of argument, he said, the most fabulously beautiful island of romance conceivable must exist, else one could conceive one more beautiful. Anselm countered this by replying that in the case of the island its existence was not necessarily included in the definition of its perfection, but he did not go on to counter a more precise objection. This was, that an argument based upon the analysis of a definition is only valid if the existence of the object defined is already known from another source. Thus, granted the existence of God, His eternity and goodness can validly be deduced from the definition of deity. But in the Anselmian argument it is existence itself that is alleged to be proved from the definition of deity. The precise point where the fallacy in the argument lies, we are told, is in the phrase 'exists in his mind (*in intellectu esse*)' when used of the concept of God by the Fool. This is merely a metaphorical phrase, for actually it is only the picture or concept of the thing which is in the mind, and this is no evidence that the thing exists; it may be merely imagined. To base an argument on intra-mental existence is to make an illicit step from the ideal to the real order of things. Doubtless; but Anselm himself specifically, and in the same context, recognized the difference between a mental and a real existence.

Realization of this has led some to maintain that the argument is not a merely logical one – the analysis of a concept – but an epistemological one. It is said that Anselm held so firmly the Platonic realism, according to which the idea is the only reality directly cognizable by the mind, that for him the presence of the idea of God in the mind implied the existence of the subsistent idea of God – that is, of God Himself, since there is no distinction of any kind in God. More recently, a personal historical approach has been made. Anselm, it is said, was a mystic, and his *fides quaerens intellectum* is the progress from a mystical or an intuitional to an intellectual knowledge. God *is* present to Anselm's inmost consciousness, and the mind, starting from the fact of his presence, goes on to analyse and deduce. Even the Fool has at least a vague, inchoate sense of God's existence. The argument would thus not be a leap from the ideal to the real order of things, but from the mystical to the rational field which, granted the intuitional knowledge of God, whether mystical or natural, would not be a fallacy. As for Gilson, he is not content with any of these explanations. His own opinion seems to be as follows. Anselm, he points out quite rightly, held that the mind could arrive at truth, which was the adequacy of the mental concept to express the being external to the mind. In other words, the external being is the cause of the concept and of its truth, not *vice versa*. If therefore a being is not only existent, but necessarily so (as is God by definition), and is in fact the only being necessarily existent ('than which no greater can be conceived') then the only true concept of this Being will be one that agrees with its definition, and the mind will recognize the adequacy of the concept and the necessity of the existence of its object as soon as it has been presented to the mind.

Anselm's argument was not directed against unbelievers, and had no apologetic design; his world was composed of the faithful, and his argument was framed for his monastic disciples. In consequence, it made little impact upon his contemporaries, and it was not till the thirteenth century that it became usual for all thinkers to notice it, either for acceptance or for criticism. Thus Bonaventure and the Augustinians in general accepted it, as strengthened by the doctrine of the divine illumination of the intellect, while Aquinas and the Aristotelians rejected it, and Scotus re-interpreted it. Ever since, indeed, it has been a touchstone of Realism, and as such accepted in one form or another by Descartes, Leibniz and Hegel, and rejected by Locke, Kant and Thomists of every kind. In recent times Karl Barth has accepted it, with an existentialist interpretation, while Geyer dismisses it out of hand as a fallacy.

We may, if we wish, accept M. Gilson's interpretation that the definition, received by faith, of God as the being than which no greater can be conceived, carries with it the existence of that being. Or we may follow Anselm's own words still more closely, and hold with him that when once the mind accepts the concept of a being than which no greater can exist, the existence of such a being – granted that we accept that there *are* existing beings – necessarily follows. We may at least feel certain that if we try to give Anselm's argument an intuitional or a mystical turn, we are departing from his intention. While it is very probable that Anselm was attracted towards, and strengthened in, his conviction of the validity of his argument by his saturation in Augustinian thought, and by his consequent omission to draw a clear line between the reasoning of the 'natural' man and that of the enlightened Christian mind, yet it must be repeated that his argument, when set out in its bare terms, without any reference to his own experience or views, is couched in terms of pure dialectic,

and must stand or fall by its sheer dialectical force. A principal reason
of our difficulty in appreciating its power may well be that pure
dialectic makes but a weak appeal to our minds.

CHAPTER NINE
The Question of Universals

During the later decades of the eleventh century and the first part of the twelfth, the topic most keenly debated by masters of logic and dialectic was that of 'universals', that is, of the degree of reality and significance attributable to the mental perception of a similarity between groups of individual beings that can only be expressed by a term common to all, such as man, horse or rose, with its abstract equivalent such as 'humanity' or 'human nature'. Sixty or seventy years ago, in the pioneering epoch of the history of medieval thought, this topic seemed to writers such as Hauréau and Rashdall to bulk so large in the writings of the thinkers of the time as to be a characteristic, if not a defining, note of the whole period. This was a misconception. The debate on universals passed through its acute stage in half a century, after which the topic took its place among the many other philosophical questions of the age. It owed its apparent paramountcy to the circumstances of the schools at the end of the eleventh century, and fell into the background when the field of philosophical speculation was broadened. Nevertheless, for fifty years or more it exercised the minds and developed the talents of the most eminent masters, and deserves notice in any account of their thought.

The subject was not wholly a novel one; it is, especially in its metaphysical implications, basic to any system of thought, but it emerged as something new to the masters of the age of Anselm, and as one to which their text-books gave no complete answer. They were logicians and took it up, so to say, by its logical end, and in so doing gave it a new look. The Greek thinkers, taking it up on the physical level, had been led on to the levels of epistemology and metaphysics, and ultimately to that of theology. The early scholastics approached it as a matter of terms and concepts, and it was some time before the metaphysical and epistemological implications became apparent.

The problem of universals, in its simplest form, is this. On the level of speech and grammar we say that Socrates is a man, and has a human nature. On the level of logic we say that he is an individual being or substance, one of a numerous species, to which we give the name man, of individuals who are united in the possession of common qualities, a common nature. Socrates, the individual being, has a right to his name; he comes before us, and a name designates him. But what of 'man' or humanity? That does not come before us, it is we who 'isolate' or 'invent' it for purposes of classification or argument. Has it the same logical worth as the name of the individual? The problem can scarcely be left at this level. Is a different mental process involved? Granted that any mental perception is valid, we have a direct perception of the individual man. But by what process do we recognize and define in thoughts and words the resemblances between two individual beings which lead us to say that each is a man or a rose? Is it a merely visual process? Or an intuitive one? Or some kind of recognition or memory or inward light? Or is it what we call an abstractive process of the reason? But this is not the end of the problem. What, in the last resort, are the individual being and its 'nature'? Are they no more than mental divisions of one thing? Is the individual more 'real' than its 'nature'? Or is the 'nature' the only reality, and if so, what is the relationship between it and the individual? Or, if they are both real and extra-mental, what is their relationship and how does the mind achieve knowledge of them? Plato, as we have seen, following up the attempts of the pre-Socratics to find an answer to the problem of identity amid change in the physical universe, found his own answer in the intellectual and real world of Forms or Ideas, of which the physical universe and its content, the individual objects of our experience, are either reflections or participants. Though thus throwing out a metaphysical theory of great and permanent fruitfulness, he never answered – he did not even consider – the precise problem of 'universals', for he never asserted, and it would indeed be absurd to assert, that a real and subsistent 'form' existed in relation to every 'universal'.

Aristotle, having to his own satisfaction demolished the Platonic subsistent forms, took up the problem as he took up all problems, on the level of the observed physical universe. His world was one of 'substances' and 'essences', of intellectual concepts of physical beings, the concepts being less real than the physical substances in their motions and activities, but more real as expressing the reason, order and purpose of all things, which alone gave meaning to all and were in the deepest sense the constitutive principles of all. When Aristotle descended from metaphysics to epistemology, he saw the mind as abstracting from individuals the 'essence' or 'nature' which constituted them what they were – a real entity present in each individual substance which the mind could grasp and possess in all its intellectual fulness. For Aristotle this analysis of the process of cognition was bound up with physics as well as metaphysics by his doctrine that the 'essence' or definition attained by abstraction was also a scientific description that could be used as an instrument of research and knowledge on the physical level, but this part of his system can be cut off without necessarily implying the destruction of his epistemology.

Aristotle was also the author of a massive system of logic, which was consistent with, and indeed geared to, his epistemology and metaphysics, but as a lower discipline it could be used without reference to the higher levels of philosophy. In the event, the later Platonists and Neoplatonists retained this logic while adopting a modified form of Platonic epistemology and metaphysics which were, as we have seen, adopted, with further modification, by Augustine. Boethius, as we have also seen, intended, but never achieved, a vast presentation and final synthesis of Plato and Aristotle, but in fact left to posterity no more than an important section of Aristotelian logic. This logic, while on the one hand it was scarcely compatible with a Platonic epistemology, was not incompatible with a metaphysical scepticism, though Aristotle himself was no sceptic. Thus at the birth of scholasticism, as at its death, we find Aristotelian logic as the queen of the schools, and at both periods it was sometimes used in a critical or Nominalist sense.

The masters of the eleventh century knew nothing of Aristotelian metaphysics and scarcely anything of Plato's Forms. They were moving only on the level of grammar and elementary logic. Nothing perhaps reveals more clearly the mental awakening of the age than their reaction to their text-books. For five centuries their predecessors had read the tags of Porphyry and Boethius and had remained asleep. Now, the same words produced an explosion. Boethius, translating Porphyry, had written: 'Now concerning *genus* and *species*, whether they have real existence or are merely and solely creations of the mind, and, if they exist, whether they are material or immaterial, and whether they are separate from the things we see or are contained within them – on all this I make no pronouncement.'[1] In this

[1] The celebrated sentence of Porphyry translated by Boethius is in Migne, *PL*, lxiv 82.

celebrated passage Porphyry, as will have been noticed, is moving on two levels without distinguishing them. *Genus* and *species* are here purely logical terms. In physical nature, the same individual being falls, in different relationships, into both, and indeed into an indefinite series of such classes. 'Eclipse' is a horse, a mammal, an animal, and so forth. This was something Plato had never discussed. On the other hand Porphyry goes on to apply to *genus* and *species*, at least as a possibility, the Platonic doctrine of transcendent and immanent forms. This confusion was not without its influence on the debate about universals. Similarly, the well-known pronouncement of Boethius, that the treatise about the Aristotelian 'predicamants' (i.e., substance, accident, etc.) was a matter of words, not of things,[2] was equally a source of confusion. No ancient metaphysician had ever held that the components of the logical analysis of a substance were reflections of ideas or forms, nor even that they possessed an 'essence' or a real existence in their own right. But by using the terms 'things' and 'words' Boethius, even while denying real existence to the predicaments, seemed to imply that there was a possibility for a debate similar to that about *genera* and *species*, or about universals in general, while on the other hand his opposition of 'words' and 'things' was transferred to the 'universal' debate, and the alternatives of 'things' and 'words' were sometimes treated as exhaustive.

Nor were other elements of confusion lacking. On the one hand there was the influence of the grammarians and the later cult of *Sprachlogik*, with the doctrine that words have an essential relationship to the things they denote. On the other was the application of logical theories to theological topics. Thus, in particular, views as to the relationship of the individual to the universal were applied to the Persons in a single Godhead, either to confirm an opinion, or as a corollary of a particular view, and it was not to be expected that the theologians would remain silent in the matter.

The origins of the medieval debate on universals are still uncertain, but it seems clear that Roscelin of Compiègne (died *c.* 1125), who taught at Tours and elsewhere, was, though probably not the founder of Nominalism, at least its first influential advocate. His only surviving writing is an unattractive letter on the Trinity to Abelard, and much of the scanty information we have of him comes from references by Anselm, including the familiar but much discussed description of the 'dialecticians, nay rather the heretics of dialectic,

---

[2]Boethius, *In categ. Aristot.* I (Migne, *PL* lxiv 162).

who consider universal substances to be no more than vocal sounds'.[3] Anselm was not himself a professional dialectician, and he was condemning, and with reason, the application of a questionable logical doctrine to the transcendent mysteries of the faith. His own use of the then ambiguous term 'substance' as applicable to universals invited confusion. Recent scholarship has tended to credit Roscelin with opinions less superficial than sheer Nominalism. He was reacting, we are told, against the current extreme realism which found subsistent reality in qualities and accidents of every kind, so that the individual existing being was merely a chance collection of characteristics, while reality lay in a world of multitudinous ideas. Roscelin, wishing to assert the reality of the existent individual, could only do so by asserting that any analysis or classification of the individual beings of our experience was a matter of words, not of things, in the well-known Boethian dichotomy. This may be so, but undoubtedly many of those who attacked him, or who subsequently wrote of him, understood his nominalism in a less subtle, more radical sense.

Among those who reacted against him was William of Champeaux, born *c.* 1070 and the pupil successively of Manegold of Lautenbach (Paris), Anselm of Laon (Laon) and Roscelin (Compiègne). He himself taught in the cathedral school at Paris, whence he was driven by Abelard's attacks and entered the Augustinian abbey of St Victor, where he was one of the founders of the Victorine school of theology. His conversion, to Abelard's embittered mind, was a case of *reculer pour mieux sauter*; he did in fact emerge as bishop of Châlons-sur-Marne, where he became the trusted friend of St Bernard until his death in 1121. Abelard's familiar phrases have turned the attention of most readers away from the solid reputation that William of Champeaux won for himself as a theologian. In the matter of universals, he originally taught extreme realism, that the nature of a being (e.g., humanity) was essentially and wholly present at one and the same time in every individual. When Abelard objected that this destroyed individuality, by leaving room for no particularity, William emended his thesis by substituting the Boethian term *indifferenter* ('in a similar fashion') for *essentialiter* in his account of universals. This he explained by using the term *status*. Each individual had the same kind of essence or substance. This was far from being a satisfactory philosophical position, and it was under

---

[3]Anselm, *Epistola de Incarnatione Verbi*, c. 1 (ed. Schmitt, ii.9): 'Illi ... nostri temporis dialectici, immo dialecticae heretici, qui non nisi flatum vocis esse putant universales substantias.'

Abelard's subsequent attacks that William of Champeaux, so we are told, withdrew from the fray.

How then does Abelard himself stand in the long story of the problem of universals? Here the excavation and publication of his dialectical treatises, chiefly by B. Geyer over fifty years ago, changed the whole picture of his activities and made of him a much more important figure in this field than he had previously appeared to be. Abelard was *par excellence* a logician, and it is not surprising that the publication of his works on logic should have enhanced his reputation. Reacting both against the realism held by almost all his predecessors and contemporaries, and exploding it with the dictum *rem de re predicare monstrum* – 'it is absurd to predicate a *thing* about a *thing*' (e.g., 'Charles', the individual, 'is man', the universal) – and *nullam rem de pluribus dici sed nomen tantum* – 'only a name, not a *thing*, can be applied to a group' – he wished also to avoid what he, at least, seems to have considered the sheer, material, nominalism of his first master Roscelin. Hence his early formula, 'the universal is a mere vocal sound (*vox*)', was soon changed to 'the universal is a mental word (*sermo*)'. This mental representation is more indistinct than the thing itself, for it omits all that the individual does not share with other individuals, and is within the mind, not outside it. Nevertheless, it is an adequate representation of the nature of the thing; it is not something other (*aliud*) than it, but the same thing perceived in different wise (*aliter*). The mind takes, 'abstracts', certain features from the thing which are identical with those seen in others of the group. Abelard, it should be added, remains throughout his logical works on the logical plane; he never discusses the metaphysical implications. Yet, when it is remembered that he knew nothing of either the *De anima* or the *Metaphysics* of Aristotle, his anticipation of the Aristotelian doctrine of abstraction and moderate realism is very striking. Even Aquinas did little to develop this particular aspect, and indeed uses phrases which recall, if they do not exactly repeat, the phrases of Abelard. It may be added that Abelard, here also followed by Aquinas, while abandoning the Platonic ideas as a logical or metaphysical coefficient, retained them as an exemplary cause of created beings in the mind of God.

Abelard's celebrity precisely as a logician must have helped to plant his teaching firmly in the schools, but there is very scanty logical or metaphysical literature in the period that follows save from the School of Chartres. The Chartrains were throughout Platonists, so far as any thinker could be truly Platonist at a time when only the *Timaeus* (or at least a great part of it) was available from among all the dialogues of Plato.[4] Naturally, therefore, they were extreme realists in the matter of universals, and made use, in one way or another, of the Platonic ideas. Bernard of Chartres, the first of the twelfth-century masters, evolved a doctrine of logic, epistemology and metaphysics which was accepted with some modifications by his successors at Chartres, and upon which his logical presentation of universals depended. It was an endeavour to harmonize the teaching of Plato and Aristotle as he understood them.

According to Bernard, there were three kinds of being apart from the Being of God, viz., the eternal ideas or forms of all created being, which were present to the mind of God from all eternity, and which had no contact with the material universe; the created ideas (*nativae formae*) based on the eternal ideas, examples of an exemplar, which, when subsistent in matter, made up all perishable things; and formless matter. These *formae nativae*, created with the creation of each separate thing, had a universal mode of existence and remained the same amid all the flux of sensible things. They alone were corporeal being and were known by the mind in their own form. A later master, Thierry, accepting in part the doctrine of forms, posited a Form of all the other forms, and asserted that the Form of God contained all other forms. This, the 'pantheism of Chartres', was taken up by Thierry's successors, though it never rose to be a formal heresy.

The greatest of all the masters of Chartres, Gilbert de la Porrée, was likewise a pupil of Bernard. He took over almost in its entirety Bernard's teaching on universals, but endeavoured to amalgamate Plato and Aristotle, joining together Aristotle's conception of a universal as that which by nature is predicated of many things (*quod natum est de pluribus praedicari*) with Bernard's conception of *nativae formae*. His chief contribution to epistemology and metaphysics was a distinction derived ultimately from Boethius between substance (*quod est*, that which is) and subsistence (*quo est*, that by which a thing exists). Universals are subsistences but not existing substances; subsistences play the part of forms to the substances. The understanding abstracts or collects (*colligit*) the universal, which is but which does not subsist (*quod est sed non substat*), from particular things which both are and subsist (*sunt et substant*). To this was added the doctrine of eternal ideas in God, and the whole formed a strong metaphysical realism, though the mental process of knowing was by abstraction from particulars, not by

---

[4] Plato's *Meno* was translated in the twelfth century, but did not become widely read.

intuition of the ideas. To this opinion John of Salisbury adhered in general, while remaining without a decided opinion on many points where doubt was permissible through disagreement among authorities.

With Gilbert de la Porrée the topic of universals reached its fullest exposition and ceased for a time to occupy the interests of the schools. What may be called the Aristotelian-Boethian period had come to an end. The logicians, using what they could of Aristotle and the Aristotelian writings of Boethius, had come, in the person of Abelard, very near to the position of Aristotle himself, metaphysics apart. The philosophers and theologians, using what remained in Boethius and in Augustine of the Platonic tradition, had built up a system that was a distant reflection of the Platonic ideas. It was only a distant reflection, since it lacked full Platonic influence on the levels of epistemology and metaphysics. Almost all thinkers of the mid-twelfth century had adopted one version or another of the Aristotelian abstraction; for none was the Platonic conception of the world of ideas as the only real world, the goal of the mind's endeavour, a reality or even an hypothesis. In so far as the subsistent ideas remained, they remained as exemplars in the mind of God. Had Aristotle remained the only philosopher to be known, and known ever more and more fully by the West, there might well have been a complete reception of his thought. As it was, the re-entry of Neoplatonism, the re-examination of Augustine by technically skilled minds, and the contaminated doctrines of the Arab writers, ensured that in all departments of philosophical thought there should be disagreement and controversy, and among the controversial topics there occurred once again the question of universals.

CHAPTER TEN

Peter Abelard

With the opening of the twelfth century the spring promise of Anselm's genius was followed by a period of expansion of the greatest variety in literature and thought; it is the golden age of early scholasticism and of literary humanism. It is the age of St Bernard and William of St Thierry, of John of Salisbury, Otto of Freising and William of Malmesbury, and during the first four decades of the century the intellectual field is dominated by Peter Abelard.

Abelard, ever since the days of Petrarch, has been a focus of interest to many who care little for medieval thought and institutions, or for the lives of medieval saints, but who continue to be fascinated by the hero, or, as perhaps he might more justly be termed, the protagonist in one of the most celebrated dramas of passion in the Western world. Abelard, indeed, thanks to Petrarch, to Pope, to Rousseau, to Walter Pater, to George Moore, to Miss Waddell, and to many others, has long since broken out of the historical framework into the land of myth and romance.

With this aspect of his fame we are not concerned. But even when Héloise is restored to her right proportions in Abelard's life, the story is not immediately made a simple one, for he has in the course of centuries acquired among another section of readers a second mythical eminence as the leader of free thought and rationalism against the obscurantism and intolerance of St Bernard. Moreover, the sources for the history of his life are themselves enigmatic, for besides a variety of contemporary judgements and accounts hard enough to harmonize, we have his own very full yet often tantalizingly silent autobiography, the *Historia calamitatum*, which, though it is of the highest value for its historical, psychological and human interest, presents in an acute form, as might be expected from its author's character and career, all the difficulties of interpretation which are inseparable from the autobiographical form. Finally, the series of letters which have done most to give Abelard fame in the modern world – the exchange between himself and Héloise – are the subject of a critical controversy of their own; the authenticity of those ascribed to Héloise has been impugned, and the whole collection has been imputed either to a later forger, or to Abelard himself.

Peter Abelard (the origin of his second name is uncertain) was the son of a land-holding knight of some position, named Berengar, and of his wife, Lucia. Both his parents ultimately took the vows of religion. He was born in 1079 at Le Pallet or Palais near Nantes; from his native village came the sobriquet, Peripateticus Palatinus, by which he was later known to John of Salisbury. Avid of knowledge from childhood, he resolved on a clerk's career, and *c.* 1095 studied under the celebrated Roscelin at Loches, and later *c.* 1100 under William of Champeaux at Paris; he criticized both these teachers severely for their handling of the question of universals. Precocious in genius, to use his own simile, as his own native soil was precocious in blade and flower, excelling in dialectic and all the arts of verbal controversy, he was intensely stimulating and exercised over young minds a peculiar charm which remained with him all his life, and which recalls the partly similar, partly very different, fascination of the young Newman at Oxford. After breaking with William of Champeaux he set up as master on his own account first at Melun (*c.* 1103), then at Corbeil, and finally in the cathedral school at Paris. There he resumed his attacks on his old master, William of Champeaux, who (1108) retired into the monastery of St Victor which he had founded; this withdrawal, according to Abelard, writing perhaps with venom, was one of wounded vanity nursing ambition. Abelard himself about this time removed to the Mont Ste Geneviève on the left bank of the Seine, destined thereafter to be the resort of students, the *quartier latin*. Victorious over William but still harassed by his supporters Abelard decided to take a more ambitious step and to join the ranks of the theologians. The masters with the highest reputation at that moment were the two brothers Anselm and Ralph of Laon; the former had been a disciple of his namesake the saint at Bec. Historians in the past were willing to accept Abelard's contemptuous estimate of Anselm as smoke without a flame and as an old oak cumbering a rich cornfield. More recent work, however, as well as the appreciation of contemporaries such as Innocent II who referred to him as the light of the Western world, show that both the 'severe simplicity' of Anselm in defining the faith, and his wide methodical influence on the compiling of glosses on the Bible and manuals of theology are seen in the careers of numerous and distinguished followers, like Gilbert the Universal, bishop of London, and Robert Pullen, the first English cardinal. Nevertheless Abelard, now thirty-five years old, soon became impatient and set up a school of his own at Laon. According to his own account, he began his teaching with a brilliant exegesis of Ezechiel, composed overnight in answer to a challenge, and thus drew away the *clientèle* of his master. Attacked by two notable pupils of Anselm, Alberic and Lotulf, he decided to return to Paris (1113–14), where he was offered a chair in the cathedral school, and began to write his books on *Theology*. He was now at the height of his powers, still young and unmolested, and he might well have entered upon a peaceful career. Instead, his vanity and overbearing self-confidence turned to self-indulgence of all kinds, and his career was sharply interrupted by the fatal *dénouement* of his association with Héloise.

Abelard was at this moment a canon of Notre Dame and was not by canon law free to marry. Héloise gave birth to a son but marriage would almost inevitably have ruined Abelard's prospects as a teacher of theology. It is a measure of the devotion and admiration of Héloise that she steadfastly dissuaded him from this solution to their problem. They were in the sequel secretly married to satisfy Fulbert, the uncle and guardian of Héloise, but Fulbert divulged the marriage and persecuted his niece, whereupon Abelard persuaded her to become a nun at Argenteuil, however stoically and unwillingly, while he took monastic vows at St Denis. His experience, however, had done nothing to abate either the inveterate combativity or the irresistible magnetism of Abelard. Allowed by Abbot Adam to open a school, he published his first theological treatise on the Trinity. This was seized upon by his old opponents Alberic and Lotulf and at a council in the presence of the papal legate at Soissons (1121) Abelard was condemned to burn his book and return to monastic life under 'house arrest'. Back at St Denis he stirred up a hornet's nest about his ears by denying that the patron of the abbey was St Denis the Areopagite, bishop of Athens. Compelled to leave, he was allowed by the great Suger, newly elected abbot, to choose his place of retreat, and selected Quincey, a desert spot in the wild country near Nogent-sur-Seine, with the expressed intention of leading a hermit's life. Crowds of pupils, however, flocked to him, and he built for them and for himself the church and house of the Paraclete (1122). Here, according to his own account, which is not substantiated by other evidence, he was threatened with molestation, perhaps by St Bernard and St Norbert; it may have been this feeling of insecurity that led him to accept the abbacy that was offered him by the monks of St Gildas, an uncouth community near the Breton coast by Vannes.

Meanwhile Suger had undertaken the reform of the unsatisfactory nunnery of Argenteuil, which belonged to St Denis, and Héloise found herself likely to be homeless. Abelard therefore made over the Paraclete to her, and in 1131 the foundation was confirmed by the pope, then in France, and was visited by St Bernard, who also met Abelard. The latter now began the extant correspondence with Héloise, and acted as legislator and spiritual adviser to her and the nuns of whom she became abbess.

The strange *ménage* at St Gildas soon proved unworkable. Abelard attempted to reform the coarse and unruly Bretons with penalties and excommunications, and they retorted, if we believe him, with attempts on his life. In *c.* 1132 he left them for good, and for the next four years his movements are lost to sight. It was at this juncture that he composed his *Historia calamitatum*, which is therefore not available as a source for the last phase of his life. He reappears in daylight on the Mont Ste Geneviève at Paris in 1136, when he had John of Salisbury among his hearers, and in 1139–40 Arnold of Brescia, almost his equal in combativity. These were years of great literary activity, in which he published his *Theologia christiana* and its successor *Theologia 'Scholarium'*, his ethical treatise *Scito te ipsum* and (probably) his *Sic et non*, all of which he was constantly re-writing. It was at this time that versions of these works fell under the eyes of William of St Thierry, then a Cistercian of Signy, who related them to his formidable friend, the abbot of Clairvaux. Abelard, after defying his opponents, faltered in his defence before bishops and others at Sens, and was condemned by the synod there in 1140. He appealed to Rome, and set out for the threshold of the Apostles, preceded by a bunch of the fiercest and most devastating letters ever written by St Bernard, but was intercepted on the road by Peter the Venerable, abbot of Cluny, who received him with characteristic sympathy, gave him a home in his own great abbey, and advised him to retract what was clearly erroneous or rash in his teaching. Abelard, with what searchings of heart we know not, took the wise if unexpected decision to follow this advice, and at a meeting with St Bernard complete harmony was established in personal relations, though Abelard's retractation stopped at the minimum possible, while in a final apologia he gave the abbot of Clairvaux as good as he had received. Back at Cluny, well over sixty and an invalid, he was still active as a writer. He had been condemned by the pope, but Peter, furnished with his retractation, obtained permission for him to remain undisturbed at Cluny. His last year was a surprising and moving contrast to his earlier life; he lived in submission and simplicity till April 1142, when he died in peace in a priory of Cluny at Chalon-sur-Saône. It was then that Peter the Venerable wrote to Héloise that most remarkable letter in which, besides expressing his admiration for herself and Abelard, he refers to their old association and anticipates their reunion beyond the tomb,

'where, beyond these voices, there is peace'.

It is altogether impossible to pass a summary judgement on Abelard's actions, character and achievements, almost every detail and facet of which has been, and still is, a subject of controversy. He is, indeed, one of the most difficult of men, whether medieval or modern, to assess: as a French historian justly remarked, he is a Proteus, who slips through our hands and takes another shape before our description of him is complete. If in Anselm all powers of mind and soul form a luminous, harmonious whole, and merge into a single principle directing and inspiring all his actions, so with Abelard all is in disarray, with characteristics and motives good and bad inextricably mixed, until the winds fall with the calm sunset. Possessed of all the external gifts of person, handsome in face and carriage (as both he himself and Héloise tell us), eloquent and seductive in speech, he combined an unrivalled brilliance in controversy with a daring only equalled by his lucidity in criticism and exposition, justifying at every turn the epithet, which recurs as an *epitheton constans* among his contemporaries, of *subtilis*. With all these gifts, he remained vain, sensitive, intemperate, restless and self-centred, never doubting of his own mental powers. 'I reckoned myself as the only true philosopher left in the world', he wrote,[1] and Otto of Freising adds that he was so arrogant, so self-confident, that he would scarcely consent to demean himself by listening to any of his masters. Wholly lacking in reverence for his seniors, he remained nevertheless (or perhaps for this very reason) supremely attractive to the young. Alone among the outstanding figures of the age, in which theologians and men of letters mixed intimately together, he had few friends, and there is a flicker of ridicule in the title given him by John of Salisbury, yet wherever he appeared pupils flocked to him. Fulques

[1]*Historia calamitatum.* ed. J. Monfrin, 2nd edn. (Paris, 1962), p. 70.

of Denil gives a long catalogue of the distant countries from which they came, the future masters and bishops and popes – Peter the Lombard and perhaps Gerhoh of Reichersberg; John of Salisbury, Celestine II, Celestine III, Otto of Freising and Robert of Melun certainly, among them. An independent chronicler speaks of him as the master of the most distinguished school, to which men of letters flocked from almost every part of Christendom, and Peter the Venerable sums all up in a sentence: 'he was renowned almost the whole world over for the weight of his learning, and his fame was universal'.[2] Selfish and sensual in his early relations with Héloïse, he captured and retained her selfless and passionate devotion, and he himself in later years, by his care for her when he was an abbot and she an abbess, did much to redeem his selfishness, just as by his unassuming carriage and simple faith in his last year of life he seems to obliterate the memory of his early arrogance and intolerance.

Until very recent years all discussions of Abelard centred upon his alleged heretical and rationalistic teaching. At the present day, as a result both of research among unpublished manuscripts and of critical methods applied to his works, he can be seen as a figure of positive import, as a logician of supreme ability and as the originator of ideas as well as of methods that were to have a long life. Not only is it now possible to grasp more fully than before what Abelard taught and thought, but it has been shown conclusively that throughout his life he was constantly rewriting and reconsidering his works, and that his opinions grew more orthodox and more carefully expressed with the passage of the years.

Was Abelard a rationalist? The question has been variously answered. Eighty years ago, the rationalists of the nineteenth century, Renan among them, saw in Abelard a herald of their enlightenment, and some of the historians of the day agreed with them; such was the opinion of Charles de Rémusat and Victor Cousin, and to their names, with some reserves, may be added the more recent opinion of Maurice de Wulf: 'Exaggerating the rights of dialectic in theological matters, Peter Abelard established the relations of theology and philosophy on rationalistic principles'.[3] Others, even, have not hesitated to reverse Anselm's motto for Abelard; he would have said: 'I understand in order that I may believe'. Nevertheless, even at the beginning of this century some of the most distinguished names were found among Abelard's advocates, among them those of Harnack and

[2]*Letters of Peter the Venerable*, ed. G. Constable, 2 vols. (Cambridge, Mass., 1967), I, no. 115, p. 307.
[3]*Hist. philosophie médiévale* (1 ed.) I 202.

Portalié, the latter of whom remarks: 'In theory at least, Abelard never desired to give a philosophical demonstration of a mystery of the faith; still less did he profess himself a rationalist.' This, expressed in various forms, is the almost unanimous verdict of recent scholars – Geyer, Chenu, Grabmann, de Ghellinck, Gilson – and we may agree with the judgement of the last-named of these, that the legend of Abelard the free-thinker has now become an exhibit of the historical curiosity-shop.[4]

Of a truth, Abelard was never a rebel against the authority of the Church, and never a rationalist in the modern sense. He never persisted in teaching what had been censured, even though until censured he may have protested vehemently that he had been misrepresented. Similarly, he never intended that his dialectic should attack or contradict or replace the doctrines of the Church as formulated by tradition. In this, full weight must be given to his words in his last treatise on *Theology*: 'Now therefore it remains for us, after having laid down the foundation of authority, to place upon it the buttresses of reasoning.'[5] This is unquestionably a genuine expression of his programme, as are also the celebrated and moving words of his letter to Héloise after the condemnation of 1140: 'I will never be a philosopher, if this is to speak against St Paul; I would not be an Aristotle, if this were to separate me from Christ . . . . I have set my conscience on the corner-stone on which Christ has built his Church . . . if the tempest rises, I am not shaken; if the winds rave, I am not fearful . . . . I rest upon the rock that cannot be moved.'[6] These are not the words of a deliberate heretic or of a professed rationalist.

There are in fact, two quite distinct questions. Did Abelard intend to formulate the doctrines of the faith in terms of dialectic, and to establish or invalidate them by this means? And, did Abelard in fact, in his writing and teaching, err from the orthodox teaching of the Church?

As we have seen, the answer to the first question, if it were needful to give it in a single word, would be negative. Such a simple answer, however, does not meet the complexity of the matter. We have already seen that Anselm, though undoubtedly orthodox in intention, probably overestimated the part that dialectic, the strict argumentation of logic, could play in explaining, and in a sense proving, the mysteries of the faith. Abelard knew Anselm's work, and though he does not mention his motto, *credo ut intelligam*, would certainly

[4] *La Philosophie au moyen âge* (ed. 1944), p. 281.
[5] *Theologia 'Scholarium'* lib. 2. (*PL* clxxviii 1039).
[6] *Ep. ad Heloissam*, ep. 17 (*PL* clxxviii 375–8).

have echoed it, though perhaps on a slightly more superficial level and with more emphasis on the last word. But Abelard, besides having his full share of the contemporary trust in dialectic as the mistress of all truth, had a far greater acquaintance with, and trust in, the current *Sprachlogik*, the conviction that just as words and terms and methods could be found to express truth with absolute fidelity, so all speculation, and indeed the nature and modes of acting of things in themselves, must follow and in a sense be modified by, the words and terms used by the skilled dialectician. *A fortiori*, the theological expression of religious truths must conform to dialectical practice; only so could any discussion or explanation of the mysteries of the faith be practicable. This postulate was probably at the root of Berengar's controversy with Lanfranc. It was certainly a prime cause of misunderstanding between Bernard and Gilbert de la Porrée. So it was with Abelard. By genius, choice and practice he was a dialectician, and a dialectician he almost always remained. The dogmas of the faith are not for him wells of infinite depth, the reflection in words of luminous supernatural truth. Rather, they are so many propositions or facts thrown, so to say, to the Christian philosopher, upon which he may exercise his ingenuity and to which he can apply no laws but those of logic and grammar. A modern analogy may perhaps be found in the attitude towards the gospels of many sincerely religious scholars, who subject the texts to the rigours of 'form criticism', without any regard to the interpretation of past ages, and without any explicit consideration of the words as bearing a deep and divine weight of meaning which can only be grasped by one whose mind and heart are attuned to a spiritual purpose.

As to the second question, Abelard was unquestionably technically unorthodox in many of his expressions. Though his opponents, and in particular St Bernard, may have erred in the severity of their attacks and in the universality of their suspicions, and though recent scholarship has shown that some, at least, of his expressions can, in their context, bear an orthodox interpretation, and that Abelard became more, and not less, respectful of tradition as the years passed, yet many of his pronouncements on the Trinity, the Incarnation, and Grace were certainly incorrect by traditional standards and, if carried to their logical issue, would have dangerously weakened the expression of Christian truth. The catalogue of erroneous, or at least of erratic, propositions in his writings drawn up by Portalié eighty years ago cannot be wholly cancelled by explanations of a verbal or logical nature. Error, however, is not always heretical. In the theological controversies of every age there have always been two families among those accused of heresy. There are those who, whatever their professions, are in fact attacking traditional doctrine, and those who, despite many of their expressions, have, as we may say, the root of the matter in them. It is the difference between an Alfred Loisy and a Friedrich von Hügel, and there can be no doubt to which of the families Abelard belongs.

Abelard's genius was versatile, and left a mark on everything he touched. We have already considered his important contribution to logic, and in particular his solution of the problem of universals. In methodology he marked an epoch with his *Sic et non*. This unusual treatise, composed perhaps in its earliest form *c.* 1122, is probably the most celebrated (though not necessarily the most important) of Abelard's contributions to the development of medieval thought; it has in decades past been the occasion of a number of controversies. It consists of a relatively short prologue explaining its purpose and giving rules for the discussion of what follows; then comes a series of texts from Scripture and the Fathers on 158 theological points. The texts are given in groups, and in each case are apparently mutually contradictory. The essence of the work is the exposition of methodical doubt. As Abelard has it, 'careful and frequent questioning is the basic key to wisdom', or, as he writes in the same prologue: 'By doubting we come to questioning, and by questioning we perceive the truth.'

Opinions have been divided as to how far the *Sic et non* is original, how far it is an instrument of scepticism, and what was its influence on the development of scholastic method. It was for long the common opinion that it was completely original, an innovation with resounding consequences as great in its own field as the invention of the spinning-jenny or the mechanical reaper in the world of economics. This view, usually held in conjunction with that which saw in Abelard the first great apostle of free thought, was convincingly refuted by the researches of Fournier and Grabmann, who showed that the juxtaposition of seemingly contradictory authorities was already a method in common use in Abelard's day by compilers of canonical collections, who had not only amassed texts but given rules for criticism and harmonization. Bernold of Constance and Ivo of Chartres in particular had employed this technique, and the *Decretum* and *Panormia* of the latter were shown to have furnished Abelard with some of his quotations from the Fathers.

As regards the primary aim of the *Sic et non*, there have been two views. Many in the past, Harnack among them, have seen in it an attempt to undermine tradition by showing its essentially self-contradictory character, in order to make way for a more rational approach. Others, and among them the greatest names among historians of medieval thought, have strenuously opposed this view, seeing in the *Sic et non* simply an exercise for explaining and harmonizing discrepancies and difficulties in the authorities. This opinion gains additional support from the fact that the work was never used by his opponents as a stick with which to beat Abelard. Such a view might well allow that *Sic et non* was a reaction against the purely traditionalist teaching of the day, and that it was intended to open a wide new field to dialectic, for which only a few samples were given.

As for the influence of the work upon the schools, the verdict of the early historians was summary, and Abelard was hailed as the creator of the scholastic method, and even Denifle in his early days regarded it as the basis of the method of question and disputation. As we have seen, all now admit that the borrowing was on Abelard's side; the disputation was long in becoming standard practice in the schools, and John of Salisbury, writing some years after the death of Abelard, gives pride of place as a teacher of dialectic not to Abelard, but Aristotle in the shape of the recently introduced *Topics*. In short, we may say that Abelard, by the *Sic et non* as well as by his own practice, gave a keen impulse to the dialectical treatment of theology, but that the evolution of the formal and obligatory technique of the disputation – arguments pro and con, judgement and reply to arguments – took place principally after the rediscovery of the 'new logic', the Analytics, Topics and Sophistics of Aristotle.

In theology, the main achievement of Abelard was to discuss and explain, where others merely asserted or proved, and to provide an outline of the whole field of doctrines. It would seem, indeed, that he was the first to use the Latin word *theologia* in the sense that is now current in all European languages; the word had previously borne the connotation familiar in the Greek Fathers and the pseudo-Denis, of the mystical or at least the expert knowledge of God and His attributes. By giving, in versions of increasing length and scope, an 'introduction' or survey of Christian teaching, Abelard's writings are an important link in the development of the *summa*, the typical medieval survey of theology.

When thus 'introducing' his disciples to theology, Abelard met, as he himself tells us, a genuine demand for an explanation of the mysteries of the faith, and he gave this explanation with opinions that were often original, and which aimed at being reasonable.

Abelard was in many ways a humanist; he stressed the exemplary purpose of the Incarnation and Crucifixion at the expense of the redemptive, and minimized the conception of original sin, regarding it as a penalty rather than a stain and regarding grace as an assistance rather than as an enablement. He reacted against all legalistic interpretations, such as the opinion that the death or blood of Christ was a discharge of the rights claimed over mankind by the devil. In his Trinitarian theology, which was the head and front of his offending at Soissons and remained a charge at Sens, the principal accusation was that in reaction from the 'tritheism' of Roscelin he founded the distinctions within the Godhead upon the traditional 'appropriations' ('power' of the Father, 'wisdom' of the Word, and 'love' of the Holy Spirit) thereby either reducing them to aspects of the one Godhead (Sabellianism) or, by an exclusive appropriation, limiting the equality of the persons. He was further accused of obscuring the personal union of the divine and human natures in Christ by treating the humanity as something assumed, as it were, as a garment by the divine Son. This, and other questionable propositions, make up an impressive total of erroneous opinions, and although some were due to faulty terminology and others were tacitly dropped from later versions of the same work – for Abelard, resembling other lecturers before and since, was always rewriting and adding precision to his treatises – too much smoke remains to allow the cry of fire to be ignored. Above and through all else was the charge that Abelard left no place in his system for faith. Not only did he suggest that the sages of old had at least a vestigial conception of the Trinity and Incarnation, and that unaided reason could go far towards demonstration of the mysteries of Christianity, but in his eyes, it was said, faith that had not been shored up by reason was merely an opinion, a supposition (*existimatio, aestimatio*). Here, again, a careful examination of Abelard's utterances shows that his real meaning was often more orthodox than his use of unfamiliar words might suggest. A general ignorance of the Greek Fathers deprived the twelfth century of the careful technical vocabulary they had evolved. Moreover, Abelard's excessive admiration for the very imperfectly known philosophy of the ancients, added to his tendency to see the Christian revelation and morality as merely the crown or, so to say, the 'production' of natural reason and ethics, caused him to see too readily in heathen philosophy an outline of Christian doctrine, including even the Trinity. And finally, Abelard's thought, like that of St Anselm before him, lacked clarity because theologians had not yet carefully delimited the provinces of faith and reason; Abelard undoubtedly extended the province of reason too far.

In yet one more important field, that of ethics, Abelard was destined to leave a durable mark. In his discussion of moral problems in *Scito te ipsum* he showed his originality in such a way as to be one of the founders of scholastic moral theology. Reacting against the view then current which placed moral goodness solely in the conformity of an act to the declared law of God, and which tended to see sin as the factual transgression of the law, even if unknown or misunderstood (e.g., the obligation of certain degrees of fasting on certain days), Abelard placed goodness wholly in the intention and will of the agent, and saw sin not as the actual transgression of the law, but as a contempt of God the lawgiver. This, properly understood, was an enlightened and health-giving view, at least for men of intelligence. It soon became a commonplace among scholastic moralists in the modified form that at the final moment of decision a man must choose what seems to him to be right and that by so doing he performs a good action, even though had he fully known how the law or the circumstances stood, he would have acted otherwise. Abelard did not wish to deny that the completely good act, the act both 'materially' and 'formally' good, only existed when the judgement of conscience was in harmony with the law of God, that is, with either the natural law of morality or God's positive commandments. He would not have accepted in a purely subjective sense that 'there's nothing either good or bad, but thinking makes it so';[7] but he made at least the first movements towards positions that were to be developed by later medieval thinkers. Thus his strong emphasis on the completely deliberate choice of the free will as a *sine qua non* of the sinful act minimized human ignorance and weakness, and the hardening and blinding effects of past failings. Abelard, in commenting upon the text, 'Father, forgive them, for they know not what they do', tended to excuse wholly from sin the agents of the Crucifixion, stressing 'they know not what they do' rather than the implicit sin that needed forgiveness. This shocked current susceptibilities, and was one of the charges against him. In another direction his opinions minimized the conception of the law of God and of the absolute ethical goodness of particular actions. Abelard, anticipating with strange exactness the opinions of some fourteenth-century 'voluntarists', suggested that with God as with man the good depended upon the free choice, and

---

[7]It need scarcely be remarked that Hamlet (Act II, Sc. ii, 251) was not proclaiming ethical relativity, but simply the possibility of different opinions as to the amenities of life in Denmark.

that God might have established canons of morality other than, and even contrary to, those of the Hebrew and Christian revelation.

Look at him how we will, and when full weight has been given to the impression of restlessness, vanity and lack of spiritual depth given by his career and some of his writings, Abelard remains, both as a teacher and as a thinker, one of the half-dozen most influential names in the history of medieval thought. As a master of unrivalled powers of attraction he did much to raise the intellectual level of the schools of his day, and by his lengthy sojourns in Paris, did more than any other single teacher to ensure the primacy of the city as a centre of student life. Prince and paladin of dialecticians, he made of the 'arts' a discipline of high intellectual content, besides originating a theory of epistemology that was to have a great future. It was no fault of his that the dialectic of his day was outmoded by the rediscovered Aristotle, and that theological speculation based upon it not only shocked contemporaries, but failed to attract posterity. As a theologian, he was the first to see his subject as a whole, and to conceive the possibility of a survey or synthesis for his pupils, thus taking an important part in fixing the method of teaching. Finally, and perhaps most significantly, he approached theological and ethical problems as questions that could be illuminated, explained and in part comprehended by a carefully reasoned approach, and still more by a humane, practical attitude which took account of difficulties and of natural, human feelings, and he endeavoured to solve problems of belief and conscience not by the blow of an abstract principle, but by a consideration of circumstances as they are in common experience. Abelard failed to become a much-cited authority by reason of his double condemnation and the attacks of celebrated adversaries, but his ideas lingered in the minds of his disciples, and many of them came to the surface, unacknowledged, in the golden age of scholasticism. It would be difficult to instance any other theologian, accused so often and justifiably of error, who has given so much of method and matter to orthodox thought. Yet despite all this, Abelard falls short of the highest achievement. In logic and dialectic, he came too early to enjoy the complete legacy of Aristotle, and he practised a logic that was soon to fall out of favour. In theology, he lacked both the constructive power and the depth of spiritual insight that informed an Augustine, an Anselm, a Bonaventure and an Aquinas. While they enriched and deepened the exposition of the Christian mysteries, Abelard could only explain and criticize on the lower level of human wisdom and experience. On that level, and as a teacher and master who for forty years could draw a multitude with his magic wand, Abelard was unsurpassed; his only rival, in a field that bordered upon his own, was the great abbot of Clairvaux.

CHAPTER ELEVEN
The School of Chartres and John of Salisbury

The fame of Abelard's teaching was probably a considerable factor in the establishment of the reputation of Paris as an intellectual centre. We shall see later how its fame was consolidated by the school of St Victor and by Peter the Lombard and others. To the contemporaries of Abelard, however, it did not as yet seem inevitable that Paris should become the intellectual centre of France and Europe. London, we remember, despite its wealth and population, and its importance as the administrative, financial, judicial and social capital, never had a student population in the middle ages, if we except the young lawyers of the Inns of Court in the fourteenth and fifteenth centuries. In the first half of the twelfth century, in similar wise, the intellectual life of France was centred at a dozen or more cathedral cities. Among these pride of place must be given to Chartres, which for more than fifty years had a succession of masters of unrivalled celebrity, and which preserved far into the following century its own tradition of teaching and culture in a rapidly changing world.

Chartres, a small cathedral city some fifty miles south-west of Paris, had first risen to fame, as we have seen, under its bishop Fulbert, the pupil of Gerbert of Aurillac, and himself later the master of Berengar, but during the latter half of the eleventh century it had been no more distinguished than a dozen rivals. Chartres continued, however, to preserve more purely than others its literary, humanistic tradition, and this was developed, with a corresponding attention to philosophy, by a series of eminent masters. The training in letters led on to a course of dialectic which, while abreast of the latest additions to the Aristotelian corpus, was based on Boethius and on the Platonic *Timaeus* and such other indications of Platonic and Neoplatonic tradition as were available.

Though never, it would seem, a resident at Chartres, the Englishman Adelard of Bath is usually reckoned along with the School of Chartres in the early decades of the century. A restless traveller, who made contacts with Arabic and Greek science and thought both in south Italy and the eastern Mediterranean, he was, as we shall see in a later chapter, a significant figure in the history of medieval mathematics and natural science. He was also, in his treatise *De eodem et diverso*, a champion of the use of reasoning and dialectic in theology. In the matter of universals, which for him bordered on metaphysics, he aimed at combining Plato and Aristotle. Universals, i.e., genera and species, were immanent in the individual things, which were cognisable by the senses, and from which the genera could be abstracted by the mind; these latter existed as ideas in the mind of God.

Of the Chartrain masters, the first of the new school was Bernard, master at Chartres by *c.* 1119 and chancellor by 1124, dying perhaps by 1126. No complete work of his has as yet been discovered and published, but John of Salisbury has left more than one description of his doctrines and methods of teaching. Among these is the famous and oft-quoted simile (not, in fact, original to Bernard) of the moderns as dwarfs who can see further than the giants, the ancients, on whose shoulders they are perched. There is also a vivid and attractive account of his manner of literary teaching, with its evening memory-exercise, reading and prayer, and its morning repetition and composition. John quotes his list of the six keys of learning: humbleness of heart, love of inquiry, a peaceful life, silent meditation, poverty and exile from home, and remarks that he was the most finished Platonist of the age. As a Platonist Bernard distinguished between the Ideas, which are eternal, and the Forms, reflections of the ideas, created by nature with the things which they specify. It was he who originated the phrase 'native forms' (*formae nativae*).

Bernard was succeeded as chancellor of Chartres by the teacher who, after Abelard, must be ranked as the most eminent thinker of the century and who, as an ecclesiastic, was considered by no less a judge than John of Salisbury, his erstwhile pupil, worthy of a full-length comparison with St Bernard. Gilbert de la Porrée is, indeed, an example of a type recurring throughout the ages, of an eminent man who to his contemporaries appears among the very greatest of an epoch, *nulli secundus*, but who fails in the judgment of posterity, either through want of genius or through some lack of central humanity, to remain a man of all time, and who consequently becomes a figure of merely historical interest. Perhaps, in the eighteenth century, Voltaire and Hume may be similarly instanced as contrasting with Burke and Johnson. Born *c.* 1080, Gilbert was a pupil of Bernard of Chartres, and succeeded him as chancelloɪ by 1126. By 1141 he was in Paris, where he taught, among others, John of Salisbury, becoming in 1142 bishop of Poitiers; he died a year after St Bernard in 1154. He is best known to history as the object of an onslaught by the abbot of Clairvaux, who wished for a condemnation of his teaching on the Trinity, and as such he is the 'obscure opponent' of the saint in Matthew Arnold's sonnet. In the later middle ages he was celebrated as the reputed author of the *Liber sex principiorum*, a thorough study of the six predicaments or categories left unexamined by Aristotle (i.e., action, passion, place, time, position and habit). The book became a classic, was commented upon by Albert the Great and others, and remained a text-book till the end of the Middle Ages, when it attained the distinction not only of print but of translation into Ciceronian Latin. The attribution to Gilbert, however, first explicitly noted in Albert's day and accepted without question till our own, has been convincingly refuted in recent years.

Gilbert de la Porrée is remarkable both as an expounder and as a practitioner of the early scholastic method, and as an original metaphysician. In both capacities he draws freely upon Boethius, upon whom he wrote a detailed commentary, and from whom he drew the distinction between the two meanings of substance, 'that which is' and 'that which makes a thing what it is'. Following his master, Bernard, he took something from both Aristotle and Plato. Like Plato a strong realist, he distinguished between the exemplary, unchanging Idea, and the created Form which gave its nature to individual things, but in the process of knowing he followed the Aristotelian theory of abstraction. His conflict with St Bernard arose from an application of his metaphysical doctrines to the Trinity. While allowing, with the constant tradition of the Fathers and the Church, that God was an entirely 'simple' Being, he nevertheless held that the three Persons were one God only by reason of the 'form' of divinity common to all, while on the other hand, just as 'humanity' is not the individual man, though it constitutes him as such, so the divine essence, though constituting each Person God, is not itself God. It was in opposition to this that Bernard made his celebrated declaration: 'Let it be written with iron upon adamant, let it be carved upon flint, that the divine essence, form, nature, goodness, wisdom, virtue and power are each truly God' (Migne, *PL* clxxxv 590).

We are not here concerned with the theological implications of the controversy, nor with the personal charges that each party made against the other. Quite apart from these, the incident is of interest as yet one more example of uncertainty of method in the dialectical explanation of theological truth. The account given of Gilbert's position in the last paragraph might convey the impression that the trouble arose merely on account of his transference to theology of his Platonic doctrine of ideas and his Boethian doctrine of subsistence. This, however, would seem to do less than justice to the intellectual stature of the bishop of Poitiers. A better explanation might be that Gilbert, like Abelard, and perhaps also like Berengar and Roscelin before him, failed to distinguish between logic and metaphysics, and also between physical and transcendental reality. On this view he would have held, in a way common to the logicians of his day but hard for us to appreciate, that words and logical predicates and categories had their exact counterparts in extra-mental reality. They were in this way extreme realists, as Duns Scotus was to be, later, in a somewhat different fashion. They did not distinguish between a real, and a merely logical, distinction or relationship. If the mind could consider God only by separating his goodness from his justice, his nature from the three persons, then these were, in fact, separate in some way. To dialecticians with this point of view the formulas of the faith, though sincerely held, seemed dialectically inadequate. Neither they, nor the theologians, had as yet reached the point of clearly delimiting truth accessible to the unaided human reason, and truth surpassing the grasp of the reason and attainable only by faith or the divinely illuminated intellect, and of realizing that formulae applicable to the former would be useless when applied to the latter kind of knowledge. Bernard, sincere in his action and right in his essential judgement as a theologian, failed to see that Gilbert was involved in what to him was a very real intellectual problem. Gilbert, for his part, while genuinely anxious to preserve orthodoxy, was unwilling to abandon a dialectical technique which was clearly causing trouble to those not adept in it, yet which seemed to him to be valid and indeed essential to any rational discussion of the subject.

Returning a little in chronological order, we may note two other distinguished Chartrains. William of Conches (*c.* 1080–*c.* 1154) was a pupil of Bernard of Chartres and the tutor of the young prince, later Henry II of England; he also had John of Salisbury for a time amongst his disciples. He was an extreme Platonist, and his early identification of the Holy Spirit with the world-soul was attacked by William of St Thierry and retracted. This academic trend towards pantheism, which had no counterpart in the theology of the persons concerned, was continued by Bernard Silvestris, or Bernard of Tours (who is not to be confused with the chancellor of Chartres from 1156 and the bishop of Quimper (1159–67)). He went far towards becoming a complete philosophical pantheist, holding that everything in the world derived its origin from a world-soul, an emanation of the divine reason. Such views, though in many ways a consequence of trends at Chartres, were not typical of the School, which continued to exist as a focus of fine letters and natural science for more than a century after the death of Gilbert de la Porrée.

Among the luminaries of the School of Chartres at this time may fitly be included the most accomplished scholar and stylist of his age, who for subsequent centuries has seemed to embody the literary and philosophic culture which we find so copiously displayed in his writings: the Englishman, John of Salisbury. John of Salisbury is one of those men who, by a happy disposition of circumstances, both represent and describe for us the higher mental life of an age. He is the Erasmus, the Johnson of the twelfth century. The friend or acquaintance of almost all the celebrated men of north-western Europe at an epoch when men of genius abounded, and when the society of the literate was more extensive in space and more homogeneous in spirit than ever before or since, he was a keen observer, a watchful but not a malevolent critic, and the master of a clear and idiomatic style perfectly adapted to the revelation of a sane, sincere, cautious and somewhat sophisticated mind.

Born at Old Sarum *c.* 1115, he received his first schooling from a parish priest and then spent twelve years in France, frequenting doctor and sage. Abelard, Robert of Melun, William of Conches, Thierry of Chartres, Robert Pullen and Gilbert de la Porrée, with many others, were among his masters, and his rich and manifold correspondence shows him to have been on easy or friendly relations with many of the great ecclesiastics, cardinals, bishops and abbots, of his time. From 1148 he was a frequent visitor to the papal court, and was present at the council of Rheims in 1148 when the teaching of Gilbert de la Porrée was impugned, but not condemned. Already in 1147 he had become chaplain and secretary, with a testimonial from St Bernard, to Archbishop Theobald of Canterbury, and thenceforward most of the archbishop's correspondence was in fact his work and often his design. It was of these years, when Theobald had around him at Canterbury a group of canonists, theologians and men of letters, that Stubbs wrote so eloquently, and to this group the name even of university has been applied – perhaps that of a medieval All Souls College would be nearer the mark. Always *persona grata* with the Roman Curia, and the intimate friend of the English pope, Hadrian IV, it was John who at Benevento obtained the papal grant of Ireland to Henry II, but he mysteriously fell under the king's displeasure: probably Henry thought that he was too much the friend of Rome, and John retired somewhat from his public activities. This gave him time for writing, and these years saw the completion of his two most considerable works, the *Policraticus*, on the faults and foibles of those in high life, and the *Metalogicon*, a treatise on Aristotelian logic, ranging widely over contemporary trends and personalities in the schools, and John's own experiences. These books were both finished about 1159 and dedicated and despatched in that year to the author's friend and late colleague, Thomas Becket, then serving as chancellor with his master at the siege of Toulouse. On Theobald's death John continued at Canterbury in the entourage of archbishop Thomas; he was one of those sent to receive the pallium from the pope, and he went into exile ahead of Thomas in 1163 or 1164. To this exile, mainly spent with his friend Pierre de Celle, abbot of Rheims, belongs his third important work, the *Historia pontificalis*. Throughout the six following years his letters are one of the most valuable sources for the history of the struggle between archbishop and king. John consistently supported the archbishop, though his very different mind and character kept him from sharing to the full either the impetuosities or the heroic self-sacrifice of his master. He was present at the interview between the knights and the archbishop in his hall at Canterbury on 29 December 1170, and remarked characteristically that the archbishop was the only one of the party who seemed to wish to die for the sake of dying. He probably fled just before the murder in the cathedral, but from the first moment afterwards devoted his energies to vindicating for his friend the titles of martyr and saint. In 1176 he was elected bishop of Chartres, largely on account of his close ties with St Thomas, and spent the last four years of his life in diocesan administration, dying in 1180. There is a certain fittingness in this official association with Chartres and its rising cathedral of one who stands in the history of thought as an *anima naturaliter Carnotensis*.

John of Salisbury first received serious attention from two distinguished scholars, R. L. Poole and C. C. J. Webb, who gave us, in addition to articles and summaries, a biography and elaborate editions of some of his works; more recently the *Historia pontificalis* and the letters have been re-edited in Nelson's (now Oxford) Medieval Texts. His works, though written in a Latin style unsurpassed in purity and flexibility by any writer of the century, and though reflecting on every page the cool, urbane and critical outlook and fine discrimination of their author, do not make easy reading. This is in part because, like all free compositions of the Middle Ages, they are very discursive and without sequence of topic and crescendo of interest, partly because the world to which they introduce us is so unlike our own, and the outlook more alien to us than the simpler, more emotional and puritanical outlook of St Bernard, and partly because they deal in so many places with the technicalities of an outmoded phase of philosophical training. They are, nevertheless, a mine of information on personalities and doctrines. The *Policraticus*, or *Statesman's Guide*, nominally a criticism of the pursuits of courtiers, develops into a treatise of political thought, the first of its kind in medieval England, in which the character and duties of the ideal prince are set out and contrasted with the behaviour of a tyrant. The *Metalogicon* is a defence of logic, particularly of the formal discipline of Aristotle, without which all argument and all philosophy is clumsy, amateurish and vain, but John, though a believer in sound technical training, deplored an absorption in arid and superficial disputes, and the prostitution of dialectic for monetary gain. Here and elsewhere he attacks a type of clerk, and their representative Cornificius, hitherto unidentified, who study for purely utilitarian ends. The *Historia pontificalis*, which has survived incomplete in a single manuscript, was intended to be a continuation of a chronicle based on Sigebert of Gembloux, which took the history of the Church down to the Council of Rheims. John at that time was in attendance at the papal Curia; and his history carries the story down to 1152, shortly before the death of Eugenius III. It is full of vivid character sketches, scenes drawn from the life in the midst of great events, and shrewd judgements. Nothing, perhaps, shows better the finished product of the humane literary education of the twelfth century than his description of the rival champions at Rheims, Bernard of Clairvaux, the saintly reformer, and Gilbert de la Porrée, the learned and revered master and bishop.

> Both were exceptionally learned and extremely eloquent, though their interests differed. The abbot, as his writings show, was a preacher of such excellence that I would think no one since St Gregory the Great could bear comparison with him. He commanded a singularly attractive style, and his acquaintance with the Scriptures was such that he could expound everything he had to say most happily in the words of the prophets or the apostles. He had indeed made the Scriptures all his own so fully that he could scarcely talk or preach or write letters without using their language. I cannot recall reading anyone who more aptly answered Horace's description:

'You'll write wonderfully, if by a deft selection you make a familiar word look new.'

He had, however, little knowledge of secular learning, in which, as was commonly thought, the bishop had no rival in our day. Each had an acute mind which he employed in interpreting the Bible, but the abbot was more experienced and efficient in practical matters. As for the bishop, though he had not the scriptural vocabulary at his fingertips to the same extent, yet he knew the doctors of the Church, Hilary, Jerome, Augustine and their like, better than Bernard, in most men's opinion. His teaching might seem obscure to newcomers, but when they had advanced somewhat it appeared both more solid and more economically expressed. He made use of every kind of learning as opportunity served, knowing that all of them together mutually supporting each other made up a whole. Even in theology he illustrated the properties of words and figures of speech by examples taken from poets as well as from philosophers. When speaking at his ease he seemed heavy, but when stimulated by contradiction and hard hit by arguments he showed himself able to be both clear and copious. You would wish he might always be roused, so that his mental fire and strength might illuminate you and set you also on fire. There have been many attempts to imitate each of these men in their particular province, but I cannot think of a single instance where either has been equalled .... Opinions have differed regarding Bernard, and judgements have varied on his conduct in pursuing two men so celebrated for their learning as Peter Abelard and Gilbert with such animus as to get one condemned and to do his best to undo the other. But for myself, I cannot believe that so holy a man lacked the true zeal of God, or that such a learned and virtuous bishop should have written anything without reasonable ground, even if many failed to follow him, for he was a man of the acutest mind who had read everything, and by my reckoning had spent almost sixty years in reading and critical work, and was so practised in the humane arts that no one surpassed him in them all; nay, rather, it was he who was considered to surpass everybody. And, as I suppose, he is no longer at variance with the abbot and other holy men, for they all together now gaze upon the truth they had always desired to see.[1]

John of Salisbury was not, like most of those whom we have passed in review, a professional philosopher or theologian. He stood to them as, yesterday and the day before, a Gladstone or an Asquith stood to professional classical scholars or Platonists – as adepts, *jam rude donati*, who could speak from without with knowledge and wise criticism. So John of Salisbury could criticize his age, and the burden of all his writing is a defence of the ideal of Chartres, and of its literary and philosophical education – as it might be the old 'Greats' school of

[1]John's judgments on Bernard and Gilbert are in *Historia pontificalis*, ed. M. Chibnall (Nelson, Edinburgh, 1956; revised edition, Oxford Medieval Texts, 1986), pp. 26, 16–17. The translation is mine.

Oxford – not as a preparation for acquiring wealth or place or as a niche for academic research, but for a full life of Christian humanism. And so before we leave 'the central figure of English learning', this man of Wiltshire whom all accept as the finest flower of European culture of his age, this Englishman who was bishop of Chartres when its lovely cathedral was in the building, we may note that all who have written of medieval thought agree on the main lines of their portrait of him as of 'a mind delicate rather than powerful, but so finely tempered, so rich, so ripe, and so exquisitely cultured that its presence, when we reflect on it, elevates and ennobles the image of a whole epoch'.[2]

NOTE. The very existence of a 'School' of Chartres has been questioned by Professor R. W. Southern in his *Medieval Humanism and Other Studies* (Oxford, 1970), pp. 61–85. He does not of course deny that there was a celebrated episcopal school at Chartres, but he maintains that the philosophical and theological 'School of Chartres' was largely the creation of R. L. Poole, *Illustrations of the History of Medieval Thought* (1884; 2nd edn, 1920) and Abbé A. Clerval, *Les écoles de Chartres* (1895), who thought to find a solidarity of philosophical and theological doctrine in a succession of masters, especially Bernard of Chartres, William of Conches, Thierry of Chartres and Gilbert de la Porrée. Southern points out that the first of these was a school master rather than a thinker, and that the others, whatever their connection with Chartres, were equally connected with Paris, and their thought was in no important respect different from that common to most masters of their epoch. Southern's case is strong and probably a valid revision of the matter, but I hesitated to re-write the whole chapter while the problem is still *sub judice* among scholars, as such a re-writing would have made necessary a critical discussion out of place in a short account. Whatever the final decision, it will not affect the analysis of the thought of the masters concerned.

[2]I have translated M. Gilson's judgment from the French edition. His own translation of the passage may be read in *History of Christian Philosophy in the Middle Ages* (London, 1955), p. 153.

CHAPTER TWELVE

The School of St Victor and St Bernard

The remarkable fecundity and variety in intellectual genius of the first half of the twelfth century is strikingly demonstrated by the rise at Paris of an influential school of thought, with a method of exposition of its own, wholly distinct on the one hand from the critical, dialectical and in some ways unspiritual school of Abelard, and on the other from the literary, humane, Platonizing School of Chartres. This was the so-called – and perhaps unfortunately so-called – mystical school of the Victorines.

The Augustinian abbey of St Victor, on the left bank of the Seine, took its rise from the small group, headed by William of Champeaux, who had retired in 1108 to join some hermits. William had been persuaded by Hildebert of Lavardin to resume his teaching, and the house had flourished in numbers and good fame. It reached a higher eminence fifteen or twenty years later, when one of its young canons, Hugh, began (c. 1125) his career as teacher. Hugh of St Victor, and his successor and disciple Richard, have attracted less attention from modern scholars than many of their less celebrated contemporaries, partly perhaps by reason of their reputation in the pages of nineteenth-century historians for mystical and (in the case of Richard) extravagantly allegorical treatment of the Scriptures and liturgy. They had, indeed, till very recently, fallen between two stools: mystics among the theologians, they were theologians among the mystics, and while most historians of medieval thought have been concerned with its intellectual rather than with its mystical content, the recent historians of mysticism have tended to fight shy of speculative theology. Till recently it was the fashion to regard mysticism and scholasticism as mutually incompatible, indeed as contrary the one to the other, and the Victorines were tacitly ignored as being a compound of two elements that could be studied only in isolation. The contemporaries and successors of the Victorines, however, had no such illusions, and saluted Hugh, as indeed he deserves to be saluted, as one of the greatest in an age of the great. Certainly, if a criterion of greatness is to be cited and praised by those whom all agree to call great, Hugh has every claim to the title. Known to his contemporaries as 'the new Augustine', for St Thomas his judgements were magisterial; they had the force of authority - *robur auctoritatis*. A recent critic is at one with his contemporaries; Père de Ghellinck writes of his delicacy of touch and of the freshness of his style, dwelling upon his warmth of tone, his accurate psychology and his elevation of mind, in which the contemplation of truth is reflected in the justice of his judgements and the accuracy of his expression.

The title of mystic as applied to Hugh is misleading unless the word is carefully defined. If by mystic we understand one who, like Ruysbroeck or John of the Cross, is distinguished by his descriptions of the union of the soul with God, then Hugh is not a mystic. His title is justifiable, if at all, only because for him the pursuit of divine truth is intimately bound up with the pursuit of virtue, and because he teaches that one who grows in virtue becomes more like God and therefore sees more clearly: 'blessed are the pure in heart, for they shall see God.' Far from being hostile to reason and science, Hugh welcomes all knowledge. 'Learn all you can,' he writes, with a rare reference to his own experience as a beginner, 'you will find later that nothing is wasted': and again: 'all human learning can serve the student of theology.'[1] This last sentence, perhaps, so quintessentially medieval in its implications, supplies a reason for the modern neglect of Hugh, for his two chief postulates, that all arts and sciences can be acquired from books in the cloister, and that all natural knowledge is an introduction to theology, are so foreign to all our ways of thought as almost to deter us from the attempt to understand one who uttered them.

The early life and personality of Hugh escaped the attention of the writers of the day, who tell us much about Abelard and St Bernard. It seems probable that the tradition of noble ancestry in Saxony is unreliable, and that he came from humble sources in northern France or Flanders, even if, as seems certain, he spent some years in a monastery in Saxony as a boy. Of his life at St Victor, where he was never prior, scarcely a mention remains, but there is a full account by an eyewitness of his edifying last hours. He was the correspondent

[1] Omnia disce, &c.' See *Didascalicon* VI 3.

and counsellor of some of the most famous men of his time, from St Bernard downwards, but his surviving letters, which are not numerous, have not been printed as yet in a collected edition. On the other hand, his writings give a clear picture of a lucid intelligence and a deeply spiritual, but moderate and conservative, outlook.

In the history of scholastic thought Hugh is chiefly of importance for his two works, one relatively short, the other bulky, the *Didascalicon*, a programme covering the whole field of education, and the *De sacramentis christianae fidei*, the first attempt on the grand scale – for Abelard's almost contemporary *Theologia* is a scantier outline – to give a really comprehensive view of theology in all its branches. The *Didascalicon*, which became a *locus classicus* for subsequent writers on education and method, is noteworthy for its inclusion of all the known arts and sciences, including that of dialectic, in the curriculum of the finished theologian. The *De sacramentis* is important for its influence on theological teaching; joined to the different approach of Abelard, it became the grandmother of all the *Summae* of the following hundred years. It is also important as being an extension of the Anselmian rather than of the Abelardian use of dialectic. Hugh employs logic and speculation to penetrate and to establish the doctrine rather than to build up an edifice of ingenious conclusions and deductions. In his approach, as in his style, there is much of Augustine, and he would have subscribed fully to the Anselmian *credo ut intelligam*, but though he is more orderly and 'scholastic' than Anselm he is by no means fully 'Augustinian' in the sense attached to that term by later theologians, and he knows nothing of the divine illumination of the intellect as the explanation of the cognitive process. The mind acquires knowledge by abstraction; the mind, in fact, does with all being presented to it what it does with the entities of mathematics. As when dealing with a line, a plane, a point, it abstracts from objects all that is accidental and imperfect, and then uses the intellectual concept as a basis for scientific argument. This position, and his doctrine on universals, are very near that of Abelard. So in his proof of personal existence, the Augustinian direct perception of thought and the thinker, and in his argument for the existence of God, which again follows Augustine, there is nothing that could correctly be called mystical. His description of faith as 'the will to assent to things unseen with a certitude greater than that of opinion and less than that of direct knowledge' was to become classic.[2] It is only on the higher

---

[2]Hugh's definition of faith is: '*Fides est certitudo quaedam animi de rebus absentibus supra opinionem et infra scientiam constituta*' (Migne, *PL* clxxvi 330).

levels of theology that Hugh becomes a 'mystical' theologian, and even there his 'mysticism' does not affect his epistemology. He does not maintain the divine illumination of the intellect as an epistemological condition of its functioning. He holds merely that there are three ways of progressive perfection in the grasp of theological truths: there is faith, which is in some ways blind; there is the deeper knowledge of the theologian, using his intellect to explore the content of the truths held by faith; and there is finally the God-given power of the mind of one who loves God to recognize and penetrate the mysteries of the faith and then in part show them to others. This, indeed, is common Christian teaching, though not always expressly asserted, but it is a different conception from that of Abelard, who tended to regard the intellect as a searchlight capable of discovering all truth, even that of mysteries declared only by revelation. Hugh of St Victor would rather have said: 'if anyone doth the will of the Father, he will know within himself what is the meaning' of the truths held by faith. In this he is in the full stream of the purest traditional teaching, elaborated by St Thomas. The Victorine element in Aquinas is indeed very large.

Hugh's successor was a teacher of almost equal medieval celebrity, Richard, about whose origins and life little is known. Traditionally a Scot by birth, he spent all his adult life at St Victor's, of which he became prior, dying in 1173. In his main lines of thought the resemblance to Hugh, whose pupil he was, is clear, but recent examination of his writings has found in them a degree of originality and of speculative power greater than that shown by Hugh. In particular, he takes further the doctrine of St Anselm that 'adequate, convincing arguments' (*rationes necessariae*) can be found for the mysteries of the faith. He finds a principal argument for the existence of God in experience: all that we experience has a beginning and end; but there must be a Being whose existence is self-caused, else nothing could have come into existence; and a Being who is the cause of his own being must be without beginning or end. Similarly in the matter of the Trinity, to which he devoted much of his thought, in his efforts to elucidate the mystery with 'necessary arguments' he showed a boldness and a subtlety hitherto unrivalled among strictly orthodox theologians, and found a definition of 'person' that was more satisfactory than that of Boethius when used of the divine Persons. Yet with all his power of original thought, which has only recently won full recognition, the fame of Richard of St Victor will always rest principally upon his two treatises of mystical theology, known as the *Benjamin Major* and *Minor*, which remained for long text-books of the subject for all writers on contemplation, even after some of their teaching had been outdated by the living experience of contemplatives who wrote and taught in the new vernaculars. For Dante and for many others Richard 'who in contemplation was more than man'[3] was the very type of the Christian mystic, but not all who read his treatises will be convinced that he is himself a mystic of wide experience. He has all the scholastic's love of schemes and divisions, though by his use of the pseudo-Denis he gave a new clarity and definition to the tradition that came down from Augustine and Gregory and, possibly without being fully aware of it, gave a salutary strength to the Dionysian scheme by introducing love, and not merely knowledge, as an integral part of the contemplative life. Richard, like Hugh, reflected throughout his spiritual writings the outlook and doctrine of Augustine, on which he had been nourished, but in the two *Benjamins* he is not so much the theorist of the Christian intellectual life as the spiritual master writing for the individual soul of the degrees of the contemplative life. In this, and in his description of the ascent from meditation to contemplation and from contemplation to ecstasy, Richard shows clearly the powerful influence of the pseudo-Denis, whose writings were even then being made available in a new translation. He is, however, no mere copyist. While the final ecstasy is Dionysian, he revises altogether the Neoplatonic concept of the super-essential God as a 'cloud of darkness' with whom union is possible only fleetingly. With Richard the cloud is the barrier of forgetfulness between the soul and creatures and the cloud of unknowing whence God emits rays of his light: a conception which was to have great success in the following centuries. Moreover, and with still greater significance for Christian mystical theology, the Dionysian intellectual process becomes almost exclusively the work of the will, and hence of love. Richard here shows at least the indirect influence of Bernard and the Cistercian school, and while he gave a new lease of life to the Augustinian tradition by translating it into the scholastic idiom, he gave a new turn to its expression by his emphasis on the primacy of the will in love.

In the second half of the century others besides Richard devoted themselves to mystical theology. Johannes Sarracenus, the friend of John of Salisbury, made a new translation of Dionysius that was to be widely known, while Thomas Gallus (d. 1246), a canon of St Victor who became abbot of Vercelli, wrote a commentary on his works that had a wide and deep effect upon spiritual writers. Thomas Gallus,

[3]Paradiso X, 131-2.

indeed, not only developed the part of the will in the contemplative life, but foreshadowed much of the teaching that was to be adopted by the later medieval mystical writers and to pass into the common inheritance of Christian spirituality.

Strangely enough, St Victor's towards the end of the century gave birth to a frankly, even furiously, anti-dialectical polemist in Walter of St Victor who was the author of a tract against the 'Four masters of Confusion in France' (*Contra quatuor labyrinthos Franciae*, 1177–8). The four were Abelard, Gilbert de la Porrée, Peter Lombard and Peter of Poitiers; the only common factor being a supposed reliance upon Aristotle as against traditional dogma. Walter's imprecation on the Lombard: 'May your grammar be your damnation!' (*Grammatica tua sit tibi in perditionem!*) is well known and characteristic. Before Walter's day, and more in harmony with Hugh and Richard, were a group of hymn and sequence writers, of whom the foremost, Adam of St Victor, is by general agreement at the summit of his restricted but very flexible form of art.

It would be unpardonable, in glancing at the various intellectual currents of the twelfth century, to omit all reference to the dynamic personality of one who, though never precisely a teacher of the schools, was capable, alone of all his contemporaries, of drowning or, if the expression be allowed, of 'jamming' all other voices, and who, on the great web of medieval religious thought and sentiment, changed and formed more patterns than any other man of his century. It is at first sight a paradox that one who, when all is said and done, affected his contemporaries more universally and more profoundly than any of those we have mentioned in the last two chapters, should stand entirely apart from, and should in some ways be positively hostile to, learning of all kinds. In many ways, indeed, the reputation of St Bernard for ferocious mental puritanism is the outcome of a piece of supreme, if unconscious, bluff. Historians and critics have been so occupied in registering their disapproval and framing replies to Bernard's attack on the wordy volubility of philosophers (*verbosa loquacitas philosophorum*) and worldly wisdom that teaches only vanity (*scientia mundi quae docet vanitatem*), or in admiring his profession that his only learning is the cross of Christ, that they have failed to note that they have to deal, not only with a speculative theologian of wide reading and great intellectual power, but with a literary genius of the first order, the greatest master of language in the Middle Ages, who, alone of all this age, has a power equal to that of Demosthenes, of Cicero and of Burke, to carry us with him on the gale of his eloquence, intoxicated as much as by his virtuosity as by his dialectical skill. Gilbert de la Porrée, in the heat of battle, might refuse to argue with one who had little knowledge of advanced grammar, but the ordinary antagonist found Bernard, merely as a technician, more than his match. Nothing, indeed, is a more impressive testimony to the widespread literary culture of the early twelfth century than the emergence of a Bernard from a small provincial school. Here we cannot hope to consider even in barest outline the work of 'the last of the Fathers' – so-called because he is the last to write upon great theological issues with no apparatus of dialectic – but we must always bear in mind that his massive personality and his written works, read by all, whatever their rank or order, in some such way as, let us say, the words of Bossuet and Newman were read by all cultivated contemporaries, had a very great, if imponderable, influence in containing the floods of rationalistic dialectic.

Bernard, indeed, as historians are beginning to realize, was more even than a skilled and sophisticated master of language. Several of his treatises, and even a large part of his *Sermons on the Canticle*, consist of closely knit arguments, and many of his sermons must have been a severe tax on the intellectual, as well as on the spiritual, capabilities of his hearers. In addition Bernard had acquired, from a source not yet identified, a working knowledge of the Greek mystical tradition in Gregory of Nyssa and the pseudo-Dionysius, while at the same time he proposed the mystical union as one of love and of unity of will rather than one of knowledge, and this concept, which suited Christian tradition and traditional ascetic teaching so well, was to have a profound effect, if not on Richard of St Victor, at least in mystical writers of the fourteenth century. Bernard, in fact, was no mean antagonist, even if his sanctity and prestige are left out of the reckoning.

His onslaughts on Abelard and on Gilbert de la Porrée will always remain celebrated and controversial topics. In the case of Abelard historians are no doubt right in stressing irreducible differences between the outlook, the psychological make-up, and the 'records' of the two men, even more distinct than those of other pairs of opponents such as Bossuet and Fénelon, Manning and Newman. But there was a more acute and tangible difference in both controversies. Even the undoubted theological inaccuracy of Abelard and, to a lesser extent, of Gilbert was not the deepest cause for Bernard's mistrust. The overt, and in some respects the real rock of scandal was the use by both of a new, and as it turned out a passing, conception of the functions of grammar and logic when applied to theological or ethical topics, and a conviction that dialectic was capable of expressing with some adequacy the objects of Christian revelation. Perhaps an analogy may be found in the attitude of many natural scientists sixty or seventy years ago to all spiritual reality: they wished to express it in scientific terms or not at all. Both Abelard and Gilbert, even though unwittingly and in different degrees, were in effect bordering upon rationalism. They were attributing to dialectic, in the particular form in which they practised it, an absolute metaphysical value, and they were at least in practice ignoring the gulf between truths accessible to reason and those beyond the grasp of reason. Their universe of knowledge was, so to say, constructed from grammar and logic upwards; for Bernard it was framed from divine revelation and faith downwards.

PART THREE
The New Universities –
The Rediscovery of Aristotle

CHAPTER THIRTEEN

The Origins of the Universities

The medieval Latin word *universitas* has no reference to the scope of the curriculum of studies; it stands for the whole gathering, the whole body, of a particular class of persons, and indeed stands very near in meaning to the modern 'union' in the term 'trade union'. It is all but synonymous, for legal purposes, with the Latin word *collegium*, and for social comparisons, with the old English word guild. The *universitas* was first of all the whole body either of the masters or of the students, and then very naturally came to mean their self-governing guild or society. The word did not acquire its local or educational connotation till the last phase of the Middle Ages. Our word 'university' would best be rendered in medieval Latin by *studium generale*, where *studium* denotes 'facilities for study' or organized school, and *generale* has reference, not to the subjects taught, but to the provenance of the students, as we might say 'of general resort' or 'international'. As in many such evolutions, a purely neutral descriptive term later became technical. *Studium generale* at first stated a fact, it did not provide a legal definition, and though the two original universities, Bologna and Paris, were from the first *studia generalia* above all others, there was nothing to prevent the title being applied to, or assumed by, other schools, as indeed it was. Yet gradually, towards the end of the twelfth century, two further conceptions were attached to the term: that it was a school where one, at least, of the three higher faculties – theology, law and medicine – was in existence, and that a considerable number of masters were engaged in teaching there. From *c.* 1200 onwards a further idea gained ground, that of the universal validity of its licence to teach – the *jus ubique docendi*. This privilege, which in the case of the original universities was a spontaneous, prescriptive recognition of fact, was later taken to be the most important feature in the recognition of a new university, and the right to issue this permission was reserved to the papacy.

Throughout the latter half of the medieval period medicine, law and theology were recognized as the only three branches of higher study, and, somewhat surprisingly to modern minds, the organized teaching in these faculties began chronologically in the order given above, and made of Salerno, Bologna and Paris the separate *foci* of celebrity.

Salerno, though its fame endured for less than two centuries and was soon challenged and eclipsed by Montpellier and Bologna, must therefore be considered first. While the ultimate, dynamic reasons for the rise of its school must be sought in the mysterious foundations of the awakening of Europe, it is possible to suggest why medicine was the subject and Salerno the site of the earliest appearance of an organized professional training. The renaissance was in every case that of a young mind working on old material, and nowhere was this available in greater profusion than in south Italy and Sicily, that *Magna Graecia* or Greater Greece which had remained in touch with the more civilized Eastern Empire throughout the 'dark ages', and where the four streams of Greek, Latin, Jewish and Arabic met. It is probable that Roman, that is, Greek, traditions of medical practice had never wholly died out in a region where material civilization had always lingered, and Salerno was famous for its climate and its springs. There the most notable physicians collected, and gradually a tradition of teaching grew up among them; it found, as has happily been said, 'a voice' in the translation of Hippocrates, Galen and other classics of Greek medicine from the Arabic by Constantine the African, who is by no means such a mythical source of influence as Rashdall suggests. Salerno was at the zenith of its fame *c.* 1100, the date of the well-known *Regimen sanitatis Salerni* or 'Salerno's rules for health'; it never developed at that time into an organized university, and was not formally recognized as such till Frederick II made pronouncement in 1231. It never possessed other faculties in its early days and declined rapidly in the thirteenth century. Arabian medicine, combined with the rise of other medical schools in flourishing universities such as Montpellier, left Salerno high and dry, though it continued a shadowy existence till its suppression, along with other venerable millenarians, by Napoleon I.

Bologna, on the other hand, was not only the first fully-fledged university, but the first of the two types or families that spread all over Europe. Before coming to its origins, it may be well to look briefly at the two kinds of law, Roman law and canon law, of which it became the exponent.

Roman law, the greatest of all historical legal systems and the sole great legacy in things of the mind that was bequeathed to posterity by the Roman people, was the outcome of a long evolution over a thousand years (753 B.C.-A.D. 300) of composition, and a further 250 years of amelioration and codification. The mass of legal declarations embodied in the final codification, and known thereafter as Roman law, and later as civil law, was a mixture of ancient Roman custom, explicit declaration (both republican, senatorial and imperial) and court decisions, together with the addition of a vast body of comment, interpretation and theoretical disquisition that was the work of the great legists of the early Empire such as Papinian and Ulpian. This enormous, unmanageable mass of material was rough-hewn into shape in the West under Theodosius the Great in 438. The Theodosian code was adapted to Germanic conditions in 506 by Alaric II in his *Lex Romana Visigothorum*, the so-called *Breviarium Alaricianum*, an unscientific and (by later and earlier standards) unintelligent epitome. Henceforward the gradual watering down of Roman law continued, along with a parallel process by which borrowed Roman principles contaminated northern folk-law. Roughly speaking the populations of central and northern Italy, and of southern France in the early Middle Ages (that is, before 1000) were under various laws more or less predominantly Roman in origin, but with a weaker mixture as one passed from south to north. The northern parts of the Carolingian empire and its successor-states were under customary law, less technically perfect and containing a strong infiltration of Roman principles. The two regions were represented in the familiar division of Western Europe into the *pays du droit coutumier* and the *pays du droit écrit*. Everywhere, however, the practice, familiar to Rome in the past, of personal, not national or regional, liability to a code was the rule, with the result familiar from the remark of Agobard of Lyons (d. 850) that when five men were gathered in a single room each of them might have a separate law. This intermingling was rendered still more confusing by the over-riding principle that ecclesiastics everywhere were liable to Roman law.

Meanwhile in the Eastern Empire a further and far more scientific codification had been effected by commissioners appointed by Justinian in 533. Their labours resulted in four compilations, viz., the *Code*, or collection of statutory laws and imperial decrees; the *Digest* or *Pandects*, a substantial selection of the teaching and comments of all the great Roman lawyers; the *Institutiones* or manual of general principles for students; and the *Novellae* or *Authenticum*, being additional decrees subsequent to the Code. This collection became the governing law for the Eastern Empire and for such parts of the West as owed allegiance to Byzantium, but although copies were sent by Justinian to Rome and other Western cities, it never superseded the Theodosian code in the West.

Ancient Roman law had probably ceased, several centuries before 1000, to be taught authoritatively and from ancient texts in Italy, and had become in the manner, though not in the perfection of its transmission, like customary law or medieval English case law. Nevertheless, it continued to find a place in the educational *trivium* as part of dialectic, and fragments of the old codes were copied in monasteries and schools. Municipal life had never wholly died out in Italy, and when, in the general revival of the eleventh century, schools of Roman law at Ravenna and Bologna, and of Lombardic law at Milan, Verona and Pavia began to flourish, law became the crown of the modest educational curriculum in northern Italy.

Why, when and how the change came about whereby the whole of Justinian's work of codification was adopted in Italy as the authoritative legal text-book is not certain. The old story was that the Pisans, at the capture of Amalfi in 1135, had discovered a codex of the *Digest* which the Emperor Lothair III had immediately enforced as a code and as a text-book. A less improbable account had it that when the law-school of Rome was broken up towards the end of the eleventh century, after the great burning of the City by the Normans in 1084, the fugitive lawyers took a *Codex* with them and this, added to the influx of numbers at Bologna, started the revival. The truth would seem to be that the rediscovery of Justinian's work was part of the movement everywhere in progress to return to the authentic documents of the famed and fabled past; the same movement had set the papal reformers looking for the ancient canons and decrees, the Italian monastic reformers restoring the practices of the Egyptian desert, and the early Cistercians observing the letter of St Benedict's Rule. It was, in fact, part of the critical movement to get hold of the old authentic documents and then to observe them. But it would seem certain that a single teacher was particularly connected with the revival, the great Irnerius who flourished at Bologna from *c.* 1112 to 1125. He was probably the first to take as his text-book the whole Justinian corpus and to normalize the commentary and glosses upon it. His notes, from being merely marginal or interlinear comments or 'glosses', became a full-sized commentary, just as had Abelard's commentary on St Paul, and he adopted the method, already familiar in canonist circles, of giving series of texts for and against a particular opinion (the ancestor of the *sic et non* method), and an occasional *quaestio* which gave a firm decision on a doubtful point. In so doing Irnerius made of the study of law, or at least of the Justinian corpus, something more scientific, technical and professional than before, and established it firmly and finally as a subject for higher education, not merely as a part or appanage of the *trivium*. This had, almost immediately, a twofold practical result: it provided a basis, at once scientific and manageable, for the study, popularization and diffusion of a single code of law for the whole of continental Europe, and it increased greatly the prospects of law as a career, thus increasing also the number of law students.

At almost the same moment a different process of crystallization was taking place at Bologna in the codification of canon law. The ancient canon law of the Church, that is, the disciplinary decrees of general councils and of popes, had reached a high degree of elaboration in the age of Popes Gelasius I and Hormisdas shortly before and after A.D. 500, when higher life in the West was on the eve of collapse, and this law had been codified by Denis the Little (early sixth century). This and similar collections based upon it had traversed the early Middle Ages in a more intact and operative condition than had Roman law, but in the middle of the ninth century the whole corpus had been contaminated by the work of a group of ecclesiastical reformers, working probably in the neighbourhood of Le Mans, who, in order to enhance papal power at the expense of the local archbishop, produced the tendentious and in part spurious collections known as the False Decretals and the False Capitularies. A little later, numerous collections appeared in Lorraine and southern Germany, and the contest between the Empire and papacy set the papalists searching for old and original sources in support of their case. In the course of this search many perfectly genuine documents were unearthed, but considerable confusion ensued as the discoveries and collections multiplied, and even the highly gifted Ivo of Chartres (d. 1115), who endeavoured to give a conspectus of the law in his *Panormia*, was not wholly successful in his endeavour.

What greater men had failed to do was accomplished by Gratian of Bologna, an Italian master in the canon law but not also, it now appears, a Camaldolese monk. Rashdall, writing in the 1890s, described it as 'one of those great text-books which, appearing just at the right time and in the right place, takes the world by storm'.[1] This

[1] H. Rashdall, *The Universities of Europe*, ed. Powicke and Emden, I, 127.

judgement, which would have been a tolerably just estimate of the work of Peter the Lombard, is not a wholly adequate description of Gratian's. Whatever his intention, the scholar of Bologna produced both a text-book and a code, and by his treatment of the problems involved was the father of a long and distinguished succession of masters of a new branch of legal science.

The history of the origins of the university of Bologna, while it is inseparably bound up with the story of the revived study of the complete Roman law, was conditioned by the character of existing Italian education. This was, at least in most of the cities between Rome and the Alps, predominantly municipal and in the hands of laymen. It was predominantly grammatical and rhetorical in content, and was directed towards the practical ends of drawing up documents and pleading and judging in the courts. City life had never wholly perished in the peninsula, and at the beginning of the twelfth century municipal life was everywhere becoming freer and more vivid, and careers were opening to the layman to which the key was the study of law. In Italy, also, the city nobility, in contrast to the militant aristocracy of Normandy and Germany, had always been literate, and now there was a growing demand for legal knowledge, stimulated first by the need of weapons in the struggle between Empire and papacy, and then by the adoption of Roman law as the imperial code. This last fact had as a result the arrival at Bologna of a growing number of ultramontanes to study law at the fountain-head.

We may be inclined to ask why Bologna, rather than other cities, took pride of place? When Lanfranc was young, Pavia was famous for its legal studies, and so, a little later, was Ravenna, where connections with the East had been long and intimate, and where Peter Damian the papalist had a brush with the imperial lawyers. The schools of Bologna, the most Roman in north Italy, were in fact principally celebrated for their literary training, and their expertise in this persisted long after the legal revival, especially in the technique which formed a bridge between the two faculties, the *dictamen* or carefully regulated style for official acts and notarial work. It is natural, also, in discussing its rise to fame, to point to the situation of the town which, then as now, is the cross-roads of Italy, and one of the calling-places of most Romeward-bound pilgrims from Germany and Austria, and of many from France and the north; in the early Middle Ages it was a meeting-place of currents from north and south, as also from the Eastern Empire, while its own comparative insignificance made it naturally hospitable to students and refugees. Nevertheless, the proximate cause of its rise to fame would seem to have been due to an influx of lawyers from Rome and, still more, to the fame of Irnerius and, somewhat later, of Gratian. Henceforward, the city was *Bolonia docta*, the 'mother of scholars', and her coins bore the legend *Bononia docet* and *Bononia mater studiorum*.

The stages in the evolution of the university are not easy to discover. At Bologna, in the early years of the twelfth century, there were three types of school: the episcopal and municipal schools of letters; the lay schools of Roman law; and schools of canon law at one or more of the monasteries. The second of these classes, by far the most important even in early days, fell entirely outside the control of the bishop and the Church. This fact, and still more the circumstance that a majority of the students of law were much older than the normal students of arts in the north, and were in many cases family men with means, preparing for a lucrative career, helped to influence the shape taken by the university.

This organization, of which the most striking feature was the direction of a university and the control of its teachers by the students, becomes a comprehensible and even a natural growth when looked at closely. Italy was a land of small political divisions, with rapidly multiplying communes, and citizenship was a possession of great price. Almost all the teachers of law were, by birth or permanent residence, citizens of Bologna. On the other hand, the vast majority of the substantial multitude of students were adult aliens, without any status or civic rights, and, according to contemporary ideas, they were subject to the laws of their respective countries. They were therefore interested in strengthening their position *vis-à-vis* the city, and in securing the right of judgement at the hands of a compatriot. In an age when guilds of all kinds were being formed, it was natural that the Bolognese students should come together to form national groups or 'universities'. In this their principal aims were: to secure exemption from the municipal tribunals and amenability to their own; to secure freedom from municipal taxation and market dues; to secure the right of fixing prices for lodgings, lecture-rooms and books; and to win the right of regulating the teaching and horarium. They therefore grouped themselves into 'nations', originally twenty or so in number. These were later amalgamated, without losing their identity, into two large groups – the *Citramontani* or Italians, consisting of the Tuscans and Lombards, and the *Ultramontani*, with thirteen or more national groups. Finally, in the thirteenth century, the two large corporations merged to form the *universitas scholarium*. Long before that, the nations had received recognition from the Emperor in the Authentic *Habita*, given to all the students of Lombardy, by which he took them under his protection and provided that in any proceedings against a scholar the defendant could, if he wished, be cited before the bishop (if he were a clerk) or his master. Later, citation before the rector became the norm. In any case, those who were absent from their homes in search of learning were recognized as deserving of rights as against the municipal authorities.

The nations forming the university were made up of law students of extra-Bolognese provenance, and of these alone. This left three other groups in the schools: the native-born law students; the students and masters in other faculties; and, most important of all, the teachers of law. The first group had the worst of both worlds. Lacking any bargaining power against their own civic officials, they were forced into the arms of the nations through their desire of sharing their academic privileges, and were made to pay scot and lot without receiving an active or passive voice in the government of the university. The second group, excluded by the jurists from any share in their privileges, ultimately formed a university with a rector of their own; this was a second student university run on the lines of the existing university of law students. As for the teachers, they were in the first instance excluded from the organization as being, with few exceptions, Bolognese citizens. As resident citizens and laymen, often married and with families, they were in quite different circumstances from the clerical, foreign, ever-changing masters of Paris and the northern schools in the mid-twelfth century, and in early days they threw in their lot with the city, as opposed to the students, in order to have civic support in keeping their body exclusive and confined to citizens. The two divisions of law each in time formed a college of doctors, and at first their fees were settled by collective bargaining with the students, but later the city found it to its advantage to make sure of retaining the most eminent masters by the offer of a fixed salary. At first the student university asserted its powers here also, and elected to the professorial chairs, but later the city obtained control and ultimately all the teaching was done by salaried civic professors. This, more than anything else, served to differentiate Bologna and the Italian universities as a group from Paris, Oxford and their progeny. The doctors as such ceased to be teachers; teaching fell entirely into the hands of salaried professors, and in consequence the task of instruction never shifted down from the central authority to the colleges, as it did in Paris and England. The only major rights retained by the 'university' of Bolognese doctors were those of examination and of conferring the doctor's degree. The bachelor's degree was conferred by the rector of the student university.

In all other respects the professors were kept in absolute and even humiliating subservience to their students. They had to swear obedience to the student rectors and to the student-made statutes, which bore very hardly upon them, e.g., the professor was fined if he began his teaching a minute late or continued a minute longer than the fixed time, and should this happen the students who failed to leave the lecture-room immediately were themselves fined. In addition, the professor was fined if he shirked explaining a difficult passage, or if he failed to get through the syllabus; he was fined if he left the city for a day without the rector's permission, and if he married, was allowed only one day off for the purpose. The city, for its part, took a hand in controlling the professors, and they were forced to take an oath not to leave Bologna in search of more lucrative or less onerous posts. If we ask how the students succeeded in gaining and maintaining such power in the law schools we may find an answer on two levels. On the one hand, the readiness with which contemporary society accepted the formation of self-governing bodies, and the existence in a city or country of groups or classes ruled by their own statutes and officials, can be seen in many other walks of life, such as the alfonduke and consuls of the Mediterranean commercial nations. On a lower level, and in the particular case, the foreign students possessed *vis-à-vis* both city and doctors a powerful weapon in the threat of secession or of boycotting individuals. The former threat was a very real one, and the exercise of the power led to the foundation of Padua and other Italian universities by seceding groups. The city, indeed, endeavoured to obtain a hold upon the students by exacting oaths of residence and imposing penalties for attempting secession, but the papacy intervened, as at Paris in a somewhat different context, and in 1217 Honorius III espoused the cause of the students against the city.

Such, then, was in its main lines the situation at Bologna in the thirteenth century; a university of law students, governed by its own statutes and under the control of a rector (who was always a clerk, so as to be competent to exercise jurisdiction over clerks) biennially elected and with civil and criminal jurisdiction; this university had the power of giving bachelor degrees and of regulating all details and prices of lodgings, books, lecture-rooms, horaria, syllabus, and the rest. Over against this there were the colleges of doctors with control over admission to their body but never powerful, since the more eminent of their numbers received salaries from the city, while all had strong ties with the place.

Finally it must be noted that at Bologna there was absolutely no connection between the law university and the other faculties of arts, medicine and theology, the last-named of which was at Bologna practically confined to the schools of the religious orders. These other faculties, as has been said, in time established student universities of their own.

The university of Paris was the direct outgrowth of the cathedral school of Notre Dame. In Abelard's days there were three schools in or near the city proper – the cathedral, the collegiate church of Ste Geneviève, where Abelard taught, and the abbey of St Victor; the last-named had ceased to exist as a school and Ste Geneviève was in decline by 1200; the university arose from the cathedral alone. Nevertheless, it was the fame of all three schools in the early twelfth century, and Abelard's dazzling personality, that first attracted great crowds to Paris. Before the age of Abelard Paris was not superior to, and scarcely the equal in scholastic eminence of, Chartres, Rheims, Laon and perhaps other cathedral schools; by 1150 it was the premier school by a comfortable margin. Once begun, the immigration continued. Paris, in later years the beloved city of so many, was, as all who write of her agree, a delightful place to live in even in the twelfth century, with her river, her gardens and her vineyards; more beautiful, more civilized, more comfortable and better supplied with material and social advantages than any other northern city. The kings of France appreciated the economic and political value of a cosmopolitan student population, and did their best to encourage their residence.

The process by which the schools of Paris grew into a university was a slow one. The cathedral school of Notre Dame, on an island in the Seine which formed the heart of the old city and still bears its name, was controlled, as were all cathedral schools, by the bishop's chancellor. No one could teach without his licence. This monopoly, in the first half of the twelfth century, was a source of income for the chancellor, but the need for schools and the value set on learning by the higher authorities of the Church, and in particular by the papacy, helped to prevent any taxation of learning. As early as 1138 a council in London had forbidden the farming out of a school for money payment, and in the Third Lateran Council of 1179 the chancellor of a cathedral school was forbidden to charge a fee for the licence to teach; the Council also decreed that permission to teach should never be refused to a properly qualified applicant. Although the chancellor of Paris successfully resisted for a time the obligation of granting licences without fee, he could not refuse to licence a qualified man who paid, and in time free licensing became the rule. The control of the chancellor and the right of a qualified man to receive a licence are the two basic points of the whole system at Paris.

When this right was recognized and the demand for education continued to grow the number of both students and masters multiplied at Paris, and the majority of the students entered the arts school, which provided the only general education then available, and which was also an indispensable preparation for theology, law and medicine. Paris, in fact, rapidly became a city of students, the first of its kind in Europe; they filled the island around the cathedral, spilling over upon the left bank of the river, the later *quartier latin*. Yet the evolution of the university was slow. At first the chancellor not only gave the licence but himself examined the candidate, a routine which had no influence in creating a professional guild. Nevertheless a corporate feeling began to grow up among the masters in arts, for no one could teach without having followed the school of a master, and the formal entry upon teaching on the part of a new master, the so-called 'inception', was a social ceremony which marked the admission of a new member to the group. As the number of students grew, so did the number of masters, and so did the value of a degree and of association with others, but the guild of masters developed its organization very slowly, and as late as 1208 had no statutes and no head.

The first privilege granted to the students of Paris, that given by Philip Augustus in 1200, was the result of an attempt on the part of the Provost of Paris to punish the culprits in a brawl. The king, when appealed to, guaranteed to any student trial before an ecclesiastical judge, and immunity of his property from confiscation. Ten years later (*c*. 1210) a bull of Innocent III sanctioned the restitution to the society of masters of one who had been expelled for a breach of the statutes. This shows that at that date statutes and a society existed, and further evidence is provided by a bull of Innocent III, himself once a Paris master, empowering the society to elect a proctor to represent them at Rome during the struggle with the chancellor then pending.

It was this struggle with the chancellor, which was one of life and death for the young university, that led, as such controversies often lead, to constitutional advance. The chancellor had begun the fight with considerable advantages. He could not only grant or refuse a licence, but he could deprive a master of his licence and a scholar of his status; he claimed to be judge-ordinary of the scholars and could excommunicate them; he even claimed the right of issuing ordinances for masters and scholars. Nevertheless, the university also had a foothold. The chancellor was not a member of the university, and could not compel the masters to admit to their society one whom he had licensed; in this, and in their power to compel a new master to swear obedience to their statutes, lay the university's strength. In this matching of opposed powers, in which the victory would probably have been with the chancellor, the papacy intervened to tip the scales. In 1212 a suit was pending at Rome; the chancellor had endeavoured to force the masters to take an oath of obedience to himself; had he succeeded he would have become head in fact of the masters' guild. Innocent III intervened to forbid the oath, and to require the chancellor to grant a licence to all candidates recommended by the masters in the various faculties. In 1215 the cardinal-legate Robert de Curzon, another past master of Paris, followed up these provisions and recognized the right of the university to make statutes of its own. Subsequent papal bulls confirmed these rights.

Alongside the university another organization was appearing, that of the nations. These, which were perhaps a conscious imitation of the nations at Bologna, came into formal existence in the first half of the thirteenth century. They were made up solely from the masters of arts and were four in number – France (i.e., the Ile de France), Normandy, Picardy and England. Each had at its head a proctor, but at first there was no common chief; then, by 1245, the faculty of arts had one in its rector. Meanwhile, the masters of theology, canon law and medicine were forming separate groups independent of the artists, and the four divisions thus created, which included arts, became known as the Faculties. Thus by 1250 the university of Paris consisted of a federal corporation of four distinct bodies; one of these was subdivided into four nations, into one of which four groups the nationals of every country were fitted. Each faculty save that of arts was presided over by a Dean; the arts alone had a Rector; and by slow but sometimes violent stages this Rector gradually advanced to the headship of the university. Deliberations were always carried out within the various faculties; voting was by faculty, and inside the faculty of arts by nations; in every case a majority prevailed.

Twice during the long struggle for autonomy the heroic step of decreeing a dispersion was taken. In 1229 this was directed against the Provost of Paris, and resulted in the Bull *Parens scientiarum* of Gregory IX (1231) which much reduced the power of the chancellor. In 1253 the same step was taken against the friars, who wished to hold university chairs without submitting to the university statutes; in this case the papacy was on the side of the friars, and the eventual compromise was in reality their victory.

Although it is often stated that the college is a peculiarly English institution, and although it is true that in Europe the only surviving continental college within a university is the Spanish college at Bologna, very few medieval universities were without them. Even student universities followed the fashion. Paris, however, is the mother of the college. In origin simply an endowed hospice or hall for students, and originating in the last decades of the twelfth century, they were stimulated by the example of the great houses of studies of the friars and the older religious orders; these provoked the foundation in 1257 of a college at Paris for secular theologians, the illustrious Sorbonne, named after the chaplain of St Louis, Robert de Sorbon.

Obscure as are the constitutional origins of Bologna and Paris, the early history of those universities is luminous when compared to that of Oxford. It is indeed strange that in an age when such a galaxy of chroniclers existed in this country, and when such a variety of charters of every kind were being issued and preserved, the most notable gathering of teachers and students in England should have left so few traces in the records. So complete is the absence of genuine history that the myth, medieval in its sober origins, but forced and bedded out and nursed to luxuriant growth by the great Oxford antiquaries of the seventeenth century, which attributed the foundation of Oxford to Alfred the Great, to Charlemagne, yea, to exiles from Troy, had open soil on which to grow. More recent attempts to derive the university from a monastic or canonical school have likewise failed to convince, both because there is no evidence for such a school at Oxford, and because the university, when it does emerge into daylight, has at its head a chancellor elected by the masters even if representing the bishop's authority; that is, an official who is neither monastic nor episcopal in origin.

Oxford had a school with perhaps a hundred clerics before 1120, and Robert Pullen, later cardinal, was teaching scripture (that is, theology) there in 1133; Gerald of Wales found masters and pupils there in 1187–8. But the town was not alone in possessing a school, and although its favoured position as a royal borough in the centre of England, situated between Northampton and Southampton at a great crossroads, was in its favour, there is no intrinsic reason why it, rather than Exeter or Lincoln, should have become the only *studium generale*. Nor does Rashdall's opinion, that a single reference to an expulsion of English students from Paris during the Becket controversy in 1167 implies a mass migration to Oxford, seem at all convincing. War with France after 1193 was more important.

As regards university organization, the *terminus ante quem* for the existence of a number of teaching faculties is the well-known passage, supported by other references, of Gerald of Wales, where he described his feat in reading his description of Ireland, the *Topographia Hibernica*, to the students and doctors of various faculties at Oxford in 1187–8; he there describes Oxford as the most celebrated centre of learning in England. Abbot Samson of Bury entertained the masters of the schools there in 1197, and at about the same time Thomas of Marlborough taught civil and canon law there. In 1209, after the execution of students consequent upon an alleged murder, the masters and scholars, to the number of 3,000 according to Roger of Wendover, dispersed to Paris and elsewhere, and the schools remained deserted till in 1214 a legatine ordinance vindicated the clerks, gave them protection and placed them under the jurisdiction of the chancellor 'whom the bishop of Lincoln shall set over the scholars'. This was clearly an imitation of the Paris chancellor, and the Oxford official was a cathedral dignitary in a university town without a cathedral; the result was a kind of amalgam of the Parisian chancellor and the Bolognese rector, for the Oxford chancellor had ecclesiastical and penal jurisdiction over the masters and students, yet was in no sense the enemy of the university. Indeed, the chancellor soon became the elected 'head of the masters' guild and thus was identified with the university as against the bishop; ultimately he became for all practical purposes head of the whole university and all its interests; the bishop even lost the right of appellate jurisdiction, and appeals from the chancellor went back to the whole university. Thus Oxford, and Cambridge which followed its model, though based on a Parisian constitution, show in many respects an arrested development: the existing division of students at Oxford into northern and southern (*boreales et australes*) disappeared, and with it any hope that a student university might develop, while among the masters the faculties were amalgamated. Consequently, there emerged the strong autonomous university of teachers, which is the only type of university with which, for centuries, Englishmen were familiar. As at Paris, colleges soon multiplied, though they were commonly small, and the vast majority of students lived in lodgings or private halls.

The imaginations of Cambridge antiquaries have proved even more fertile than those of their Oxford rivals, and the origin of the university has been ascribed to a Spanish prince Cantaber, of uncertain date, and to King Arthur, whose charter is dated 531. Actually, even if schools existed in the town before 1200, the university owes its existence to the migration thither of a large group of the dispersed students of Oxford in 1209. We may still echo Rashdall's confession of ignorance: 'what attracted them to that distant [*sc.*, from Oxford] marsh town we know not .'[2] Thenceforth, growth was fairly rapid, and a chancellor is mentioned in 1225, with three active faculties, including a flourishing school of theology, by 1260, and colleges soon appearing. In general, the resemblance to Oxford is complete, but the chancellor was slower in gaining exemption from the bishop, who from Ely had no difficulty in surveying Cambridge.

In the thirteenth century there was a steady growth in the number of universities, especially in France, Italy and Spain. In Italy, the normal type is seen in Vicenza (1204) and Padua (1222), both the outcome of migrations from Bologna, of which Padua, the intellectual centre or *quartier latin* of Venetia, became the rival who ultimately surpassed her parent. Both had student-universities of four nations under four rectors. Wholly abnormal 'artefacts' are seen at Naples, founded by an administrative act of Frederick II in 1224 and remaining under immediate royal control, and the university in the Roman Curia, founded to improve the minds of cardinals and others by Innocent IV in 1244, and later adorned by the presence of Pecham and Aquinas. This last venture had faculties in theology and civil and canon law, and was governed by the papal chamberlain as chancellor. Apart from these two exceptions, the Italian universities shared the following characteristics: they were all of one type, that of Bologna, which in its most characteristic form, that of the university of 'foreign' students, was ubiquitous in, and confined to, the Italian peninsula; they were occupied prominently and almost exclusively with legal studies and medicine; they were municipal in origin and the professors were salaried by the city; they were comparatively unaffected by ecclesiastical interests, as their only corporate connection with the Church lay in the formal conferment of licences by the bishop or archdeacon. For all these reasons, and for implications which are not at first sight obvious, such as their preoccupation with practical or legal questions, rather than with speculative and metaphysical topics, the Italian universities, at least in the period from 1150 to 1350, were less interested in, and consequently less implicated in, the theological and politico-theoretical controversies than were the French and English universities.

[2]H. Rashdall, *Universities*, I, 34.

In France, leaving Paris aside, there was a steady, though not a spectacular, increase in university foundations in the thirteenth century. At Montpellier (which, though it lay in the medieval kingdom of Aragon, had close connections with France) a medical school of celebrity existed as early as 1137, and was influenced both by Salerno and by the Arabian and Jewish medical traditions of Spain. Montpellier contained three separate universities: medicine, law and arts. The medical university was as early as 1220 under a chancellor, nominated by the bishop and three masters; he was a member of the university, and the bishop reserved to himself criminal and spiritual jurisdiction and the right of giving licences – an arrangement which invites comparison (and contrast) with that of Oxford. From 1200 onwards Montpellier was and remained the medical university of northern Europe *par excellence*, though later Padua rose to parity south of the Alps.

Orleans, like other schools of the Loire valley and neighbourhood, was for long celebrated for its humanistic studies, but later became the greatest canon law school in medieval France, owing to migrations from Paris after the study of civil law there had been prohibited by Honorius III in 1219 – a prohibition that reacted unfavourably upon the study of canon law at Paris. As the legists were a late immigration at Orleans they fell under the *scholasticus*, the equivalent of the chancellor at Paris, who was both head of the masters' guild and representative of the bishop. The constitution was as a result a compromise between the models of Paris and Bologna; the university was administered by the doctors together with the proctors of the ten student-nations; the last-named elected a rector, who himself was often a doctor. Two other early universities were also primarily legal: Angers, founded by migrants from Paris in the year 1229, was a great school of civil law, with a constitution similar to that of Paris. Toulouse, the first university to be founded (1229–33) by a papal bull, was intended as a citadel of orthodoxy *in terra Albigensium*; largely legal, it had a school of theology in the hands of the Dominicans.

Of the French universities as a group (excluding Paris) it may be noted that the older ones were spontaneous growths from cathedral schools, elevated to university status by a papal bull, and with an organization which was not framed directly or solely upon that of either Bologna or Paris. In them internal government was in the hands of the masters or doctors, but the students were organized also by nations, which in time came to elect the single rector and to share in the government through proctors. The bishop in most cases was more powerful than at Paris, and the law was the principal study everywhere save at Montpellier.

The early Spanish universities, Palencia (*c.* 1208-9; it disappeared before 1300), Salamanca (*c.* 1227) and Valladolid (late thirteenth century), differed from the Italian and northern academies in owing their foundation, or at least their recognition and funds, to sovereigns of Castile and Leon, who built them into the social framework by legislation covering their constitution, rights and finances. Though internally approximating more nearly to the Bolognese than to the Parisian model, they were closely connected with the cathedral or a great church and were endowed with church funds. Coimbra in Portugal, older than any of the Spanish universities, was a spontaneous growth of the type of the early Orleans.

Concurrently with the emergence of the 'university' and the growth of its constitution went the organization of the system of degrees and preparatory studies. Scarcely any evidence exists of the stages of the gradual process from the complete freedom of Abelard's day, when a man could set up as a teacher without any formal qualification and teach whatever he wished to pupils who were under no obligation either to attend his lectures, or to pass through a set course of instruction, or to qualify themselves by satisfying any formal examiners, to the moment a century later when the studies of Paris appear as a formalized statutory series of exercises. For our present purpose, therefore, which is to indicate the background and conditions of the intellectual life of the thirteenth century, it will be sufficient to give in outline the framework of university education in its mature form as seen at Paris and elsewhere round about the birth-dates of Aquinas and Bonaventure.

CHAPTER FOURTEEN

Studies, Degrees and Text-books

While the external and corporate organization of the universities was being perfected, a parallel development was going forward in the regularization and formalization of the studies, which originally had been freely arranged by the individual master, with perhaps a certain deference to the customs and traditions of the individual schools. Here again, there is little to be seen of the gradual growth till the elaborate and comprehensive decrees and statutes appear in the first half of the thirteenth century. The sketch which follows deals separately with the legal and theological courses.

At Bologna a previous education in arts was presupposed as a condition for entry upon legal studies, but as few of the lawyers were natives of the city and old pupils of its arts school, the latter makes no such show here and in other law universities as it does at Paris, and in the thirteenth century these universities made little contribution to the development of philosophy as an autonomous discipline. In the law universities the first significant act was matriculation. This was originally peculiar to the student universities, for in them alone did membership of the university begin (as nowadays it begins in most universities) with the embarkation upon a course of study. During the course there were three lectures daily. The first, from seven to nine in the morning, was the 'ordinary' lecture on the *Codex* of Justinian or the *Decretum* of Gratian. The second and third, from two to four and from four to five-thirty in the afternoon, were both 'extraordinary', and on other parts of the law. Lectures were given either in the master's house or in a lecture-room hired by him. They consisted of a reading in the text of the law and the vulgate gloss, followed by a presentation of seemingly contradictory laws, and a decision, with a statement (known as a *brocard*) of the general questions involved. Disputations took place in Lent.

After five years study, licence was given by the (student) university for the 'bachelor', as he now became, to read on a single title of the law. After seven or eight years of study the doctors examined for the licentiate. Originally the licence was awarded solely on the authority of the doctors, but in 1219 Honorius III decreed that there could be no promotion to the doctorate without licence from the archdeacon of Bologna; this was an epoch-making decision, for it brought all universities under ecclesiastical surveillance and helped to bridge the existing gap between the Italian and French universities.

Whereas at Bologna and other student universities the arts school was an unimportant adjunct, at Paris and Oxford it was from the first large, and soon became extremely important. Not only was a degree in arts a *sine qua non* of admission to the courses leading to a higher degree, but large numbers of men departed from the university to their careers with no more than an arts degree, while possibly a still greater number departed without a degree, after obtaining a smattering of education.

At Paris, the arts course must have taken shape many years before the set curriculum of reading and study for the master's degree was stereotyped in the statutes of Robert de Curzon in 1215, which marked an epoch in European education as the first public decree of the kind. Here the course consisted of Grammar, Logic and Rhetoric, plus the fossilized remains of the old *quadrivium*. Grammar by this time consisted of rules only; the careful study of literature had gone altogether. In Logic, the old and new logic of Aristotle, together with the *Isagoge* of Porphyry, were read as 'ordinary'. The books of the *Ethics* were absorbed as they appeared in translation, but, as we shall see, the more important philosophical works of Aristotle were for a time banned at Paris. In 1215 the arts course lasted for six years, and the age of twenty was required for the reception of a master's licence. Previous to this, the student could become a *baccalaureus* (a word of unknown derivation, englished as 'bachelor') and could help with the ordinary or 'cursory' reading. After six years, informal 'responsions' in December were followed by a 'determination' in Lent. In contrast to the student universities, the grade of bachelor was bestowed within the faculty by the masters. For the final licence and mastership there was an examination within the faculty and the candidate was subsequently presented to the chancellor for the formal licence. After an interval of six months 'inception' took place. There was a solemn disputation (*vesperiae*) in the evening followed by an inaugural disputation next day. The new master was bound by oath to remain teaching at Paris for two years.

The course in theology originally consisted of eight years' study; for five years as a simple student, and for three more as a bachelor of theology, and the lowest age for the completion of the course was thirty-four, which would have implied, in a man who began his studies at fourteen and pursued them without a setback, some six years teaching in the arts school before beginning theology. A survival of this arrangement may still be seen in the course of studies appointed for the Society of Jesus in the seventeeth century, and still followed in its main lines. At Paris and Oxford the theological course was lengthened in course of time, and the baccalaureate came only after four years on the Bible and two on the Sentences. After the baccalaureate followed two years of 'cursory' lecturing on the Bible and one on the Sentences. After three or four years more came the final licence by the chancellor and then, after another year, the new doctor's *vesperiae* and the inaugural lecture or disputation. All this would have the effect of postponing the doctorate in theology to the fortieth year, and the wider effect of restricting this extremely long and elaborate training to a very few who either intended to make an academic career for themselves or who had financial means sufficient to support them in preparing for high preferment in the Church.

The basic discipline of the schools was the lecture or reading (*lectio*) of the master. In origin this was, in theology, a reading of the Bible and the 'ordinary gloss' or running notation, which comprised older material shaped in the twelfth century. Later, the reading was complicated by the addition of an exegesis such as that of Gilbert de la Porrée or Rupert of Deutz, and elaborated by each master with a mass of linguistic, explanatory or allegorical notes. The plain, unvarnished technique of 'reading' gradually took literary form in several specialized shapes; one family of these developed into running, but elaborate, commentaries on the Scriptures; another species began with short tracts on special points of theological interest, spread out into commentaries on the *Sentences* of the Lombard, and finally blossomed into the theological *Summae* of the twelfth century which covered the whole field of divinity.

Alongside the *lectio* and its developments there was also growing up, in every faculty, the *quaestio*. This was originally a simple question and answer on a difficult point of legal, biblical or theological interest, but later it developed into a *disputatio* in dialectical form. It soon came, long before the organization of the universities, to bear a technical meaning, and was defined by Gilbert de la Porrée as a pair of contradictory statements, both of which were supported by seemingly valid arguments. The *quaestio*, originally a merely oral exercise, soon came to take literary form, and it was in this form that the masterpieces of thought and expression of the thirteenth-century theologians saw the light. Originally the problem was first answered (*responsio*) by a student, and then settled (*determinatio*) by a master. There were two principal types of *quaestio*, the *quaestio disputata*, which was a formal disputation on feasts and solemn days, and tended to have as its theme some familiar but perennially difficult point, and the 'open question' or *quaestio quodlibetalis*, held in the second week of Advent and the fourth and fifth weeks of Lent. This was a freer business, with a variety of disputants, including students, masters, and distinguished visitors. Any question might be put, and it was then answered at a subsequent session. These *quodlibetales* were therefore more topical, representing subjects that were 'in the air' at the moment, and are therefore a valuable index of what was to the fore at a particular juncture of time. In the arts faculty the corresponding disputations were classified as *sophismata* and *quodlibetales*.

Thus gradually, in the course of the century between the death of St Anselm and the birth of St Thomas, the medieval university grew to maturity. In its final perfection, it was to be one of the most important and original contributions that the medieval centuries made to the civilized life of Europe, and it has proved one of the most valuable of the legacies left to modern times by the medieval past. For the University, in the sense of that word now current, was wholly a medieval creation. There had been nothing quite like it in the ancient world. In Greece there had been the study of philosophy, both as a pursuit for individuals and, later, as a way of higher education for a restricted class, but philosophy had never been publicly recognized either as one of several branches of higher education or as a preparation for some other department of higher studies. In the cosmopolitan world of the Roman Republic and early Empire, Athens was still a kind of finishing school for a small class of men, but such higher education as existed was more strictly professional, whether for orators, as in Asia Minor, or for lawyers, as in Rome. In any case, there was no institution that combined the functions of a professional educator with that of the nurse of a cultured class and that of the director of research of all kinds. If we define a university as an organized and articulated body of masters and students, in which higher instruction is given by a body of masters who follow a statutory syllabus and test their pupils by a long and searching examination before admitting them to a degree which is a fair certificate of learning, then we may say that this is an entirely medieval creation, which has survived intact in all essentials to the present day.

While the organization and formalization of the educational system of Europe was in progress throughout the twelfth century, the books used as tools by the teachers and students inevitably went through a concomitant process of development and formalization. In this the lead was taken by the law schools of northern Italy, where the manner and framework of academic teaching were stereotyped almost half a century before the process was completed in the arts and theology. This was partly due to the great practical need for lawyers, and the prizes which skill in the law could command, but it was also due to the more fully developed and sophisticated nature of the study of law at a time when theology was still in the care of isolated and private masters. The 'discovery' and appropriation of the complete legal system of Justinian and his successors presented the Roman lawyer with an admirable text to gloss and to dissect in the lecture-room. Canon law, also, was technically more developed than theology. The collections made before and during the second half of the eleventh century, originally to implement the papal reform programme, and later to cover every aspect of church life, were methodically and technically more finished and ordered pieces of work than the writings of contemporary theologians, with the exception of those of St Anselm, which were in fact outside the stream of development and had few imitators. But while the civilian had the Digest and its satellite texts, the canon lawyer had only a number of collections made by individuals for their own purposes. The way was thus open for some sort of codification, and the opening was seized by an obscure scholar of Bologna, Gratian, who until very recently was believed, but wrongly, to be a monk of Camaldoli. Gratian's immediate purpose was to give aid in the resolution of the many cases where two or more authoritative pronouncements seemed to contradict one another; this, which has always been a source of difficulty in every large body of law, was particularly so in the haphazard, disparate mass of canonical enactments, made at different times and places and by different authorities, and containing in fact a great admixture of unauthentic material. To disentangle their problems, the lawyers, as has been seen, were the first to use the dialectical method which was perfected and supplied with a logical apparatus by Abelard. It was Gratian's great achievement to compile a comprehensive if confusingly arranged body of legal pronouncements, carefully grouped under leading headings of subject and topic, and to apply to them the *Sic et non* method of dialectic, giving also in most cases a judgement on the issue and a brief discussion in which critical and legal principles were displayed.[1]

As with all medieval compilations, the amount of original matter in Gratian's work was small. He drew heavily on previous collections of Burchard of Worms, Ivo of Chartres, Anselm of Lucca and the rest, and even when he did not draw on previous collections he could make use of official pronouncements of the past and other sources which were to hand. His excellence lay in the scope of his work, in the sanity of his judgements, and above all in the skill with which he examined and controlled his materials. Rarely can any text-book have had such a success. Used from the first by masters and students, it became at once a 'text' on which subsequent writers made their comments and from which they drew problems to discuss. Indeed, it soon lost its character as a text-book and became an authority in its own right under the name of Gratian's *Decretum*, from which a whole class of commentators for more than a generation took their name of 'decretists'. Nor was this the end. In default of any official code drawn up by the Roman authorities, the *Decretum* gradually came to be treated as such by the schools, the episcopal courts and finally even by the Curia itself; it became the core to which were attached the additional collections of papal decretals that were issued officially in the thirteenth and fourteenth centuries and which were significantly entitled *extravagantes* ('strays' or 'overflows'), and before the Middle Ages came to an end it had been adopted silently as the effective body of ecclesiastical law. As such it remained through all the vicissitudes of the papacy, until it was finally absorbed in large part into the Code of Canon Law published in 1917. Gratian's work had thus gone through a process exactly the reverse of that usually exerienced by the successful text-book. As a rule, such productions are gradually revised and re-written till they retain little save the name of the original. The *Concordia*, on the other hand, lost its private name and all trace of private origin, while remaining identical in essentials and rising from the status of a text-book to that of an authentic text.

Meanwhile a parallel, but much more leisurely, progress was taking place among the theologians. Here there was, at the beginning of the twelfth century, no kind of agreement as to the form to be taken in writing or teaching theology. Alongside the freely moving, dialectically subtle, dialogues of Anselm, and the more traditional

[1] Its title was *Concordia discordantium canonum*.

literary treatises of St Bernard and William of St Thierry, were the *Sententiae*, or patristic and conciliar anthologies of the masters of cathedral schools, and the more systematic and dialectically organized 'theologies' of Abelard. The former gradually became more complete and schematic in the great *Summae sententiarum* of the third and fourth decades of the twelfth century, while in another idiom Hugh of St Victor drew the outlines of a complete picture of theology in his slow-moving, speculative, carefully composed *De sacramentis*. Contemporary with Hugh was Abelard's successor on the Mont Ste Geneviève, the Englishman Robert of Melun. Himself the pupil of Abelard and of Hugh, and the master of John of Salisbury, he was associated with Peter the Lombard in opposition to Gilbert de la Porrée at Rheims in 1148. He left Paris to teach at Melun, and eventually returned to England as bishop of Hereford in 1163. He is remarkable chiefly for his great *Liber sententiarum*, a collection of expositions, opinions and decisions covering the whole of theology, and distinguished by the purity of its doctrine and the acuity of its reasoning. Thus at Paris there were two streams of influence flowing, the one deriving from the dialectical *Theologia* of Abelard, the other from the methodical, lucid, spiritual *De sacramentis* of Hugh; they were uniting in the *Summae* of Robert of Melun and of the school of Gilbert de la Porrée to produce a new theological form, the *Summa*, covering the whole range of doctrine and embodying the two strands of *auctoritas* and *ratio*. The desire for a synthesis, a text-book, was in the air, and, as so often happens, a single writer succeeded in doing just a little better than others what many were attempting to do. His name remains, while those of his all-but-equals fade. Here, the name that became famous and joined the ranks of the immortals in Dante's *Paradiso* and Raphael's *Disputa* was not that of Robert of Melun, but that of his contemporary and fellow-bishop, Peter the Lombard,

'who, with the poor widow, offered his treasure unto Holy Church'.[2]

Peter the Lombard, born near Novara in Lombardy, was educated in the schools of Rheims and of the canonry of St Victor. He was a pupil of Hugh of St Victor and he was well known to Bernard, who had recommended him to the canons. By 1144 he taught in the cathedral school at Paris, of which city he became bishop in 1159 and died, probably, in the following year. The Lombard, round about the year 1140, had composed commentaries on the psalms and on the epistles of St Paul which became successful manuals, and in so doing had compiled a collection of texts from Scripture and the Fathers to

[2] Dante, *Paradiso*, x, 107–8.

illustrate his points. These he now used as part of the material for his masterpiece, the four *Books of the Sentences*, completed *c.* 1155–8, which dealt respectively with (1) God, (2) creatures, that is, with the creation and history of the world before Christ, (3) the Incarnation and Redemption and (4) with the Sacraments and the *Novissima*, that is, death, judgement, hell and heaven. His method was to propose a doctrinal thesis or question, to bring forward authorities for and against this thesis from Scripture, the Councils, the Canons and the Fathers, and then give judgement on the issue. Research into his sources shows that, as was to be expected, Augustine is by far the most frequently cited, with some thousand quotations, or nine-tenths of the total of personal citations. Unbalanced as this may seem, it must be remembered that Augustine is not only by far the most voluminous of the Fathers, but also the most comprehensive. Apart altogether from his great treatises on the Trinity and Grace, he touches somewhere in his writings upon almost every topic of Christian doctrine and practice. Nevertheless, the gap is wide between Augustine and the two who come next in order of citation, Hilary and Ambrose, with between thirty and forty quotations. There is a similar disproportion between Latin and Greek Fathers. Of the latter, Chrysostom is the most frequently cited, with some twenty occurrences; Origen appears a dozen times and the great Cappadocian Fathers still more rarely. A few modern masters are quoted, notably the Lombard's own teachers, Abelard (from the *Theologia*) and Hugh of St Victor; as also his 'opposite number' and inspirer, Gratian. An interesting and novel appearance is that of St John Damascene, the Greek who foreshadowed Aquinas. He had very recently been translated into Latin, and the Lombard's use of this new material is characteristic. All his quotations come from a particular section of the Damascene, and it has been shown that they are derived from a particular manuscript of the first translation that was made, which was available in Paris. Subsequently, the Lombard was able, when on a visit to Rome, to check his text against the complete translation of Burgundio of Pisa, but he made no attempt to extract from this any passages to add to his original limited selection.

It has been conclusively shown – what might indeed have been safely assumed – that the patristic quotations do not rest upon a thorough perusal of the Fathers concerned, but on previous compilations and anthologies, some of which can be identified, and on a few manuscripts (such as that of the Damascene) that were to hand. Throughout the work the influence of the two great currents is seen, those of Abelard and Hugh of St Victor. To the first is owing the technique used throughout, which is an adaptation of the *Sic et non* method, and also the rules which are applied to reconcile differences between authorities; to the second the Lombard owes his firm reverence for tradition and *auctoritas*, his love of positive dogma, and his insistence on the claims of faith. While in Abelard the tendency had appeared to take a single fact or word, such as the Threefold God or Person, on which to weave a great dialectical web, the Lombard's first care is always to set out fully all that the Church as such believes. He rarely if ever employs dialectic as a *tour de force*, and on purely philosophic or speculative points he often prefers to refrain from a decision; yet on occasion he can show himself the master of a complicated and faultless dialectic method based on the new logic.

The Lombard's success, like that of Gratian, was immediate and lasting, though the fate of his masterpiece was different from that of the *Concordia*. Within twenty years his text was being taken as the basis of elaborate commentaries, while 'potted' versions and compendia, as one might say 'the Lombard without tears', were soon made available for students, one of the most successful being by his faithful pupil Peter of Poitiers. He had his enemies, for he had given motives for attack to various groups by his use of dialectic, by his reiterated attacks on Gilbert de la Porrée, and by his approval of the Abelardian teaching on the Incarnation. There were at least two occasions when the *Book of the Sentences*, like the *Summa* of Aquinas a century later, came within an ace of sinking under the attacks of the anti-dialecticians or the supporters of Joachim of Flora. In the event, he obtained a resounding certificate of orthodoxy from the fathers of the Fourth Lateran Council in 1215, who, when defining the Trinitarian faith against Joachim of Flora, cited his name and used his formula when declaring that they believed and confessed, 'with Peter the Lombard', that such was the traditional doctrine. Throughout the thirteenth century and beyond his book was, after the Bible, the text-book of divinity, and after completing his biblical course the *baccalaureus biblicus* delivered a course of lectures on the *Sentences* as *baccalaureus sententiarius*. Not only did every young theologian lecture upon it, but innumerable masters wrote commentaries upon it in some such way, though in far greater numbers, as 'Greats' tutors at Oxford wrote commentaries upon Plato or Aristotle. The commentary of Aquinas is only the most famous of a whole army. Recent and incomplete attempts at cataloguing have shown that in England alone some two hundred such commentaries were written, while another basis of division shows that more than 150 such commentaries were written by members of the Dominican order alone. Every great library of manuscript material has sequences of entries of the Lombard's work. Indeed it is certain that no book save the Bible was copied and commented upon so often between 1150 and 1500. The *Summa* of St Thomas, besides starting the race with a century's handicap, failed to supplant the Lombard for three hundred years. Only in the sixteenth century did Cajetan Vitoria and Bañez secure for St Thomas's work the position of a text-book *par excellence*, and as late as the mid-seventeenth century theologians were still publishing commentaries on the *Sentences*.

Modern critics have naturally sought to name the formula for this phenomenal success. They have found it partly in the sane and central outlook of the Lombard. He had wide interests, no hobbies and few idiosyncracies. He was not infallible, and two or three of his positions, e.g., his 'Adoptionist' tendency, and his identification of 'charity' with the Holy Ghost, were soon discarded; they caused no scandal, and were silently pardoned, as warts on a well-loved countenance. Beyond this, his phenomenal vogue was no doubt largely due to the fortunate moment at the very beginning of a long period of expansion. There were as yet no 'schools' among the theologians such as later were to divide Augustinians and Aristotelians, Thomists and Scotists. The Lombard stood at the fountain-head, the common inheritance of all the schools. When he wrote all were feeling the need of some such compilation which might summarize the teaching of the pre-scholastic Church and cater for the growing student population and the rapidly formalizing system of instruction. Many felt the need, and were feeling their way towards meeting it, and the Lombard was ahead of his contemporaries in finding the answer. It was an epoch of text-books, and we may compare, in very different fields and epochs, the success and subsequent literary history of the Lombard and his two contemporaries, Gratian and Peter Comestor, with those of such works as Palgrave's *Golden Treasury* and Kennedy's *Latin Grammar* a century ago. Once the commenting had begun, there was no going back. In the modern world, we rewrite our text-books; in the medieval world, it was the commentaries that were supplanted.

This estimate, if correct, will allow us to assess the Lombard's significance in the history of scholasticism. The judgement of some earlier critics, that he was the originator of the scholastic method, will not bear a moment's examination. If any single thinker deserves the title of Father of Scholasticism, it is Anselm; if any are to have the credit of perfecting the technique of dialectic Abelard and Hugh of St Victor are claimants. The Lombard was merely the great *vulgarisateur.* The further question, granted his original success, as to the precise character of his influence on subsequent method, is not easy to answer. That even such powerful and original minds as Bonaventure and Aquinas were greatly influenced by his arrangement and treatment of theological matter is unquestionable, but it is going too far to say that without the four *Books of the Sentences* there would have been no *Summa theologiae.* If the Lombard had not appeared a contemporary would have filled his place less successfully and with a briefer vogue, but the general development of the technique of scholasticism would have been scarcely affected.

The last thirty years of the twelfth century were on the whole a time of lesser men. Talented expounders of the whole range of theology replaced the more specialized, and at times more erratic, men of genius. Peter of Poitiers, who abbreviated the Lombard, is a good example of the type. Two other Peters accomplished in other fields of learning, with a little less spectacular success, what the Lombard had shown to be feasible in theology. Peter the Eater (Petrus Comestor: his diet was books), Chancellor of Paris from before 1168 until 1178/9, composed an *Historia scholastica,* or sacred history of the Old and New Testaments, which was the historical handbook for centuries. Peter the Chanter, by 1173 master of theology at Notre Dame and from 1183 Precentor, dying in 1197, composed a *Summa* of sacramental and moral theology which had an equal popularity.

Thus to the contemporary the last decades of the twelfth century, a time of general decay and disorder and centrifugal strains in France and Italy, must have seemed to many, and in particular to those who, like Peter of Blois and Gerald of Wales, survived from an earlier generation, a time of decadence and mediocrity as well in theology as in letters. The culture admired by John of Salisbury had gone, as had the zest and conflict of the great days of Abelard, Bernard and Gilbert de la Porrée. Theology seemed to have become safer, more dull, and less personal. Only a very acute observer could have seen in germ two of the three great tendencies that were to make the thirteenth a century even more distinguished for the number and variety of its schools and its great men than had been the twelfth. We have considered the rise of the universities. The rediscovery of Aristotle will soon occupy our attention. The rise of the friars and their impact upon the universities could never have been foreseen, but the origins of the mendicant orders lie outside our purview.

CHAPTER FIFTEEN
The Rediscovery of Aristotle

For more than a century after the revival of learning and the beginnings of dialectical activity in the schools of Italy and France, the masters of logic and philosophy had at their disposal only that fragment of ancient thought represented by the so-called 'old Logic' of Aristotle and the group of commentaries and treatises connected with it and composed for the most part by Boethius. It says much for the native genius of north-western Europe that for more than a hundred years this meagre store sufficed to nourish a series of great thinkers and to enable them to produce works of solid and permanent value. During this period, which came to an end between 1140 and 1170, the most influential master was undoubtedly Boethius, while to those who aimed higher, as at Chartres, Plato, however imperfectly known, was 'the Philosopher'.

Towards the middle of the twelfth century a great change began, and an epoch opened which was to last for more than a hundred years; it was the epoch in which ancient Greek and more recent Arabic and Jewish thought and science became available to the West in larger and larger doses. This flood of new knowledge transformed European thought and life in more than one respect, and we shall notice this on later pages, but in the realm of philosophy the principal transforming agent was the system of Aristotle, which was revealed piece by piece until all was visible, and its author had become, in place of Plato, 'the Philosopher' to all the schools. This revelation, which began soon after 1100 and was not completed until 1270, was the result of a process of translation from the Greek and Arabic on the part of a series of scholars of every race, working almost solely from a disinterested desire for knowledge. The sources for our information of this activity, which was practically *terra incognita* sixty years ago, have recently been diligently explored and exploited, and though many details are still obscure, the main outlines are fairly clear. Two circumstances would seem to have been responsible for this new phenomenon in Western culture. On the one hand, the outward thrust of the northern peoples into south Italy, the East and especially into Spain, brought them into contact with centres of civilization, hitherto unfamiliar, which contained treasures from the past of which they had hitherto had no knowledge; on the other hand, this very expansion was part of a new energy and capability of the same peoples, which in the intellectual sphere was manifested by a new curiosity and ability to use any new aid to knowledge and thought that might be discovered.

There were, in the early part of the twelfth century, at least four centres of exchange where Western scholars might make discoveries. There was, in the first place, Syria shortly after the first crusade. A few scholars and men of letters followed in the wake of the first crusaders and settled in Eastern cities such as Antioch, where they found and translated Arabic books that had never made the tour of the Mediterranean. Thus Stephen of Antioch, a Pisan by birth, is found at Antioch translating medical works in 1114, and at a much later date Philip of Tripoli found and translated at Antioch the pseudo-Aristotelian *Secretum secretorum*, a collection of practical maxims, secret counsels and occult lore intended for the instruction of rulers and purporting to have been written by Aristotle for his pupil Alexander the Great. This mixture of the marvellous and the exotic became immensely popular; more than two hundred manuscripts are known to exist, and its fancies were transferred into sculpture and stained glass.

Next, there was Constantinople. Here both Pisans and Venetians are found at work translating from the Greek in their colonies on the waterside. Among them are two or three notable names: James of Venice translated the whole corpus of Aristotelian logic; Moses of Bergamo, a member of the Venetian group, collected Greek manuscripts (which he had the misfortune to lose by fire) and made translations which have not survived; while Burgundio of Pisa translated Chrysostom, Basil and John Damascene. It is natural to ask why Constantinople, where pure Greek culture had flourished without a break, and which would therefore seem at first sight the obvious centre for those interested in Greek philosophy, did not become the Mecca of all Western scholars. The answer is complex, and illustrates the larger question of the rift between East and West that existed all through the Middle Ages, that age-long and bitter misunderstanding between Greeks and Latins, which made close social and intellectual relationship impossible. To this must be added both the lack of a clear-cut programme among Western scholars, who were by no means agreed that they were searching principally for works of philosophy, and a lack of contemporary Greek interest in philosophy as a principal mental pursuit.

A third theatre of interchange was Sicily under its Norman monarchs. Here four races and tongues met – Latin, Greek, Arabic and Hebrew – while life was more luxurious and civilized, and minds were more inquisitive and receptive, than anywhere else in Western Christendom. Sicily, therefore, under King Roger II, was a most important centre. Thither travelled many of the scholars, such as Adelard of Bath, and there worked several prolific translators, among them Henricus Aristippus, archdeacon of Catania in 1156, who translated Plato's *Meno* and *Phaedo*, and part of Aristotle's *Meteorology*, and Eugene the Emir or Admiral, who, besides being a considerable historian under another name,[1] translated Euclid and other mathematical works. Nevertheless, despite the importance of the Sicilian translators, who had the advantage of Greek texts for translation, Haskins, a pioneer in this as in other fields, does not hesitate to say: 'the broad fact remains that the Arabs of Spain were the principal source of the new learning for Western Europe'.[2]

In the fourth theatre of operations, Spain, the conditions existed that had been wanting in Constantinople. If Aristotle there was an accepted but neglected authority, here he had been for long an object of intense and almost emotional interest to the Arabs and later to the Jews. If at Constantinople there was little interest in Western needs, in Spain there was an atmosphere of eager activity among the rulers and bishops of the recent reconquest. We shall see on a later page something of the pre-history of the Arabic version of the writings of Aristotle; here we may look for a moment at the work of the first generation of translators.

The conquest and Christianizing of northern Spain had gone fitfully forward between 1031, when the caliphate of Córdoba ceased to exist, and 1085, when the Christians reconquered Toledo, and it had brought the Latin-speaking nations into contact with the learning of the Arabs and Jews, and into possession of many of their libraries. Save for Gerbert of Aurillac few northerners had gone to Spain in search of learning before 1100, but from 1100 onwards there

---

[1] Viz., that of Hugo Falcandus. See Evelyn Jamison, *Admiral Eugenius of Sicily* (British Academy, 1957).

[2] C. H. Haskins, *Studies in Medieval Science* (Cambridge, Mass., 2nd edn., 1927), 5.

was a steady stream of northern scholars into Spain seeking for manuscripts to be translated, and something like a school of translation was established by the archbishop of Toledo, Raymond (1125–52). One of the first and most distinguished of the pioneers is Adelard of Bath whose works survive in some quantity. His personality can be seen only by glimpses, though he has been called by Haskins 'one of the most interesting and significant figures in medieval science'.[3] Born at Bath, whither he retired at the end of his life, he travelled widely in Sicily, Syria, Palestine and Spain, and was active in translation and composition between 1100 and 1140. In his philosophical treatises, which were written in early life, he aims at following Plato, whose *Timaeus* he knew, and in the matter of epistemology attempted a reconciliation of the 'prince of philosophers' with Aristotle. Aristotle, he said, was right in making the 'universals' immanent in individuals, which were perceived by the senses, but Plato was correct in placing them in the mind of God, where they could be perceived by the 'imagination'. The individuals and the Universals were therefore the same thing seen by different mental powers; hence the title of his dialogue, *De eodem et diverso*. He also wrote, among many other works, a useful treatise on falconry and a work entitled *Quaestiones naturales*, a considerable collection of observations on nature and living creatures.

Among Adelard's contemporaries were Hermann of Carinthia (*c.* 1090–*c.* 1150), who rescued Ptolemy's planisphere for the West, and Robert of Chester, one of whose principal translations was the *Algebra* of Al-Khwarizmi. Robert and Hermann would seem often to have worked in double harness, and they were both engaged by Peter the Venerable, abbot of Cluny, who turned them on to help in the translation of the Koran he was organizing. The two most prolific and influential of the translators in Spain, however, were at work a little later. They were Dominic Gundisalvi, an Italian who became archdeacon of Segovia (*fl.* 1150), and Gerard of Cremona. Gundisalvi, by translating the *Metaphysics* of Avicenna and the *Fountain of Life* by Avicebron, threw a quantity of explosive material into the schools of the West, but this is part of a later story. Some of his work, we are told, was accomplished with the help of a Jew who put the Arabic into Spanish word by word, for Gundisalvi's subsequent translation into Latin. Gerard of Cremona (1114–87) was the most indefatigable of all the translators. Having learnt Arabic at Toledo for this sole purpose, he devoted his energies to the Greeks, and is known to have translated at least seventy-odd works, among them some of Aristotle,

[3]Haskins, *Medieval Science*, 42; cf. also p. 20.

Euclid and Archimedes, and all manner of books on geometry, algebra and optics, besides the medical works of Hippocrates and Galen.

We must now consider the effect of these translations on the schools and thinkers of the West. As their primary interest was in logic, the translators naturally turned first to logical works, and these in their turn influenced the thought and methods of the schools. Hitherto, as has been said, the masters of the eleventh and early twelfth centuries had inherited from the past only the so-called 'old' logic of Aristotle, mainly in the translation, and with the commentaries, of Boethius. The middle decades of the twelfth century were marked by the arrival of the 'new' logic, which completed the Aristotelian corpus on this subject: the *Analytica priora*, the *Analytica posteriora*, the *Topica* and the *De elenchis sophisticis*. All these were concerned with the modes of propositions, the syllogism in all its forms, and the various methods of argument and of detecting fallacies of all kinds, whether linguistic, formal or frankly captious.

Of these and other works of Aristotle the translations have been and still are the objects of manifold research and some controversy. The American scholar C. H. Haskins, Martin Grabmann and his disciples and assistants, and more recently Lorenzo Minio-Paluello, have revealed not only the translations that became current, but a whole undergrowth of others which for this reason or that failed to become popular or were allowed to disappear, while they have also investigated the problem, no less important in the history of thought, of the moment when a particular work of Aristotle was effectively 'received' in the schools, at a date often considerably later than that of its potential availability in translation somewhere in Europe. Here we can do no more than give the briefest conspectus of the field as it is seen at present. Whereas the *Topica*, the *De elenchis* and probably also the *Analytica priora* were discovered in the translation of Boethius, the so-called *versio communis*, the *Analytica posteriora* appeared in a series of renderings, which included a Boethian version, almost unusable on account of scribal misspelling of Greek words, a translation *c*. 1130 by James of Venice, whose obscurity prevented any wide popularity, several others made in Toledo and elsewhere, and finally that of Gerard of Cremona before 1187 which became standard.

As regards the date of 'reception', we know that Abelard in his early writings knew only of the 'old' logic, but in later works he cites the *Prior Analytics* and the *Elenchi*. Gilbert de la Porrée likewise knew the *Prior Analytics*, and Otto of Freising, who died in 1158, knew the whole of the 'new' logic, which he introduced into the schools of Germany. Finally, John of Salisbury, writing *c.* 1159, specifically discusses the introduction of the whole body of the new logic, and pronounces upon its exploitation as a *sine qua non* for any dialectician in the future. It was, in fact, decisive in making dialectical logic, for more than fifty years, the be-all and end-all of the course in the liberal arts which so soon became the necessary preparation for all the higher studies in the nascent universities. In so doing, it canonized, for the whole of the middle ages and beyond, the *question* and *disputation* as the basic form of all teaching and discovery. These in turn rested upon the correct manipulation of the syllogism, and upon the critical technique of the 'new' logic in demolishing false argument and pressing home valid demonstrations. The syllogism, often concealed, as in the 'body of the article' of St Thomas's *Summa*, under a dress of apparently free and persuasive argument, became all pervasive, not only as the foundation of all assertion and criticism, but also as the steel framework, capable of indefinite extension, which supported the construction of so many of the medieval edifices of cosmology, political thought and theological speculation. Logic was a discipline eminently suitable as an academic subject, with its mixture of memory work and quasi-philosophical argument; it lent itself to exercises in mental agility as well as to deep speculation. When once it was established its attraction to both masters and disciples rapidly drove out the long literary exercises of an earlier day. The student now went to logic as soon as he might; a literary style and the cultivation of individual self-expression were no longer desirable, and when logic was mastered, theology or the law opened their wide vistas to the ambitious student. Even if there had been no other agency to displace the literary monastic culture of the 'Benedictine centuries', the rise of logic as an autonomous discipline would of itself have been sufficient.

In the history of thought there was something of an interlunary period between the arrival of the New Logic of Aristotle and the reception of his major philosophical works. The interval is more apparent than real, for the leading translators were at work all the time, but whereas the logical treatises of Aristotle were of immediate and vital interest to each and every master and school, the philosophical and scientific works were of no direct interest either to logicians or to theologians. Their first appeal was to curious scholars only, and it was not until individual masters of arts at Paris and theologians there and elsewhere began to use or to misuse their doctrines that Aristotelian thought began to make its impact on academic circles, where it was at first regarded with suspicion, and then avidly absorbed. Here, in almost every case, an early translation of the later twelfth century served the pioneers, while the more exigent scholars of the next generation demanded an accurate translation from the Greek. Their demands were finally met, in nearly every case, by the Dominican translator William of Moerbeke.

Thus of the treaties on natural science, the *Physics*, the *De coelo et mundo*, the *De generatione* and the *Meteora* were all translated from the Arabic before 1187 by Gerard of Cremona, to be re-translated from the Greek almost a century later by Moerbeke. The supremely important philosophical works, the *De anima*, the *Metaphysics* and the *Ethics* had a different fortune. The two first were translated from the Greek by James of Venice by *c*. 1150, but found few readers at the time. The *De anima* became, as will be seen, one of the focal points of controversy in the thirteenth century, but this was due principally to the appearance of the Arabic commentaries on the book, and to the doctrines of the Arabs on the human soul. Aristotle's work was translated from the Greek a century after its first appearance, and Aquinas based upon it his great commentary. The *Metaphysics*, a work of peculiar difficulty in both language and thought, was translated several times. James of Venice made the first version, from the Greek, but at least two further unsatisfactory translations were made before Michael Scot, early in the thirteenth century, made one from the Arabic and William of Moerbeke another from the Greek before 1272. The history of the *Ethics* which, with its frank acceptance of human values, was a work of very great importance, is particularly complicated. The oldest translation, of books ii and iii only, was made from the Greek in the twelfth century, and a second followed early in the next. About 1240 Herman the German produced a compendium of books i-x from the Arabic, but the first complete translation from the Greek was that of Robert Grosseteste and it probably dates from shortly before 1250. Finally, the *Economics* and *Rhetoric* were translated from the Greek by the mid or late thirteenth century. Moerbeke made a new translation of the latter before 1270 and himself produced the *translatio princeps* of the *Politics* and *Poetics c*. 1260-4 and 1278 respectively.

Thus the introduction of the whole canon of Aristotle to the West was a process continuing over a hundred years. The first wave, that of the logical works, was absorbed easily and avidly, for it prolonged and perfected a discipline which was already committed to the Aristotelian mould. The second wave, that of the difficult and

profound philosophical works, gave more trouble and was less easily
absorbed, though its effects were epoch-making. Finally, the ethical
and political and literary treatises presented Europe with a
philosopher who regarded human life from a purely naturalistic,
this-world point of view. Taken as a whole the translations of
Aristotle gave Western thinkers, for the first time, matter on which to
construct a full and mature system, but the atmosphere, the
presuppositions of this great body of thought were not medieval and
Christian, but ancient Greek and non-religious, not to say
rationalistic in character.

CHAPTER SIXTEEN

Arabian and Jewish Philosophy

Until the end of the twelfth century Western thought had developed by natural stages and in a single direction. It had become active in the revival of the eleventh century by examining and debating the problems of logic that had long been potentially stimulating in its text-books, and the additions to its intellectual capital in the twelfth century had been, almost without exception, the logical treatises of Aristotle which amplified and clarified what had already been known and discussed. Save for isolated attempts, inspired by the *Timaeus*, to construct a metaphysic and a cosmology on Platonic lines, almost all the purely philosophical thought had remained within the confines of logic, and the scattered translations from the Greek that had appeared in Sicily had had very little effect in changing the currents of thought. Towards the end of the twelfth century the familiar veins had been exploited so thoroughly that something of a pause ensued. What the sequel would have been had no external influence made itself felt cannot be known. In fact, the whole course of medieval intellectual life was changed and enriched by the arrival of the whole Aristotelian corpus, accompanied by other works and lengthy commentaries which introduced the West to a whole world of Arabian and Jewish thought that hitherto had remained almost entirely unknown. As a consequence of this, thinkers and theologians were occupied for almost a century, first in absorbing and explaining Aristotle, and next in examining and partially rejecting the body of Arabian, Jewish and Neoplatonic thought that arrived along with the later portions of Aristotle. The course of scholastic thought was both interrupted and profoundly modified by this infiltration, which soon became an irruption, of new material. We shall need to study somewhat closely the stages of this invasion, and the extent and permanence of its conquests, but before doing so it is necessary to consider the channels and agencies by which Aristotle reached medieval Europe. Had the works of the Philosopher been rediscovered, as was Roman law *c*. 1100, and Greek literature in the fifteenth century, in a completely 'clean' or 'pure' state, their influence would no doubt have been as great, if not greater, but it would also have been less ambiguous in its effects and more readily distinguishable from rival systems. Actually, the works of Aristotle reached the West not only in a sporadic fashion and a fragmentary state, but also heavily contaminated by additions from other sources which were then thought to be Aristotelian, and accompanied by commentaries often extremely valuable, but also frequently tendentious and even misleading.

Although, as we have seen, some of the Aristotelian writings reached the West directly from Byzantium, or from Byzantine circles in Sicily, the majority came by way of Spain, and the story of their tradition is long and extraordinary. Greek philosophy and medical science had been received in the fourth century and thereafter adopted by the flourishing Christian communities, Syrian in race, who occupied Mesopotamia, where the schools of Edessa, opened by Ephrem in 363, were famous. When, in 489, these same schools were closed by the Emperor Zeno as tainted by Nestorianism, the professors carried their philosophy and science with them into Persia. When, in the following century, Islam conquered the whole of Persia and Syria, the enlightened caliphs of Baghdad made use of the services of these Syrians, who thus passed on to the Arabs Aristotle, Euclid, Archimedes, Hippocrates, Galen, and much besides. The period 750–900 was the great age of the translators, mainly Syrian Christians, who turned Aristotle into Arabic, sometimes directly from the Greek, more often from Syriac translations of the original. Unfortunately for later critics, and perhaps also for all later philosophers, a certain number of non-Aristotelian writings passed into Arabic under the name of the Philosopher. Among these were two Neoplatonic writings destined to have great influence, the so-called *Theologia Aristotelis*, made up of passages from Books IV–VI of the *Enneads* of Plotinus, and the *Liber de Causis*, which derived from Plotinus's disciple Proclus; there was also the celebrated Peripatetic commentary on Aristotle by Alexander of Aphrodisias. The contamination of Aristotle had, in addition to its other effects, that of giving the Arabian and Jewish philosophers an excuse – indeed, we may almost say that it imposed upon them the necessity – of attempting a synthesis of the systems of Plato and Aristotle.

Besides acting as agents in the long process of transmitting Aristotelian thought from Syria and Persia through Egypt to Spain, the Arabian thinkers handed over a legacy of their own to the Latins. It has often been repeated that the Arabs were not creative thinkers, and it is true that they did not originate a totally new system of thought. It might nevertheless be claimed that the system of Aristotle underwent at their hands a change similar, if not as thorough, to that experienced by Plato's system at the hands of the Neoplatonists, or Aristotle himself in the thirteenth century at the hands of Aquinas. Certainly, two or three of their most celebrated thinkers interpreted and extended the doctrines of Aristotle to a significant degree, besides adding from other sources elements that were to prove hard to disentangle.

A century of translation into Arabic at Baghdad was thus followed by an epoch of notable thinkers. No attempt will be made to describe or even to summarize their teaching, but it is necessary to note the principal changes in the Aristotelian system, and the additions thereto, for which they were responsible.

The earliest name of significance is that of Alkindi, who lived in Persia and died in Baghdad after 870. He treated at length of the process of cognition described by Aristotle in his *De anima*, a work which did not reach the West till the thirteenth century. Aristotle had explained the process of thought as the reception by the passive intelligence of the forms of things outside itself. He had also thrown out a suggestion, which he never elaborated, of an active intelligence with a nobler nature than that of the passive intelligence, which actually framed the forms that it understood. Aristotle's most celebrated commentator in the Greek world, the late Platonist Alexander of Aphrodisias in the second century of our era, had understood this active intelligence to be a spiritual being distinct from the human soul and acting upon it. Alkindi took the idea a stage further, and made of this active intelligence a single superhuman intelligence which, acting upon individual passive intelligences, gave birth to human thought. Thus an idea thrown out by a Greek, in the climate that was to foster the Plotinian system, was taken up in Persia to become an abiding element in Arabian thought.

The next name of note, perhaps the most original mind of the Arab race, was Alfarabi, who lived and died (950) at Baghdad. He is notable as having made the epoch-making metaphysical distinction between essence and existence, thereby providing a metaphysical basis for the distinction between a necessary and a contingent being, and for the concept of a universe created by, and not merely emanating from,

God, and thus causally depending upon Him. Working upon the Aristotelian logical distinction between the nature and the actual existence of a thing, he drew the metaphysical conclusion that the concept of essence did not include that of existence. Existence he regarded as an accident of the essence, which could come upon it or depart from it. He also took over from Alkindi the notion of a single active intellect (*intellectus agens*) external to the individual human minds, and perpetually illuminating them with the forms of things. Alfarabi had thus made a fusion of Aristotle and Neoplatonism very similar to that effected by Augustine: the concepts and relationships between sense-perception and the isolation of the essence are Aristotelian; the illumination of the mind with the forms of things is Neoplatonic. As the cause of the existence of things, God, is also the cause of their intelligibility, our ideas or universal concepts are necessarily true. Similarly, the final end of man, the contemplation of God, is a blend of the Aristotelian contemplative life and the Neoplatonic return to God. Alfarabi himself was a *sufi* or mystic, and made allowance in his system for a higher and purer illumination than that available to all men in their measure. Alfarabi's work and writings were less familiar to the medieval world, and remain to-day less familiar, than those of Avicenna, but his significance is perhaps as great: in his use of Aristotelian logic and his blend of Aristotelian and Neoplatonic metaphysics he showed the way to all those who came after.

Alfarabi was followed by the most celebrated of all the Arabians, Ibn Sînâ or, as the Latin world called him, Avicenna (980–1037). Avicenna was born in Bukhara, taught at Esfahan, and died at Hamadan in Iran. A prodigy of learning from childhood, he wrote an encyclopedia as a young man, filled a number of public offices, mixed freely and with enjoyment in social life, and was a celebrated physician. He was, indeed, the most authoritative writer on the theory and practice of medicine between the age of Galen and the Italian Renaissance, and it was he who gave universal currency to the notion of a close connection between natural dispositions (the later 'humours') on the one hand, and the mingling of the four elements (earth, air, fire and water) on the other, with its consequent significance for health and medical treatment. In the history of thought his is one of the supreme names; he was, in influence at least, an epoch-making thinker who determined the course of much Western thought – for the Arabs and Jews, despite their oriental characteristics and affinities, belong to the Western tradition. Not only was Avicenna the vehicle of transmission that conveyed the thought of Aristotle to the medieval world, but in several important points of logic and metaphysics he drew out the suggestions and implications of the Philosopher in the sense that became classic among all later Aristotelians including St Thomas. His universal mind covered the whole field of thought even more comprehensively than had that of Aristotle, from logic and physics to metaphysics and mysticism. It was he who first distinguished the three modes of existence of the universals or *genera*: that in the mind of God previous to the occurrence of the individual thing (*ante res*), that when clothed with accidents in the existing individual (*in rebus*), and that abstracted from things by the thinking mind (*post res*). It was he who first gave technical expression to the two Aristotelian perceptions of reality: the 'first intention' (*intentio prima*) by which we perceive the individual thing as it exists outside our mind *in rerum natura*, and by which it is received into our consciousness but has not yet become the object of rational and scientific consideration, and the 'second intention', by which we break the individual down in our minds into essence, accidents, existence, etc., and thus make it the object of scientific knowledge. Finally, it was he who noted that the essences of things could be regarded in three ways: in themselves, as the proper object of metaphysics; in our mind, as the proper object of logic; and in individual things, as the object of science. This was a clarification of the Aristotelian position which, by correlating the metaphysical constituent of a being as perceived by intellectual abstraction with the physical constituent existing and active in the world outside the mind, tied science to philosophy and helped to canonize the deductive method as the chief instrument of scientific knowledge.

While Avicenna followed Alfarabi in many ways, he nevertheless tended to present Aristotelian thought more purely and to abandon Neoplatonic accretions. Thus he keeps 'matter' as an eternal constituent of things, while Neoplatonism regarded it as the last vanishing trace of spirit. He retained fully the Aristotelian matter and form as correlative constituents of all physical beings, extending the doctrine to every level of being in the sense that all things have a 'form of Body' (*forma corporeitatis*), over which are laid, so to say, subsequent forms such as the forms of 'animality' and 'humanity'. This was the beginning of the 'plurality of forms' that was to become a subject of burning controversy in the late thirteenth century. Avicenna, however, was not responsible for the extreme 'hylomorphism' which attributed 'matter' even to spiritual beings. On the other hand, his God is largely Plotinian in character: the unchangeable Being from whom comes the First Intelligence, whence flows a descending hierarchy of being through the (Aristotelian) spheres down to the sublunary world.

In epistemology Avicenna resembles, and is probably following, Alfarabi. The individual human intellect is capable of receiving and cataloguing sense-impressions, and of making estimative and practical judgements, partly by the memory of experiences in the past and partly by an intuition of principles, but the final act of intellection, by which the mind abstracts the universal form, which is the object of intellectual knowledge and the basis of all philosophy and science, is due to illumination by the single Active Intelligence external to the individual 'possible' or 'passive' intellect, and this active intelligence illuminates the essences or forms of things in so far as the individual intellect is ready to receive them. The human soul, which for Avicenna is in practice equivalent to the intellect, is deathless in the sense that it contains no element of decay and may be kept in being by the divine power. This divine power is the one necessary being, the first uncaused cause of the universe, the creator of a universe which is co-eternal with its creator. This being, God, is the ruler of all things, though His governance is mediated by the intelligences and spheres down which it passes, but the universe of Avicenna, like that of Aristotle, is ruled by necessity. There is no providential care for individuals, though all that is, is good; evil is the privation, the fading out, of good. In such a universe there can be no freewill. Avicenna, as a sincere and devout Muslim, superimposed upon this strictly rational system the promises, commands and revelations of the Prophet, which included the doctrine of personal immortality, but in his opinion the philosopher retains the right to translate the coarse popular conceptions of future beatitude into his own terms.

This vast and complete system of thought, the supreme achievement of the Arab genius, in which the Aristotelian framework was illuminated and rendered supple by elements from Neoplatonism, and which provided a basis of natural religion on which could be set the positive religious teaching of Islam, had much to recommend it to Christian philosophers, though there were also elements, such as the eternal universe and the necessary character of divine governance, which were to prove intractable and incapable of assimilation.

Shortly after the death of Avicenna his works made their way to Spain, whither many of the Aristotelian writings had preceded them, to be followed later by the remainder. Although Avicenna was himself deeply religious, with a sympathy for the mystical element in oriental theology, his rational scheme of things was attacked by conservative theologians in Islam, and his teaching may have passed into relative oblivion in the East. In the West, however, the conflict between reason and revelation was to become acute.

There, in the sophisticated and highly civilized Muslim society in the south of Spain, where the arts and literary and intellectual pursuits were more highly valued and developed than in any region of the Latin world, another great name appears to rival that of Avicenna. Ibn Roshd or, as he was Latinized, Averroës, was an Arabian born at Córdoba in 1126, the son and grandson of lawyers and judges and himself a man of many talents as judge, astronomer and personal physician to the caliph. Prosperous and honoured for most of his life, he was finally attacked as unorthodox and died in exile in 1198. Compared with Alfarabi and Avicenna, Averroës is not an original thinker; his eminence lies in his critical powers which are shown in his great Commentary on Aristotle, which earned for him Dante's line,[1] and in his devotion to a single significant purpose, that of presenting Aristotle whole and pure to the world.

His admiration for Aristotle was unbounded, and even when all allowance is made for Semitic rhetoric Averroës is responsible for the most impressive eulogium ever given by one great philosopher to another. 'I consider [he wrote] that that man was a rule and exemplar which nature devised to show the final perfection of man ... the teaching of Aristotle is the supreme truth, because his mind was the final expression of the human mind. Wherefore it has been well said that he was created and given to us by divine providence that we might know all there is to be known. Let us praise God, who set this man apart from all others in perfection, and made him approach very near to the highest dignity humanity can attain.'[2] The aim, therefore, and the achievement of Averroës was to purify Aristotle from Neoplatonism, even at the cost of losing the scanty religious elements in his system as currently presented. He was on the whole not only thorough but successful, though even when he had done there remained a few traces of Neoplatonism, such as the identification of the First Mover with God, and the intellectualization of the Aristotelian hierarchy of celestial bodies, while he took over from Avicenna his doctrine of the eternal universe.

On one important point of psychology, however, Averroës separated significantly from his great predecessor. Avicenna, as has

[1]*Averrois che il gran commento feo'. Inferno* iv., 144.

[2]These passages occur in the commentary of Averroës on Aristotle's *De anima*. For the precise references see Ueberweg-Geyer, 316–17.

been said, working upon the commentary on Aristotle of Alexander of Aphrodisias, held that the possible or passive intellect of man, which of itself was an individual and spiritual being capable of existence when separated from the body, was illuminated by a single external intelligence so as to perceive the forms of things. According to Averroës the potential intellect, which corresponded to the possible or passive intellect of Avicenna, was itself brought into existence in man at the moment of first contact with the external, universal, active intellect; during his lifetime it remained with him, but at his death it passed, as a drop into the sea, into the universal intelligence. Thus not only freewill, but personal immortality was excluded.

Although Averroës set out to discover the pure word of Aristotle and to follow whithersoever his teaching (equated with right reason) might lead, he certainly also desired to be, and wished himself to be thought, an orthodox Muslim. At the same time he made no attempt to subordinate reason to revelation or philosophy to faith, nor to attempt a reconciliation of their conflicting demands, but to state and if necessary recognize their differences. These he explained by affirming degrees or varying depths of truth. Religion, he maintained, is necessary for all kinds of men, and the revelation of the Prophet and the Koran is so rich that all can find nourishment in their different ways. He himself distinguished three classes of believers. There is the ordinary, uncultured man, who is only capable of, and is satisfied by, authoritative and emotional arguments: for him there is the bare and literal word of revelation. Next, there is the moderately educated man, the dialectician and theologian, who is satisfied with probable or persuasive arguments. Finally, there is the rare and highly intelligent man, the philosopher, who needs absolute demonstration. This doctrine of Averroës, destined to find an echo at more than one subsequent moment of history, has been variously explained and defended. It has been called by some the doctrine of 'the double truth'. That historically it was at least the reputed parent of the teaching that was imputed to the Latin Averroists of Paris in the thirteenth century is unquestionable, but it is by no means clear that Averroës maintained, as often stated, that he followed Aristotle with the reason while giving lip-service only to the Prophet. Still less is it true that he professed Islam outwardly in order to avoid molestation. The question of interpretation is rendered more difficult by the doubtful accuracy of the Latin translations of Averroës, but it would appear that he never asserted that both of two incompatible assertions were true: he said only that one was a necessary conclusion of the reason, and the other a declaration to which one must adhere, as being the only expression of the truth that could be apprehended by a simple mind.

Seen as a whole, the achievement of three centuries of Arabian thought was to present and interpret, and in some important respects to develop, the whole body of Aristotelian teaching, and in so doing to eliminate many, though not all, of the Platonic and Neoplatonic doctrines that had been combined with it in the early centuries of our era. An important and unforeseen effect of this process had been to emphasize, if not to exaggerate, the determinist, unspiritual characteristics of Aristotle's thought, as also to eliminate, again probably unintentionally, the traces of deist or mystical religious sentiment. Averroës in particular, both by 'purifying' Aristotle and by putting him forward as the supreme master of true thought, did much to prepare for and to hasten the advent of integral Aristotelianism among Christian thinkers.

The influence of Arabian ways of thought was not the only impact sustained by the works of Aristotle on their way through Spain to France. The eleventh and twelfth centuries were also the golden age of Jewish philosophy, which flowered in the genial climate of the caliphate of Córdoba, though it did not bear its most mature fruit until Moslem power was on the wane. The Jews, during the first millennium of our era had mingled with many cultures – Neoplatonic, oriental, Mohammedan – and had admitted many elements from them into their view of the universe. In particular, the God of the Old Testament, Yahweh, so near to men in the psalms and prophetical books, had withdrawn from His place as the ever-present Father, and a whole hierarchy of angelic ministers had come between man and God. The angelic host of Palestinian Judaism had been contaminated by Persian semi-divinities and Neoplatonic emanations. With the long evolution of Jewish thought we are not concerned, but in the eleventh and twelfth centuries two Jewish thinkers added their quota to the legacy that Spain bequeathed to Paris.

The first of these is Salomon Ibn Gabirol, a native of Malaga (1021/2-70), whom the scholastics took for an Arab and latinized as Avicebron or Avencebrol. He was a poet and moralist as well as a philosopher. His principal work was the *Fountain of Life (Fons Vitae)*, a mixture of metaphysics, cosmology and cosmogony, which combined elements of Aristotelian, Neoplatonic and Jewish thought. He is significant in the history of scholasticism for two additions or innovations to the body of thought then existent in Spain.

Firstly he adopted, probably from the Avicennan tradition, a thoroughgoing doctrine of matter and form. In this not only did a series of specific forms overlay the basic form of 'body' (*forma corporeitatis*) as might, to use a homely comparison, the various skins of an onion: this, the 'plurality of forms', was in no way a novel doctrine. Gabirol, unlike the Neoplatonists and Avicenna, had to find a place for 'angels' (i.e., pure spirits) in his scheme, and in consequence extended hylomorphism to spirit also, in the sense that 'matter' was the potentiality, 'form' the actuality of spirit. Secondly, for the intellective principle, the Mind or First Intelligence, which in Neoplatonic and Arabian thinkers was the agent that brought the universe into being and conserved it with dynamic power, he substituted the Will of God, conceived almost as a personification, a mediator between God and the essences of creatures. This, as may readily be imagined, made a greater appeal to Christian thinkers than the Arabian Mind. It was more compatible with the conception of God as revealed in Scripture, and it safeguarded both the absolute freedom and the omnipotent action of God. Both these doctrines were to be reflected in the systems of the thirteenth century.

Still greater was the influence of Moses ben Maimon or Maimonides, the son of a judge, born at Córdoba in 1135 and exiled to Palestine and Cairo, where he died in 1204. Nurtured on Aristotelian philosophy as interpreted by the Arabs he was a devoted follower of the Philosopher who, he taught, was the supreme master of human science, as the Scriptures were of divine truth. Living as he did in highly educated, sophisticated circles he saw, as Averroës had seen, the apparent contradictions between philosophy and religion, with the consequent intellectual difficulties of believers, and his greatest work, the *Guide for the Perplexed,* is a long and systematic attempt to subordinate philosophy to revealed religion, while using all the resources of rational argument to prove or to support revealed truth. His position as to the limitations of philosophy in attaining to the mysteries of religion is almost exactly the same as that of St Thomas, who in fact accepts or elaborates much of the natural theology and apologetics of Maimonides. The latter rejected the extreme hylomorphism of Avicebron, while taking over the metaphysical position of Aristotle, and he abandoned the 'angelic' universe for the neoplatonized Aristotelian doctrine of the spheres and their intelligences. In psychology he took over the Aristotelian position as interpreted by Alexander and the Arabs: man has a passive intellect only, which can nevertheless acquire and retain an intellectual capital through the actualizing power of the active intelligence (*intellectus agens*), the ruler of the tenth and lowest sphere. Men therefore are not personally immortal, but every acquisition of knowledge by individuals enriches the Intelligence common to all and is therefore a gain. This is a slight advance upon the teaching of Averroës and an opinion that was destined to appeal to later generations, as to Comtean Positivists. On the other hand Maimonides emphasized the freedom of the will and made moral, rather than intellectual, perfection the goal of human endeavour. Taken for all in all, no other alien system in the Middle Ages had closer affinity with Christian philosophy, as was fully realized by Aquinas, who treats Maimonides with the greatest respect. Only in his teaching on the mediation of intellectual life from God to man through a series of pure spirits, and his denial of personal immortality, did he come into conflict with Christian orthodoxy.

One more important source of influence remains to be noted after the great names of Arabian and Jewish thought. Dominic Gundisalvi (Gonsalez), the convert Jew who became archdeacon of Segovia and took, as we have seen, a large part in the work of translation, was besides a thinker and writer in his own right. His short treatises, often aphoristic in form and based largely upon Avicenna and Gabirol, were skilful compilations that brought the various doctrines of the past into sharp focus upon a particular point, as upon the creation in *de processione mundi* and upon psychology in *de anima*, and upon personal immortality in *de immortalitate animae*. The last-named tract in particular, with its clear enunciation of all the arguments that had been framed since Plato's *Phaedo* in favour of immortality, was taken up in its entirety into thirteenth-century thought. Gundisalvi himself admits the single active intelligence of Avicenna and Gabirol, apparently without realizing its incompatibility with Christian doctrine. Elsewhere, in his catalogue of the various disciplines (*de divisione philosophiae*), he is the first to add explicitly to the old *quadrivium* the new Aristotelian sciences of metaphysics, physics, politics, economics and ethics. Coming, as they did, from a Christian source, and often accompanying the same author's translations in the manuscripts, the works of Gundisalvi acted as a kind of harbinger or sponsor of Arabian and Jewish thought, and helped to make its introduction to the West a simple and natural process.

All this great body of ancient thought, Aristotelian, Neoplatonic, Arabian and Jewish, was to be decanted into Western Europe and particularly into Paris and Oxford between 1190 and 1260. In the past the whole movement has too often been labelled 'the introduction of

Aristotle'. The whole of Aristotle did indeed arrive, and this was in the long run the significant fact, but the manner of its arrival, and the vehicles by which it was conveyed, had a great share in determining the quality and the extent of its influence.

CHAPTER SEVENTEEN

The Problems of the Soul and the Process of Cognition

(i)

In the first century of the intellectual revival of Europe (1050–1150) the interest and the attention of the masters of all the schools were taken up for more than fifty years by the problem of universals. This problem, posed by Porphyry and Boethius, was argued and resolved in different senses without any settlement upon a single agreed solution. Abelard, using part of the Aristotelian logic, but lacking the fuller light given by the other Aristotelian writings, answered it in one way. Gilbert de la Porrée, using the same logic, with the addition of what he supposed to be the Platonic doctrine of Forms, answered it in another. Then for a season, this particular problem ceased to attract attention. More than a century later, the interest of the masters, among whom were some of the greatest of the age, was occupied by problems concerning the human soul and its faculties. We shall consider on a later page the historical circumstances that gave this topic its significance and acuity; that the debate could be prolonged for decades and take a peculiarly passionate tone was due to the body of controversial and debatable matter contained in the Aristotelian writings and in the commentaries made upon them by subsequent thinkers. It will be well, therefore, before attempting a narrative of the controversies of the thirteenth century, to glance at their prehistory in the golden age of Greek philosophy and in the later speculations of the Arabs.

We have already looked briefly at the pronouncements of Plato on the subject.[1] They were in themselves a magnificent assertion of the nobility and capabilities of the human soul. The noblest part of man,

[1] See above, pp. 9 ff.

187

the essence of his being and individuality, godlike and eternal, the soul was in fact the man himself, the real man, and the body was now a servant, now a rebel, now a prison, and now a tomb. In his earlier dialogues Plato wrote of the soul as a Christian might, using the word as synonymous with spirit, a 'simple' being, self-sufficient and self-supporting, a 'substance' in the Aristotelian sense of the word. Later, he speaks of it as using or guiding the body, and as reining in the impulses of the disorderly steed of passion. Plato recognized within the soul a threefold division, that of the sensual, the 'spirited' or self-assertive, and the rational elements, which demanded the threefold educational system of the *Republic*. Later still he spoke of the highest division, the reasoning element (τό λογιστικόν) as the immortal part of the soul, but Plato never discussed or analysed the soul from a rigorously metaphysical standpoint, or from what may be called a scientifically psychological one. He remained in this respect primarily a moralist, an educationalist and a practical psychologist. As for the process of knowing, the 'noetic' of man, this was absorbed in and conditioned by the basic teaching of Plato on the Forms. The soul had within it the 'recollection' of these, whether seen before its incarnation or intuitively recognized and aroused by its encounter with the objects of sense which embodied or reflected the Forms or Ideas.

Aristotle's teaching, as indeed Plato's before him, was regarded by the ancient and medieval thinkers as a 'closed' system, fixed and complete from end to end, but recent scholarship has done for it what nineteenth-century historians did for Plato, and it is now recognized that his thought developed and changed in the course of his long academic career, though he retained throughout several important elements of the teaching he had received from Plato, such as the immateriality, the spiritual and godlike quality, and the supreme value, of the individual soul. In his early dialogues the soul is a being or 'substance' lightly attached to the body; the body is an illness from which death brings release. Even in these early days, however, Aristotle elaborates what was to be a characteristic element in his thought throughout his life. The great differential in man as opposed to all other living beings, and his highest activity, is 'Mind' (Nûs), but at this stage Aristotle made no attempt to analyse the act of understanding. When, however, in middle life the philosopher opened his great series of biological investigations, and when the empirical, receptive approach became habitual, he was faced with the imperious problem (which Plato had never fully considered) of the hierarchy of being and the close resemblances in behaviour, faculties and metaphysical components between the higher animals and man. 'Soul', regarded as the vital principle, the ultimate internal source of movement and sensation, was clearly not something found in human beings alone. In other words, man and the animals were of a like structure. But whereas all the other degrees of living beings shaded imperceptibly into one another, man – in Aristotle's opinion – had something additional which set him quite apart from all else, namely, his reason or intelligence. At this stage of his thought Aristotle, treating of animals and men alike, made of 'soul' the final metaphysical perfection that sealed, so to say, the union of all the faculties and qualities of a human being, but outside the realm of metaphysics he continued to regard the soul as a component of man together with the body, and even as the body's guide, and he makes a comparison with the artificer and the instrument he uses. In this middle period Mind is regarded as having both an abstractive and an intuitional function in the process of understanding. At this stage of his thought, so far as it can be tentatively reconstructed, Aristotle seems to have made no attempt to integrate his biological findings and his metaphysical intuitions. To put the matter in other words, he had formulated a dilemma in his various writings without fully realizing its existence.

The fundamental difficulty was this. Metaphysically speaking, in all living things, the soul is the form that gives perfection to the congeries of faculties and potentialities that must be coordinated and unified in order to become a single 'substance'. But if this is so, the soul (psyche) is, metaphysically regarded, the same for all visible living beings, something that comes into being at the moment the substance is perfected and existent, and which vanishes when the subject dies or is destroyed. What place can be found in this context for the Mind (Nûs) whose whole purpose and function is spiritual and immaterial, which itself is 'simple' and therefore necessarily a 'substance' in its own right, and which is clearly not the purely formal element giving unity to a group of components that form the metaphysical 'matter'?

In his last period of work Aristotle develops his doctrine regarding both Soul and Mind. The Soul is the principle of actuality, the basic metaphysical perfection of the natural organic body with all its faculties. Mind, on the other hand, is at once a substance and imperishable, while also fulfilling all the functions of an intellective reasoning faculty. The dilemma outlined above remained unresolved. Meanwhile Aristotle attacked directly the cognate problem of noetic. Having abandoned altogether (at least in this immediate context) the

Platonic Forms, and all recourse to innate or reminiscential knowledge, Aristotle explains the intellectual process by an analogy based on sense perception. As the objects of sense impinge upon the bodily organs, which retain an 'impress' which still has material associations, so the intellect receives from intelligible objects their essence or rationale, which is received as a concept and expressed as a definition. The analogy, however, breaks down in an important respect. Whereas the objects of sense directly 'impress' the senses, the essence, the immaterial element of intelligible things, must be detached, 'abstracted', from the individual subject in which it resides. Since Aristotle had rejected the Platonic Forms, the universal concept had no existence in its own right. In other words, whereas sense-perception is purely receptive, intellection demands both an active (abstractive) and a receptive faculty. To supply this need Aristotle introduced the celebrated 'agent', or, as it was later called, 'constructive' intellect.

Aristotle also endeavoured to clarify his position with the aid of another analogy that was to have a long career. As under the influence of light colours hitherto neutral become actual and can then be received by the sense of sight, so the potential intelligibles hidden in objects of sense become actual under the ray of the active intelligence. Yet here again the analogy gives rise to a difficulty. Whereas physical light is an agency quite distinct from both object and sense (in the later scholastic terminology, it is the *medium quo* of vision), the active intelligence is itself a correlative to the receptive intelligence as form is to matter. Aristotle acknowledged this; indeed, he emphasized it. 'This [active] intelligence', he wrote, 'is separate from the other and pure [i.e., without any potency], being in its own essence actuality',[2] and again: 'once separated from the body this intellect is immortal, yea, eternal' [*aidios*, that is, existing before and after corporeal life].[3] Aristotle thus posited an active intelligence capable of a separate existence; that is, he posited a substance. He had previously posited a substantial Mind as an intellective principle. Are the two to be identified? If so, it would seem that the mind/active intelligence must be either a being entirely outside the human *psyche*, or else itself a *psyche* of the Platonic type, joined to a substantial body. If neither of these, what relationship then has the mind to the active intelligence? Here we find ourselves caught in the knot of questions which Aristotle frankly declared to be among those at once the most

[2] *De anima* 430 a 17–19. In what follows I have been guided chiefly by F. Neurens, *L'évolution de la Psychologie d'Aristote* (Louvain, 1948).
[3] *De anima* 430 a 22–23.

important and the most puzzling encountered by philosophers. He himself gave no clear answer in his surviving works, and thinkers in succeeding ages were forced to extend his doctrines if they wished to reach practical conclusions.

The Arab and medieval commentators gave little attention to the relation of Nûs to Psyche in the writings of Aristotle, and in consequence this topic was not debated until modern scholars had carefully collated all the relevant passages in the *De anima*. Medieval thinkers were more exercised by the problem of the agent intellect and its place in the process of understanding, and opinions were divided into two main streams. The one was that of those who held that the active intellect was an intrinsic component part of the human intelligence. This was the considered opinion of St Thomas, and several modern commentators have adhered to this view, which is indeed the interpretation of Aristotle that is philosophically the most defensible. Nevertheless, we can understand Aristotle in this sense only if we can overcome or ignore several grave difficulties. We must in the first place meet the objection that this interpretation of a crucial text[4] runs counter to the firm statements of Aristotle in which he equates Mind with the active intellect and asserts that it enters the soul from without and is 'separate' from it.[5] Moreover, we encounter the technical difficulty allowed by Aristotle himself, of explaining how the active and receptive elements of intellection can exist within one faculty. In consequence of these difficulties, most ancient and medieval thinkers before Aquinas held that Aristotle's agent intellect is an agent coming upon or into the soul from outside, though to square this with Aristotle's own words in the crucial text already mentioned they had recourse to an unusual, if not inadmissible, translation.[6]

This explanation took two main forms. The one understood by the agent intellect an external substance or power acting upon the

[4]The text is *De anima* 430 a 10–14. 'As throughout the whole of Nature there is a potential principle in every kind of being, as also an efficient cause that brings them into existence – as does each craft with respect to its material – so it is necessary to find these different principles in the soul (ἐν τῇ ψυχῇ).' The last three words in this interpretation bear a strictly determined sense = 'within the soul'.

[5]*De generatione animalium* 736 b 27–8. 'Our only explanation must be that mind alone enters from without and is alone the divine element [in intellectual beings],' And Aristotle adds, with an emphasis which is verbally unique in his writings (736 b 5–8): 'When and how and whence mind comes is a most difficult question, which we must answer carefully and as best we may.'

[6]The phrase 'in the soul' must be taken as meaning 'in the case of the soul', contrary to the normal Greek usage. Professor W. K. C. Guthrie, almost alone among present-day Aristotelian scholars, holds that Aristotle's 'agent intellect' is the Prime Mover, Aristotle's God.

individual soul: with Alexander of Aphrodisias it was the power of the divinity actualizing the human soul regarded as 'matter'; with the Neoplatonists, it was an emanation of the divinity filling the human soul; with Augustine it was a divine light enlightening the human faculty which was of its own powers capable of a lower form of knowledge only; with Avicenna, it was a soul-substance pouring its intellectual light of forms upon the human soul, which was capable of preparing itself for the reception of this light. The other explanation, which was that of Averroës, allowed to the human soul a purely receptive function, with no existence in its own right as an intellectual, spiritual being. For him, the external agent intellect was the only soul, in the full sense of the word, and the individual human 'soul' became real and individual only when enlightened by the agent intellect.

The preceding paragraphs will have shown that the important topics of the nature of the human soul and of the process of knowledge were inevitably confused owing to a lack both of precision and of final pronouncement on the part of Aristotle himself, and in particular owing to his failure to harmonize the two seemingly incompatible views of the soul as simply a metaphysical 'form' and as a mind-substance existing in its own right. In concluding this review, it may be well to set out the principal statements as to the nature of the soul made, according to the most probable explanation of his words, by the Philosopher himself, abstracting altogether from the interpretations of later thinkers. We may say, then:

First, that man, as presented to us in the living world of beings, is distinguished from all other beings of which we have knowledge by his possession of a rational intellect. This is essentially immaterial, simple, incorruptible and actual.
Secondly, that the presence of this intellect cannot be accounted for by any physical potency or generative activity. It would therefore seem that its origin must be sought 'outside' man, and that in some inexplicable way it enters the human being, and is integrated into the human animal, whose nature it then completes and rules.
Thirdly, that of itself this Mind is immortal, but as it is not of itself the human being, it would seem that its survival does not imply the survival of individual human personality.

This presentation of the human mind and soul, though of itself baffling in its conclusions, needs, as will at once be seen, only a few important precisions and amplifications, together with a little dialectic, to enable it to serve admirably as a basis for the Christian doctrine of the nature and powers and destiny of the human soul.

Indeed, little more is needed than the concept of a personal, provident deity, the creator of the individual soul, to remove all the obscurity and inadequacy of the Aristotelian outlook. At the same time, though perhaps with less facility, the Aristotelian framework could be fitted to other spiritual systems of thought – to a pantheist, to a Neoplatonic or to an Averroistic *Weltanschauung*. It is a measure of the greatness of Aristotle as an original thinker that his utterances on the nature of the soul and of the process of knowing lie behind every system of psychology in the Western world (including the Arabian civilization) from his own day to the age of Aquinas and Scotus, and that they still exert their influence upon Christian thought. We may wonder whether any other sequences of words, outside the Scriptures, have been examined and canvassed with such care and assiduity as the few broken sentences, scattered here and there in his works, in which Aristotle set down his intuitions as to the nature and qualities of the human soul.

(ii)

We must now consider the history and fortunes of Aristotle's teaching on the soul and on the process of intellection both in the ancient world and among the Arabian thinkers of the Middle Ages, for it was through them that it first reached the medieval West. The most influential of all the ancient interpreters of Aristotle was Alexander of Aphrodisias, known for many centuries as 'the Commentator' *par excellence*, who flourished *c.* A.D. 200. Many of his commentaries on Aristotle have perished, but his own *De anima* survived and was often copied in the Middle Ages, together with a part of the same work, labelled *De intellectu*, that circulated still more widely. In the ancient world he was celebrated chiefly as a logician, but in the history of thought he is significant as the author of a particular interpretation of Aristotle's doctrine of the soul. Alexander was, as regards his conception of the human being, a materialist; the soul, form of the body, is mortal. Man in his own right has only a 'material' mind – 'material', that is, in the technical sense of potential or receptive. The material mind is activated, as it were by a light, by the agent intellect (the *nûs poeticus*) which is at once an illuminant and an abstractive power. By its action the 'material' mind becomes the mind 'in possession' of understanding, the *intellectus adeptus*. Alexander identifies the agent intellect with Aristotle's 'mind from outside' (*nûs thurathen*), and this in turn with the divinity. According to him, therefore, the human being and its intellect are mortal; understanding comes directly from the action of God.

Themistius, a later interpreter of Aristotle (*c.* 317–*c.* 388), held on the other hand that the 'possible' or 'material' intellect was not a mere potency, but a correlative of the 'active' intellect; both are within the soul and both deathless; the possible intellect when acted upon by the active became the 'speculative' intellect with an incorruptible life of its own. There were thus, in the last centuries of the ancient world, two interpretations or prolongations of Aristotle's enigmatic utterances. The one accepted the need of an external agent to actualize the human mind and enable it to perceive and to grasp the immaterial constituent of the material thing observed by the senses; this external agent was the divine power, understood as Greek thought understood the divinity. The other made the human soul a self-sufficient source of knowledge and understanding, but gave no explanation how this power originated.

Of the two views, that of Alexander of Aphrodisias was the more influential; it appealed, in one way or another, to almost all succeeding thinkers, not excluding Plotinus and, through him, to Augustine. These two, however, and Neoplatonists in general, derived their doctrine of the soul and its powers primarily from Plato and his theory of Forms, though the analogy of the Sun and light as applied to the intellectual illumination in the process of understanding, which was common to both Plato and Aristotle, made it possible for Aristotelian elements, such as the doctrine of the active or agent intellect, to 'contaminate' an essentially Platonic outlook. Augustine's divine illumination of the intellect, for example, though embedded in an essentially Platonic noetic, recalls immediately the divine agent intellect of Aphrodisias, even though it is impossible to trace the historic link between the two thinkers, and we shall see that many medieval philosophers understood the Augustinian scheme in this sense.

The commentaries on Aristotle accompanied the writings of the Philosopher in the eastward journey which has been described on an earlier page, and Alexander's work on the soul, both in its complete form and in the abbreviated version, were translated into Arabic at Baghdad shortly after A.D. 800, and became the ancestors of a whole series of treatises with the same or a similar title. The first was that of Alkindi (*c.* 870), which was later to become, in Latin dress, almost as familiar to the West as its prototype, the work of Alexander. Alkindi used slightly different terminology from his predecessor, but his divisions of the intellect are clearly based on those of the Greek commentator, though his conception of the soul was widely different, being throughout spiritualistic whereas Alexander was a materialist. With Alkindi the agent intellect is a spiritual one (not expressly divine in nature), and is one and the same though acting upon all men. Thus Alexander's agent intellect, God acting upon the mind of each human being, was transformed into an external intelligence, without the character of divinity, acting as an efficient, activating intellect for all members of the human race. This outlook was adopted with modifications by all subsequent Arabian philosophers, whose doctrine on the soul and its faculties is thus derived by direct descent from Alexander of Aphrodisias, though from the beginning they gave to it a 'slant' which ultimately altered its whole appearance.

Alkindi was followed by Alfarabi (d. 950), whose psychology and epistemology represent a blend of Aristotle (as interpreted by Alexander) and the Neoplatonists. In his work on the subject, entitled *De intellectu et intellecto*, the human intelligence, immaterial and indestructible, is of its nature in potency to receive the action of the agent intellect. This latter is an external being, the lowest in the hierarchy of pure intelligences in a system based on Neoplatonism, which is continually radiating upon both the material world and the receptive intellect the intelligible forms of the material individual things of which it is cause. The metaphysical forms of things, therefore, and the intellect which gives the human mind power to understand them, have one and the same source, the lowest of the pure intelligences. The 'receptive' human intellect can prepare itself to receive the intellectual forms, either by a process of abstraction from the material being, or by a higher, intuitive, mystical knowledge, and the end of human endeavour is union with the agent intellect external to itself. Alfarabi himself was a deeply religious *sufi*, who gave spiritual content to what had been a purely intellectual system.

After Alfarabi came Avicenna who, drawing on both Aristotle and the Neoplatonists, endeavoured to combine the two conceptions of the soul as a substance and as a form, and thus approximated to what was to become the common teaching of the scholastics. He provides a very full and on the whole convincing and experiential description of the various degrees of knowledge and the means of acquiring them, and of the various powers of the soul, regarded primarily as an intellect. The soul, as a reasoning faculty, is self-sufficient for all the processes of knowledge save the highest, which is the 'abstraction' of the form from the individual thing. This last task it performs in virtue of the light (comparable to that of the sun in physical sense-perception) of the separate, external agent intellect, and it can prepare itself to receive this light; when the soul-mind has been 'actualized' by this external power it becomes metaphysically independent of the body. The soul is a radiation from the lowest of the pure intelligences that make up the cosmos, and is itself susceptible of other radiations, such as that of the forms of things, from without. Avicenna is thus inheritor, here as elsewhere in his system, of both Aristotle and Plotinus, and from both of them he takes a soul which is, when perfected by intelligence, an immaterial, indestructible being.

Averroës, commenting on *De anima*, agrees in many respects with Avicenna, but differs in his estimate of the soul. In his psychology he combines the teaching of Alexander and Themistius, dropping certain elements from both. According to him the individual human soul is a merely sensitive soul, generated by the parents and corruptible; it is united with the body, of which it is the form, and it disappears at death. Essentially different from and external to the human being is the unique intellective soul, incorruptible and immortal, which stands in relation to the human being as the Intelligence stands to each sphere of the Aristotelian cosmos – that is, in contact with them and influencing them. This intellective soul or 'agent intellect', when in contact with a suitably disposed human imaginative power 'engenders a receptivity' (to use Gilson's phrase) of intelligible truth which Averroës calls the 'possible' intellect, and which is the agent intellect rendered particular in the individual human being during the act of understanding. Averroës himself takes an analogy from the sun striking with its light various visible bodies, each of which receives light while the sun shines upon it. Thus the individual human intellect has actuality and individuality only when and while it is illuminated by the unique intellective soul, and even then its individuality is not really its own, but that of the agent intellect. Thus the individual human intelligence has no existence in its own right, though its thoughts and intellectual achievements, when enlightened by the agent intellect, help to enrich the latter, to whom, indeed, they rightly belong as to their only cause. This is the celebrated monopsychism of Averroës, which he took to be the authentic interpretation of Aristotle, and which he held as a philosopher, thus eliminating human individuality and immortality, while as a Muslim he accepted through faith, as a divine act of power, the existence of both.

One other name must be mentioned, that of Dominic Gundisalvi, the Italian scholar who became archdeacon of Segovia. Gundisalvi himself wrote a treatise *De anima* (between 1126 and 1150), in which he followed in general Avicenna. The soul is both substance and form, made by God out of 'spiritual matter'. Its intellect, on the higher levels of cognition, is actualized by the light of the agent intellect, which is God. In addition to the intellect, whose object is Form, the soul possesses wisdom, by which it has knowledge of itself, of intelligible things, and of God. Gundisalvi thus juxtaposes, without full conflation, Arabian and Christian teaching. His work was extremely popular, and helped to increase the confusion which already existed as to the nature of the soul.

This brief and over-simplified summary may at least have shown that the largely fluid teaching of Aristotle, to which precision had been given in different directions by Alexander and Themistius, had passed down the centuries as a parent stem on which successive thinkers had grafted their various elaborations. Whatever their differences, they had followed Aristotle's lead in two important respects. By concentrating their attention on the purely psychological pronouncements of the Philosopher, they had tended in their conception of the soul to neglect all that was not intellectual. The soul of which they write, therefore, has not the richness of content of the Platonic soul, still less that of the Christian soul. And secondly, partly as a consequence of this neglect and of their lack of interest in the 'personality' and 'vital force' of the individual, they had continued to feel the difficulty that had seemed insoluble to Aristotle, that of explaining whence came the power of a being which as agent actuated itself as potency. One and all, therefore, of those who followed Alexander, felt it necessary to posit an entirely external agent to actualize the potential or 'material' intellect, and the Neoplatonic system, with its emanation down the scale of intelligences, provided a solution ready to hand.

The great scholastics of the mid-thirteenth century, who had been nurtured for the most part upon an Augustinian noetic with its supernatural, mystical overtones, were now presented with a rich literature of works upon the soul and its powers, stretching back from Gundisalvi and the Arabs to the works of Aristotle. Their first impulse was to apply the system of Avicenna to clarify that of Augustine, making of the agent intellect of the former the divine illumination of the latter. Then, when Averroës appeared, with his commentary on Aristotle, they were faced with new difficulties. Some, and among them Siger of Brabant, at least in the early stages of his career, adopted the Arabian philosopher's solution of the problem. Others, and chiefly Albert the Great and Aquinas, while using both Avicenna and Averroës, based themselves on the pure doctrine of Aristotle's *De anima*, neglecting the indications that the soul, or the agent intellect, came into the human being 'from outside'. St Thomas, in particular, gave in his *De anima* a coherent and viable account of the intellective soul of the Aristotelian tradition, though even he did not have occasion to integrate this with the Christian, Augustinian conception of a richly endowed, many-sided spiritual being. After Aquinas, the attack on Aristotle had the effect of withdrawing attention from the *De anima* and the Thomist solution. but the problems of epistemology and psychology had become so much a part of the atmosphere of the schools of the thirteenth century that they remained in the forefront of the thought of both Duns Scotus and William of Ockham.

PART FOUR

The Achievement of the Thirteenth Century

CHAPTER EIGHTEEN
The Philosophical Revolution of the Thirteenth Century

The history of Western thought in the thirteenth century is dominated by the revolution caused by the introduction into the consciousness of northern Europe of the great stream of Aristotelian philosophy. The history of this revolution is by no means simple or straightforward, and it has not yet been finally grasped in all its details; in the past it has suffered from over-simplification, both as to the matter and the manner of the revolution that was effected.

In the first place, as we have seen, Aristotle was not the only arrival. He came borne upon, or rather half-submerged by, a great tidal wave of Aristotelian scholarship, the tradition of more than a thousand years of comment and criticism from Alexander of Aphrodisias to Dominic Gundisalvi. Moreover, this literature of comment was seasoned and augmented by thick layers of Arabian and Jewish thought, while as a rider upon Aristotle came a considerable quantity of pure Neoplatonic doctrine, supported by a secondary but quite separate stream, that of the newly diffused Dionysian writings. The masters of the thirteenth century were thus faced, not only with an array of new texts of ancient writers, but with an elaborate and highly intelligent body of comment and criticism upon them. These in due course were to be examined, not only as all criticism upon a text must be examined, but also for the purpose of eliminating matter which was unacceptable to any Christian thinker.

The effect of this massive influx of new material of the highest intellectual value was to confuse as well as to revolutionize all existing modes of thought, and the disturbance was rendered still more widespread by the piecemeal and long-drawn-out character of the invasion of philosophical material; Aristotle himself, logical treatises apart, was almost a century in arriving, accompanied by several pseudo-Aristotelian and Neoplatonic treatises. Half-way through the process the great commentary of Averroës appeared, and later came a new and more accurate translation of Aristotle and Neoplatonist writings from the Greek. As a result, the thirteenth century at Paris and Oxford and within the schools of the friars was an epoch of unexampled intellectual activity and ferment, with rapid changes and new alignments. It is not surprising that the modern historiography of the century should itself have seen corresponding changes of attitude and emphasis, with an overall picture showing ever more detail and depth.

When medieval thought first came to be studied intensively, in the 1870s and 1880s, the thirteenth century was regarded as having witnessed a struggle between Aristotle and Arabian thought and the forces of ecclesiastical obscurantism, in which the latter were finally defeated. But, in the 1880s, the pioneer and epoch-making researches of Franz Ehrle discovered another tension, that between the Aristotelian philosophy of Thomism and the Augustinian position of conservative theologians, principally Franciscan; the final result was the victory of Thomism. Two decades later Pierre Mandonnet stressed the novelty of the combined work of Albert the Great and Thomas Aquinas in making Aristotle viable for Christian theologians; he also showed that originally the Dominicans and Franciscans agreed in their distrust of Aristotle, and that the division between the two orders in philosophical outlook was due to the attacks of the conservatives upon Aquinas, which precipitated the formation of 'schools of thought' in the parties to the controversy. Mandonnet also was the first to exhibit the historical Siger of Brabant as the originator and the leader of the 'Latin Averroists' whom Renan had indicated but had failed to comprehend. He accepted, however, the general pattern presented by Ehrle, of an Augustinian philosophy threatened by the new Christian Aristotelian system, and he saw in Siger and his friends an advocacy of the 'double truth' derived from Averroës. More recently still, Fernand van Steenberghen has revised the picture once again. He has shown that Augustinism as a philosophical system was the reaction of a few conservative thinkers, most of them Franciscans, to the integral Aristotelian scheme of Aquinas; before the arrival of St Thomas, which came near to coinciding with that of Siger, all theologians had used Aristotle as they pleased while following Augustine in theological matters; now St Thomas accepted Aristotle, emended where necessary, as the basic authority in questions of pure philosophy. As for Siger and his friends, they now appeared primarily as integral Aristotelians, committed to the pure word of the Philosopher more rigidly than Aquinas; the influence of Averroës upon them was minimized, and the theological orthodoxy of Siger defended. On the other hand, the condemnations of 1270 and 1277, once regarded as the futile resistance of conservatism to Thomism, were now seen as an epoch-making pronouncement which cast a permanent shadow over Christian Aristotelianism, directed the attention of theologians to other interests, and put an end once and for all to the building of grand syntheses of philosophy and theology.

In what follows we shall first consider the state of the schools at the opening of the thirteenth century, then examine the attempts to 'contain' the floods of Aristotelian thought, and finally watch the infiltration of Greek and Arabian thought at Paris and Oxford prior to 1250.

The half-century that passed between the publication of the great text-books of Gratian and the Lombard and the first prohibition of the works of Aristotle at Paris in 1210, appears at first sight as an interlunary period containing few signs of important development or change, and witnessing few movements of thought. It is certainly true that for more than sixty years after the death of Gilbert de la Porrée no thinker or theologian of the first rank appeared in Western Europe, and though doubtless abundant material for the history of the age still remains unpublished and unknown, it is scarcely likely that a figure of the first magnitude remains to be revealed. The celebrities of the period such as Peter the Chanter, Alain of Lille, Robert de Curzon and Stephen Langton have all in different degrees the characteristics of the traditional 'biblical' and 'positive' theologian who makes little use of philosophy and certainly has no complete system of thought. Yet underneath this surface of tradition and mediocrity, a whole culture was changing, and the world of 1210 was a very different one from that of 1155 both in its institutional forms and in its interior spirit. The monastic centuries had ended and the age of the universities, the scholastic age, had taken their place.

Of all the agencies of change the most influential was the formalization of higher education and its close relationship to the two chief 'learned professions' of law and theology that grew so greatly in numerical strength and social importance in the latter half of the twelfth century. In Abelard's day the individual master was everything: he could, within certain conventional limits, teach what he would and how he would, and his pupils made what they could and would of his teaching. Masters often changed their place of teaching, and students still more often sat at the feet of a succession of masters. There was no formal curriculum, no set examination or degree (though in this the lawyers were probably fifty years ahead of the theologians), no set syllabus or text-book, no prescribed 'terms' or length of study. If the profession of law was already becoming a close corporation, that of the philosopher and theologian was still fluid.

By the time that Stephen Langton left Paris for Rome and Canterbury all had changed. Higher education had grown into a system recognizable as the remote ancestor of the system of the modern world. Times, terms, subjects, lectures and degrees were all on the point of becoming fixed and standardized. The cathedral schools throughout France were no longer educational centres of equal or at least of ever-varying importance; Paris had become the unique metropolis, with a numerous student population drawn from the whole of France, augmented by arrivals from England, the Low Countries and Germany. Through this mill – or at least into this mill – passed all those who hoped to earn their living by mental work or services as opposed to manual or commercial employment. One great difference there was between the medieval and the modern system of education: with the former, university education began at a stage in a boy's life only a little later than the break in modern times between the preparatory and the public school, or the lower and upper schools of the older city type. For the medieval boy the parish priest or the local grammar school or the convent school led him to the university at fourteen or fifteen.

The standardization of this curriculum had an important cultural effect which remained till the fifteenth century. Whereas in the monasteries and many of the cathedral schools a literary education had continued till adolescence or beyond, not only preceding but also accompanying the more technical disciplines of dialectic, in the new world all that was needed of a grammar school was a firm grounding in Latin grammar, syntax and composition; this once gained, the pupil was eager to begin the clerk's training of logic and dialectic, which itself in the case of abler or more ambitious students was only a preparation for the professional studies of medicine, law and theology. The literary teaching of a Bernard at Chartres was reduced to a study of language in its logical aspects – the *Sprachlogik* of the twelfth and thirteenth centuries. Hence, by the beginning of the thirteenth century not only literature, but philosophy also had become a propaedeutic discipline, to be traversed as rapidly as possible. This was unquestionably the principal cause of the disappearance of humanism and of elegant Latin literature between the age of St Bernard and that of St Dominic. A training in letters, which in the early twelfth century implied an ability to appreciate and imitate the Latin classics, in the early thirteenth century meant little more than a knowledge of the curial or notarial forms and expressions, the *dictamen*, as it was called. For the great majority of students, logic took the place of letters.

In addition to its fatal effect upon literary humanism, the systematization of the arts school at Paris had also a depressive influence on the study of philosophy. The propaedeutic character of the arts course affected both pupil and master. The former was eager to have done with it as soon as might be in order to begin the training for a career; philosophy, therefore, at least for a majority of the arts students, tended to go the way of literature, and to become a technical education in logic, logical grammar and disputation. The master also in most cases regarded his office as temporary. The less talented would pass from Paris to the lesser schools; for those who aimed higher the maxim applied: *non est consenescendum in artibus* – 'don't stay for life in the arts school'. They taught for a few years, and then passed on to take their course for the mastership in theology. There was indeed nothing at this time in the arts school that could satisfy a superior mind. Moreover, now that the artists had been separated so completely from the theologians the latter, from their position of eminence, kept a jealous watch upon their inferiors. The artists must not be allowed to arrogate to themselves any of the philosophical problems, such as the immortality of the soul, or the relationship of predestination to free will, which impinged upon theology. Any attempt to discuss the most vital philosophical problems was therefore discouraged, and we shall see that the jealous eyes of the theologians were probably directly concerned with the first prohibitions of Aristotle.

Such then was the aspect of the schools of Paris when the first infiltration of the Aristotelian treatises began: an arts course confined to logic and formal dialectic; a theological school of masters maintaining the traditional approach, themselves not greatly interested in philosophy and resolved to keep the masters of arts within the fixed bounds of their province. Their function was, in the phrase of van Steenberghen, to train the mind, not to feed it or fill it.

While recent research has shown clearly that by *c.* 1200 the bulk of Aristotle was, potentially at least, available for Western use, the currents of teaching in the arts school at Paris at the turn of the century are still obscure. It is out of the dark, so to say, that the first events emerge.

In 1210 the provincial synod of Sens, of which the bishop of Paris was a member, passed a decree against many heretics and especially against the writings and supporters of David of Dinant and Amaury de Bène; it added: 'Neither the writings of Aristotle on natural philosophy nor their commentaries are to be read at Paris in public or private, and this we forbid under penalty of excommunication.'[1] On this it may be remarked that, while it is clear that Amaury de Bène was condemned as a heretic, nothing is known of his writings or their connection with Aristotle. David of Dinant, on the other hand, is accused by both Albert the Great and Roger Bacon of using Aristotle and of interpreting him in a materialistic and pantheistic sense. As for the works of Aristotle, they are probably the *Physics,* and *De anima* and the *Metaphysics.* In the prohibition the word *legantur* ('read') bears the technical sense of 'use as texts for public or private teaching'. The private reading or use of Aristotle was not forbidden: he was not, so to say, 'put on the Index'. Furthermore, the prohibition applied only to the arts school, and was only local; it was not at that time made general by Rome. The theologians could and did read and use Aristotle; so did the arts schools of other universities, such as Oxford and Toulouse; at the latter, indeed, which only began its life in 1229, one of the advantages claimed in the prospectus was the freedom to use Aristotle enjoyed by its masters.

Five years later in 1215, Robert de Curzon, then cardinal legate, who was himself an old master of arts of Paris and a fellow-student there of Innocent III, proclaimed a set of statutes for the university. In these he laid down lists of text-books, and decreed that the masters of arts 'must not lecture on the books of Aristotle on metaphysics and natural philosophy, or on summaries of them; nor concerning the doctrine of master David of Dinant or the heretic Amaury or Maurice of Spain'.[2] This clearly depends upon the decree of 1210; the two heretics were still remembered, and the 'summaries' are probably the paraphrases of Aristotle by Avicenna. As for Maurice of Spain, a long controversy has failed to effect a decision: no teacher of that name is known, and Mandonnet's suggestion that *Mauricii* was a misreading of *Mauri,* and that the 'Spanish Moor' was Averroës, though unsupported by any evidence, is plausible, but no more than that.

So matters rested till 1231. In that year Gregory IX promulgated the Bull *Parens scientiarum* (13 April) which has been called the Magna Carta of Paris university. In it he decreed that 'those books of natural

---

[1]Denifle and Chatelain, *Chartularium Universitatis Parisiensis,* I 70.
[2]Denifle and Chatelain, *op. cit.,* I 78–9.

philosophy, which were with good reason prohibited in a provincial council, shall not be used at Paris till they have been examined and purged from all suspicion of error'.[3] A week later arrangements were made for the absolution of all who had violated the prohibitions of 1210 and 1215, and on 23 April the pope set up a commission of three to examine the prohibited books and expurgate them, 'so that when dubious matter has been removed, the rest may be studied without delay and without offence'. The committee was a strong one: the chairman was William of Auxerre, the distinguished Paris theologian, and another member was Stephen of Provins, the friend of Michael Scot the translator, who clearly was to act as the Aristotelian expert. In the event, the committee never reported – why, we do not know, but the death in the same year of William of Auxerre is probably enough to account for the lack of action. Fourteen years later, the prohibition of 1210–15 was extended by Innocent IV to Toulouse.

These decrees would seem to have been effective among the artists at Paris, for a kind of 'crammer's guide' to Paris examinations, written *c.* 1230–40, and discovered at Barcelona by Mgr Grabmann, shows that while the *Ethics* of Aristotle were taught, the *Metaphysics* and books on natural philosophy were clearly no part of the syllabus, and the contemporary commentaries on the *Ethics* show no trace of any conflict between the findings of 'philosophers' and those of 'theologians' such as developed later. Moreover, the surviving works of those who are known to have lectured in the arts school during these decades are almost entirely concerned with logic, and the remainder are ethical commentaries. There is also an apparent exception which helps to 'prove the rule'. This is the Englishman Roger Bacon, who tells us that he lectured at Paris on the *Physics* and *Metaphysics* of Aristotle, the *Liber de causis* of Proclus, and other works. The ban on Aristotle, as has been seen, never affected Oxford, and the Aristotelian writings entered there and were the subject of instruction and commentary. No doubt by 1240 the papal prohibition of Aristotle had lost its urgency, and the artists of Paris may well have felt that it was time for France to catch up with England. In any case, the tide was now flowing in favour of the Philosopher. In 1252 the *De anima* was prescribed as an examination subject by the English 'nation' at Paris, and in 1255 all the current works of Aristotle were prescribed for the whole Faculty. It is therefore at first sight surprising that on 19 January 1263, Urban IV, when confirming the

[3]Denifle and Chatelain, *op. cit.*, I 138, 143.

bull *Parens scientiarum* of Gregory IX, should have reproduced in full its prohibition of 'those books on nature which were prohibited' at Sens in 1210.[4] Various explanations have been given: Mandonnet saw in it the papal reaction to the transgression of the earlier decrees, but such a move would seem both tardy and futile, and would in any case have been worded more drastically. Ehrle, after long consideration, took the view that it was directed against the first manifestations of 'Latin Averroism', but against this it may be urged that the pope would have done something more effective than to exhume a decree thirty years old without any comment. Perhaps the best explanation, so simple as to be overlooked by earlier scholars, is that of van Steenberghen: that the pope gave directions for the bull *Parens scientiarum* to be reissued (a common practice with the Curia), and that the Chancery copied it out in full, the clerk perhaps not even realizing that Aristotle (who was not mentioned by name) was stigmatized by Gregory IX. Certainly by 1250-60 the Philosopher was being treated in many quarters as a kind of precursor of Christ, an intellectual Baptist, and Roger Bacon could say that he was now called antonomastically 'the Philosopher', just as St Paul was called 'the Apostle'.

Meanwhile, among the theologians who had never been hindered from a free use of Aristotle, a new type was appearing, that of the academic master who, during his career as teacher, produced a comprehensive manual or *Summa* covering the whole of theology and used philosophy and the dialectical method to a greater or lesser degree to deduce or explain his conclusions, thereby revealing to the historian his standpoint in regard to his contemporaries and to the questions in debate at the time. For all these men the tradition of the Church and the Scriptures, largely as interpreted by Augustine, formed the nucleus of their thought; to explain and develop this they drew upon the accumulated and ever increasing stock of philosophical ideas, Neoplatonic, Arabian and in ever growing measure Aristotelian. These they attempted to harmonize as best they might.

The first examples of this type are three masters William of Auxerre (d. 1231), Philip the Chancellor (from 1218; d. 1236), and William of Auvergne (bishop of Paris 1228; d. 1249). All three use the new literature, Aristotelian, Arabian and Neoplatonic; William of Auvergne is in addition a thinker of considerable originality and power, the first of those who, in the course of the thirteenth century,

---

[4]Denifle and Chatelain, *op. cit.*, I 278.

strove to form a synthesis of Christian theology and philosophy. He knows Avicenna well and uses him, though he opposes his teaching on the eternity of the world and on the separate active intelligence. His greatest praise is, however, reserved for Gabirol, 'the unique, most noble of all philosophers', whom he thought to be a Christian, and Maimonides. He follows Avicenna in using the distinction of *esse* and *existentia* to prove the absolute simplicity of God and his distinction from all other beings, but avoids Arabian determinism by adopting Gabirol's doctrine of the Will of God as the creative power. In epistemology he adopts the Aristotelian teaching on sense-perception, but for intellection he takes the Augustinian illumination, understood as the presentation to the mind by the Word of God of the first principles and ideas of all things external to the mind. He thus abandons altogether the Avicennan teaching of a separate 'agent intellect', and makes of the soul a single, simple intelligence reduced to act by the divine illumination just as the sense of sight is reduced to act by the light of day. Similarly, he follows Augustine in finding the first principles of knowledge and the sciences as reflected from the mirror of the divine mind upon the human intelligence, thus rejecting the Aristotelian reliance upon abstraction and experience as the sources of knowledge.

In the last years of the lifetime of William of Auvergne a new epoch began at Paris as a result of a movement that the most clearsighted could never have foreseen. This was the appearance of the two first and most influential of the orders of friars, followed within a few years by their arrival at the universities of Paris and Oxford, an event which was itself followed shortly by the transference to their ranks of a number of the most eminent masters, and the steady intake, for almost a century, of the most brilliant minds of north-western Europe. As a consequence, of the dozen names of theologians that would occur most readily to the historian in the hundred years between 1250 and 1350 only one or two at the most would be those of secular priests. That during the same period only one or two of the dozen would be Frenchmen was partly due to the same circumstance, and partly to the unique reputation of Paris, which drew to itself, either as student or master, every ambitious and superior mind. The paramount position of Paris in the first half of the century is strikingly shown in the opening words of the bull *Parens scientiarum* of Gregory IX. 'Paris,' the pope began, 'mother of the sciences, like another Cariath Sepher, city of letters, shines clear; where, as it were in wisdom's special workshop ... those prudent in mystical eloquence ... fit and decorate the spouse of Christ with priceless jewels.' This eminence of Paris had the result (paradoxical at first sight) that almost all the great Parisian theologians of the century following the death of William of Auvergne were foreigners: the specifically French character of Parisian thought ceases, not to reappear till the age of Gerson.

The arrival of the friars, besides the noisy controversies to which it gave rise, resulted in the gradual emergence of definite schools of thought divided from each other with some sharpness and jealously maintained by *esprit de corps*. This last result, however, did not make itself apparent until the last quarter of the century.

The two first and greatest orders of friars arose almost simultaneously. Though St Dominic, a Spaniard, was considerably older than St Francis, the latter had received his call to the life of poverty and preaching before Dominic had composed the constitutions for his followers, and though the Preachers were organized as an order before the Minors, each influenced the other in a variety of ways during their first decades of existence. Dominic had from the first intended his followers to be a body of theologically trained priests: they were the first religious order to make of study an essential feature of their life, and in their constitutions it was laid down that individuals were to be dispensed from fasting and liturgical duties if these interfered with application to study. Every Dominican convent was in fact a school, and according to the constitutions contained among its members a master of theology. Each province was to support one or more houses set up as *studia particularia*, to which friars of promise were sent, and certain convents, usually but not always in university towns, were *studia generalia* to which were sent the most brilliant young men from all over the order. Paris, Oxford, Cambridge, Bologna and Cologne were among such houses.

The Franciscans, whose original task had been to preach penance (i.e., moral reform) not doctrine, and whose founder had expressed himself strongly against book learning, soon adopted many of the aims and most of the organization of the Preachers, and from *c.* 1240 onwards the two orders – the two 'student orders' of Roger Bacon – were intellectually indistinguishable, and very soon the other friars, Carmelites and Augustinians, were assimilated to them. At first not even the Preachers had intended to form part of the academic movement of the age, but events were more powerful than designs. Within a few years of their arrival in Paris (the Preachers were there in 1217; the Minors on the outskirts in 1219) a number of the most successful secular masters joined them. In 1225 the English doctor

Haymo of Faversham, with three other masters, joined the Minors in Paris; John of St Giles took the Dominican habit under dramatic circumstances *c.* 1231, and about 1235 or 6 the most celebrated Parisian teacher of his day, the Englishman Alexander of Hales, became a Franciscan. These were far from being the only recruits of note. In England, for example, the two most celebrated Minors, Adam Marsh and Roger Bacon, both joined the order when already men of position, and every master who joined carried with him and subsequently attracted numerous disciples. The conquest of the schools by the friars was indeed complete, and for almost a century no theologian of the very first rank (for Grosseteste was middle-aged when the friars arrived) arose from outside their orders either in England or France.

This sudden shift of balance from the university of secular masters to the schools of the friars inevitably produced rivalry and jealousy. From the first the friars were a law unto themselves and demanded the best of both worlds, which the seculars were in no position to deny them in face of the support of the papacy. They not only refused to take part in the great dispersion of the university of Paris in 1229, but the Dominicans took advantage of the departure of the secular masters to throw open their own school to the students who remained, and Roland of Cremona thus became the first regent master from among the Preachers. When his erstwhile pupil, John of St Giles, joined the order two years later he continued teaching from a second chair. Similarly when Alexander of Hales became a Minor he continued to teach at the Cordeliers. Both these innovations had been made without the consent of the Chancellor, and for twenty years this state of things continued, the friars incepting under their own doctors, who had never received formal licence to teach from the Chancellor. Meanwhile, both orders sent their most brilliant members to the Parisian chairs, which were held in due course, to name but three or four occupants, by such eminent men as Bonaventure, Aquinas, Kilwardby and Pecham. This uneasy truce was broken by the outbreak of hostility to the friars in more than one quarter. The bishops resented their invasion of the fields of preaching, confessing and directing, supported as they were by papal privileges ensuring their liberty of action. The secular clergy in general, both inside and outside the universities, began to challenge the right of the friars to perform priestly and pastoral tasks and to assert a theoretically superior poverty, which in fact implied a sheltered life of study. In consequence, the mendicants became, about the middle of the thirteenth century, the focus of two controversies at

Paris, one on a practical question of privilege, the other on a theoretical problem of vocation. The friars had come to Paris before the regulations of the university had crystallized, and had from the beginning sat very loosely to all ordinances. Their first doctors had come to them from outside and they had continued to fill the chair or chairs in their convents without formal application to the chancellor and without formally becoming members of the college of masters. At the same time, they had insisted that the course in arts should be made by their subjects either before reception of the habit or in a house of studies of the order. The matter came to a head in 1253-4, when the friars refused to obey a decree of the university that lectures should cease pending the settlement of a quarrel between the university and the civic authorities; this was followed by a refusal to take an oath of obedience to the university. In consequence of this, the Dominicans were formally expelled from the university. They appealed to Rome, and the papal decision was ultimately given in their favour. It was this quarrel that delayed the public admission of Bonaventure and Thomas to the master's degree, and it was by papal command that they were finally admitted. Meanwhile an attack on the level of pulpit and pamphlet had been made on the friars by a secular master, William of Saint Amour, and others, impugning the ideal of poverty and mendicancy, and denying the right of the friars to take any part in the pastoral work of the church. This attack had as one of its results the production of elaborate defences of the friars from both Bonaventure and Thomas, while St Amour's book was condemned by the pope in 1256. Of themselves, these controversies had little direct effect on the course of intellectual life at Paris, but it is worth remembering that the great works of Bonaventure, Albert and Thomas, which, taken in their bulk, leave an impression on the reader of pondered and serene intellectual activity, were composed at a centre of violent, bitter and even deadly controversy, when, for Aquinas at least, his academic career, his status as friar and his personal integrity as an orthodox teacher were endangered.

CHAPTER NINETEEN

The Franciscan School at Paris

The Friars Preachers arrived in Paris in 1217; the Friars Minor in 1219. The former came primarily to learn theology, the latter to preach penance; in the event, both remained to teach, and it would be hard to say, as between the university and the friars, which of the two parties was captor and which captive during the next hundred years. Both orders drew great masters into their net, and the masters, resuming their teaching in the friars' convents, drew their brethren in turn back into the sea whence they had been drawn. To the Franciscans came, among others, Haymo of Faversham, Alexander of Hales, Adam Marsh and Roger Bacon, Englishmen all; to the Dominicans, John of St Giles, Robert Bacon and Richard Fishacre.

For our present purpose Alexander of Hales is of the greatest importance, not only in his own right as a distinguished master, but more particularly as the first regent master in the Franciscan convent at Paris, as the teacher of John de la Rochelle and St Bonaventure and, finally, as the patriarch and fountain-head to whom Pecham and others, fifty years later, traced back the characteristic doctrines of the Franciscan, or as they would have it, the Augustinian school of thought. His great *Summa*, 'heavier than a horse, and not his at that', as Roger Bacon remarked bitterly,[1] is, as we have it, a compilation from several hands, but the additions made by John de la Rochelle and others confirm its right to be regarded as the original Franciscan text-book. Alexander sampled all of Aristotle that was available in his day, but he drew also upon the Neoplatonic teaching of Augustine and the Victorines. From Avicebron he took the doctrine of 'spiritual matter', and from Anselm, probably by way of William of Auvergne, his 'ontological' argument for the existence of God. Alexander,

[1] *Opera inedita*, ed. J. Brewer (Rolls Series 15), p. 326.

indeed, has no system, only a 'complex' of doctrines, and he made no thorough use of Aristotle. John de la Rochelle, on the other hand, though his pupil and successor, has a personal outlook, especially on the soul and on the process of knowledge. In the latter question he adopts the Aristotelian abstraction for the lower forms of knowledge, and for these man uses an 'agent intellect' of his own. For the highest truths, and those which exceed the capacities of human nature God is the 'agent intellect', and the Augustinian divine illumination enters in.

The young friar who regarded himself as the disciple of these two masters far surpassed them in gifts and in achievement. With St Bonaventure (Giovanni Fidanza of Bagnorea in Tuscany) we reach one of the twin summits of medieval theology, the Seraphic Doctor who appears as the equal of St Thomas in the *Paradiso* of Dante and in the *Disputa* of Raphael. The poet, indeed, displays the two friars as the representatives of their respective religious families and of Christian theology, and each of them praises the Founder and the genius of the other's order. Whatever may be the historical truth of their personal relationship, Dante, a younger contemporary of those of whom he sang, saw with the prophetic eye of genius the eminence and the lasting significance of the two great doctors who after seven centuries remain, like Plato and Aristotle, supreme in their leadership and their rivalry of systems.

Of the two, Bonaventure is at first sight the more clearly seen.[2] Much is known of his life and actions, and of the judgements of his contemporaries, and some, at least, of his writings are both personal in tone and of great literary charm; in addition, he was concerned with many more public acts of government and administration than was St Thomas. Healed, it was said, as a child by St Francis himself, he followed the arts school at Paris and became a friar in early manhood, when he heard the lectures of Alexander of Hales and perhaps John of Parma and taught as a 'bachelor of the Bible' (1248) and as a 'bachelor of the Sentences' (1250), in which capacity he composed his great *Commentary*. He proceeded as master of theology in 1253 and held the Franciscan chair at Paris, but his solemn reception as master by the university was delayed by the controversy between the seculars and mendicants till August 1257, when he took his degree in company with St Thomas. Shortly before this, in February 1257, he had been nominated and elected minister general of his order at the age of forty or so, and thenceforward was much

[2]Bonaventure was b. *c.* 1217; studied at Paris 1236–42; became a friar 1243; followed theological studies 1243–8.

occupied with its business. In 1273 he was named cardinal bishop of Albano by Pope Gregory X, who owed his tiara to Bonaventure's recommendation; he died at Lyons during the Council in 1274.

Bonaventure was thus a public figure for much of his life. All agree as to his angelic purity of life, his amiability and his outstanding intellectual powers, and all his writings bear the same impress of a lucid and keen intelligence; they show also a consistency and a power of conception and execution of great designs rivalled only by St Anselm and St Thomas, and an ability to erect a theological edifice of many parts and perfect harmony which is surpassed by St Thomas alone. Regarded more closely, however, he is not so easily comprehensible as are the two other saintly doctors just mentioned. He did indeed earn the title of second founder of his order by his skilful government at a time of crisis, by his constitutional work at the chapter of Narbonne, by his commentary on the *Rule* and by his *Life* of St Francis, and undoubtedly his wise presentations of the *via media*, accompanied as it was by an example which all could agree in calling holy, did more than any other agency to make the Franciscan ideal viable for a great order. His programmatic replacement of the ascesis of manual work and scanty sustenance by that of intellectual discipline was, many would say, a salutary inspiration of genius. Yet others will feel that the *Rule* and the *Life* of St Francis, as expounded by Bonaventure, conceal and at times contradict the message, the ideals and the personal commands of Francis himself, that Bonaventure's treatment of his own saintly predecessor John of Parma, and of some conservative friars, was harsh, and that he exercised his authority in a way that would not have been approved by the Founder.

Be this as it may, the writings and the thought of Bonaventure have a richness, a cohesion and a maturity hitherto unknown in the schools. These qualities are seen most clearly, perhaps, in the *Commentary on the Sentences* and in the short *Itinerarium mentis ad Deum*, but they are present everywhere and bear the stamp of genius. When the youth of the writer of the *Commentary* is borne in mind the achievement appears even more remarkable. The character of Bonaventure's use of non-Christian philosophy reflects so clearly the early date of his theological work, and his outlook is in such strong contrast, not to say contradiction, to that of Aquinas that in the early stages of the neoscholastic revival he was neglected, and to most non-Catholic readers in the modern world his views are uncongenial, if not distasteful. More recently, however, the skilful advocacy of his confreres of to-day and the sympathetic presentation of his thought by M. Gilson have gone far to redress the balance. Bonaventure, whether fortunately or unfortunately for his reputation, was called at an early age and irrevocably from his chair at Paris, and that precisely at the moment when the whole intellectual climate of the age was about to be changed by the writings of Albert the Great, of Thomas Aquinas, and of Siger of Brabant. He lived long enough to witness a great part of this revolution and to show his disapproval of much that he saw, and a controversy, not yet ended, has arisen as to the extent of his knowledge and disapproval of the new ways. The two adversaries in chief are no mean pair; they are M. Gilson and Canon F. van Steenberghen. As is the way with controversies between reasonable men, the distance that separates the two parties is smaller now than it was, but the difference remains, as we shall see later in this chapter.

Bonaventure was in a very real, if not in an historically or spiritually integral sense, a devoted follower of St Francis; he was a theologian, and he became also intellectually and spiritually a disciple of St Augustine. The two fundamental and characteristic marks of St Augustine's thought were first, his exclusive concern with the human soul (his own soul writ large) and with God, and, secondly, his view of the whole of human life, individual and social, as a divinely planned and assisted progress towards the vision of God. In both these respects Bonaventure was a faithful disciple. His two absorbing interests – which in fact coalesce – are to penetrate the revealed mysteries, and especially the mystery of God Himself, as a theologian, and to describe the progress of the individual human soul towards union with God. He writes and thinks throughout his work implicitly, if not explicitly, for those who, like himself, have no other interest and purpose in life, and who share his faith, his assumptions and his desires. He is a friar, a devoted religious, studying and writing theology for the benefit of his own soul and those of his brethren. Philosophy, and in particular pagan philosophy, is to be used when it can help towards this end, but a pagan philosopher has at best a very limited authority and value: he does not know the truths of faith and he has not God's direct help; he must therefore often err. Moreover, knowledge without faith and about purely secular matters is in itself worthless. Bonaventure's field of interest is narrow (though not shallow) compared with those of both Augustine and Aquinas. Augustine was a pastoral teacher, a great controversialist, a philosopher of history and an individual with a keen interest in others. Aquinas, though he too has with Bonaventure a goal which is almost exclusively theological, has a wide concern with every human activity that affects or is affected by a man's religion – law, politics, the civic virtues, every object and pursuit that is part of the life of a Christian, whether bishop, religious or lay, whether pope or king, whether active or contemplative. It is his concentration upon the one important reality that has made Bonaventure difficult reading for historians to-day. On matters touching the life of a friar he can be both copious and extremely realistic and practical, as may be seen in some parts of his *Commentary on the Rule*, or in his list of reasons for not lending books, noted by Gilson, but on the interests and pursuits, the virtues and the sins of ordinary human life he is less explicit. The world is seen as a reflection of God, and human life as a progress towards the ecstatic vision.

Yet Bonaventure is far from being merely an ascetical or a mystical theologian; he is an intellectual, and not of the least. To come to him from William of Auvergne or Alexander of Hales is to move from one climate to another. The reader is at once aware that he is listening to one who has a clear programme, and a mind capable of ordering and illuminating every topic. His achievement is in its way as notable as that of Aquinas. He draws together all the strands of his learning to give an account of God, of creation, of the angelic choirs, of the soul and its nature, knowledge and virtues, of grace and the Gifts of the Holy Spirit, of the progress of the soul and its union with God; and all this is seen by a mind of great clarity and creative power. His was the first great synthesis of thought and doctrine. It has often been said that we have only a fragment, a youthful master's first sketch, of a system, and that had Bonaventure not been snatched from Paris to rule a great order when barely forty, he might well have given us a corpus of theology, and even of philosophy, as complete as that of St Thomas. Where should we be, it is asked, if Aquinas had died soon after writing his *Commentary on the Sentences*? The argument has force, and doubtless Bonaventure would have produced more than one theological masterpiece had he remained in the academic world. Yet it is clear that his genius was precocious, even more than that of St Thomas, while on the other hand it is not at all true that his election to high office ended his public career as theologian. Works such as the *Hexaemeron* and the other conferences, and the *Itinerarium* itself, broaden and deepen the teaching of his *Commentary on the Sentences*, and his sermons continue to his last years without giving any indication whatsoever of any change of outlook.

While all the Paris masters had regarded Augustine as the supreme master in theology and while all had adopted parts of the Aristotelian and Arabian philosophies as need arose, Bonaventure is the first to declare that he is professedly following Augustine's thought as well as his theology. In this he differs entirely from Anselm, who had declared that he followed Augustine in all things, but shows no trace of adopting the characteristic Augustinian epistemology. Bonaventure for his part builds his system on the three most significant doctrines of Augustine: the metaphysic of light, the divine illumination of the intellect, and the seminal tendencies in matter (*rationes seminales*). The two first of these were in origin Neoplatonic; the third is a Platonic suggestion amplified by the Stoics. The light-metaphysic, adumbrated by Augustine following Plotinus, and adopted in another line of development by Alfarabi, Avicenna and the pseudo-Aristotelian *Liber de causis*, probably came to Bonaventure from Alexander of Hales. For Bonaventure light is the ultimate metaphysical constituent of all visible bodies; it is the *forma substantialis corporeitatis*, and beings differ in nobility in proportion to their participation in light. As for the doctrine of seminal tendencies, a key doctrine of Augustine, Bonaventure regarded it as a metaphysical necessity to account for formal and substantial change. Only the presence of an aptitude for this or that 'form' could explain how a secondary agent (in contrast to God the Creator) could change one substance into another. A nominal pre-existence 'in the potentiality of matter' would not, in his opinion, suffice. Finally, and most characteristic, is Bonaventure's teaching on the process of knowing. Here he adopts a duality of methods which has behind it a long history reaching back to Plotinus. On the level of sense perception he adopts the Aristotelian theory of abstraction, by which the sensible object is 'purified' for entry into the intelligence. In the next stage, in opposition to the Arabs, he holds both agent and possible intellect to be faculties of the soul, and the possible intellect is in his opinion able to accept as true the intelligible species which is presented to it by the agent intellect. This is sufficient for our knowledge of things when it is a question of mere comprehension, but by a third process the mind is able to recognize the truth of a thing understood (i.e., its correspondence with reality) by virtue of an innate light which is a reflection of the divine ideas; this light supplies the standard, the criterion of truth (*regula veritatis*). As with Augustine, so with Bonaventure, the necessity for this divine light is to be found in the eternal, immutable nature of truth, as opposed to the mutability of all created things and agencies; this truth we can only see by virtue of the *rationes aeternae*, the illumination of the divine ideas. We have therefore two kinds of knowledge, the uncertain knowledge of things and the certain knowledge of intelligible truths. We can see here behind Augustine the Platonic distinction between 'opinion' and 'knowledge'. Similarly in the practical sphere we can make a practical judgement of our own powers, but the ultimate judgement of right and wrong, and the conviction of conscience, must come from the divine illumination.

Besides these important doctrines, Bonaventure has some others adumbrated in Neoplatonism and Augustine. One such is the multiplicity of forms. To St Bonaventure a form is not, as with St Thomas, an actuation which is at the same time a limitation; it is for him a perfection of a being which makes it possible for further substantial perfections to come upon it. Another doctrine is that of 'spiritual matter', which on analysis signifies little more than the potential element in a spiritual being. Strange and unreal as may seem to us the care devoted by medieval theologians to a consideration of the angelic beings, the matter is of crucial importance to those who are convinced of the reality of another kind of spiritual being, the human soul, for in the 'angels' the being of an incorporeal spirit can be isolated and discussed without the complications caused by a material body. Moreover, this discussion has a particular bearing upon the matter of human individuality. If an angel, or a human soul, has no 'matter', no potential metaphysical constituent, which it possesses in common with all or certain other spirits, how is the individual to be distinguished? Each angel, St Thomas was to answer, is a species by itself; each human soul is individualized by its body when this is united with the soul, and by its relationship to the body when the two are separated. To many, these answers have appeared as the weakest elements in Thomist psychology, and it is unquestionable that the Neoplatonic-Augustinian doctrine on the soul and its powers is more easily compatible with Christian teaching and practice than is the Aristotelian.

St Bonaventure is often described as a mystic. If by this it is implied that he himself was in the fullest theological sense an experiential mystic and that this influenced his doctrine and method of presentation, it can only be replied that nowhere in his writings does he claim this or give clear evidence of such experiences. If, on the other hand, all that is meant is that St Bonaventure regarded the mystical experience as a foretaste of the vision of God to which every Christian must aspire, and as given to some souls here on earth, and that, writing for religious and regarding theology as primarily the science of a holy life, he includes in his teaching much that now would be called 'mystical' as distinct from 'dogmatic' theology, the title may be allowed, though perhaps it would be better to call him a mystical theologian than a mystic. Certainly he teaches in the

Itinerarium that the end and crown of the progress of man's soul towards God is the unitive ectasy of love, as instanced in the *Life* of St Francis. In his description of the last stages of this progress Bonaventure uses the language of the pseudo-Denis and of Richard of St Victor, and the ascent of the mind and soul to God follows the stages of the Neoplatonic ascent. We are therefore presented once more with the problem that faces readers of Plotinus, of Augustine, of the Victorines and of all those who employ the Neoplatonic phraseology: how far is the experience described a fully mystical, supernatural experience in the sense attached to that phrase by the classical mystical writers and theologians? Is the writer speaking of what he knows from his own life? Or is he doing no more than an expert in mystical theology might do, though perhaps more vividly? Certainly there is in the *Itinerarium*, as in much Neoplatonic and Dionysian writing, a hint of intellectual effort and of schematic advance which has little reference to St Francis and Monte La Verna.

In recent years the question has often been asked: how far is St Bonaventure in agreement with St Thomas? Or, to take another aspect of the problem: how far is St Bonaventure hostile to Aristotle and to philosophy in general?

When a group of eminent Franciscan scholars undertook the so-called Quaracchi critical edition of St Bonaventure's works (1882–1902), they worked with the sound of Leo XIII's recall to Thomism still in their ears, and tended in consequence to adopt a 'concordist' policy of reconciling all apparent differences between Bonaventure and Thomas. It was not long, however, before the great Dominican historians such as Denifle and Mandonnet found themselves forced to underline the revolutionary nature of St Thomas's thought and the consequent differences between him and Bonaventure, and in due course a new generation of Franciscan writers, such as Ephrem Longpré, so far from smoothing away the differences, took pride in them and defended the position of Bonaventure when he appeared to differ from St Thomas. A different slant was given to the controversy by M. Gilson in his study of Bonaventurian philosophy. He saw in St Bonaventure a determined enemy of Aristotle and of all merely human thought or science; he also used the then accepted chronology of the lives of Bonaventure and Albert to show that the former was directly opposed to the latter in his use of Aristotelian thought and methods. This last point was taken up by Fernand van Steenberghen, who had no difficulty in showing that as Bonaventure's principal work was composed before St Albert had formulated his Aristotelian position, it could not be said that St Bonaventure 'refused to allow himself to follow Albert'. He then went on to underline once more the radical agreement of the two, and denied that Bonaventure's hostility to Aristotle was as thorough as Gilson had suggested. Bonaventure's position, in fact, like that of St Thomas, could be described as Aristotelian affected by Neoplatonism.

While it is clear that on more than one historical point and possibly also on some points of philosophy van Steenberghen had successfully revised Gilson, many readers will feel that the overall judgement on Bonaventure of the latter is more valid than that provided by his critic from Louvain, at least in his earlier works. No doubt it is true that Bonaventure uses Aristotle freely, not only as the supreme master in logic and dialectic, but also as the philosopher who put into currency so many basic concepts and technical terms, such as matter and form, potency and act, active and 'possible' intellect and the like, and that therefore his thought is in fact saturated with Aristotle. This however, could be said of almost every great thinker from Plotinus downwards. Aristotle's logic was the common heritage of all philosophers down to our own day, and some of his basic metaphysical concepts were likewise common property. What differentiates Aquinas from Bonaventure is the attitude towards human intellectual activity. The whole scope of Bonaventure's thought might be summed up in the title of his most celebrated work: the journey of the mind to God. For him the aim of all teaching was the approach of the mind, the will and the soul to God. Philosophy, faith, theology, contemplation and ecstasy were stages in the journey which the Christian doctor was himself making and teaching others to make. All teaching, all knowledge, therefore, was dynamic, progressive, teleological. All conception of philosophy or even of theology as a purely intellectual discipline was entirely alien to his mind: a *fortiori* the claim that philosophy was capable of satisfying the Christian's mind or was in any sense an end in itself. Philosophy for Bonaventure was always heteronomous, an adjunct, an instrument, of theology. In this he differed little from St Thomas the theologian, but whereas Thomas had elaborated a system of pure philosophy, which lay behind and beneath his theology, even behind his mystical theology, Bonaventure had done nothing of the kind, and whereas Bonaventure tends to choose philosophical opinions that suit his theological ideas, Thomas corrects and extends his philosophy to harmonize with his presentation of Christian teaching. While Bonaventure eliminates those who differ from him by using theological arguments, and substitutes for Aristotle other thinkers more patient of a Christian interpretation, Thomas meets his opponents on the level of human reason, and gives rational arguments for his position.

Indeed, although Bonaventure may use the mechanics of Aristotle, and although his system may seem, when broken down and catalogued, to be an amalgam of elements taken from Aristotle and others, such an impression would be in truth an illusion. Bonaventure may use Aristotelian terms, but he never adopts the mind and spirit of Aristotle. His forms are not Aristotelian forms, and he has none of the empirical, commonsense humanism of the Greek. Bonaventure throughout his work remains upon what was for him the real plane of thought and on this plane little or nothing is Aristotelian. Both soul and body are formally complete substances, and the spiritual nature of the soul is no bar to this, for spiritual substances, as well as corporeal ones, are composed of matter and form. Yet these two substances can combine into one, for in virtue of the doctrine of multiplicity of form a superior form can come upon and 'cover' or absorb an inferior one: in this instance the soul becomes the form of the body, which still retains its own forms of corporeity, animality and the rest. This metaphysical combination is brought about by the desire (*appetitus*) that body and soul have for each other; the soul perfects and animates the body. Since the soul and its powers make up a self-sufficient unity, there can be no direct impact of external material objects upon the soul or its powers; sense-perception is a purely bodily function. Nevertheless, the soul, united with the body, can register and pass judgement on the action exerted upon the sense-organ by the external object, and thus begin the process of knowing. As for our knowledge of God, He is not only more real in Himself than we are, but also nearer to us, more present to us, than we are to ourselves. He is in consequence more directly perceptible to us than any other being, and He is logically the first to be known to us; without a knowledge of being which is its own source (an *ens a se*) no other kind of being can be known. This knowledge of God is innate, whereas the knowledge of external beings comes to the soul from without, and indirectly, by means of a judgement upon the experiences of the corporeal senses.

M. Etienne Gilson, in one of the most illuminating passages of his great study of Bonaventure's thought, isolated for us three of the principal philosophical differences between him and St Thomas.[3] They are fine points, but they are very significant. He quotes

---

[3] *La philosophie de St. Bonaventure* (ed. 1945), pp. 412–13; trans. Sheed and Trethowan (1938), pp. 428–9. The passage in St Thomas is *Quaestiones disputatae de Veritate* qu. XI art. 1 ad Resp.

Aquinas, who here as elsewhere refers to his opponents without mention of names: 'The difference of our opinions can be seen in three questions, namely: the bringing of forms into being, the acquisition of virtues, and the acquisition of knowledge', and then continues:

'The Thomist "form" begets a form in matter; it imposes that form upon a matter which submits to it; the Bonaventuran form rouses to life in the bosom of matter a potential form which that matter already contains. The Thomist intellect forms intelligibles out of sense-impressions and creates the first principles, which in their turn are the instruments by which it builds the entire edifice of knowledge. The Bonaventuran intellect finds within itself the intelligible, which it has not framed out of sense-perceptions, but has received from One within it who is more "within" than its own interior life. The Thomist will acquires "natural" virtues which owe their development, *qua* natural, to exercise and habit; the Bonaventuran will waits for grace to descend upon these virtues, *qua* natural, in order that it may complete them.'
And on another page he writes: 'St Bonaventure began by reducing the whole of metaphysics to three essential problems: emanation, exemplarism, and the return to God by enlightenment.'

Nevertheless, Bonaventure marks an epoch in the evolution of speculative theology, for he is the first to pour the whole body of Christian teaching into the mould of a system which, if not precisely a philosophical system, is at least a mould – the mould of an outlook, a *Weltanschauung*, that in theology is that of Augustine, and in philosophy is in large part that of Christian Neoplatonism.

Bonaventure's significance in the history of thought derives principally from two qualities in himself and in his work. He had the mental power – and he was the first to show mental power enough – to construct a cohesive system which, despite what may be called mechanical faults, was a logical and comprehensive whole that could be presented to others and taught as a system, and could be attacked only by those who were prepared and able to deny and to disprove some of the most hallowed postulates of the traditional heritage. Beyond this, Bonaventure enjoyed the personal reputation, not only of an eminent scholar and master, but of an ecclesiastical statesman of the first rank, and, what is more, of a saint. All this gave to his thought a cachet, a personal recommendation, that no one in the schools had hitherto enjoyed. He was, indeed, the last and one of the most eminent of a long series of thinkers, from the fourth to the thirteenth century, who regarded all forms of knowledge and learning as subservient to theology and useful solely in that ancillary function, and who also regarded the progress from letters to philosophy and from philosophy to the Bible as stages in the growth of Christian Wisdom, which was also Christian virtue. This, the ideal of the late patristic and early monastic centuries, had reached its crowning point between Lanfranc and Bernard. Bonaventure's vision was in a sense a new one, with philosophy taking the place of letters and speculative theology (in part) that of the Bible. But it was essentially the traditional position, the inward-looking study of theology as a discipline for the individual. Such an aim, such an ideal, were becoming obsolete with the growth of the universities and the rise of a Christian population possessed of education and economic independence, and surrounded on many sides by the infidel. Theology was now a science, and there was need of both apologists and publicists to defend the faith and to expound it. Bonaventure was in some respects the end of a chapter as surely as he was in other ways a beginning and a source. We may add that Bonaventure's cast of mind, which had a natural harmony with the Augustinian conception of Wisdom, and which could elevate all it touched to the theological, the spiritual, even to the mystical level, was triumphantly successful in presenting a view of theology and of the Christian life which had, and still has, a strong appeal to many minds. In him, if anywhere, we find the Augustinian vision of a Christian Wisdom and a Christian's dedicated advance to the knowledge of God, set out in terms acceptable to the medieval mind, and in part, perhaps, to certain minds of the modern world, and of every age.

The academic and administrative eminence of Bonaventure as member and head of a great religious order helped to make him the unofficial founder of a school. Among his pupils two in particular diffused his ideas. John Pecham, an Englishman (*c.* 1225–92), adopted all the features of his teaching, and attached particular importance to the multiplicity of forms. As regent in Paris, and later as archbishop of Canterbury, he was to define and defend his position – which he identified with tradition – against the attacks of Christian Aristotelianism. His contemporary, Matthew of Aquasparta (*c.* 1237–1302), an Italian, was equally distinguished and perhaps more gifted. He succeeded Pecham in the chair at the Roman Curia and became a cardinal and supporter of Boniface VIII; as such he appears in the *Divine Comedy*. He developed Bonaventure's doctrines, and in particular held that the mind has direct knowledge of individual beings by means of individual (i.e. not universal) intelligible 'species'.

The group of faithful disciples was followed by a series of

Franciscan masters who allowed Bonaventure's doctrines to be contaminated to a greater or less degree. Thus the Englishman Roger Marston explained divine illumination by identifying the agent intellect with God (thus following Avicenna), while yielding to Aristotle to some extent by positing an 'impression' upon the mind from the divine light. Richard of Middleton (*fl.* 1280s) adopted an Aristotelian epistemology while maintaining an intellectual knowledge of the individual being, as also universal hylomorphic. In general, and especially in England, the reign of Bonaventure was short, and Duns Scotus, who came to maturity in the climate of Oxford, was to find the way prepared for a new interpretation of metaphysical reality in his order.

CHAPTER TWENTY

Albert the Great

The Dominican theologians, in the early decades of their teaching at Paris, had shown no characteristics that might distinguish them from the seculars or the Franciscans. They had been forbidden by their constitutions of 1228 'to study the books of pagans and philosophers, though they might give them a passing glance',[1] and although their first Paris master, Roland of Cremona (1229-31) had a wide acquaintance with Aristotle, and their great encyclopedist, Vincent of Beauvais (d. 1264) made considerable use of Greek and Arabian writers, most of their theologians before 1250 showed a distrust of Aristotle similar to that of the conservative Franciscans. Their most distinguished master of the mid-century, the Englishman Robert Kilwardby (prior-provincial 1261-72; archbishop of Canterbury, 1272/3-8; d. cardinal 1279), was a conservative eclectic, holding the doctrine of seminal tendencies and opposing, as we shall see, the Aristotelian doctrine of the unity of form in beings, including man. Albert himself could write of those of his own habit who wished by all means in their power to oppose philosophy, 'as brute beasts, blaspheming in matters wherein they are ignorant'.[2] The language might be that of Roger Bacon, and we are reminded by it that two of the most active minds of the day, though so far apart from each other in aims and sympathies, were in fact aware of the crucial problem of their age, and of the opposition with which all innovators would meet. Yet if there was little original matter in early Dominican

[1] Denifle and Chatelain, *Chartularium Universitatis Parisiensis*, 1, 112.

[2] The passage is from his commentary *In Epist. B. Dionysii Areopagitae*, Ep. vii (see *Alberti Magni . . . Opera omnia*, t. xxxvii, 2 (Münster i. W., 1978), p. 504, 11, 28-32). It is cited and discussed by P. Mandonnet. *Siger de Brabant* (1899), p. 50. The wording is ambiguous and can be translated in more than one way. Some think that Albert is not referring to the Dominicans.

thought, one external circumstance and one mental attitude distinguished the Preachers even in their early days: their whole *raison d'être* was to learn and preach theology, for which end they were the first to perfect a system of higher education throughout their order; and from early days they had a conception of all knowledge as forming a body of ascertainable truth. This is seen even in the writings of the conservative Kilwardby. While to the Franciscan Pecham the new Aristotelianism is impious and untraditional, to Kilwardby it is sheer untruth.

The life of Albert the Great, like that of several of his most eminent contemporaries in the schools, is very imperfectly known. Though the course of his later life can be seen fairly distinctly, the chronology of his early years and of some of his writings is still a matter of debate. Two dates for his birth have been, and are, defended by opposing scholars, 1193 and 1206–7. While the evidence seems strong for the later date, other indications would suggest that he was a very old man (that is, well over seventy-three) when he died in 1280. In any case, it has been established that he was probably a son of a *ministerialis* of the Hohenstaufen. He studied for a few months at Bologna and Padua in 1223, and joined the Dominican novitiate at the hands of Jordan of Saxony in the same year. Roger Bacon, who had a particular animus against him, is thus correct in saying that he had never been through a course in arts; he had to construct his philosophy for himself. He was sent to study at Cologne and he taught theology in Germany in the 1220s and 1230s, then in Paris in the 1240s, becoming regent master in 1245. It was during this period that he had St Thomas as his pupil, and when he returned to Cologne to found a *studium generale* he took Thomas with him (1248–52), and from 1254 to 1257 he was prior provincial of Germany. Appointed bishop of Ratisbon (Regensburg) in 1260, he resigned in 1262, and for the remainder of his life he was chiefly at Cologne, where he died in 1280. During the last few years of his life his powers were failing.

Albert's output of writing was enormous, filling thirty-eight volumes in the Paris edition of 1890–9. Many points of chronology are still undecided, and the matter is of some importance, as ten years one way or the other in the dating of his work on Aristotle would change the whole history of Latin Aristotelianism and of the controversies of 1266–77. Mandonnet placed the commentaries on Aristotle in 1245–6, which would imply that Bonaventure could have known them, but nevertheless ignored or rejected them in his writings. Pelster places them 1256–70, and present-day scholarship has tended to accept this, with the implication that at Paris extreme

Aristotelianism was well on its way before the impact of Albert was felt. If we accept this view, Albert's literary activity will fall into four periods, the first (Cologne and Paris, 1228-48) devoted to theology, the second (Cologne, 1248-54) to the writings of Dionysius and the *Ethics* of Aristotle; the third, the Aristotelian period (1254-70), to the philosophy and scientific writings of Aristotle; and the fourth, to a return to theology (1270-*c*. 1275) when Albert wrote his *Summa theologiae*, ignoring that of Aquinas.

If we know little save administrative details of Albert's life, his mental characteristics and tastes stand out in his writings, which contain many personal references and autobiographical details; we have a clear impression of a massive, outspoken, fearless man of warm emotions, while his works show him to have had in full measure the Teutonic industry and zest for the absorption of knowledge. Known to his age as 'the Great', chiefly by reason of his seeming omniscience and a fecundity remarkable even among theologians, he was regarded by his contemporaries primarily as a man of immense learning, a scientific encyclopedist, the *doctor universalis* who wrote with authority about everything. To us his importance is that of the thinker who marked an epoch, not so much by the force and originality of his own thought as by his definition and steadfast recognition of natural human knowledge, and in particular philosophy, as a valid and useful perception of truth, and hence as a discipline of value, autonomous within its own sphere. Hitherto, to Christian thinkers of the West, the true philosophy had been the divine message of the Old and New Testaments, illuminated by meditation and contemplation, using the bankrupt and largely erroneous wisdom of the pagans to assist and explain on the human level. Now, Albert accepted philosophy as the Arabs and Jews had accepted it, as a vision of truth on the natural level, valid within certain agreed limits and therefore to be sought for its own sake as a part of the knowledge of creation given to man as his birthright and heritage. The principal guide and repository of this knowledge was Aristotle, and Albert proposed to himself, when at the height of his powers, the task of presenting the whole of Aristotle to the West, a task which he pursued to the end. His aim was to edit Aristotle with a running commentary on the Avicennan model, which should be in part informative and in part critical, and in so doing to strip away the Arabian and Jewish additions when they ran counter to Christian sentiment or tradition. In addition, Albert added all the cognate information he could collect from any and every source, including his own observations, with some careful notes on birds and the use of dialect names for the fauna of the Rhineland. Roger Bacon, who did not stint his abuse of Albert, is a valuable witness to the position he had attained among his contemporaries long before his death. 'He is', he says, 'cited in the schools just like Aristotle, Avicenna and Averroës, and while still alive is counted as an authority, unlike any other man.' And again: 'Although he is still alive he is given the name of doctor at Paris, and is cited in the schools as an authority.'[3]

Contemporaries were not mistaken in their estimate of Albert's significance. Stupendous as was his design, he accomplished it in essentials, displaying a vast erudition, familiar with the Arabian, Jewish and some of the Neoplatonist writers, and yet able to choose and make personal decisions in accepting their thought. It is little wonder that Ulrich of Strasbourg should refer to him as the wonder and marvel of his age.[4] While presenting and explaining Aristotle he also remained, as it were, in the background, as his judge. Albert is never the slave of Aristotle: the Philosopher is not a Christian, and he can err.

The judgement of historians on Albert has changed twice in the past eighty years. In the nineteenth century he was regarded as the great encyclopedic amasser of facts; Mandonnet and other Dominicans successfully enlarged this view, and endeavoured to show that he was also the first consistent Aristotelian, not only the master of Thomas, but the co-creator with him of what was somewhat ponderously called the Albertino-Thomist synthesis. This, it has been said with justice, is to give Albert both more and less than his due: more, because he was far from being purely and consistently Aristotelian, and had probably been anticipated in this respect by several years by Siger of Brabant; less than his due, because his receptive and genial mind swept up such a mass of ideas that he was able to make a present of bunches of them to at least two other groups besides that of the Thomists – to the theologians in the tradition of Thomas of Strasbourg, and to the Neoplatonists led by Dietrich of Freiburg.

At the same time it must be remembered that Albert himself made no attempt to create a system or make a synthesis. He illustrated the whole Aristotelian corpus from all available sources, but in his own writings he was neither a consistent Aristotelian nor a perfectly consistent thinker. While opposing and directly attacking the monopsychism of Averroës, he nevertheless showed himself hesitant as to the unicity of form in man; he seems to have admitted a *forma*

---

[3]*Opera inedita*, ed. J. Brewer (Rolls Series 15), pp. 30, 327.
[4]Cited by M. Grabmann, *Zeitschrift f. katholische Theologie* (1905), p. 91.

corporeitatis and some kind of 'spiritual matter'. While treating Aristotle (to use Dante's phrase) as 'the master of scientific knowledge', he nevertheless understood and used Neoplatonic teaching, and in theology greatly developed the traditional teaching on the Gifts of the Holy Ghost. His doctrine of universals and of the process of knowledge is pure Aristotle, but much of his teaching as to the nature of the soul is Platonic. 'One can be a perfect philosopher', he remarks, 'only if one knows both Plato and Aristotle; if we consider the soul in itself, we follow Plato; if we consider it as the animating principle of the body, we agree with Aristotle.'[5] Forward-looking in so many ways, he was nevertheless more than once lamentably out of touch with his world: he could republish, at the crisis of Latin Averroism, a tract against Averroës which had no relevance to the burning issues, and his defence of St Thomas a few years later failed entirely to grasp the real needs of the situation.

Nevertheless, Albert remains a great and significant figure. Above all, beyond the heritage of his immense learning – his encyclopedia of information, his exposition of Aristotle, his comprehension of the import of Neoplatonism – beyond, even, the impulse and the guidance he gave to St Thomas, there stands his acceptance of natural philosophy, in the traditional, widest sense of the terms, as an inescapable, necessary basis of the Christian vision of the universe. The purely theological conception of Augustine, which had held sway for eight hundred years, was about to be challenged by a vision that was, or that could be, purely naturalistic. While retaining in fullness all that Christianity taught of the God-given, supernatural life of the soul, Albert admitted also as a primary, valid, autonomous field of mental exercise, the realm of Nature, which included Man, as grasped by the faculties given man at his creation as part of his natural endowment by the God of Nature.

[5]*Alberti Magni Opera* ed. Borgnet vol. xxxv pp. 16, 34. Cf. Gilson. *History of Christian Philosophy*, 283 and notes.

CHAPTER TWENTY-ONE
St Thomas Aquinas

St Thomas Aquinas has been hailed by common consent in the modern world as the prince of scholastics, not only the *doctor angelicus*, but also, as he was acclaimed soon after his death, the *doctor communis*. To Thomists of pure blood, as to many others besides, he appears as the authentic voice of reason, interpreting and defending tradition, as the greatest medieval representative of the *philosophia perennis*, the way of thinking that is ever ancient and ever new.

The newcomer to Aquinas who is unacquainted with the language and preoccupations of medieval theology, or whose reading in philosophy has lain among the ancients or the moderns, will probably be dismayed or frustrated by the form of his writings. He will find none of the literary charm that the writer of a dialogue or treatise can diffuse; the great doctor goes remorselessly forward through things great and small, following for the most part an invariable sequence of objection, solution and argument; there is no emphasis, no high lighting, no difference between points that seem trivial or otiose and the supreme problems of existence. All is settled by a personal assertion, with little apparent distinction between what is substantial and of common belief, and what is only a possibility or an opinion. It is this apparent lack of discrimination that repels or confuses many readers of to-day, and it must be admitted that some of the admirers and followers of St Thomas have done him a real disservice by their failure to realize themselves, and to communicate to others, the fundamental characteristics of the spirit and doctrine of the master. A rigid and unspiritual Thomist can be the worst of guides to St Thomas.

For the greatness is there. The judgement of his contemporaries and posterity has not been false. As we read, with sympathy and a receptive mind, on and on in the two great *Summae*, the pattern unfolds and the cardinal principles of thought recur and are used, like keen knives, to separate the truth from all else. We come to expect, and never fail to find, a justice and lucidity of thought and expression that thrills and stimulates by the impression it creates that a veil has fallen away and that the pure light of reason and reality is streaming into our minds.

The peculiar greatness of Aquinas, as a master of technical method, lies in his combination of fearless strength of reasoning with an entire absence of personal bias, and in his ability to recognize and produce harmony and order – to recognize them in the universe, and to produce them in his own thought – to a degree without parallel among the great philosophers of the world. The two *Summae* have been compared, not inaptly, to the whole mass of the medieval fabric and furnishings of such a building as Salisbury cathedral, their exact contemporary. The design, the symmetry, the sublimity and the beauty flow from the genius of Aquinas; the basis upon which the soaring structure rests is in the main the work of Aristotle.

St Thomas stands apart from all the other scholastics to the modern world. He is not only recognized by all as a figure of importance, one who can stand alongside of Dante as a representative of medieval genius at its height, but he has stood, ever since his lifetime and never more than now, as a master to a large body of thinking men. As such, he has, during the past eighty years, broken clean out of the scholastic framework. This creates difficulties for the historian. Thomism, the philosophico-theological system derived from the writings of St Thomas, and itself divided into what may be called its integral and its eclectic subdivisions, may well be a logical and legitimate derivation, but it is not in all respects and unquestionably to be found in the writings of Aquinas, which alone are of interest to the historian. Philosophers and theologians have rarely been historians. They have tended to treat the works of St Thomas as a single timeless text-book, from which the desired answer can be extracted, as from a dictionary, by a use of the elaborate indices provided by editors. Only in the past sixty years, largely owing to the work of Martin Grabmann, have the works of St Thomas come to be regarded historically, as a series of writings conditioned by all kinds of local, intellectual and chronological circumstances, and as the work of a mind always ready to modify an opinion or an argument in the face of new information or valid criticism. While it is true that the writings of Aquinas present considerably less evidence of change or development than do those of a Plato or a Russell, they are not a monolith; there is a distance between the *Sentences* and the Second Part of the *Summa theologiae*, and those who study his thought on, e.g., the eternity of the world, or the Immaculate Conception, will find that it changes, and sometimes returns yet again to its starting-point. Here we are concerned only with the Aquinas of history. As such, his significance appears in two principal achievements. He integrated Aristotelian philosophical principles with traditional speculative theology, and he created, by remoulding and rethinking existing materials and old problems, a wholly new and original Christian philosophy.

As a follower of Albert who outran his master he accepted human reason as an adequate and self-sufficient instrument for attaining truth within the realm of man's natural experience, and in so doing gave, not only to abstract thought but to all scientific knowledge, rights of citizenship in a Christian world. He accepted in its main lines the system of Aristotle as a basis for his own interpretation of the visible universe, and this acceptance did not exclude the ethical and political teaching of the Philosopher. By so doing, and without a full realization of all the consequences, St Thomas admitted into the Christian purview all the natural values of human social activity and, by implication, a host of other activities such as art. All these activities were indeed subordinated by him to the supernatural vocation of man, and were raised to a higher power by the Christian's supernatural end of action, but they had their own reality and value, they were not mere shadows or vanities.

Aquinas did not merely adopt and 'baptize' or 'Christianize' Aristotle. He had, indeed, no hesitation in extending his thought, in filling gaps within it and in interpreting it in accord with Christian teaching. He also took many elements from elsewhere. But he did more than this: and Aristotle, had he been restored to life to read the *Summa contra Gentiles*, would have had difficulty in recognizing the thought as his. For indeed Aquinas stood the system of Aristotle on its head or, to speak more carefully, supplied the lack of higher metaphysics in Aristotle by framing a conception of the deity which was in part drawn from Judeo-Christian revelation and which when proposed in Thomist terms embodied all that was most valuable in the metaphysic of Platonism. While Aristotle, the empiricist, looked most carefully at the universe of being as it was displayed to the senses and intelligence, and explored in his *Metaphysics* the veins and sinews of substance, he became imprecise when he rose to consider mind and soul, and hesitant when he looked up towards the First Cause of all things. His God is a shadow, an unseen, unknown, uncaring force and reason necessary to give supreme unity to the universe. In the Aristotelian system reality, existential reality, is strongest in the world of everyday experience; the loftier the gaze, the weaker the reality. With Thomism, on the other hand, the infinitely rich, dynamic existential reality is God, the creator and source of all being, goodness and truth, present in all being by power and essence, holding and guiding and regarding every part of creation, while as the one subsistent Being, the uncaused cause, the *ens a se* in whom alone essence and existence are one, He takes the place of the Platonic forms and exemplars as the One of whose Being all created being, its essence perfected by its God-given existence, is a reflection and (according to its mode as creature) a participant. It is only on a lower level that the Aristotelian universe of being is found, but the two visions of reality are fused by Aquinas under the light of the unifying principles, first proposed by the Greeks, of cause, reason and order.

Thomas, a younger son in the large family of the lord of Aquino, and related through his mother to the Emperor Frederick II, was born in the castle of Roccasecca, in the broad valley above Cassino, in 1224 or 1225. Of his life, as of Shakespeare's, we know surprisingly little. His personal letters, if he wrote them, have not been preserved; there is not a single personal reminiscence in his voluminous works, nor a single expression of personal taste or feeling, if we except a rare word of disapproval in one of his last works, and, what is stranger still, the greatest thinker and theologian of his age, recognized as a saint by all who knew him, found no adequate biographer.

His parents offered Thomas in 1230/1 as a child of the cloister at Monte Cassino; no doubt he was destined for the monastic life and perhaps for the abbacy; he was in any case bereft of what many would think the most gracious memories of childhood, though he remained throughout life in close contact with his family. Many monks were expelled from Cassino by Frederick II in 1239, and Thomas became a student at the newly founded university of Naples, where he is known to have been taught by a devotee of Aristotelian thought. Taking the Dominican habit in 1244 he was destined for Paris, but as with St Clare of Assisi thirty-two years previously his family intervened and he was held in confinement for a year. When released he proceeded to Paris and Cologne; at the former he may have been, at the latter from 1248 he certainly was, a pupil of St Albert. From 1252–6 he taught as bachelor at Paris, and in 1256 he incepted as master, but could not proceed master on account of the conflict then raging between the mendicants and the university, though he acted as regent in the

Dominican house from 1256–9. In 1257 he was admitted to his degree by papal command, along with St Bonaventure. From 1259 to 1268 he was in Italy, teaching and writing while following the papal court at Anagni, Orvieto, Viterbo and Rome; St Albert was with him for part of the time, and he formed a friendship with another fellow-Preacher, the Greek scholar William of Moerbeke, whom he interested in the translation of Aristotle. He returned to Paris for another regency in January 1269, and soon became a rock of scandal to the conservative theologians who engaged him in dispute, while with the other hand he was occupied in attacking Siger and his friends; these years were a time of great literary activity. Called away from Paris in 1272, perhaps on account of mounting opposition, he organized studies at the university of Naples, and died on 7 March 1274, at the age of 48/9, at the Cistercian abbey of Fossanova, on his way to the Council of Lyons. Few personal details are known of him: he was corpulent and silent – the 'dumb ox' – and a celebrated anecdote shows him preoccupied with speculation even in company with St Louis. Other stories recall his simplicity and gentleness in disputation, even when provoked. The Office and Mass of Corpus Christi, surely the most admirable liturgical service ever composed to order (1264), show him not only as an exact theologian and a scriptural anthologist of peculiar felicity, but also as a master of prosody. The hymn *Adoro Te*, if his, touches a note of deep emotion which is still nearer to great poetry.

Aquinas, in common with all the great scholastics, was a tireless and voluminous writer, and every treatise, however small, bears the mark of his luminous and penetrating genius. Careful modern criticism has shown that he willingly and often modified his opinions on reflection, and that he applied critical methods to his authorities and abandoned a text (such as the pseudo-Augustinian *De spiritu et anima*) if he had convinced himself that it was not authentic. While many of his shorter works, such as *De ente et essentia, De veritate* and *De unitate intellectus* show all his superior qualities present to an eminent degree, pride of place must be taken by his three large works, the early *Commentary on the Sentences* (1252–7), the *Summa contra Gentiles* (*c.* 1258/9–1264), probably written for the use of Dominican controversialists in Spain, and the *Summa theologiae* I and II (1266–72) and III (1272–3), left unfinished at his death. Of these the *Sentences* is of interest as showing the early stages in the development of his thought, with the main lines already firmly drawn; the *Contra Gentiles*, a work of maturity, is of especial importance by reason of the very full development of his metaphysical positions: the arguments of natural religion and apologetics are forcefully developed and subjected to a more detailed criticism than was to be possible in the *Summa theologiae*. Nevertheless, the last-named has always been recognized as his masterpiece – a masterpiece of architectonics, of logical thought, and of deep and genial pronouncements, in which almost every question of theology and morality is touched upon.

The qualities which give Aquinas individuality as one of the very greatest of the world's thinkers are perhaps his exquisite lucidity, which is derived not from an impoverishment or dilution of thought, but from the domination and diffusion of light over a whole landscape of ideas; his sense of proportion; and his ability to construct a great edifice which is a perfect whole and is informed by a few simple but pregnant leading principles. This is not the place to attempt a survey of his system of thought; several good studies exist, though no single account can be described as perfectly satisfactory. We shall merely glance, as historians, at a few of the most significant ideas and characteristics.

St Thomas followed his master, Albert, in a resolute separation of the spheres of reason and revelation, the natural and the supernatural. While on the one hand this recognized the autonomy of human reason in its own field, it also limited its competence severely. Pure mysteries, such as the Trinity and the Incarnation, were no longer susceptible of proof, of comprehension, or even of adequate explanation. The human mind was now bounded by its contacts with the external world, according to the axiom *nihil est in intellectu, nisi prius fuerit in sensu*.[1] It was from observation of external reality, not through the soul's direct consciousness of its own or of God's existence, that a proof of the First Cause could be found. It was from contact with external reality, not from a divine illumination or contact with the divine ideas, that a knowledge of truth came. This was in harmony with a key proposition of Aquinas: *quicquid recipitur, secundum modum recipientis recipitur*, which in the field of epistemology became: *cognitum est in cognoscente per modum cognoscentis*[2] – God is known from His works not in Himself – but it might well seem to theologians of the traditional Franciscan school a despiritualization of religious thought. Yet it gave a new dignity to the human reason by lending philosophical support to a conviction

[1]'The mind can perceive nothing that has not previously been perceived by the senses.'

[2]'Whatever is received, is received according to the mode of being of the receiver', as for example, the sound of a clock striking is heard merely as a sound by an animal, but as a time-signal by a man. 'What is known is in the mind of the knower according to his mode of being.'

common to all men, viz., that our knowledge comes to us directly or indirectly from the universe of being around us, and that neither our senses nor our reason play us false when they function normally. In other words, the activity of the human mind is as much a factor in the dynamics of the universe as are purely material or mechanistic activities. The human reason is a perfectly adequate precision instrument for perceiving all truth in the world of matter and spirit around it, within the limits of its range. Aquinas thus set his face both against any kind of 'double truth' and against the Platonic conception of the world as a mere shadow and symbol of true reality. The realms of reason and revelation became separate, and the bounds of theology and philosophy, faith and natural knowledge, stood out sharp and clear. There is only one truth, but there are realms of truth to which the unaided human mind cannot attain; there is only one truth, and we can recognize it when we see it; it is therefore not possible for a man to have faith and natural certainty about one and the same proposition, still less can faith and natural certainty be in opposition. Moreover, all being and therefore all truth comes from a single source; there is therefore an order and harmony in all the parts. In the celebrated and characteristic phrase of Aquinas: 'Grace does not destroy nature; it perfects her.'[3]

Yet though Aquinas followed Aristotle he also went beyond him with new intuitions and principles, such as the unicity of form in all beings, man included, and the distinction between essence and existence. How novel these principles appeared to contemporaries can be seen clearly enough in the words of two contemporaries. The one, Guglielmo da Tocco, the earliest and most reliable biographer of the saint, who had lived with him during his last years at Naples, wrote: 'in his lectures he propounded *new* theses, and discovered a *new* and clear manner of proof, bringing forward *new* reasons, so that no one who heard him teaching these *new* doctrines and settling doubts by these *new* reasons could doubt that God was illuminating him with a *new* light, ... that he to whom *new* inspiration was given should not hesitate to teach and write *new* things.'[4] John Pecham, the Franciscan archbishop of Canterbury, who had been regent at the Paris house of his order – the 'opposite number' to St Thomas – was equally convinced of the novelty, though less inclined to attribute it to divine inspiration.[5]

[3]*Gratia non tollit sed perficit naturam. (Summa theologiae* 1 8 ad 2, and elsewhere.)
[4]*Acta Sanctorum*, March i, 663. Vita S. Thomae c.3.
[5]Peckham (Pecham), *Registrum Epistolarum*, ed. C. T. Martin (Rolls Series 77) III 901, ep. dcxlv. 'Quae sit ... solidior et sanior doctrina, vel Bonaventurae ... vel illa novella quasi tota contraria.'

One of these new doctrines was undoubtedly his metaphysic of being. The leading idea running through his whole system is that every finite being is made up of act and potency, essence and existence. Existence brings the potency of an essence into act, but is itself limited by that potency. This distinction between essence and existence is vital; it is the shibboleth of Thomism. It is because God alone is subsistent being, without distinction between His essence and existence, that He is all-perfect, and it is ultimately from contingent being that we deduce the existence of God. Nothing of which we have experience is a self-caused being, an *ens a se*;[6] it must therefore depend on a cause which exists of itself. In other words, a contingent uncaused being is a contradiction in terms. This conception of being throws light also on the nature of God. Subsistent being is above all created natures, it is therefore supernatural being, unattainable by any created or creatable intelligence. God is therefore in essence transcendent, though He is also, by essence, power and presence, immanent. But if God is a supernatural being, how can we have any knowledge of Him by natural powers?

Aquinas answers this question by his profound doctrine of analogy, which again depends upon the distinction between essence and existence. The qualities or perfections of creatures, such as being, truth, goodness, beauty and the rest, are in God not only virtually, as the source of creative power, but, as the technical phrase goes, *formaliter eminenter*: that is, they are really present in the Godhead, but in a manner inconceivable and inexpressible by the human mind – beyond its limit, as one might say. Goodness, for example, is not predicated of God and ourselves univocally – men are not good as God is good – nor is it predicated merely equivocally – the same word with a different meaning – but analogically. It is thus that Aquinas avoids both agnosticism and anthropomorphism.

Indeed, the thought of Aquinas, if considered from one point of view, is almost always a mean between two extremes, though the mean is not a compromise between the extremes, but a summit which overlooks them. Thus in the oldest of all metaphysical controversies, typified in ancient Greece by the systems of ceaseless flux (Heraclitus) and static monism (Parmenides), Aquinas adopts the philosophy of 'becoming', of potency and act, of indeterminate matter and determinant form, of essence and existence. We shall see that his epistemology is a moderate realism, between Plato and the Nominalists. In another field he holds the mean between a

[6]*Ens a se* = 'a being which is its own cause and origin'.

mechanistic and a dynamistic analysis: the universe is neither the sum of colliding and pressing atoms, nor of immaterial energy, but a compound of both, with energy as form gradually assuming greater and greater importance in vegetable, animal and rational shape, for in contradiction to the materialists Aquinas sets his axiom that form, energy, determines all: action follows being (*agere sequitur esse*). Finally, in the great controversy of ethics he stands between determinism and moral agnosticism. The will is determined by the good; it cannot choose evil as such; but it is not determined by individual good things or designs; it can choose at the bidding of reason, but its choice is always, really or apparently, good.

St Thomas's theory of knowledge is that of Aristotle, rendered somewhat more explicit. The mind is a *tabula rasa*. External things impinge upon the senses, which present the individual object to the mind; this strips off all that is individual and accidental, and grasps the essence or nature. We see Smith, and recognize in him manhood, the nature of a rational animal, man. The essence of the individual abstracted by the mind is in one way less real than it is in the individual himself, for it only exists fully and in its own right in the individual. But in another sense it is more real, for to Aquinas, as to the Neoplatonists, immaterial being, spirit and thought, is more real than physical, material being; it is a higher mode of being and is logically prior to anything physical. By reaching the essence we reach the formal cause of a being, the expression in rational shape of the spiritual idea which is ultimately its constitutive agency.

We have alluded to the thorough acceptance of Aristotle by Aquinas. This leads him to assert, or rather to assume, what has been called the primacy of the intellect. Reason and order throughout the universe reflect the unchanging mind and law of God. Hence the celebrated doctrine of the various kinds of Law. Just as with man nothing can be willed before it is known (*nil volitum quin praecognitum*), and therefore reason is of the essence of freedom, so with God it is His knowledge, His unalterable law, that logically precedes His decrees. Consequently Aquinas, like Avicenna and Aristotle before him, has a strong bias towards determinism, and in one of the bitterest of all theological controversies his interpreter, the great Bañez, was accused of near-Calvinism.

Yet Aquinas's acceptance of Aristotle, though thorough and epoch-making, is neither uncritical nor absolute. He accepts his metaphysics almost in entirety, but his world-system only with reservations, and for all the higher levels of Christian life he repeatedly asserts Aristotle's incompetence. Similarly, while taking over bodily from the Jewish Maimonides much of his natural theology, he takes only part (and that with cautious reservation) of his and others' Jewish and Neoplatonist teaching on the information of the heavenly spheres by intelligences or angels, and he firmly rejects the series of creative causes posited by Avicenna, and the emanations of the Neoplatonists. At the same time, Aquinas admits far more from non-Aristotelian sources than appears at first sight. Thus the Platonic ideas, resolutely banished in their familiar form from epistemology and metaphysics, remain 'in the heavens' (to use a Platonic phrase) where Augustine had seen them, as the eternal, exemplary, creative ideas in what we call 'the mind of God'. Moreover, as we have seen, the 'exemplary' and participatory function of the ideas is assumed by the Thomist doctrine of essence and existence. Similarly in ethics, alongside the everyday virtues of Aristotle are the four cardinal virtues taken from Plato and the Plotinian specification of all the virtues on the three levels of ordinary life, proficiency in virtue, and the state of perfection. These many undertones and overtones in the thought of Aquinas are important; they give it a richness and a flexibility which it might not otherwise possess.

Indeed Aquinas makes so much use of ways of thought that are ultimately Platonic that it may almost be said of him that he achieves that fusion of the Academy and the Lyceum that so many of his predecessors and contemporaries were attempting. He accomplishes this, however, not by a synthesis, but by using elements from Platonism mainly in the higher levels of metaphysics. Thus by his use of the principle that all creatures participate in being, though in varying measure, by his use of exemplarism in which the creature reflects the creator, by his doctrine of metaphysical composition, and by his assertion of the self-sufficing being of God, he makes of God the centre and cause of a universe of manifold being, and in ethics the creator, lawgiver and providential Father of each human soul, thus placing the centre of gravity, so to say, at the summit of being, and revealing a radiating centre, a living principle and a final goal where Aristotle points merely to an abstract postulate. In this way he adds all that is true in Plato's idealism, other-worldliness and spirit of love to the common-sense, rationalistic empiricism of Aristotle.

To this copious fund of material taken from older thinkers, and to the many, and as yet not fully catalogued, debts which Thomas owed to his immediate predecessors and masters, another rich source must be added, the self-revelation of God in the Old and New Testaments. This revelation is not indeed philosophy, but, as M. Gilson has finely shown, it gives a clear and simple answer to several of the problems that all philosophers must face; it directs attention to the sovereign importance of others which they might neglect; and it brands as false many conclusions to which some thinkers in every age are prone. In all these ways the Christian religion, in a mind profoundly receptive of its influence, must present the philosopher with a view of the universe different in many respects from that of Plato and Aristotle. Whether this view, and the intuitions and axioms it encourages, are fuller and more true than any purely natural outlook could be, is of course a matter on which universal agreement will never be reached, but it is undoubtedly a constitutive element, and not mere colouring matter, in a philosophical system.

From all these constituents of Aquinas's thought there emerged the first original philosophical system that Christianity had seen – neither Platonism, nor Aristotelianism, nor Augustinism, but Thomism. Henceforward this presentation of the universe of reality could be regarded, not only as a phase in the ever-changing outlook of thinking man, and as a phenomenon of thirteenth-century intellectual life, but as a system to which men could return to study, to adopt and to amend. It is still a common belief, and a common error, that the teaching of Aquinas, besides being the most complete and coherent and in the opinion of many the most intellectually satisfying system of the middle ages, was in addition the most characteristic and the most influential. This belief has been considerably strengthened by the great, though often misrepresented, influence exerted by Aquinas over the single supreme poet of the middle ages. Dante knew his *Summa* well enough, and could apply it to any situation he wished, but he is even less of a pure Thomist than Thomas is a pure Aristotelian. Moreover, Dante speaks for himself, not for his world. When he began to write, and still more when he died, the academic climate had changed from that of the decade of his birth. Thomism, from 1290 to the early sixteenth century, was only a unit, and at times a small unit, in the European pattern of thought. It was only with the counter-Reformation, and still more with the nineteenth century, that the thought of Aquinas came to be regarded as in some respects synonymous with Catholic philosophy. As Gilson remarks with great felicity, at the end of his review of Aquinas, in the thirteenth century 'St Thomas may not have been fully acclaimed by his age, but time was on his side: "These things shall be written in another generation than ours, and a people yet to be created shall praise the Lord." '[7]

[7]Psalm 101 (Vulgate), v. 19. '*Scribantur haec in generatione altera, et populus qui creabitur laudabit Dominum.*'

The preceding observations, as indeed the whole tenor of the modern presentation of St Thomas, have stressed his significance as a philosopher to the detriment, or at least to the overshadowing, of his wider reputation. We must not forget that St Thomas was also, indeed was primarily, a great theologian. Though, true to his own principles, he uses philosophical arguments to defend and to explain some of the most obscure mysteries of the faith, such as the Trinity, the personal union of the divine and human natures in the Incarnate Word, and the real presence in the Blessed Sacrament, while his methods were later applied by others to the problems of Grace and Predestination, the careful reader of the *Summa* becomes aware of other qualities in the philosopher, of a wide and living knowledge and an unusually felicitous use of Scripture wholly different from that of St Bernard, but no less impressive; of an unexpected tolerance of Dionysian elements of thought, and of a clarity of exposition which makes many of the Trinitarian articles unrivalled as precise statements of the Christian faith. It is not uncommon for those writing on St Thomas to point to his hymns in the office of Corpus Christi as evidence that the Angelic Doctor joined devotion to his metaphysics. Even the sympathetic Rashdall could write of 'the cold, rationalistic orthodoxy of Thomas'.[8] St Thomas, it is true, eschews the purple patch of piety and his words have on their surface less unction than have those of St Bonaventure. But still waters run deep, and if he uses the language of cold human reason in matters where rational argument suffices, he does not thereby leave out of the reckoning a higher and entirely supernatural light that directs the purified mind to a higher truth. In the words of an eminent modern Thomist, he distinguishes the various degrees of knowledge only to unite them without confusion.[9] We speak of the dialectical aridities of the schools, but for St Thomas there is a knowledge more perfect than dialectic. Hear him speak of wisdom, the noblest of the Gifts of the Holy Ghost:

> Wisdom by its very name implies an eminent abundance of knowledge, which enables a man to judge of all things, for everyone can judge well what he fully knows. Some have this abundance of knowledge as the result of learning and study, added to a native quickness of intelligence; and this is the wisdom which Aristotle counts among the intellectual virtues. But others have wisdom as a result of the kinship which they have with the things of God; it is of such that the Apostle says: 'The spiritual man judges all things.' The Gift of Wisdom gives a man this

[8]*The Universities of Europe in the Middle Ages*, ed. Powicke and Emden, III, 260.
[9]*Distinguer pour unir* (Paris 1932) is the title of M. Jacques Maritain's great book, translated into English with the title *The Degrees of Knowledge* (London, 1937, 1959).

eminent knowledge as a result of his union with God, and this union can only be by love, for 'he who cleaveth to God is of one spirit with Him'. And therefore the Gift of Wisdom leads to a godlike and explicit gaze at revealed truth, which mere faith holds in a human manner as it were disguised.[10]

The pages from which these words are taken are perhaps among the most eloquent in the whole of the works of Aquinas, though they occur at no climax, and show no difference in formal arrangement, from any other page in the vast work. We feel as we read them that he is speaking of what he knows, and we can understand why, some months before his death, he ceased from his occupation with academic theology, and we can believe him when he said, only a few days before his death, that all that he had written of divine things was mere trash compared with the truth of which he now enjoyed another and a more direct and certain vision.

[10] *Commentary on Book III of the Sentences*, D. 35, q. 2, art. 1.

CHAPTER TWENTY-TWO

Siger of Brabant and the Faculty of Arts

We have now briefly considered the two first syntheses or systems of thought and theology, the conservative, 'theological', spiritual presentation of Bonaventure, and the more thorough, philosophical, intellectual system of Aquinas, building upon, and extending, the intuitions of Albert. In the former, the thought of Aristotle was used only partially and occasionally; in the latter, it was the basic, though not the sole, philosophical element, but the doctrines of Aristotle incompatible with Christianity were either eliminated, or extended and explained in a way conformable to traditional doctrine. A third leader of thought has now to appear who, though gifted, was scarcely the peer of the three just mentioned, but who was nevertheless destined to do more than any other agent in the way of sharpening rivalries and bringing the currents of opinion, hitherto moving freely under the sole direction of individual masters, into collision with authority of one kind or another. While it would be ridiculous to describe as harmonious and uneventful the decades at Paris that had witnessed the long-drawn birth pangs of the Franciscan order, the rivalries of Minors and Preachers, the quarrels between the mendicants and the universities, and between the friars and the bishops, it is nevertheless true that in intellectual matters and academic circles men had hitherto been free, within the limits of traditional orthodoxy, to choose their own path and follow it to the end. The time was soon to come when rigid 'schools' of thought appeared and authority of every kind challenged or condemned all deviation. The immediate cause of the altered state of opinion was the emergence at Paris of a group of what have been called integral, radical and unorthodox Aristotelians, whose leaders were Siger of Brabant and Boethius of Dacia.

The rediscovery of this school and of its first and most celebrated exponent has been the work of half-a-dozen eminent scholars over the past 150 years – Renan, Hauréau, Mandonnet, Baeumker, Grabmann and van Steenberghen – and is one of the most remarkable 'historical revisions' in the field of medieval thought. Renan, in his pioneer work on Averroism, was the first to appreciate and even to exaggerate its importance, but progress in the study of its history was blocked by the existing confusion of its standard-bearer, Siger of Brabant, with a younger contemporary, a Thomist in outlook, Siger of Courtrai. This identification was destroyed by Hauréau and Mandonnet, and the latter was able to construct in outline the career of the authentic Siger. Subsequently, reliable evidence of his teaching was made available by the discovery and criticism of some of his writings by Grabmann and others, and within the last fifty years F. van Steenberghen, both by his publication and identification of further works, and by his judgement on the whole character of his thought, has given a new interpretation of his significance. Whereas Mandonnet and his followers had seen Siger as a follower of Averroës, a disingenuous proclaimer of the 'double truth', and a heterodox Aristotelian, van Steenberghen sees him as an upholder of integral Aristotelianism by no means committed to an acceptance of the doctrines of Averroës, a sincere Christian faced with a genuine intellectual problem. The debate on these latter points has continued in recent years, with Gilson and van Steenberghen as the opposing champions. Van Steenberghen has certainly caught his opponents out on a number of small points, and has established with some certainty the career of Siger and the content of his thought. Gilson, on the other hand, would seem to have been successful in showing the pervasive influence of Averroës before and during the acute years of controversy, and until the canon and chronology of Siger's works are fully established further discussion is likely to be unprofitable, especially in a matter where the climate of opinion needs to be analysed. As Gilson remarked, the debate will be settled by historical discoveries, not by dialectical victories.

Before giving an account of the crisis at Paris, it will be well to glance at the sequence of events there and the movements of leading personalities in the schools. By the middle of the century the complete Latin translation of the works of Averroës was available to accompany the study of the complete corpus of Aristotle's philosophy. Whereas fifty years earlier the teaching of the masters of arts had been restricted to grammar, logic and dialectic, and all attempts to exploit the newly arrived intellectual capital, or to expatiate on topics of 'natural' theology, had been strenuously resisted by the theologians, now, when the whole system of Aristotle, accompanied by a considerable satellite literature, was available and indeed was compulsory teaching matter, the masters of arts had matter for thought to last for a lifetime and to provide material to satisfy the keenest intelligence. Moreover, circumstances had combined to leave something of a void to be filled in the mental life of Paris. In 1248 Albert had left for Cologne, without having begun his commentary on the Philosopher; two years later Bonaventure began to compose his *Commentary on the Sentences* in the traditional manner, and two years later again it was the turn of Aquinas. Both these works give the impression of having been written in a peaceful and uncontroversial atmosphere. Within a few years Albert at Cologne began his great work of paraphrasing and commenting upon Aristotle, while Thomas in the *Summa contra Gentiles*, begun in 1258, produced a major synthesis of theology and philosophy based entirely upon Aristotle. Meanwhile Bonaventure had been removed from the schools by his election as minister-general (February 1257) and two years later Thomas was called away to Italy. Thus the three great theologians had disappeared from the scene at Paris, and there was no one of the first rank to replace them, in an atmosphere where the thought of Aristotle was fermenting on every side. The teaching of Aristotle, though in so many ways lucid even to self-evidence, is on many points ambiguous or fragmentary. Even to-day, when we possess uncontaminated texts of the Philosopher and his predecessors, illuminated by five centuries of careful criticism, the difficulties and lacunae remain, and they are most noticeable precisely on two or three points of essential significance to all religious thinkers – the existence and nature of God and of our knowledge of Him, the individuality and immortality of the human soul, and the nature of free-will. The Paris artists, who were not fully aware of the extent of Aristotle's silences, were not without assistance in filling the voids. They now had before them, not only the writings of Avicenna, but the great commentaries of Averroës, who had himself noted some of the difficulties and had resolved them by interpreting his texts in a non-religious sense. The masters in arts were not friars or priests, and had no theological training; theoretically, they had no authority to teach any part of philosophy that impinged upon divinity. In practice, however, it was inevitable that when vast tracts of pure philosophy were being illuminated for them, the artists, hitherto starved of material, should extend their grasp to every region of metaphysics, psychology and cosmology, while at the same time emphasizing their intention of remaining philosophers and nothing more. This claim was soon to take upon itself a new and peculiar colour.

Siger, called 'of Brabant' (d. 1284), began his career in the arts faculty about 1260. He appears first in the records as a fomenter of disturbance and faction in 1266, and from his first writings appears as a follower of Aristotle *au pied de la lettre*. The dangerous and heterodox tendencies among the artists were attacked by St Bonaventure in his Lent conferences on the Ten Commandments and the Gifts of the Holy Ghost in 1267 and 1268, and among the erroneous doctrines he mentions are several found in Siger's works, such as the eternity of the world, and the unicity of the human intellect – that is, the existence of a single intelligence common to all men. At the beginning of 1269 St Thomas returned to Paris, and a period of great productive activity ensued, culminating, for our purpose, in his masterly attack on the Averroist doctrine of monopsychism in the *De unitate intellectus* (1270).[1] In the same year (10 December), the faculty of theology, now thoroughly alert, procured the condemnation of the obnoxious teaching of the artists by the bishop of Paris, Etienne Tempier, lately himself a member of the faculty. In this act Tempier condemned thirteen articles which proclaimed the unicity of the human intellect, determinism of the will, the eternity of the world, the mortal nature of the soul, the complete detachment of God from all knowledge of the universe, and the negation of divine providence.

This condemnation had only a superficial effect within the faculty. Siger himself submitted and would seem to have been influenced both by it and by St Thomas's arguments against monopsychism, and to have modified his extreme teaching on this and other points; others denied that they had ever intended to oppose orthodox teaching. Some may even have repeated what they took to be the tactics of Averroës and maintained that philosophical truth could exist side by side with a contrary theological truth. Meanwhile, either in 1269 or 1270, Aquinas had been hard pressed by opponents among the conservative theologians, and particularly among the Minors, for holding doctrines on the soul and on the eternity of the world which they considered indistinguishable from those condemned by Tempier. After both Siger and Aquinas had put out their views on the

---

[1] 'Monopsychism' and 'unicity of the intellect' are almost synonymous terms at this period, owing to the Aristotelian use of the word *Nûs* as the equivalent of 'soul' in many passages of his writings; the usage spread to his Arabian and medieval commentators.

origin of the world the latter, in 1272, left Paris, never to return, while Bonaventure, in a third series of conferences, on the Week of Creation, in 1273 denounced the perils of philosophy and specifically of Aristotle in forcible, not to say, extravagant, terms. Neither he nor Aquinas lived to see the sequel: both died in 1274. Meanwhile the parties in presence continued their activities; agitations and divisions continued in the faculty of arts, and the theologians kept up their attacks. To these years belong the *Errores philosophorum* of the individualistic Giles of Rome (*c.* 1270) and the consultation of Albert in Cologne by Giles de Lessines, a Preacher and disciple of St Thomas, which evoked from the old oracle a reply characterized by van Steenberghen as 'deplorably inadequate to meet the situation'.[2] Meantime, while Siger continued his writings, seemingly anxious to keep within the pale of Christian orthodoxy though prey to a genuine intellectual struggle, his ally, Boethius of Dacia, began to attract general attention. His particular field was ethics, and in the two short works first published by Grabmann, especially his *De summo bono*, he sought to establish that the supreme happiness of man is the philosophic contemplation by the natural reason of the First Principle, to which the mind rises from the multiplicity of things around it. This is clearly, like Siger's programme in another field, a presentation of Aristotle's teaching in a pure and simple fashion, but modern scholars are divided here, as also in the case of Siger, as to the implications latent in it. While some, with Mandonnet, see in his treatment sheer rationalism in an undiluted form, surpassing anything in the Italian Renaissance, and foreshadowing Fontenelle and the age of Enlightenment, others consider that Boethius was treating simply of natural beatitude and excluding from his purview all mention of the supernatural life, which for a Christian under the present dispensation is inextricably bound up with the natural life, just as Aquinas discusses the powers of human nature as such, without considering its present fallen, wounded, state, the result of original and actual sin. Others will agree with Gilson that there is a warmth of expression, untinged by any nostalgic religious emotion, in Boethius's account of philosophic beatitude, which is hard to reconcile with the supposition that the writer was, as a private person, a fervent Christian.

Whatever the personal position of the two leaders may have been, it would seem certain that there was a great deal of questionable teaching and naturalistic criticism current in the faculty of arts, in

---

[2]'Elle [*sc.* Albert's reply] est lamentablement inadaptée à la situation.' F. van Steenberghen in Fliche et Martin. *Histoire de l'Eglise* XIII (1951), p. 268.

addition to the factions among its leaders. Pope John XXI, who as Peter of Spain had taught in the arts faculty thirty years previously, heard of the troubles and instructed the bishop of Paris to make enquiries. Tempier, moving with remarkable, not to say improper, despatch, and improving on his instructions, collected complaints from all quarters and, after only three weeks' delay, issued, precisely on the third anniversary of the death of Aquinas, a list of 219 propositions taken largely from the teaching of the masters of arts, prefacing his decree by a prohibition of the doctrine of the double truth as a loophole of escape. The condemned theses were a mixed grill; Avicenna, Averroës, Aristotle, Aquinas and the rules of the Love of Courtesy were among them; the only common factor apparent is a tendency to naturalism to the exclusion or contempt of religion. Some of the propositions might well have dated from the France of Voltaire or the Italy of the Synod of Pistoia: they contained statements that theology rests upon myth (*quod sermones theologi fundati sunt in fabulis*), that religion is a bar to enlightened education (*quod lex Christiana impedit addiscere*), that no profession is superior to that of a philosopher (*quod non est excellentior status quam vacare philosophiae*), and that there is no happiness save in this life (*quod felicitas habetur in ista vita, non in alia*). More significant for the future was the condemnation of various Averroistic or Aristotelian propositions seeming to limit the freedom of God, or His ability to come into direct contact with individuals; it was in reaction from these and similar theses that the theologians of the next generation extolled and ultimately deformed the concept of God's freedom of action, and combated the Thomist teaching of a God bound by the 'laws' of His own nature. The condemnation of certain propositions attributed to Aquinas will be dealt with later.

Whatever may be thought of Tempier's action (and the pope showed no sign of disapproval), this second condemnation ended Siger's career. Wanted by the Inquisitor, Simon du Val, he had left France in 1276 for Italy where he appealed to the Curia hoping to receive milder treatment. Siger was acquitted of heresy by the next pope, Nicholas III, but kept under house arrest in the papal Curia, only to be murdered, some time before the end of 1284, by his demented secretary. Siger, an enigma in life, is thus an enigma also in death – and even beyond the grave, since a celebrated verse in Dante has given birth to a small literature of its own. For in Paradise, and near to Aquinas himself among the greatest theologians, near to Denis the mystic, Isidore the encyclopedist, Bede the Venerable and Richard of St Victor, is another shining spirit, no other than Siger, 'who in weighty thoughts enwrapped, thought he went all too slowly to death'; Siger 'who, in his lectures in the Street of Straw [the abode of the artists at Paris] proposed in faultless form truths that earned him the hate of the envious rivals'.[3] And who is it, of all men, that speaks thus? No other than St Thomas himself. Was Dante, then, an Averroist? Or did Siger, as has been held, become in his last years a convert to Thomism? Or was Dante searching, as van Steenberghen holds, for a prince of pure philosophers to set beside the theologians?

Siger's reputation among contemporaries was high, and he is at least once entitled 'the great' by a fellow philosopher. How far this is justified can only be decided when all his works have been unearthed and authenticated; those now accessible in print show a keen and uncompromising mind, though one without great powers of original thought, or of the higher wisdom which soars above dialectic. The distinguishing traits of his doctrine are insistence on the autonomy and value of pure (i.e. natural) philosophy and an attachment to what is thought to be the genuine teaching of Aristotle. He aimed at being a pure Aristotelian, and is in fact a faithful exegete, filling the gaps on peripatetic principles, uninfluenced by experience or religious teaching. He was also influenced by Proclus, Avicenna and Averroës, and later by Albert and Thomas, whom he mentions as princes of philosophy. He did not hesitate to add to Aristotle a Supreme Being and First Cause from Proclus, and the Neoplatonic doctrine of creation by intermediaries.

Modern scholars have been divided, as was in part contemporary opinion, on three important points regarding Siger. Was he an Averroist? Were he and his friends sincere in maintaining that their aim was simply the academic presentation of the pure word of Aristotle? And did he and they proclaim the theory of the 'double truth'?

On the first point there was universal agreement from the days of Renan to the appearance of van Steenberghen's study, and the name Latin Averroism was accepted as a title for his system. Van Steenberghen argues at great length that Siger was never called, or regarded by contemporaries as, an Averroist, that the term was not in fact current till after his death, and that the specifically Averroistic doctrine, that of the unicity of the human soul, or 'monopsychism', though held by Siger for a time, was greatly modified under the pressure of St Thomas's arguments. Van Steenberghen has probably succeeded in clearing Siger of the charge of integral Averroism, and if a ticket must be applied to him, that of integral and heterodox

[3] Dante, *Paradiso*, X, 134–8.

Aristotelian is perhaps more precise, but he has not fully succeeded in disproving the existence of a conviction at Paris that Averroistic teaching was a public enemy, nor in disproving that the faculty of theology acted with this conviction in pressing for the two condemnations.

As for his sincerity, since all his actions as at present known are consistent with both sincerity and hypocrisy, no certain decision can be reached. We can only say that Siger categorically asserted that he sought the mind of Aristotle rather than the truth – a dictum to which St Thomas retorted that the aim of philosophy was not to know what men thought, but where the truth lay. If, as seemed clearly the case, some of the conclusions of Aristotle ran counter to Christian teaching, Siger made no attempt to explain or to remove the discrepancy; he stated the Philosopher's position as *necessarium* (i.e., unavoidable if one proceeded logically) on the natural level, though contrary to the affirmations of the faith, which alone were true. As for the doctrine of the 'double truth' which he adopted, according to Mandonnet and many others, to escape condemnation, van Steenberghen has argued cogently that no extant work by Siger contains either the phrase or the doctrine which it expressed. A statement seemed to natural reason inescapable, its contrary was made known by revelation; as a Christian, he accepted the latter. Whether all his followers were equally precise and consistent is another matter; but the precautionary condemnation of the double truth by Tempier is presumptive evidence that some, at least, were ready to exploit the phrase. It may be added that van Steenberghen seems on occasion to simplify unduly the question of Siger's sincerity. To profess Christian orthodoxy when denial would spell disaster need not necessarily imply either whole-hearted belief or sheer hypocrisy. It may be merely the practical decision of one who has neither deep religious conviction nor any inner compulsion to reject his status as a member of the Church. As for van Steenberghen's further claim, that Siger and his friends were led into difficulties by following Aristotle, not by following the interpretation put on him by Averroës, and that had Averroës never existed Siger would have come to all his heterodox conclusions from perusing Aristotle alone, opinions will probably continue to differ. To one outside the controversy, it seems hard to suppose that the true text of Aristotle would have led to such drastic conclusions, as also that the many heterodox opinions of Averroës should have had no influence upon minds with a critical and revolutionary bent.

CHAPTER TWENTY-THREE

England in the Thirteenth Century

We must now return to consider the English scene in the first century of full university life. England, until very recently, has fared ill at the hands of historians of thought. The great majority of these have been scholars of continental countries, and their interest was for long devoted to the great figures of Paris such as Aquinas and Bonaventure, with their predecessors and successors, while the rare English student, such as A. G. Little, often ploughed a lonely furrow without fully correlating English and continental movements. Since the 1940s the late Dr Beryl Smalley and Fr Daniel Callus O.P. have helped to draw attention to English scholastics, and (what is almost as significant) continental scholars have begun to absorb their conclusions, but there is a need for further intensive research by specialists before full justice can be done to the thought of Oxford before the advent of Scotus.

In truth, the share taken by England in the intellectual life of the twelfth and thirteenth centuries appears the more remarkable the more closely it is examined. The undisputed European primacy of Paris during this period has tended to obscure the real importance of Oxford and of men of English provenance. Continental scholars have often unwittingly conveyed the impression that the intellectual achievement of Paris was in a sense the achievement of France, whereas the university of Paris was in every way fully international, and examination shows that the number of eminent masters of French provenance was surprisingly small. England, on the other hand, besides contributing a lavish quota of her sons to the teaching body of Paris, was the only region in Europe possessing a school of arts and theology that could be considered in any way as a rival. Indeed, any list of the dozen or so most influential masters of the period 1200–1350 would be found to contain the names of more Englishmen than of any other nationality. No such list could omit Alexander of Hales, Robert Grosseteste, Roger Bacon, Duns Scotus, William of Ockham and Thomas Bradwardine, while Italy would contribute only the two greatest, St Bonaventure and St Thomas, and France would be hard put to it to find a companion for William of Auvergne. Even among the next dozen names Stephen Langton, Adam Marsh, Thomas of York, Robert Kilwardby and John Pecham would not be the only English competitors for a place.

Moreover, England had from early times an intellectual tradition of her own, which developed steadily throughout the twelfth and thirteenth centuries, until it became dominant in the fourteenth. Whereas until 1280 there were always some English thinkers who, like Alexander of Hales, Kilwardby and Pecham, entered fully into the continental stream, thenceforward it was England, with Scotus, Ockham and the Mertonian mathematicians, who exported her methods and doctrines to Europe. In general, and throughout the thirteenth century, Paris remained the mistress of theology and pure philosophy, and most of the English names in this field are of those who spent a great part, if not all, of their working lives abroad. The peculiar strength of England lay in logic, mathematics and science, and here Oxford held a unique position for more than a century.

From the very beginning of the twelfth century there had been a succession of scholars in England interested in the mathematical and natural sciences. Though few in number, they made up a real intellectual succession, which came in time to find its focus in the rising university of Oxford. The first of these, and perhaps the most original mind of them all, was Adelard of Bath (*fl.* 1116–1162), a pioneer who travelled to south Italy and Syria in search of Greek and Arabian science and thought, and who translated several of the classics of the two civilizations for the West. Adelard was a versatile and a very learned man. As a philosopher we have seen him, in his *De eodem et diverso*, trying to combine Plato and Aristotle in the matter of universals and epistemology, while remaining primarily a Platonic realist, in so far as he could grasp Plato's thought. In another field he is well known as the translator from the Arabic of Euclid's *Elements*. In yet another field he wrote excellently on the astrolabe, translated the Khorasmian astronomical tables, the work of Al-Khwarizmi (whence 'algorism' = decimal system of numerals), and in his *Quaestiones naturales* dealt with all kinds of biological and physical problems. While following the Arabs where they seemed to him to have improved upon the Greeks, he exhorted his nephew to follow reason against authority and to seek natural causes rather than to assume lightly a supernatural explanation. Such passages have rightly attracted attention, but it must always be borne in mind that Adelard was writing of natural science, not of theology. An earlier contemporary, Walcher, prior of Malvern (d. 1125), had devoted himself to astronomical observations and made use of the astrolabe, and a younger man, Robert of Ketton (or Chester) was among the first translators in Spain, where he became archdeacon of Pamplona, translating the algebra of Al-Khwarizmi and a revised version of his tables. Roger of Hereford (*fl.* 1178–95) carried on the astronomical tradition, as did also Daniel of Morley (*fl. c.* 1180), while Alfred of Sareshel (*fl.* 1200) commented on the *Meteorologica* of Aristotle and showed a particular interest in psychology. The writings and translations of all these men were known and read in England rather than at Paris, whereas the early translations of the philosophical works of the Arabs and Jews were first 'received' at Paris.

Oxford became an organized school of arts and theology shortly after 1200. There Aristotelian studies had a considerable start over Paris, since the faculty of arts was not affected by the prohibitions against the use for teaching purposes of the newly arrived translations and commentaries of the physical and metaphysical works of the philosopher, and in consequence the absorption and comprehension of Aristotle, beginning early in the century with John Blund, continued to grow and develop for some sixty years. This early use of Aristotle, added to the mathematical and scientific traditions that have been mentioned, helped to give a permanent and characteristic 'slant' to Oxford and English intellectual interests for the following two hundred years. This tendency met with no immediate competition, for there was no tradition at Oxford of a speculative, dialectical approach to all mental disciplines such as Abelard, the Victorines and others had long made endemic at Paris. The atmosphere of the Early Oxford schools was comparable rather to that of Chartres, only with a greater interest in the positive sciences. Had the evolution of Oxford continued as it had begun in the two first decades of the century, these characteristics might have made the English universities wholly different in spirit from those of France. The purely domestic growth was, however, greatly changed by the advent of the friars. Not only did they, here as at Paris, attract almost all the keenest minds of the century, but their international character brought to England a considerable dose of Parisian material and method, and in the event two currents flowed side by side in Oxford without ever fully intermingling their waters. The primary interest of the friars was in theology; they made of that, rather than of philosophy or mathematics, the crown of their achievement. Moreover, the constant interchange of regent masters between Oxford and Paris tended to standardize the teaching of theology in the Parisian mould. Thus Kilwardby and Pecham were regent masters in Paris before returning to teach or govern in England, and in later years Duns Scotus and others who passed from Oxford to Paris, are figures in the European, rather than in the Oxford tradition. It is perhaps significant that the secular masters, Grosseteste in the thirteenth century, and in the fourteenth Bradwardine and other Mertonians, were known to their contemporaries as theologians and as mathematicians and scientists. Roger Bacon, though a friar, is no exception, for much of his scientific and experimental work was completed, and his interests formed, before he became a Minor, and when he was a friar his attempts to continue his favourite pursuits led to nothing but trouble and frustration.

The first great Oxford teacher of whom we have adequate information, Robert Grosseteste, was in many ways the noblest Englishman of his age, and he impressed his personality upon Oxford in a way that no single master ever imposed himself upon Paris. All recent study tends to confirm and justify the opinion of his contemporaries in his regard, and if he is now only a name, whereas Bonaventure and Aquinas and Scotus are still influential masters of thought, it is partly because he lived just before the time of the integration of Aristotle into Christian thought, but more because his chief work was done in fields where he could light a torch and hand it on, but could not himself be a burning flame for ever.

Grosseteste was born near Bury St Edmunds in Suffolk *c.* 1170 and was teaching in Oxford from 1225, at first in the secular schools of the university and from about 1230 in the newly established community of Franciscans just outside the city walls. In 1232 he gave up his archdeaconry of Leicester which he had held since 1229 in order to follow more closely the Franciscan way of life. His main interests were shifting away from science to theology. From 1235 till his death in 1253 he was bishop of Lincoln, and thus diocesan of Oxford. His career for these eighteen years belongs to the history of England and of the papacy. As a theologian Grosseteste was not of the older school of Peter Comestor and Stephen Langton; he had his own way of reading the Bible and its main expositors. He was the first Englishman to absorb the greater part of the Aristotelian corpus, and the first to give Europe a complete translation of the *Ethics*. One of his greatest distinctions was to know Greek well: besides Aristotle, he translated works of the pseudo-Denis and St John Damascene, and he continued his work as translator even when at Lincoln, as he did also his advocacy of a knowledge of languages on the part of the theologian. For all his interest in Aristotle, Denis and Augustine gave his thought a strongly Neoplatonic flavour, and he accepted the Augustinian illumination of the intellect by the divine ideas. His Neoplatonism appeared not only in his abstract philosophy, but in his cosmology and ontology. He was a convinced expositor of the 'light-metaphysic', regarding light both as the first metaphysical constituent of bodies and as the genetic power of all being. Divine and intellectual light, which to us are no more than analogical applications of the physical term, were to him different manifestations of the same entity. There was for him, therefore, no gulf, no partition between metaphysics and physics such as existed for his thoroughgoing Aristotelian contemporaries, and sciences such as mathematics, geometry, optics and astronomy were an essential part of the philosopher's equipment. It was only a stage from this, easily traversed under the guidance of Aristotle, to take interest in the subject-matter and methods of science for their own sake, and in order to enlarge and perfect positive knowledge of all kinds. This stage was rapidly attained by Roger Bacon and other pupils and they rightly claimed Grosseteste as their standard-bearer. He gave them two principles of permanent value: the use of mathematics as a means of description, not (as they were to Plato) as revealing physical or metaphysical causes of things; and the use of observation and experiment controlled by logical methods of analysis and verification. The characteristics of his teaching were: a close attention to the study of the Bible, read textually and critically, as the basis of theology; the study of languages, especially Greek; an interest in securing faithful translations of all ancient works as a necessary part of a scholar's equipment; and, above all, an attention to mathematics and kindred sciences.

Grosseteste, like the other eminent scholastics of his age, lacked the qualities and tastes of a humanist. His treatises and private letters are wholly without beauty of form and language. Indeed, the element of charm and the impress of personality are almost entirely absent from his correspondence; it is not easy to instance any other man, equally and as justly celebrated for his mental and moral qualities, of whom such a judgement can be made. To us, there is a massive quality about his learning that borders on the ponderous, and an aridity that hides from us the appeal of his holiness. Yet to acute contemporaries, to Adam Marsh, Roger Bacon and Geoffrey of Fontaines, he is the great master, the most learned man of his day, *homo magnus in sanctitate vitae, claritate sapientiae.*

To Grosseteste's abiding influence of personality and teaching at Oxford must be added yet another title to fame. By welcoming the Minors and acting as regent in their school he became in a very real sense the father of the great family of Oxford Franciscan theologians and thinkers. This was more significant than a contemporary could ever have guessed, for at Oxford, as at Paris, the friars from their arrival attracted and formed the finest minds of the time. There was, however, this difference between the universities, that whereas at Paris Minors and Preachers shared with some equality the potentialities of genius and talent, at Oxford, at least for a century, the Franciscans had more than their share of both. Grosseteste, therefore, by becoming the father of the Franciscan school, became also *reduplicativè* the father of Oxford thought.

Among Grosseteste's friends in early days at Oxford had been the wealthy secular master Adam Marsh who at last, like Alexander of Hales and others, took the Franciscan habit. On his return to Oxford Adam took up the threads of his old friendship, and constant correspondence with Grosseteste, unbroken till the bishop's death, was maintained by letter when they were apart. Marsh, by general consent, was all but Grosseteste's equal as a scholar and teacher, and the two are frequently coupled by that stern critic, Roger Bacon, as the two greatest clerks in the world. The two men have much in common; the letters of Adam Marsh, like those of the bishop, are wholly wanting in personal charm and any indication of a sense of beauty in life, nature or letters. There is also in each a touch of hardness and an overtone of bitterness which seem to deprive their exemplary and austere lives of the finest bloom of sanctity.

Marsh was followed as regent master by a succession of able teachers, Richard of Cornwall, Thomas of Wales, Thomas of York. The most celebrated name of the younger generation is not, however, that of a regent master but of a friar unhappy in his life and legendary after death. The writings of Roger Bacon soon fell into oblivion, but within a century of his death he acquired an extraordinary reputation for necromancy which endured for nearly three hundred years. This he shared with a highly respectable colleague, Master Thomas of Bungay, and the two friars ultimately appeared together on the Elizabethan stage, as did Bacon and the bishop of Lincoln in *Hudibras*:

'Yet none a deeper knowledge boasted
Since old Hodg Bacon and Bob Grosted.'

Roger Bacon's equally undeserved reputation as a prophet and martyr of free thought, and his celebrity (probably also unmerited) as the inventor of gunpowder and the telescope, and as the foreseer of the motor and the aeroplane, have attracted to him the attention of both English and foreign scholars. In his extreme sensitiveness, in his intolerance of the obscurantism, real or supposed, of those in high place, and in his flashes of real insight, he has affinities with Abelard and with de Lammenais. His work shows many of the peculiar characteristics of Grosseteste: an interest in positive studies, an attention to observation and experiment, and an independence of outlook in the face of all the conventions of contemporary thought.

The writings of Bacon long remained unprinted, and a critical edition of the whole corpus is still wanting. Moreover, though much has been written on his work and personality, the sequence of his writings and the chronology of his life remained critically unexamined until quite recently. He was born by *c.* 1219 of a well known land-holding family, and studied arts, perhaps at Oxford, from about 1230. He rapidly acquired a wide philosophical learning, and an understanding of Aristotelian psychology and metaphysics superior to that of any Paris master of the day. To Paris he went before 1237 and was the first to lecture on the hitherto banned books of Aristotle, and he began there his study of theology. Later he resumed his theology, perhaps at Oxford *c.* 1247, under Adam Marsh and Thomas of Wales, but, doubtless under the influence of Grosseteste, he abandoned his intention of proceeding master and became wholly absorbed in natural sciences and experiment. His bitter criticisms of theologians are in part at least a revelation of his sense of inferiority. Henceforward he devoted himself entirely to his sciences, spending large sums on apparatus and materials for his experiments, perhaps chiefly in alchemy and optics. In 1257 or thereabouts be became a friar – why, must remain a mystery, since he must have known that his expensive laboratory work would be no longer possible.

As a friar he was hampered in his chosen pursuits not only by the poverty which forbade expense and by a general lack of sympathy for his favourite studies, but also by the decree of the chapter of Narbonne (1260) forbidding a friar to publish anything without permission and careful censorship. Bacon for his part did little to mollify superiors and contemporaries, and his sharp and often intemperate criticisms were directed principally against theologians, including some of the greatest. In 1260 the influential cardinal Guy de Foulques, who had heard that he had a great work ready, asked to see it. Bacon, taken by surprise and without funds as he was, spent a wretched four or five years preparing for his *opus. magnum*, a wide programme for the reform of studies and theology, traversing the whole field of his interests and schemes and frustrations. When, in 1265, his patron became pope, Bacon sent him a message that he had advice of importance for the church. Clement IV, ignorant of the type of book that was coming, commanded him to produce it, and Bacon, writing in great haste and secrecy, finished and sent the *Opus Maius* in 1267, followed by the *Opus Minus* and the *Opus Tertium* in 1268, the two latter being explanations of the first. Unfortunately, the pope died in November, 1268. What followed is uncertain, but in 1277, in circumstances of which we know little, Bacon was condemned by his superiors to some sort of restraint. His general had been Bonaventure, who had little sympathy with science and still less with astrology. Moreover, Bacon had made so many personal enemies by his reckless abuse that the wolves were howling about him, and he may have been thrown to them for the sake of peace. How long he was in confinement we do not know, but before 1292 he was at liberty, writing his *Compendium studii theologiae* with all his old verve and recklessness. The outspoken critic of St Albert and St Thomas, and a trouble to St Bonaventure, he had lived right through the golden age into another climate pursuing an ideal other than theirs. He died *c.* 1292, probably at Oxford.

Bacon was a strange and erratic genius. Almost alone of the celebrated scholastics, he is remembered principally by works that were not composed for the schools, and for the greater part of his mature life he took no part in university life. His early work shows him a philosopher of unusual ability and modernity, but of the normal type, part Aristotelian, part Neoplatonist, with a strong dosage of the light-metaphysic which he perhaps drew from Grosseteste, and had he proceeded to theology, he might have developed still further along normal lines. Instead, he turned, a 'spoiled theologian', to experimental science, a pursuit foredoomed to frustration in that age, and what with his own sense of inferiority, his constant financial stringency, his conflict with authority and his own temperament, he passed from one period of distress to another. He was, to all appearances, irresponsible and neurotic and as such, perhaps, unmanageable and friendless. Yet he had great intuitive genius and rare critical power. He seized with precision the basic faults of later scholasticism, which did in the event bring the building down. He deplored the divorce of pure thought from life and experience, and the insecurity of the basis of faulty texts, jealous tradition and bookish learning on which it rested. Yet the ultimate aims, the philosophical prepossessions and the outward form of his writings are purely traditional, and careful research has set him in his place in the sequence of Oxford Franciscans. Moreover, his science included alchemy and astrology, and he was both extremely credulous and unreasonably assertive of their possibilities. The originality noted by historians in the past often consists of little more than irresponsible hits at contemporaries and the flouting of some of the most eminent thinkers and the deepest problems in philosophy. His criticisms, outspoken as they are, and often palpably unjust and ill-informed, are often, when they can be checked, found to be inaccurate. Yet he remains the most insistent medieval advocate of the value of experiment in science, and of experience and intuition in human life.

Throughout the period of a century, over which the active lives of Grosseteste and Bacon extended, a series of theologians at Oxford were engaged in the task of adapting the new philosophical material to their needs. St Edmund of Abingdon (*c*. 1170–1240), later archbishop of Canterbury, and John Blund (d. 1248), elected but subsequently disqualified for the same high office, seem to have been between them the first to lecture on the new logic and the *libri naturales* of Aristotle at Oxford. The latter is noteworthy for his knowledge of Avicenna and his rejection of the hylomorphism of Avicebron and of the plurality of forms. Adam of Buckfield in the middle of the century commented on almost the whole of the Aristotelian corpus. Meanwhile the Dominican masters Robert Bacon, friend and biographer of St Edmund, and Richard Fishacre were well known names; Fishacre was a prominent Aristotelian. Their contemporaries among the Franciscans, Adam Marsh and Thomas of York also used the new literature, but the latter claimed to be a Platonist and followed Avicebron among the philosophers and William of Auvergne among the moderns. From Oxford came also the unique and very interesting *Summa philosophiae*, of which the authorship is still unknown. It contains a history of philosophy and also a very detailed analysis of the various schools of thought in presence when the author was writing. He himself, while realizing the intellectual value of Aristotle's system, prefers to follow Plato on many important points. Robert Kilwardby has been put forward as the author of this treatise, and the outlook is certainly akin to his, but the style and spirit of the work do not show much resemblance to the authentic writings of Kilwardby.

In the years when the Minors and Preachers at Oxford were developing their schools, English members of the two orders were learning and teaching at Paris. Pre-eminent among them were Robert Kilwardby (d. 1279) and John Pecham (d. 1292). Kilwardby studied arts and taught at Paris before becoming a friar *c.* 1245 and as a Preacher held the regency at Oxford before becoming prior provincial (1261) and archbishop of Canterbury (1272). A very prolific writer and a methodical thinker who knew Aristotle but did not follow him exclusively, Kilwardby belongs to the group of traditional theologians from all the orders who instinctively opposed the integral Aristotelianism, whether Thomist or heterodox. He was regarded in his order as a leading theologian, to be set beside St Thomas, and they served together in the Dominican organization of studies. His share in the attack on Thomism will be mentioned later. John Pecham's career was somewhat similar to that of Kilwardby, save that he became a friar when a boy and spent all his academic life abroad, chiefly at Paris, where he was a pupil and disciple of Bonaventure and ultimately regent from *c.* 1269–71, at the height of the controversy between the Aristotelians and the conservative theologians. He then became in turn minister provincial in England, lector in theology at the papal court and archbishop of Canterbury in succession to Kilwardby. Pecham might stand for a text-book portrait of an Augustinian; indeed, he is credited by van Steenberghen with having given the school its fixed programme. Professing to follow Alexander of Hales and Bonaventure, he isolated the characteristic philosophical doctrines which he considered to form the framework of the Franciscan school: divine illumination of the intellect, multiplicity of substantial forms, 'seminal tendencies', and the substantial nature of the spiritual soul of man. He also clashed with St Thomas in Paris, and with his disciples in England. Though neither Kilwardby nor Pecham had a mind of the first order of creative genius, each represented to perfection the class of conservative theologians who were to oppose the synthesis of Aquinas so stubbornly.

PART FIVE

The Breakdown of the Medieval Synthesis

CHAPTER TWENTY-FOUR
The Aftermath of Aristotle

In the five preceding chapters we have considered different strands in the great and varied fabric of the intellectual life of the schools in the decades around the middle of the thirteenth century. The years between 1250 and 1270 form the brief high summer, the brightest moment of the golden age of medieval philosophy and theology. The short summer ended as abruptly as it had begun. St Thomas and St Bonaventure were prematurely overtaken by death in 1274, by which time St Albert, his great work accomplished, was no more than the shadow of a mighty name, while Siger, hard hit and shaken, was about to be driven from Paris. In the preceding chapters we have reviewed the positive achievements of these men; we must now consider the causes and results of the antagonism between the three Paris teachers. Albert stood apart from the main stream of the controversy whose significance, it would seem, he did not fully appreciate.

In the decades before 1250 the theologians of Paris had continued to discuss the great topics of their science with the aid of a greater or less amount of philosophical material. All of them regarded Augustine as their supreme master in theology and Aristotle as their guide in the technique of reasoning and dispute. Each drew upon the newly available legacy of the past: Aristotelian metaphysics and noetics, Arabian and Jewish comment and criticism, Neoplatonic treatises were used as seemed opportune, and it was natural that many of the elements of the new material should be attributed to a wrong source, and should be regarded as part of the Augustinian inheritance. Among the philosophical and theological doctrines received from Augustine by all, or almost all, the Paris theologians were the creation of the world by God, the seminal tendencies or bias (*rationes seminales*) in the matter of which earthly being was composed, the concept of the soul as a substance complete in itself, though inhabiting or informing a body, and the divine illumination of the intellect. Along with these, though not derived from Augustine, had come the so-called extreme hylomorphism, which consisted in part of the thesis that all being, even if purely spiritual, was composed of 'matter' and 'form', and in part of the thesis of the multiplicity of co-existent forms within a single being. This last, in the case of the human being, implied forms of sensitive and vegetative life, and a form of bodiliness (*forma corporeitatis*) existing simultaneously with the intellective form of the soul.

St Thomas, by adopting Aristotle as the authoritative basis of his system of philosophy, which was itself the most complete medieval system and synthesis, came ultimately into collision with the conservative theologians on all the points just mentioned. He taught, with Aristotle, that the eternity of the world was philosophically an acceptable doctrine, that matter was pure potency, that the soul was the constitutive form of the human being, that there was only one substantial form in beings, the substantial form that made a being 'one', and that all human knowledge was derived by contact, by means of the senses, with the external world: there was, on the natural level, no divine illumination of the intellect.

Wholly unconnected with St Thomas, the brilliant but intemperate Siger had taken as his programme the resolve to follow Aristotle to the letter, without any reference to the teaching of the theologians. For him, therefore, the world was eternal, not created, matter was pure potency, human knowledge came through the senses, and the world, physical and intellectual, was ordered and governed by the immutable design of the First Mover. In one important matter, moreover, he went beyond Aristotle under the influence of Averroës: he taught that there was a single soul for the whole human race, which vitalized the 'possible' intellect of the individual. The so-called human soul was therefore no more than the form of the sensitive, vegetative being possessed of a 'possible' intellect, and it ceased to exist when separated from its body. The intelligent human being consisted of two substances – a bodily substance vitalized by a sensitive-vegetative soul, and a spiritual substance common to all men. These two did not form a substantial unity, but a unity of operation only, though this operation implied intimate association. In the process of knowing two intellects took part, the 'agent' and the 'possible' intellects, the latter being a mere capacity to think and to receive determining species abstracted from sense-pictures by the active intelligence. The single world-soul never in fact existed in separation from the unending procession of human intelligences to which it was joined.

The foregoing paragraphs will have shown that in the twenty years (1265–85) of acute controversy, which resulted from the reception of the complete Aristotle, two closely related topics came to the fore and remained for a generation at the centre of all controversies, as had the problem of universals almost two centuries earlier. The one concerned the nature of the human soul, its metaphysical content and its relations with the body in life and death; the other concerned the process of intellection. Both were ultimately traceable to the radical differences between Plato and Aristotle, and to the failure on the part of Aristotle to give a clear and satisfactory statement of his position, and both were brought to the fore by the impact upon Parisian masters of the *De anima* of Aristotle, the treatise on the soul of Dominic Gundisalvi, the epistemological opinions of the Arabs, and, last in time but not in importance, the monopsychism of Averroës. During the decade 1265–74 both St Thomas and Siger returned again and again to a discussion of the nature of the soul and the intellective process. The discussion continued after they had passed from the scene, but the interest of the participants, as will be seen, concentrated itself chiefly upon the single point of the unity of substantial form in beings.

It is not possible to discover the exact moment when controversy broke out within the university of Paris between the Aristotelian artists and the conservative theologians, but fairly exact limits can be assigned to our uncertainty. St Bonaventure was elected minister-general in February, 1257, and for almost a decade after that took no discernible part in domestic controversy at Paris. St Thomas left Paris in 1259 with his first great philosophical survey, the *Summa contra Gentiles*, only in its beginnings, and not to be finished before 1264, in Italy. Siger began writing *c.* 1265 and was giving trouble at Paris in 1266, the year in which Aquinas began the *Summa theologiae* in Italy. In Lent 1267 came the first of the series of attacks on pagan philosophy launched by Bonaventure; in January, 1269 St Thomas returned to Paris and in the same year John Pecham became regent in the Franciscan convent there. The years 1269–71 were a time of intense activity in which Aquinas put forward his teaching on the soul and on epistemology, opposed the monopsychism of Siger, and defended the philosophical opinion of the eternity of the world. On this a public disputation took place between Pecham and Aquinas and Pecham also challenged his view of the subject of the unicity of form in man. At the end of 1270 came the first condemnation of Siger, in which, so Giles of Lessines said, the Thomist doctrine of the soul came near to being involved. The years 1269–71 may therefore be considered as seeing the first open collision between St Thomas and the conservative theologians headed by Pecham.

The head and front of offending on the part of St Thomas would seem to have been the matter of the unity of form in man, that is, that the soul, a spiritual substance (and therefore simple and without 'matter') stood to the body as form to matter, and superseded all other forms, such as the 'form of bodiliness'. This was not a new doctrine. It was based, as we have seen, upon the teaching of Aristotle, that the soul is the 'first entelechy' or perfection of the body, and it had been held by several masters at Paris and Oxford during the early decades of the thirteenth century, but it had been contaminated by the prevailing Augustinian conception of the soul as a complete entity acting upon the body and never pressed to its full metaphysical conclusion. The concept of a single substantial form for every being was obscured, and in default of a clear distinction between substantial and accidental forms, and between the real and objective, and the merely logical, decomposition of a being, the door was left open for the admission of an indefinite number of 'forms' of equal metaphysical significance. The human soul was at the same time regarded in many quarters as a composite of matter and form, while the body had also its form and the vegetative and sensitive principles were regarded either as having essential forms of their own, united under the one life-form of the intellective soul, or as possessing an autonomous existence of their own and as only extrinsically united to the soul, or, finally, as forming a hierarchy in which the highest and directive place was taken by the soul. In opposition to all these theories St Thomas set his thesis, which developed and clarified that of Aristotle, that the soul, as pure form, actualizes the body as its matter, and that the intellective soul contains in itself in an eminent degree all the perfections of the sensitive and vegetative souls, which it supplants in the embryo of the human being at the moment of its creation.

Pecham contended that this doctrine was invented by Aquinas, if indeed he had not taken it from the Paris Aristotelians. The latter suggestion can be refuted from the writings of St Thomas; his doctrine on the soul appears in them several years before the rise of the integral Aristotelians. The former contention is also, as has been seen, incorrect. Nevertheless, it can be said in defence of Pecham that the matter had been hitherto considered from a psychological rather than from a metaphysical angle. St Thomas realized the full importance of substantial unity as a metaphysical reality, and had extended its application to cover all compound beings. 'Nothing', he observed, 'is purely and simply a unity unless it has a single form that determines its being, for a thing derives its being and its unity from a single source.'[1] It thus became one of the pillars of his metaphysical structure and it was, in this sense, a real innovation.

The question was not a purely speculative one. Under the old conception of the soul as a substance in its own right, a rich life of faculties, virtues, and superior potentialities had been developed. The soul was the immortal, personal part of man which could not die, but might be lost. In Aristotle there was little of this. As with his cosmos, so with his microcosm, the highest part is seen the most faintly. The first mover is little more than a necessary postulate, the soul is a mere form or principle of life, necessary only as a metaphysical keystone to hold together the various intellective and moral powers of the human being. Aristotle is not interested in a life after death, and his views on it are uncertain. The tenuous nature of the Aristotelian soul and the questions of its individualization and its relationship to the body have indeed remained ever since his day, as we have seen, one of the most debatable points in his system,[2] while in the realm of scholastic disputation a number of theological arguments could be pressed home, such as the relationship of the soul-form to the body after death, and thus to the dead body of Christ between death and resurrection, or to the body of Christ as present in the consecrated bread after transubstantiation had taken place. Once the question had been transferred to this level every kind of criticism, genuine or captious, might be made. Aquinas was even accused of agreeing with the monopsychism of Siger.

No Thomist thesis was included in Tempier's list of December 1270, either explicitly or by implication, though it is possible, as Giles of Lessines asserted in his letter to Albert at Cologne, that the teaching of Aquinas on the unity of form and the simplicity of purely spiritual beings came near to condemnation. Little more than a year later, about May 1272, the great Preacher left Paris, never to return, and in the same year Pecham departed to become regent at Oxford. Bonaventure, so far as is known, had made no overt move in the attack on Thomas, but when his character and official position and the reiterated expressions of devotion to him on the part of Pecham are

---

[1]*Summa theologiae*, I² Q. lxxvi, art. 3, corp. art.: '*Nihil enim est simpliciter unum nisi per formam unam, per quam habet res esse: ab eodem enim habet res quod sit ens, et quod sit una.*'
[2]See above, ch. xvii.

borne in mind, it is difficult to suppose that the minister general, often residing in the convent where Pecham was regent, can have disapproved of the attitude of his order's most active spokesman. Bonaventure died in 1274, and thereafter the controversy was continued by lesser men.

As has been seen, Tempier and the conservative theologians of Paris, among whom Henry of Ghent must be counted, were not satisfied with the result of their action of 1270. Though Siger may have become more moderate, his associates continued to utter extreme opinions, and a spirit of rationalism and cynicism was clearly abroad in the arts school, though perhaps only among a minority of the artists. Early in 1277 came the second fulmination. This time a larger number of theses were included in the miscellaneous slaughter, but as the name of Thomas did not occur, and as throughout the list the various contributors seem to have instanced conclusions drawn from doctrines rather than the authentic words of the party responsible, there can be a fair difference of opinion as to the number of Thomist propositions condemned.[3] In general the doctrine of individualization of the soul by the body, the determination of the will by the good, and the Thomist theory of knowledge were the principal objects of attack. The unity of form did not figure, though it was closely connected with more than one of the opinions condemned. The omission was shortly made good elsewhere. Ten days after Tempier's decree, and undoubtedly in collusion with him, Archbishop Kilwardby 'visited' the university of Oxford.

Robert Kilwardby, St Thomas's senior by some ten or fifteen years, was perhaps the most distinguished master of his order before the rise to fame of Albert and Thomas. He was a learned commentator on many of the works of Aristotle, and possibly, as we have seen, the author of a *Summa philosophiae* which outlined an eclectic and interesting system drawn from all sources but on the whole opposed to Aristotelian opinions. Kilwardby had known Aquinas and had shown no enthusiasm for his work. Back in England as regent at Oxford, then as prior provincial and finally archbishop of Canterbury, he had hardened in his conservatism and still cherished most of the doctrines affected by Bonaventure twenty years earlier. He had observed with displeasure the infiltration of Thomist opinions among the younger friars in the school at Oxford where he had once ruled. One Richard Knapwell in particular had recently advertised his conversion from the traditional teaching to the Thomist doctrine

[3]Mandonnet reckons twenty such, Hissette only one.

of unity of form. Kilwardby therefore demanded assent to a series of propositions, among which were the *rationes seminales,* and the assertion that the human soul was not simple but composite.

Aquinas, however, though dead did not lack for powerful friends. One of these, the Preacher Pierre de Conflans in Rome, wrote to Kilwardby taking him to task and setting out the doctrine of substantial form. Kilwardby fought back, but he was shortly recalled to Rome and created cardinal, perhaps as a measure of papal disapproval; he died within a few months. As for Tempier, who had wished to echo Kilwardby's Oxford demands, his hands were tied by the cardinals who administered the curia on the death of John XXI. Meanwhile Kilwardby had been succeeded at Canterbury by his and Thomas's old opponent John Pecham. Pecham, an able theologian of the second class, a disciple of Bonaventure but inelastic of mind and irritable of temper, had consistently opposed both Thomas and the Paris Aristotelians, and may well have briefed the pope in 1277. The continued activities of Knapwell at Oxford goaded him to action, and in 1284 he announced that he in his turn would repeat Kilwardby's exploit of visiting the university, and the prior provincial of the Preachers, himself a Thomist, tried in vain to dissuade him at an interview in which both parties practised considerable economy of the truth. Arrived at Oxford, he reiterated Kilwardby's decree, adding nothing save an express condemnation of the unity of form, alleging the guiding example of Kilwardby and asserting that the opinion of the unity of form had originated among dangerous innovators, and specifically from the teaching of Siger of Brabant. Fortunately for historians, the archbishop felt it incumbent upon him to defend himself in a series of letters to Oxford, Lincoln and Rome which are among the most valuable documents of the century for the historian of scholastic thought, giving as they do the views of an eminent contemporary on the revolution produced in the schools by Aquinas and, incidentally, cataloguing the notes of traditional Augustinism.[4] These letters were, in fact, the *pièces justificatives* of Ehrle's epoch-making article on the contest between Aristotelian and Augustinian thought, and if historians now tend to reject Ehrle's inclusion of earlier theologians under the blanket of Augustinianism, they agree in seeing Pecham as the principal propagator, if not the originator, of an 'Augustinian' system of philosophy. Among much that is of interest Pecham's note of time is particularly valuable: the changes, he says, writing in 1285, began

[4]The letters were first printed in 1885 by C. T. Martin in the Rolls Series edition (No. 77) of the *Registrum Epistolarum* of Pecham. See especially iii 864–8, 870–2, 896–902.

twenty years ago, and this date would take us back a little before the year (1266) in which Aquinas began the *Summa theologiae* shortly before his return to Paris.

Pecham was an obstinate man, and regardless of consequences, and in spite of the appeal which the Oxford Preachers had lodged at Rome, he proceeded in 1286 to pronounce a solemn judgement against a batch of Thomist propositions which included the unity of form, signalized as the source of all the mischief. This time the 'errors' were branded as heresies, and their supporters declared excommunicate and to be shunned (*vitandi*) by all. The Preachers appealed to Rome on the point of privilege, but by the time the case came on a Franciscan, Nicholas IV, was pope, and Knapwell was condemned to perpetual silence. The Dunstable annalist says he died insane; a more reliable source tells us that Pecham also in the last weeks of his life became enfeebled of mind and subject to fits of fury.

The series of condemnations at Paris and Oxford, especially those of Tempier in 1277, marks something of an epoch in the history of medieval thought. Too often in the past they have been considered merely as a malicious attempt on the life of infant Thomism, and as such doomed to a speedy reversal. It is true that they failed to do any direct harm to the system of Aquinas; on the contrary, by provoking its adherents and stimulating the order's *esprit de corps* they were a principal cause of its becoming the official doctrine of the order as early as 1278. But they were certainly instrumental in 'precipitating' the counter-philosophy of the conservatives, who now strengthened their defences with a system explicitly based upon that of Augustine and the other saints of old. This in turn soon gave place to the novel synthesis of Duns Scotus, and henceforward the Friars Minor rested upon a blend of his teaching and that of Bonaventure. But the rift between Minors and Preachers, always threatening to become a chasm, had now widened formidably, and as Pecham remarked, 'the doctrine of the one order is in almost every particular the contrary of the other, save in the fundamentals of the faith'.[5] It was the beginning of the fragmentation of speculative theology into schools with an excessive *esprit de corps*, which may indeed at certain periods have given life and stimulus to their activities, but which has been responsible also for much sterile controversy and frustration.

Neither did these condemnations strangle heterodox Aristotelianism, which was the principal public enemy against which they were directed. Siger and his personal friends were indeed eliminated, and

[5]Pecham, *Registrum Epistolarum* (Rolls Series) iii 902.

others were silenced, but their spirit was reincarnated, half a century later, in Jean of Jandun, Marsilio of Padua, and the Averroism of the north Italian universities. What was of still greater importance, the condemnations strengthened unduly the conservative theologians who had maintained for twenty years that this was what would come of taking up with Aristotle, and their success created a widespread phobia of Aristotelian philosophy as tending towards determinism and a necessitarian cosmology. Moreover, by setting a stigma upon philosophy, and particularly upon Aristotle, the most 'rational' of philosophers, they did much to shatter the vision of a great synthesis. That Tempier's decrees against Thomist propositions were rescinded, and Thomas himself canonized, might satisfy the Preachers and benefit posterity, but by the time this satisfaction was given Aquinas's own order was far from being united in maintaining the great principles of his system. As Gilson finely remarked: 'After 1277, the aspect of the whole of medieval thought is changed. After a brief honeymoon [one might almost have said, before the wedding breakfast was over] theology and philosophy think they see that their marriage was a mistake. While waiting for the decree of divorce, which is not long in coming, they proceed to divide their effects. Each resumes possession of its own problems, and warns the other against interference.'

CHAPTER TWENTY-FIVE
Henry of Ghent and Duns Scotus

The principal, or at least the most vocal, opponents of Thomism in the years around the condemnations of Paris and Oxford were the Friars Minor, of whom the leading spokesman, both at Paris and in England, was John Pecham. They opposed to the novelties of Aquinas the teaching of the fathers and saints of old, specifically St Augustine, Alexander of Hales and St Bonaventure, and they elaborated a system which they took to be wholly in agreement with the Augustinian tradition. As we have seen, this system in its fulness maintained itself for less than two decades, for in the increasingly critical and controversial climate the defenders of certain points of Augustinian doctrine, and in particular the theory of epistemology involving divine illumination of the intellect, had difficulty in withstanding the arguments of the Aristotelians. The Augustinian school, therefore, and even its contingent within the Franciscan order, was gradually eroded by a new movement of eclecticism. These new eclectic thinkers, however, were no longer concerned with choosing philosophical doctrines to insert here and there in their theological speculations, but with constructing a complete system to which both Aristotle and others might contribute. Unlike their predecessors earlier in the century, who could ignore the instructions given to the artists, they now had before them as directives the condemnations of Etienne Tempier.

Among the most notable in this group was the secular master Henry of Ghent, who was perhaps the first secular master since William of Auvergne to stand among the great figures of Paris. Notable in his own right, he is still more significant for the historian as at once a harbinger and an object of criticism to Duns Scotus.

Henry of Ghent was one of the theologians in Tempier's panel of

1277, and he was a leading influence at Paris between that date and 1293. He was an Augustinian, but with a considerable difference; he was also, like earlier Augustinians, a sympathetic reader of Avicenna. The second half of the thirteenth century was a great age of metaphysics, and Henry, like Thomas Aquinas and Thomas of York and Scotus himself, gave much attention to the philosophy of being. For Henry, being was not, as it was for Aquinas, a richly endowed, diversified entity, but an indefinable something immediately recognizable by the mind; it was everything that is. There were for him two kinds of being, uncreated (God) and created, and from the latter we can argue to the former; still more readily, our mind, in its first conception of being, sees it in the first of the two types just mentioned, viz., uncreated being, and to this extent Henry would have accepted the Anselmian argument for the existence of God. All being, therefore, *is* in one way or another, and there is no distinction between a being and its existence.

On the vexed question of individuation Henry of Ghent meets the difficulty with an assertion; an existent being is given the status it has by its cause, and in virtue of that status it is individual. It is, as we recognize, both a unity in itself and distinct from everything else. In the matter of the metaphysical composition of the human being Henry, who admitted the unicity of substantial form in general, made an exception in the case of man. The soul, divinely created and infused, does not interfere with the *forma corporeitatis*. As for the process of knowing, Henry abides by the Augustinian principle that no 'sincere' or pure truth can come by means of the senses, but that natural knowledge acquired by the intellect abstracting from sense images is in normal circumstances true; but it is not the pure and full truth, which can only be attained by contact with the 'rules of eternal light'. These are displayed by God when he wishes and to whom he wishes, though in a natural, not a mystical way.

We can see Henry of Ghent carefully avoiding the dangers of integral Aristotelianism, and still attracted by the outlook of Augustine, but fully conscious of the difficulties of the traditional philosophy and willing to accept Aristotle when no essentials are at stake. We can see him also making allowance in his system both for intuitional knowledge, for the frank acceptance of convictions which we cannot rationalize, and for the acceptance of uncertainty in our forecast of divine action. Some of these tendencies will reappear in an accentuated form in Duns Scotus. The epistemology, in particular, of the neo-Augustinians was a focus of difficulty. On the one hand, the classical dictum of Augustine, deriving ultimately from Plato, that 'no pure truth can be expected from sensation', made them distrust the empiricism of Aristotle, with its Thomist corollary, that 'nothing is in the intellect that has not first come through the senses'. On the other hand, the doctrine of the divine illumination of the intellect, which alone guarded an Augustinian from a general scepticism when the pure Platonic doctrine of ideas had gone, was a tenet extremely hard to defend philosophically, particularly in the critical mental climate of the 1280s. In this predicament, the conservative theologians, or at least those of their number who belonged to the order of Friars Minor, received an uncovenanted assistance from the genius of Duns Scotus.

John Duns the Scot, who took his name from a small Border village in Berwickshire, was until recently a homeless figure, and even now the account of his origin that follows would not be accepted by all Scottish historians. According to this account, which in some particulars depends upon evidence that cannot be traced to a medieval source, John Duns was born at Maxton in Roxburghshire in 1266 and received his early schooling at Haddington. Entering the Franciscan convent at Dumfries, where his uncle was guardian, in 1277, he received the Franciscan habit in 1281, as Gilson noted, in the church that was to be desecrated twenty-five years later by the blood of the Red Comyn shed by Robert Bruce. He was ordained priest by Bishop Oliver Sutton at Northampton in 1291 (here we are on certain ground), and studied at Oxford (1290–3), Paris (1293–6) and Oxford again (1297–1301), where he began his teaching life and wrote the first redaction of his commentary on the Sentences, which when rewritten became the *Opus Oxoniense*. In 1302 he returned to Paris where he composed his second commentary and was banished, along with others, for taking the part of Boniface VIII against Philippe le Bel, a circumstance that has been emphasized, not to say exploited, by his modern confrères. He returned in 1304 and became doctor in 1305, but in 1307 was sent to Cologne where he died in the autumn of 1308 at the age of forty-two, already the author of a great bulk of writings.

Duns Scotus, the sharp-witted (*doctor subtilis*), is by common consent a difficult thinker, and when both M. Gilson and his Franciscan editor-in-chief, Fr. Balić, agree to call him so, others need feel no shame in pleading occasional bewilderment. There are several reasons for this, in addition to the extreme acuity of his mind. In the first place, the short life of Duns ended before he had given a full and reasoned presentation of his system. On many points, therefore, we know what he held, but not his reasons for holding it. These have been supplied in many cases by his disciples, but the historian is not concerned with them. Secondly, his works are textually in a far worse condition than those of Bonaventure or Thomas. Some are preserved only as taken down by his hearers, and such versions often disagree; moreover, the business of separating the spurious from the genuine is only now approaching completion. And, finally, Duns, unlike Bonaventure and Thomas, not only devised a new metaphysical approach but also coined novel concepts and the terms to denote them, such as the celebrated *haecceitas* and the *distinctio formalis naturalis ex natura rei*. Thus a second mental effort is imposed upon the modern reader after his initial task of mastering the normal scholastic terminology.

John Duns, it must be remembered, began his studies in a climate conditioned by the pronouncements of Tempier, Kilwardby and Pecham. Averroës and certain doctrines of Aristotle were therefore anathema, while on the positive side the Franciscan school at Oxford had inherited the mathematical and empirical tradition of Grosseteste as well as the Augustinianism of Bonaventure and Pecham. Duns therefore tended to separate the provinces of philosophy and theology, in agreement with Avicenna, whom he revered and often followed, while at the same time he was deeply interested in metaphysics. Metaphysics deals with being *qua* being, but being as such, according to Duns, eludes comprehension by the human mind, which can only attain to such delimitations of being as it can abstract from the data of sense. Consequently, at the very beginning Duns parts company with Aquinas. For the latter being (*esse*) is not a univocal notion, with the same signification whenever used, but a notion admitting an indefinite succession of degrees from a relationship or quality, through material, vegetable, animal and spiritual substances up to God. Created being is therefore a reflection (*analogatum*) of God's Being, and therefore the mind can rise from created being to find in God the source (*analogizans*) of all. Being is therefore something extremely positive; in fact, the only really positive entity.

With Duns, being is the same wherever found, and has no positive content. As he says, it is everything that is not nonentity (*se extendit ad quodcumque quod non est nihil*). It has neither depth nor degrees, and there is no room in his system for the distinction between essence and existence; as Duns observes roundly, such a distinction is a sheer mistake (*falsum est quod esse sit aliud ab existentia*). If therefore we wish to prove the existence of God as the cause of univocal being (within which God Himself, as known to us, is included) we cannot get outside the physical order of things; we have simply proved the existence of the keystone of the arch, of the first cause behind all other causes. As in Aristotle's system, the First Mover is within the universe moved by him. Duns therefore, searching for an argument of God's existence, proceeded on the high metaphysical plane: all beings of which we have knowledge are contingent and composite of matter and form; contingent, multiple and finite beings demand a cause that is necessary, single and infinite; infinity implies the possession of all perfections, including existence, provided, as we can show, that there is no self-contradiction in such an infinite being. This being is God. This, it will be noted, has a strong kinship to the Anselmian argument, which in fact Scotus did not reject, but it is both a stronger and a clearer argument than Anselm's for those to whom metaphysical reasoning is acceptable.

In epistemology Duns is, with Aquinas, an empirical Aristotelian. The mind attains knowledge by abstracting the essence from the object presented by the senses, thus attaining to the concept. Within its sphere the human reason can attain truth without any direct divine illumination. In one important respect, however, Duns differs from Aquinas. He holds that the mind has a direct, though not a clear, intuition of the individual, whereas for St Thomas the mind knows the individual only by a reflex reference to the memory and the senses. An intellectual intuition presupposes an object susceptible of intellectual comprehension, and this Duns finds in the 'form' of the individual. This form or 'thisness' (*Haecceitas*) is a novel notion; it is the ultimate intelligible factor beneath the generic and the specific, the basis of individuality that makes a being different from all else and present to our consciousness here and now. For Duns the first attainment of the understanding is the singular, not the common, essence.

This doctrine again is closely linked with Duns' teaching on form. Taking from his Franciscan masters, and ultimately from Avicebron, the hylomorphism which implied the multiplicity of substantial forms, he was a realist and in a sense a more thoroughgoing realist than St Thomas. Not only did he teach that the universal exists in threefold wise, in the mind of God before creation, in the individual and in the concept, but he also held the reality and 'formality' of all the modes and distinctions actually recognized by the mind as present in things – that there is in the structure of things a correspondence to the structure of thought. Duns therefore gave reality and formality to something between a real distinction and a mere distinction of the reason as admitted by Aquinas. He could therefore admit the plurality of form in man, and assert the *forma corporeitatis* beneath the substantial form, the soul. The whole of being is thus covered, as it were, by a metaphysical network of forms, the 'inscape' of metaphysics, to use the term coined by the poet Hopkins, himself a disciple of Scotus. This doctrine helped Duns to maintain his own version of the 'Augustinian' teaching on the actuality of matter.

John Duns stood firmly against the Aristotelians and Thomists in his conception of the relations between intellect and will. The Friars Minor, whose first inspiration came from one whose life was a response to the love of God as seen in the Incarnation and Passion of Christ, found it natural to consider a human being as primarily a will directing the intellect to this or that, and this outlook was, if anything, strengthened by the adoption of Augustinian theology, wherein the will played so large a part. The Aristotelian, on the other hand, remembering his definition of man as a rational animal, looked always to the intellect as the royal faculty of man, and this attitude was reflected in the ordered, unchangeable universe of Aristotle, and emphasized by the determinist 'slant' of Averroës. The Thomist, therefore, held that the will was a blind faculty (which he sometimes compared to a blind man led by a child) and was determined by the good, once this had been seen and recognized by the mind, though he added that in this life the reason could direct the will to a lesser, or a relative, or even to a supposed good, for everything that is, has something of good in it.

Scotus, on the other hand, came near to ethical indeterminism in his teaching that the last word rested with the will *qua* will. Knowledge of the good is only a condition *sine qua non*, it is not a cause. The whole cause of the will's willing is purely and simply the will (*causa totalis volitionis in voluntate nihil aliud a voluntate est*). When applied to God, this had the effect of finding the ultimate source of God's action on creatures and of his law as transmitted to mankind in his will alone (*nulla est causa quare voluntas* [*Dei*] *voluit hoc, nisi quia voluntas est voluntas*). The only limit is that God cannot will two contraries. When applied to man, this doctrine has important consequences. Whereas for Aquinas the external law is a reflection of the 'mind' of God, and human acts are good because they are a realization of human nature, and are directed towards man's proper end, for Scotus only the commandment to love God is concerned with something good in itself; all other acts are good simply because they are commanded by God. He does indeed say that in the prohibitory commandments the acts are prohibited because they are evil, but he goes on to explain that they are evil only because they are the contrary of what is positively commanded. For Scotus therefore it is the Legislator, not the Law, that is eternal, and acts of themselves can be in the strictest sense indifferent – a proposition denied by St Thomas. Although in practice Scotus made no change in his assessment of moral worth, for he relied in this upon the direct commands of God, his insistence on the absolute freedom of God, and his introduction of the 'absolute' as opposed to the 'covenanted' power of God, are distant pointers towards some of the later developments that we shall have to consider.

To the credit side of the doctrine of the Primacy of the Will must be set some of Scotus's most eloquent and attractive pages, where he outlines the law of love in God's action in the world. It was passages such as these that led Rashdall to write that 'in the depth of its religious feeling his writing contrasts favourably with the cold rationalistic orthodoxy of Thomas', and we may accept the first part of his sentence without subscribing to the latter judgement.[1] Scotus was in fact led by his emphasis on love to a celebrated point of disagreement with Aquinas. The latter, when he put to himself the question whether the Incarnation would have taken place had there been no sin to redeem, answered with some hesitation in the negative. Scotus, on the other hand, answers affirmatively. God, he says, first of all loves Himself; then he desires to love and to be loved by others; finally he desires to be loved by the One who can love Him to the limit (*summe*), and so he willed from all eternity the union of His Son with the created nature that was fitted so to love Him.

Scotus was for long considered, as author of the *Theoremata*, to have relegated to the company of rationally unproven propositions many of the basic theses of 'natural theology'. Whether or not the authenticity of this work is accepted, it is clear from the principles enunciated in his authentic writings that Duns, denying the competence of philosophy to reach beyond finite being, would deny that natural certainty is obtainable on such matters as the immortality of the soul and the attributes of God. This is in part due to the Scotist definition of being which, in the framework of his empirical epistemology and his metaphysical proof of the infinity of God, removes from the realm of truths accessible to the human mind in its fallen state here below the intuition or apprehension not only of infinite being, but of pure (i.e., intellectually perceptible) being. There is a gulf between the universe of sense, which we can apprehend and know, and examine with mathematical certainty, and the infinity of God; and the human reason cannot cross this gulf with

[1] *Universities of Europe in the Middle Ages*, iii 260.

any arguments save those of probability nor with any certainty save that of faith. Though there is nothing of the sceptic in Duns, and though his theology is in all its basic principles the same as that of Aquinas, the realms of philosophy and theology are beginning to fall apart each into its own focus, in a way unfamiliar to the traditions of both Bonaventure and of Aquinas. Duns is in no direct sense the ancestor of Ockhamism, and his followers have in the sequel arrested any tendency towards Nominalism in their school by combining the theological systems of Bonaventure and Scotus, but in the realm of pure philosophy Duns, in reacting against a rigid, cramping, physical interpretation of Aristotle, did in fact narrow the capacity of the unaided human intelligence. Though himself a metaphysician, he narrowed the scope of metaphysical attainment; it was left to his successors to begin the flight from metaphysics as such.

Though Duns Scotus early became the mainstay of the Franciscan school he never became their official doctor in medieval times, and though Scotism claimed more followers in the schools than Thomism from 1350 to 1650, with the consequence that Duns men (or 'dunces') were the prime objects of obloquy to Erasmus and the Reformers, Scotus fell into an eclipse even more complete than that which overtook Aquinas in the age of enlightenment, and when scholasticism again became the mode a century ago Thomism took pride of place. John Duns, though in fact Aquinas was only one among the many predecessors and contemporaries whom he criticized, had always been the adversary *par excellence* for the Thomists, the *fons et origo mali*, the first exhibit in the chamber of horrors, and it was some time before he was presented anew to the modern world. Even his warmest admirers did not find it easy to bring him forward, along with St Thomas, as the incarnation of sweet reasonableness and inspired common sense. To a layman and one unfamiliar with Catholic theology Scotus presents all the generic difficulties of St Thomas with a generous ration of specific additions of his own. This will probably always be so, but in the past half century the ardent advocacy of Franciscan scholars has combined with the impartial approach of critics such as M. Gilson, to reveal anew the true Duns and to manifest his greatness. This indeed is undeniable. Though Duns lacks the limpid clarity of the deep waters of Aquinas, many of his phrases strike undertones and overtones, and he is throughout a great theologian as well as the incomparable critic who put his finger unerringly on the weakest spots in Christian Aristotelianism. He is the only thinker of the thirteenth century who can challenge a place alongside the three saints and Doctors; probably all would agree that he is less massive than Albert, less creative than Thomas, less luminous than Bonaventure, but his titular epithet was not lightly bestowed in an age which, if any other, knew what exact and critical thought demanded of a master. It is strange, but not unfitting, that one of the most exquisite tributes to Oxford, and the only lines of great English poetry inspired by a scholastic thinker,[2] should centre upon John Duns,

> 'Of realty the rarest-veinèd unraveller; a not
> Rivalled insight, be rival Italy or Greece.'

[2]G. M. Hopkins, *Duns Scotus' Oxford.*

CHAPTER TWENTY-SIX
The Breakdown of the Synthesis

The forty years that followed upon the deaths of Aquinas and Bonaventure were a time of great intellectual activity and ecclesiastical ferment. The spirit of contention among the Friars Minor which led to the crystallization of the parties of the Spirituals and their opponents the Conventuals, and which broadened into the controversy which shook all Europe on the poverty of Christ and then to the later controversy on Dominion and Grace, began soon after the moderating influence of Bonaventure had been removed, while towards the end of the century the abdication of Celestine V and the extravagant claims of Boniface VIII blew into flame the smouldering fires of the old controversy between Church and State. This led in France to the anti-papal measures and propaganda of Philip the Fair and his minister Nogaret and to the violence of word and action that marked the last years of the pontificate of Boniface VIII. In Italy it led to further divisions between Guelf and Ghibelline and to the imperial dreams of Dante, while a little later the secularist propaganda of Marsilio of Padua allied itself with the schismatic Spiritual general of the Franciscans and the political ambitions of the Emperor Lewis of Bavaria in raising accusations of heresy against Pope John XXII.

While in these public controversies the note of bitterness is steadily rising in intensity, and all parties pursue their ends with a drastic logic that carries them far beyond the limits of common sense and the horizon of practical politics, the period in the schools is marked by a number of divergences from the main lines hitherto pursued, and by the emergence of a number of able free-lances who criticize, often with damaging effect, many of the theses of the great ones of an earlier generation, and hew out torsos of new systems which never achieve, and perhaps were never intended to achieve, completion. Of all the schools that of the Friars Minor continued for the longest span to produce a succession of notable masters, though Scotus partially, and William of Ockham more thoroughly, shook the foundations on which much of the older Franciscan thought had rested. The Friars Preachers, for whom Thomism had become the official doctrine as early as 1278, produced no doctor of the first rank for two hundred years, though in the second or third class the two Englishmen, Thomas of Sutton, a very able theologian, and Nicholas Trivet, the literary critic and historian, were prominent.

The most notable of the pupils and personal disciples of Aquinas were outside his own order. Foremost among them was Giles of Rome (*c.* 1243/7–1316), who became an Augustinian Hermit and was the pupil of St Thomas in the latter's second period of regency at Paris. Later, Giles was the first regent of the Augustinian house in Paris, and his teaching was honoured as early as 1287 by its adoption as the official doctrine of the order. In 1292 he became general of the Augustinian Friars, and in 1295 archbishop of Bourges. As a young man Giles had been the stoutest defender of Thomism at Paris, and in particular of the doctrine of unity of form against bishop Tempier and his friends, and had been forced into exile in consequence. Some years later he returned, perceptibly sobered, and though he remained in most essentials a faithful Thomist, he drew his master's teaching out further in some respects than Aquinas would have authorized, while in others he departed from it altogether. His intransigence was especially noticeable in the papal-political field, where his *De regimine principum*, Aristotelian and Thomist in its argument, works up to an assertion of the right of the pope to sole and supreme dominion over all activities in church and state. So fully was Giles recognized as a leading papalist that his ideas and phrases were embodied wholesale in the bull *Unam sanctam*, though the doctrinal conclusion of the bull is distinctly more balanced and traditional than the arguments and pleading of Giles might have seemed to demand or warrant. Giles was the immediate or remote master of a succession of distinguished Augustinian friars who held with fair fidelity to Thomism; the last of them, Thomas of Strasbourg, a general of the order, was responsible for keeping his flock untainted by Nominalism.

A more important and a more localized colony with Thomist affinities is seen at Cologne. That city, the metropolis of the Rhineland, was early chosen as one of the *studia generalia* of the Dominicans and it was also an important scholastic centre for the Franciscans. Thither came some of the most eminent friars to learn and to lecture, among them Albert the Great, Thomas Aquinas and Duns Scotus, and Cologne remained for more than a century an intellectual focus of the first importance, though it was not the seat of a university till 1388. In the history of scholastic thought it is chiefly notable as the home of a school of Neoplatonist theologians who were also originators and leaders of a school of mysticism both theoretical and practical.

The origins of this school can be traced in large part to the influence and teaching of Albert in his Neoplatonic phase of interest, but it was given an altogether new vitality by the translation of the works of Proclus from the Greek by William of Moerbeke the Dominican between 1268 and *c*. 1286. These books made an immediate appeal to the German mind in the Dominican friaries, and the first to feel the pull was Albert's favourite pupil, Ulrich of Strasbourg, who in turn, together with Albert, influenced Dietrich of Freiburg. Dietrich, noted for his researches and discoveries in natural science – he was the first to propound the correct explanation of the rainbow – was also a distinguished philosopher, partly Thomist, but chiefly Augustinian and Neoplatonic in outlook.

A still greater name is that of Master Eckhart (*c*. 1260–1327). Eckhart may have been a pupil of Albert at Cologne and was later a contemporary lecturer at Paris with Duns Scotus. He had a distinguished career as regent and provincial in the Dominican order, and though his last years were disturbed by accusations of heresy he died, after declaring his willingness to submit fully to the Church, two years before the condemnation of a number of propositions drawn from his writings. Eckhart has long been, and still remains, a figure of controversy. Hailed by Luther and others of the German Reformers as a fountain of national, mystical, un-Roman religion, and by more recent German thinkers and historians as an undenominational mystic, he was set in his context by Denifle, who had no difficulty in showing the scholastic Thomist framework of his theology. Denifle, whose active, pugnacious, concrete mind was unsympathetic to speculative mysticism, was inclined to treat all that was not Thomism in Eckhart as mist or moonshine. Scholars since Denifle have been divided, some regarding Eckhart as a mystical scholastic, others as a scholastical mystic. The former is probably the more correct estimate. Though he uses the scholastic, and even the Thomist dialectic and technical terms and knows all its positions, Eckhart employs the negative, apophatic Neoplatonist method in his theology, and is undoubtedly at least verbally unorthodox and pantheistic both in his assertion of the absolute non-entity of all creatures, and of the existence of a centre or spark (*Fünklein*) of the soul which is uncreated and divine and which tends always towards reunion with or absorption in God. That Eckhart was nevertheless fundamentally orthodox is seen both in his own normal life and spiritual teaching and in the impression he made upon his disciples.

Eckhart, besides his theological treatises and his administrative occupations as prior provincial, was a frequent preacher and spiritual adviser to devout persons in the Rhineland. In the cities and towns of the region numerous communities of women had come into being, with a fervent religious and spiritual life, and at the request of the papacy, their direction had been assumed by the Dominicans. The friars were greatly influenced in this task by the writings of the pseudo-Denis which, taken in conjunction with the Neoplatonic doctrines of the Albertine school, gave a characteristic colouring to the Dominican tradition, which in its theology of grace and the virtues was strictly Thomist. The two great disciples of Eckhart, John Tauler (*c.* 1300–61) and Henry Suso (*c.* 1295–1366) were both Dominicans, both broadly speaking Thomist, and both entirely orthodox; they tacitly abandoned the Master's Neoplatonist superstructure and all traces of pantheism, while retaining his spiritual and mystical teaching as applicable to the individual. The teaching of the school, which belongs to the history of spirituality rather than to that of philosophy, spread not only to the Low Countries in the person of the Flemish Jan van Ruysbroeck (1293–1381) but to England in the teaching of *The Cloud of Unknowing*, and two centuries later the teaching of Tauler had a considerable influence upon St John of the Cross and other Spanish spiritual writers. The Rhineland school is, indeed, the source of the medieval and modern school of Dominican spirituality which, partly from its origins and more completely since the sixteenth century, has been closely linked with Thomist thought.

A very different strand of development, noticeable chiefly in France, was the emergence of a number of distinguished theologians, critical and eclectic, who moved in great affairs and were familiar with the papal court at Avignon. More than one of them spent the last years of his life as a diocesan bishop. While in the present state of our knowledge it is rash to see in this one or the other a germ of Nominalism, everything goes to show that many of the tendencies that are patent in Ockham and his followers were present in a latent solution in the writings of thinkers from the days of Duns Scotus onwards. Attention to our perception of the individual, the undemonstrability of certain truths of 'natural' religion, the absolute freedom of God, and the interest taken in his 'absolute' power – these topics are all suggested by John Duns, and were to become principal matters for discussion among his successors.

One of these, Durand de S. Pourçain (*c.* 1275–1334), was a Dominican who repeatedly fell foul of the authorities of his order on account of his anti-Thomist opinions and his resolute independence of all his predecessors. He retracted his obnoxious views under pressure, but when he became bishop and *persona grata* at the Curia he felt free to reassert them. His elevation to the see of Limoux (of which he was apparently the first and last bishop) took place in 1317; he was translated to Le Puy in 1318 and to Meaux in 1326. In 1325 and the following years he served on the commission that examined and censured the writings of Ockham. His most important work was a *Commentary on the Sentences*, of which three editions exist, the first and last unorthodox from a Thomist standpoint, the second inoffensive. In the history of ideas his most significant thought was on the question of relationships and the process of intellection.

According to the traditional logical doctrine accepted by Aquinas, 'relation', that is, the reference (*habitus, respectus*) of one being to another (e.g., father to son, left to right, &c.,), was one of the 'accidents' of substance, though presenting certain peculiarities, for the relationship might be real (father-son) or merely mental (right-left). Durand made of it a third mode of being (i.e., substance, accident, relation), and gave the full title of relationship only when some kind of dependence or causality existed, such as father and son, mover and moved. This was to go half-way towards the Ockhamist teaching which turned causality into mere relationship: the father was not the cause of the son; merely, as a matter of experience, he always appeared as preceding and claiming him. Durand's teaching, when applied to the Trinity, where according to traditional theology the Persons are distinguished only by their relationships, got him into trouble. In epistemology his teaching was that the intelligence was a power seizing upon the individual object and knowing it as an individual, not in the form of an abstracted concept. The cause of cognition was not the object, but the cognitive power. All existing things are singular; the universal is not a reality or an entity, but the sum of what can be said about a group of individuals 'seen' by the mind. Hence the Thomist view that truth is the matching of the object with the mind had no sense for Durand. In his view truth was the conformity of the thing as known with the thing as it is in itself. The individual being and the universal are not identical, nor is the universal transcendent or immanent. The universal and the individual object are *related* and truth is the relation of a being to itself in the two modes, that of the real thing and that of the thing as understood. There is therefore no room for exemplary ideas in God: He is simply the cause of things.

A contemporary of Durand, Pierre Auriol (*c.* 1280–1322) was his Franciscan counterpart. He attacked with equal impartiality Bonaventure, Aquinas and Scotus, and ended his life as archbishop of Aix-en-Provence. He was peculiarly eclectic, neither a Platonist nor an Aristotelian, neither a Thomist nor a Scotist. Auriol, unlike Durand, was a conceptualist: that is, he refused to hold, with Aristotle, Aquinas and other 'moderate realists', that the object known is present in essence in the mind of the knower; he held it to be there only in appearance; as he put it: the concept is the appearance of the thing in the mind. Individual beings have, according to Auriol, a form and a resemblance or similarity to one another. The active intellect accepts this as a concept, but the concept has only a phenomenal being, not a real one. No essence is abstracted from the individual, only an image; the *species* is a fairly clear picture, the *genus* a dimmer one. He makes his meaning clear by saying that the form, which experience teaches us that we are seeing when we understand what we mean by a rose, is not something real impressed upon the mind, but is the thing itself (the rose) which has a visible mental being (*esse intentionale conspicuum*). In other words, there is no intellectual abstraction, but only the picture of the thing in the mind, and terms (e.g., rose) are merely names which we give to the pictures. Individuals alone exist, and are known by direct vision, which is nobler and clearer than the pictorial mental image. On other points, also, Auriol had opinions of his own which seemed to him to render some truths of natural religion (e.g., the immortality of the soul) indemonstrable. These he was prepared to believe without understanding, as if they were mysteries.

Others besides Durand and Auriol held views strikingly similar, though not, as it would appear, directly derived from the two Frenchmen. Thus Henry of Harclay (died 1317), an Oxford doctor, accepted the *haecceitas* of Duns, but denied that the nature common to several individuals was anything more than a confused form of 'thisness'; the universal exists, but as a confused, not as a clear concept, analogous to the visual appearance of Socrates at a distance, which the eye recognizes simply as 'a man'.

These three thinkers, and many more like them, are all engaged in an endeavour to give intelligibility, as well as reality, to the individual, while at the same time they have abandoned all attempts to find that reality outside the individual (realism) or at least abstracted and presented in intellectual form in the mind of the knower (moderate realism). All of them, nevertheless, agree that some kind of form or picture of individual reality is present in the mind of the knower, whether it is form such as *haecceitas,* or a picture, or a confused image. All agree, likewise, that there is in the individual something that can be called nature or universal, even if it is only distinguishable from the individual as such by a conventional mental recognition. It remained for Ockham to deny anything common or universal in the essence of the individual, and thus to deny any intelligibility in the true sense of the word to the objects of our experience.

CHAPTER TWENTY-SEVEN
William of Ockham

We have now to meet the last of the great medieval thinkers who influenced the course of European thought. William of Ockham is a difficult philosopher, whom many have studied recently and many others are discussing at the present moment, without having attained as yet either full agreement among themselves or, it may be, a perfect understanding of their subject. Though the chronology of his life, long in confusion, has now been straightened out in its main lines, the chronology of his writings is still uncertain at several points, while the writings themselves still remain in part unprinted and in part uncritically edited. Moreover, Ockham was a daring thinker and a swift writer, and his chequered career took him into turbulent waters; in his later writings logic, philosophy, theology, political history, questions of Franciscan poverty and papal and imperial claims all jostle one another in his pages, and although he can scarcely be said to have adorned with literary charm all that he touched, he certainly left upon it the impress of his keen and mordant mind.

He remains even to our day a controversial figure. Hailed by his younger contemporaries and their successors as the herald and hierophant of a new era, he was attacked in his lifetime by those who detested his opinions and later by those who reacted against his technique while preserving many of his opinions. Neglected in his turn for centuries, save as a bogy to scare young Thomists, he was re-discovered as an historical figure by the students of medieval thought who, followers as they were of Thomas or Duns, regarded him as Apollyon, the grand deceiver and destroyer who ruined the fabric of the golden age of medieval thought. Others again, in more recent years, have seen in him one of the great creators, one of that group of contemporaries in whose writings Cartesian philosophy, anti-papal reform, modern science and the secular state can be seen in embryonic form. More recently still, within the past two decades, members of his own order have endeavoured and still endeavour to destroy what they regard as the myth of Ockham's destructive genius, and to show him as the great logician, fundamentally traditional in thought and doctrine, who rejuvenated Aristotelian logic and who never intended that his daring hypotheses should do more than provide material for intellectual debate. This last opinion will probably find few supporters. It is true that the most original and lasting contribution made by Ockham to medieval thought was within the province of technical logic, while on the other hand he did not make, or intend to make, any innovations in his treatment of purely theological truths, but he never confined himself to 'pure' logic, and from his early days he propounded an epistemology that was not only novel and revolutionary, but which closed the door against any knowledge of being *qua* being or, in other words, of any possibility of metaphysical knowledge. In addition, he was intellectually as ruthless and unflinching in the realm of thought as some of his contemporaries were in the realm of political action, and in his refusal to admit into his system any term or concept which was not demanded by what seemed to him strict necessity (the celebrated 'razor of Ockham'), he arrived at a simplification of the business of thinking which differed little from a complete sterilization of the traditional powers of mankind to describe and analyze the universe of being.

William of Ockham, one of the half-dozen British philosophers who have profoundly influenced the thought of Western Europe, was born at Ockham in Surrey, a village lying near the modern Portsmouth road between Wisley and Ripley, about the year 1285. Nothing whatever is known of his family or early life, save that he became a Franciscan as a boy, and studied at Oxford *c.* 1310–17; from the latter year he lectured on the *Sentences* and on the Bible, and between 1319 and 1324 he composed his logical writings and his *Commentary on the Sentences*, which he rewrote at least twice in the years immediately following. Although it was an age, as we have seen, of eclectic thinkers and independent minds, an ex-chancellor of Oxford, John Luttrell, was clearsighted enough to realize that there was something not only novel but potentially dangerous in Ockham, and in 1324 he delated the young friar to the papal curia at Avignon, and his career in theology was thus arrested when he was already lecturing, but had not yet proceeded to his master's degree. Ockham followed his accusers to Avignon, and for more than three years the brilliant young man had the mortifying experience of waiting upon the delays and debates of his judges, with his high hopes dashed, and in the demoralizing surroundings of a city of luxury and intrigue, where the atmosphere was rendered permanently electric by the irascible septuagenarian autocrat Pope John XXII, an untiring generator of storm and lightning. While waiting, he was drawn into the orbit of Michael of Cesena, minister-general of his order, then at odds with the pope, and he was given by him the task of scrutinizing the papal pronouncements and the other literature of the controversy on the poverty of Christ and the domestic politics of the Franciscan order, and became in consequence persuaded of the lack both of wisdom and orthodoxy in the papal decisions. Meanwhile, the quarrel between John XXII and Lewis of Bavaria was working up to a climax, and early in 1328, the Emperor entered Rome, with Marsilio of Padua as his vicar *in spiritualibus*, and deposed the pope in favour of a schismatic friar. High politics, Franciscan controversy, and Ockham's own private fate came together to a climax at one and the same moment. When arrest seemed imminent at Avignon, William of Ockham and the now rebellious general of his order, who had appealed from the pope to the Church of Rome, decided to wait no longer. On the night of 26 May 1328, they left the convent for the wharf and took boat secretly down the Rhone. At Aigues Mortes an imperial galley was ready to take them to the Emperor. It was a decisive moment in the history of European thought, comparable to the secret despatch of Lenin from Switzerland to Petrograd in a sealed train in 1917. 'Protect me with your sword, and I will defend you with my pen.'[1] The words may be mythical, but they well express the reality of facts. Henceforward Ockham was in opposition to the head of the Catholic church on a double count, as a schismatic Franciscan and as a protégé of the Emperor. He was forthwith excommunicated and remained under the ban for the rest of his life. At about the same time the commission at Avignon, of which Durand of St Pourçain was a member, reported, condemning a few of Ockham's propositions and questioning others, but treating him on the whole far more leniently than would have been the case thirty years later. Meanwhile Ockham and Michael of Cesena had joined Marsilio of Padua and Jean of Jandun at the court of Lewis at Munich, and for the next fifteen years a stream of pamphlets issued from Ockham's

---

[1]'*O Imperator, defende me gladio, et ego defendam te verbo*'. The saying cannot, it seems, be traced back beyond the late fourteenth century. See J. Miethke, *Ockhams Weg zur Sozialphilosophie* (Berlin, 1969), pp. 222–3.

pen, bearing on every aspect of the quarrel with the papacy. When Lewis and John XXII were dead, movements may have been made for a reconciliation with the papacy, and a form of absolution survives, doubtfully genuine. It is extremely doubtful whether this reached, or was accepted by Ockham before his death, which took place in 1346/9, possibly as a victim of the Black Death.

Ockham's principal gift to his generation was his new system of logic, expressed in his *Summa totius logicae,* in which he joined to the Aristotelian logic the terminist logic of William of Sherwood and others, thus bestowing upon his contemporaries a technique of great subtlety resembling in some respects the symbolic logic of our own day. His ultimate fame, however, rests upon the overflow from logic into epistemology, which made of him the founder of the school known as Nominalism, or in its broader aspects the 'modern way' (*via moderna*) – so much so, indeed, that the title given him by his immediate followers, that of *venerabilis inceptor,* the best that could be done in the way of honorifics for one who never became a doctor in theology, was misunderstood to imply that he was the originator of a way of thought that conquered the greater part of Europe.

Although the immediate parentage of the distinctive doctrines of Ockham has not yet been indicated, and may indeed not exist, the similarity of so many elements in his thought to that of the eclectic innovators of the early fourteenth century is so close, and the main topics that interested him are so often shared with his immediate predecessors, that the final, but truly original, step may well have been taken by Ockham alone. This was the complete abandonment, not only of every form of realism, but of every kind of intellectual abstraction, in his account of the process of cognition. The mind of the knower does not abstract essence or nature from the thing known because neither the mental process of abstraction, nor the existence of any nature to abstract, can be shown to exist. All that is known is individual and singular, and the process of knowledge is purely intuitional. There is no such thing as a universal, and it is nonsense to speak of the thing known as present in an intelligible form in the mind of the knower. 'This I say,' remarks Ockham, 'that no universal is existent in any way whatsoever outside the mind of the knower.'[2] He attacked realism vigorously both in its extreme Platonic and Scotist forms and in its more moderate Thomist dress. If the universal is transcendent, as in the Platonic 'ideas', then it is not universal but individual; if it is immanent, then it is not individual but plural. Duns's individual form, his *haecceitas,* and his multitudinous forms

[2]*In 1 Sent.* d. 2, q. 8 (U-Geyer, 577).

in general are mere super-subtleties, to be abandoned in obedience to the principle of economy. The universal is something purely intra-mental, the concomitant of the intuitional realization of the individual thing. A given thing, a dog or rose, evokes in the human mind a mental 'sign' (*signum naturale*) which is the same in all men, as is a laugh or a cry; each race of men then gives to this sign a verbal sign or term or name in its own language, which we attach to our mental image and which recalls that image to our mind. As Ockham has it: 'nothing can be known in itself naturally save by intuitional knowledge'.[3] The universal is not something real which has subjective being (that is, of its own right) either in the soul or outside the soul; it has only an objective being (that is, as the object of thought), and it is a kind of mental artefact (*et est quoddam fictivum*) having being as an object of thought corresponding to the being which the thing itself has of its own right. In other words, the universal only exists because it is framed by the mind, and the term or word (dog, rose, &c.) is a sign which we attach to our mental intuition, and which recalls it for us. As there is no such thing as a universal, and as everything whatsoever is an irreducible individual, being does not exist as a metaphysical entity, and therefore no metaphysical knowledge is possible; metaphysics in fact does not exist.

From this it follows that none of the truths of so-called natural religion are demonstrable. God cannot be known intuitionally by man using only his natural powers, and as intuition is the only form of true knowledge this means that God cannot be known by us at all. Hence no demonstrative proof can be given of God's existence. Similarly with the divine attributes: nothing can be demonstrated as we have no direct knowledge and no way of arguing from creatures to God; we must be satisfied with what faith and revelation tell us.

Then Ockham proceeds to the soul. Here we have intuitive knowledge of our own experiences, such as joy and sorrow, but no intuition of the soul itself, its essence, its immortality and the rest, still less about that troublesome question of form. As Ockham put it: 'there is no way of knowing with clear certainty either by reason or experience that such and such a form is within us, or that such and such a substance within us has the property of intelligence, or that such and such a soul is the form of the body . . . . We hold these three truths by faith only.'[4]

[3]*In 1 Sent* dist. 3 q. 2 F (U-Geyer, 579).
[4]*Quodl.* I q. 10, *Opera Theologica*, IX, ed. J. C. Wey (St Bonaventure, New York, 1980), pp. 63–4.

In consequence of this delimitation of the mind's capacity, Ockham throws open the widest field to God's action, and we can see the first examples of the methodical use of the absolute power of God to eliminate certainty on the normal level of human experience. Scotus had been the first to use the traditional doctrine of God's omnipotence as a positive, and not merely as a concessive, element in an argument, but it was left to Ockham to use it in a destructive sense and to begin the custom, so greatly developed by his followers, of transferring every argument into the stratosphere of God's absolute power and thus eliminating the Aristotelian (and Thomist) application of the concepts of divine order and law and predictability to the working of the universe. The old, and hitherto platitudinous statement that God can effect by his immediate action all that he does by a mediating or secondary efficient cause, is used to prove that an observed 'effect' has not necessarily got a finite, natural 'cause'. We have, in fact, no means of knowing when the effect is a natural one or not, or even whether our intuitive knowledge on any given occasion is, or is not, implanted directly in our minds by God, even when the object of intuition is non-existent *in rerum natura*. In Ockham's words: 'Even if a thing has been destroyed the intuitive knowledge of it may be given to us [by God] and so intuitive knowledge is not of itself and necessarily the knowledge of something that exists; it may well be of something that does not exist.'[5] Hence, any argument for the existence of universals based upon our intuitive knowledge is without force, for if the things themselves do not exist, *a fortiori* the universals are non-existent.

This methodical use of the absolute power of God is a corollary of the emphasis on the absolute freedom of God first emphasized in a tendentious manner by Scotus. Ockham followed Duns here, stressing the primacy of the will and the concept of freedom both in God and man. As we know nothing by pure reason of God's attributes or way of acting, and as the first article of the creed is an assertion of the omnipotence of God, ethics becomes entirely dependent upon revelation, which is the only channel by which God's will becomes known to us. Acts are not good or bad of themselves, but solely because they are commanded or prohibited by God. Not only murder and adultery, but even hatred of God could become ethically good actions at God's commands. Where there is no known ethical good there can be no merit and no reward, and thus the divine dispensation of beatitude or damnation bears no intrinsic causal relationship to

[5]*In Sent. Liber I, Prol. Q.1, Opera Theologica*, I, ed. G. Gál, O.F.M. (St Bonaventure, New York, 1967), p. 36.

conduct in this world. Since merit is not strictly necessary for reward, and since God is absolutely free and can reward any action he chooses and give beatitude where no merit exists, the theological conception of grace as a quality of the soul is superfluous, together with all the structure and hierarchy of the virtues. The Holy Spirit, the Gift of God, is grace; all else can be cut out.

It would, however, be a serious error to regard Ockham as an intellectual sceptic. He held that the universe of being existed, altogether apart from the mind that came into contact with it; he held also that the mind had valid intuition of individual things. His assertion that God could produce the intuition in the mind when no reality was before it was not meant to open the door to scepticism. There was a natural, normal effect, as well as a supernatural one; Ockham's only point was that since God could produce the same effect as an external thing could produce, it was not valid to argue back from the reality of the intuition to the reality of the thing. While the Thomists had taught that truth is attained by the reception into the mind of the object known, and that the knowledge of a being is more true and noble than the mere registration of its existence, Ockham reduced all knowledge to intuition, and held that all purely intellectual apprehensions were concerned with a form of reality other than that of extra-mental beings. Intuition attained the individual, which alone existed *in rerum natura*. All judgements of value, therefore, and all arguments from causality were meaningless save as notes of observations of individual facts. It was permissible only to say: this is good, and that is exceedingly good: this happened, and that happened subsequently. On the other hand, scientific and logical argument was valid within its own sphere but this was not the sphere of real existing things, but of the suppositions or terms by which they were represented in our minds. To argue back from supposition to existence is illicit. The only valid logical demonstration is of a conclusion implicitly contained within its premises.

We are always relieved when we are able, or think we are able, to point to a single doctrine or, still better, to a single man as the cause of any specific evil we deplore, and those who prize the intellectual and religious achievements of thirteenth century scholasticism have often in the past found in Ockham and Nominalism what some have found to-day in Marx and Communism, the fount and source of all that is ill done. In both cases, as in all similar circumstances, the complex of ideas and tendencies is far too wide for any 'ism' to contain, and an individual, however great his genius, is always a representative and an heir as well as being an originator. We must beware, therefore, of regarding Ockham as responsible for all the philosophical and theological agnosticism that came after him. Yet undoubtedly the influence of the venerable inceptor was very great. The consistency and the ruthlessness of his thought, like that of Kant in the late eighteenth century, fascinated his contemporaries and successors, and they used his technique to go further than he had gone. Though not himself a philosophical sceptic, he gave powerful assistance in the work of shattering the already trembling fabric raised by the Christian Aristotelians, and to disperse the conception of an ordered, interlocking universe which in its turn was permeated by, and dovetailed into, the economy of supernatural grace. To Bonaventure, Thomas and Scotus alike the Christian life was human life raised to an essentially higher power. To Ockham, or at least to his radical followers, it remained a human life, though assisted by God and rewarded by him according to his choice, without any necessary reference to the quality of that life in itself.

CHAPTER TWENTY-EIGHT
The Harvest of Nominalism

William of Ockham left Oxford and England, never to return, still young and under a cloud that did not lift. His teaching was criticized and censured and he himself returned no more to the schools, but lived and died an excommunicate and an exile. Yet within a few years of his departure from England his methods and doctrines were spreading like oil, and before many years had passed he was revered as the originator of the 'new way', the *via moderna* which had changed the whole outlook of the schools and which, under the name of Terminism or Nominalism, was to impregnate so many centres of academic thought for almost two centuries. Such a success is itself a proof that Ockham was no solitary innovator. His name and his works became famous because they exactly suited the temper and the tendencies of his age. It was his achievement to do boldly and see clearly what others were attempting or only dimly discerning.

The most original and powerful thought of Ockham was contained in his logical writings, in which he professed and doubtless intended to reinterpret the traditional logic of Aristotle as transmitted by Boethius and elaborated by the terminist logicians of the thirteenth century. No great thinker, however, can remain a mere logician; as has been seen in our own day, the very restriction of thought to logic is itself a criticism of metaphysics and much else. Ockham, moreover, explicitly propounded a new epistemology, and it was this aspect of his work that exploded, as it were, and changed the whole landscape of contemporary thought by denying to the philosopher all right to any knowledge of the extra-mental universe save the intuitive knowledge of individual things, each of which was so irreducibly individual as to be unsusceptible of any intelligible relationship or connection with any other individual.

This principle, applied with remorseless logic to every field of thought, acted as an immediate solvent, and when applied with the maxim that nothing must be assumed to exist unless an unanswerable reason could be given for its existence, led forthwith to the demolition of Thomism and Scotism alike. With the dictum *entia non sunt multiplicanda praeter necessitatem* – the so-called 'razor of Ockham' – the most venerable philosophical entities could be shorn away. Once Ockham's epistemology had been admitted realism was doomed, causality was reduced to the observation of happenings and the central concepts of nature and substance disappeared.

The consequences were equally serious in the realm of theology. The whole fabric of natural theology, of the deductions from theological propositions, and the analysis of theological terms, rested ultimately upon the validity of universal concepts and the possibility of basing valid arguments upon them. When they were removed a spectacular deflation of theology followed. Moreover, Ockham and his followers, though many of them were trained theologians and all were professedly orthodox, approached all problems from the opposite end, so to say, to the way followed by a Bonaventure or an Aquinas. Whereas the latter regarded the universe *a parte Dei*, from God downwards, Ockham worked from the human mind upwards, and in fact was unable to ascend on account of his own criticism of human knowledge. The truths of 'natural' theology, which had formed the chains binding the dictates of reason to the declarations of revelation, melted into thin air. Neither the existence of God, nor the immortality of the soul, nor the essential relation between human action and its ethical worth, could be held as demonstrable by the reason. The essentially supernatural life of the Christian, seen in action in divine faith and love, and derived from a totally new and God-given principle of grace which had inspired and dominated the work of an Anselm, a Bonaventure or a Thomas, was now relegated, as unknowable and inexpressible, to the purely religious sphere of belief, and in practice ignored. The Ockhamists drew as sharp a line as did Thomism between the realm of reason and the realm of faith, but unlike Aquinas, who here stood fully in the line of traditional Christian theology, they did not regard the life of grace as a prolongation and elevation of the natural powers directed by a new principle. Grace for them, like the immortal soul itself and the new life of the Christian, was lifted out of the purview of the Christian thinker into that of the Christian believer, and the affirmations of faith were of no interest or value to the Christian philosopher. Consequently theology, the ordered, speculative theology of the schools, disappeared. The preacher and the pastor might use the Creeds and the Scriptures; the theologian was left with an unknowable and absolutely free God. Theologians had always distinguished between God's way of acting as revealed in Scripture and the commands of Christ and the general government of the world, and his 'absolute' power, but their interests had always lain with God as known to us by reason or revelation, and the 'absolute' power was no more than a formal saving clause. The Ockhamists, on the other hand, were not interested in what to them had no intellectual content, and concentrated all their attention on what may be called the 'pure mathematics' of God's absolute power.

Within William of Ockham's lifetime his disciples were pushing his principles to their logical conclusion. The Dominican Robert Holcot, who taught at Oxford, taking his stand on the doctrine that all knowledge comes from sense-experience, denied the possibility of proving the existence of either the soul, or pure spirit, or God: while faith tells us that God is omnipotent and supremely free, then it follows that God can command anything, even that man should hate Him. John of Mirecourt, a Cistercian who fell under condemnation at Paris in 1347, took the same view of God's power, and reduced certainty to immediate experience and philosophical knowledge to the principle of contradiction. All else is no more than probable. Nicholas of Autrecourt, whose teaching incurred Roman condemnation in 1346, went even further in his denial that our judgement of cause and effect was anything more than a record of sense experience. For him neither substance nor form nor matter nor the faculties of the soul or mind exist, nor can we conclude from the existence of the world to the existence of God. It is true that these men were formally condemned at Paris, but others were teaching similar doctrines elsewhere without condemnation, and the basic principles of Ockhamism, from which theologians drew extreme conclusions, were never formally condemned and became, indeed, the common opinions of the arts schools soon after the middle of the century.

In the first flush of its novelty, Ockhamism was all but supreme in France and England. Secular masters and all the four orders of friars felt its attraction and even extended its territory. Some teachers, however, refused to capitulate. Some of the older masters saw its implications and succeeded, as we have seen, in obtaining several condemnations, and the university of Paris, followed by a papal behest, decreed a global condemnation of his teaching in 1339 and 1340. In England Thomas Bradwardine stood firmly for what he conceived to be the traditional teaching against the 'Pelagians', and

Wyclif followed him in upholding realism. The schools of the friars, who already had their assigned 'doctors', held on, or swung back, to tradition despite notable defections to the modern way. Thomism was never completely submerged, though it did not regain its place as a clear-cut system until the early fifteenth century, when Capreolus, *princeps Thomistarum* (*c.* 1380–1444), wrote his great commentary and defence of Aquinas. Scotism likewise survived, and alongside it a devotion to Bonaventure. Even in the mid-fourteenth century the Austin Hermits, whose first schools had been given a Thomist colour by Giles of Rome, continued more than any other order to remain outside the orbit of Ockham, and their traditional outlook was clinched by Thomas of Strasbourg, their general in the middle of the century. On the other side of the fence Averroism in north Italy and elsewhere held to a rigid, naturalistic Aristotelianism, while at the end of the century Hus, the disciple of Wyclif, kept Prague and other central European universities within the realist camp. But by and large the universities of Europe were Nominalist of lighter or darker shading by the end of the fourteenth century, and whatever may have been the gain in other fields, such as those of scientific and mechanical thought, and whatever may have been the achievements of the fourteenth-century theologians within their own discipline, the blow dealt to metaphysics and constructive speculation by Ockham and his disciples must be held largely responsible for the arid academic climate of the fifteenth century and the justified disrepute into which the technicians of theology fell.

No mention has yet been made of one who stood outside the ranks of the philosophers and theologians, but who nevertheless was to stand as a guide to the things of the mind and spirit for the intelligent lover of literature and even for some academics, both in his own world and in the centuries that followed. Dante, in the first decades of the fourteenth century, had given a magnificent advertisement to Thomism, not only by his presentation in the *Paradiso* of St Thomas as the theologian *par excellence*, but also by his acceptance of Thomist philosophy and theology at numerous points of the *Divine Comedy*. Nowhere perhaps does the poet display more strikingly his genius for seizing upon the immortal significance of the characters who inhabit the world of his imagination than in his designation of Thomas and Bonaventure as the twin summits of medieval thought, at a moment when both were losing ground as masters among their own confreres, and when Scotus and Ockham were driving the main theses of the two great doctors into a long exile from Paris and the academic arena. Dante, we may be told, was a pupil of the

Dominicans who had never caught up with the advanced thought of his day; he was writing, not as an accredited world-poet but as an exiled party-leader of Florence. Even if it be true that his is the authentic voice of medieval religious culture in its finest hour, yet he does not necessarily represent a numerical majority of his countrymen any more than Shakespeare, the creedless poet of secular humanity, may be said to represent the age of the Puritans, of Richard Hooker and of the Catholic martyrs. Moreover, the Thomism of Dante is often considerably below proof, and he can be shown to have drawn elements of his thought from Neoplatonic and still more suspect sources. Nevertheless, Dante, who became a classic to his countrymen far more rapidly than Shakespeare, must have had a large share in creating the 'myth' of St Thomas which, like many similar myths, undoubtedly had a share in moulding the later history of Thomism. For the period under review, however, the system of St Thomas had no great influence on the intellectual life of the fourteenth century. It influenced notably a group of spiritual teachers connected with his order, of whom Henry Suso and Catherine of Siena are the most eminent, and the fact that a majority of the judges of the Inquisition were drawn from the Preachers helped it to maintain its place as an agent of rigid orthodoxy, but it would certainly be unjust to debit Thomism with the numerous shortcomings chargeable to scholasticism by Wyclif and the later Reformers and humanists.

The Ockhamists, without any intention of changing the religious sentiment of their world, had in fact a twofold influence upon it. By denying the possibility of a rational demonstration of the truths of 'natural' religion, and by regarding revelation as something arbitrary, to be accepted with unreasoning submission and left without comment or explanation, Nominalism, under the guise of a devout humility, left the door open for agnosticism or incredulity as well as for a fideistic acceptance of religious teaching. At the same time, by neglecting tradition and appealing solely to the literal word of Scripture and of papal pronouncements, its supporters left their disciples without any clear knowledge as to what was of immemorial tradition in the Church and what was the speculation of recent schoolmen or the claim of papal propagandists. It was only a step to reduce revealed doctrine to the message of Scripture alone, and this step was in fact soon taken by Wyclif and his followers. For others the void left by the disappearance of rational argument was filled by a recourse to mystical certainty. The fourteenth century was an age of great mystics, and of prophetesses.

Yet if the effect of Nominalism was destructive in philosophy and theology, this does not imply any lack of mental power or critical acuity in the men of the age. If thinkers avoided the widest issues of metaphysics, they showed their powers in the discussion of such important topics as free will, the reconciliation of God's freedom with his foreknowledge and Providence, and the relations between merit and grace. Thomas Bradwardine, Gregory of Rimini and Jean Gerson are names that would add distinction to any epoch. Even more significant as prefiguring much that was to follow, was the work of the scientists. We saw how at Oxford in the thirteenth century Grosseteste and his disciples combined an interest in natural science with their philosophical and theological pursuits. They were influenced partly by the close connection between the 'light-metaphysic' which they favoured and geometry and optics, and it may be thought also that Oxford had not as yet suffered from that exclusive attention to logic which prevented the masters of Paris from straying into other fields. This had changed by the beginning of the fourteenth century. Oxford was taking the lead in logic from Paris, and the Mertonians were interested in pure mathematics rather than in science. At Paris, however, the impact of Ockhamism seems to have caused many of the masters in the mid-fourteenth century to turn from theology to the old problems of physical science, and to answer them differently from Aristotle. Thus Jean Buridan (*c.* 1300–d. after 1358; rector of Paris 1328 and 1340), Albert of Saxony (*c.* 1316–90; rector 1357 and 1362) and Nicole Oresme (*c.* 1320–82) are notable in the field of science. Buridan successfully disproved the Aristotelian explanation of violent motion in space as caused by the direct and continued application of force by the 'mover' – initially by immediate application and thereafter by the pressure communicated by the air. For this he substituted an 'impetus' communicated once for all to the body at rest, which thenceforward continued to move until slowed down by the friction of the air and the pull of 'gravity'. This by implication rendered the Aristotelian motive intelligences of the spheres otiose and meaningless. Albert of Saxony, continuing the study of moving bodies, noted that the centre of gravity of an object did not necessarily coincide with its centre of magnitude. Oresme, the greatest of the three, was the first to formulate the law of acceleration in falling bodies, and to bring forward cogent arguments for the diurnal movement of the earth and to maintain that the Aristotelian conception of a moving 'sky' or 'heaven' was an unproved hypothesis.

The fourteenth century has often in the past appeared to historians as a century of disasters and decline, notable only for its savage warfare and its sterile controversies, crowned by the *débâcle* of the papacy and the futile manœuvres of the conciliarists. Seen from another, and perhaps a less superficial angle, it is one of the most genial centuries in European history, in which the fields of art, literature, natural and political science, and even of theology, were fertilized by achievements and ideas that were to give foundations to a new world, the world of 'modern Europe', which is at the present moment in our own day dissolving into something wider. The fact that in almost every department of cultural life save that of the visual arts a strange standstill of almost a century was to intervene between seedtime and harvest must not make us forgetful of the generation that sowed the seed. We may indeed well consider the fourteenth century more prolific than the thirteenth in those *idées-forces* that were to determine the course of European intellectual life. While the great minds of the age of Bonaventure and Aquinas were engaged in fusing and transforming the whole of ancient thought as they knew it into an interpretation of the Christian universe, their successors sought new answers to questions of another kind. The fourteenth century saw the extreme assertion of papal claims by Augustinus Triumphus and Giles of Rome answered in different ways by Ockham, by Wyclif and by Gerson; it saw a frontal attack launched on both the City of God and the Vicar of Christ by Marsilio of Padua and John Wyclif; it gave birth to the discussions of divine providence, of divine freedom and omnipotence, and of God's knowledge of free futures, of grace and merit, congruous and condign, and of justification and predetermination by Bradwardine, Gregory of Rimini and others; it produced the sequence of great Mertonian philosophers and mathematicians at Oxford and the revolutionary opinions of Buridan and Oresme in statics and astronomy at Paris. This age, considered only in the realm of pure thought, must be counted one of the most fertile and influential in medieval Europe, while in the realm of literature and art its paramount importance has never been questioned.

It was a century also of great controversies. While those of the preceding age were either political or restricted to academic circles, those of the fourteenth century, among which the contest between the publicists of Boniface VIII and Philip the Fair may rightly be reckoned, were in essence public to the whole of Europe, and were conducted by individuals separated from each other by space as well as by nationality. The issues between the pope and the king of France, between the papacy and the Empire; the manifestoes of Marsilio of Padua; the social-theological controversies over the Poverty of Christ,

Dominion and Grace; the Eucharistic and other wrangles of Wyclif; and, finally, the great conciliar question – all these were of immediate interest to all educated men in Europe, and either threatened or succeeded in breaking out into the realm of practical politics. In these controversies, a sign of the times was the intransigency and the ruthless logicality with which the ideas and arguments were pushed up to and beyond the limits of what was practically possible and intellectually tolerable.

Nevertheless, as historians of philosophy we have to recognize an end as well as a beginning. With the death of Aquinas a whole age began to draw to a close, and when William of Ockham died it had ended. It was not merely that the effort of the Paris masters to unite the findings of human reason and the data of revealed truth had failed to establish its achievement and to commend it to their world; not merely that metaphysics and indeed 'philosophy' as such were in retreat. The outlook of a whole age was slipping away; the moment was as significant in its own limits as the not wholly dissimilar rupture of unity in Europe at the Reformation. From the age of Augustine to the death of Aquinas there had been a conviction, shared by all the schools, and expressed by all implicitly, if not explicitly, that there existed a single reasoned and intelligible explanation of the universe on the natural level, and a single analysis of man and his powers, that could be discovered, elaborated and taught, and that it was valid for all men and final within its own sphere. A corollary to this conviction was the prevailing opinion that the ancients – who in this particular context were the Greeks, with Cicero and Plotinus – had said if not the final, at least the most authoritative word in this as in so many other fields, and that the Christian thinker's task could be achieved by a study either of Plato or of Aristotle or of an amalgam of the two, eked out by such further discussions as might be made necessary by the higher wisdom of the Christian revelation. Within twenty years of the death of Aquinas this conviction was changing shape. Duns Scotus and some of his contemporaries were still convinced that an explanation of the universe in terms of thought was possible and desirable, but in their view it had not yet been found, and it was the task of the philosopher to try new ways of finding it. Thirty years later the Ockhamists were challenging both the conviction and its corollary. The universe neither needed nor was susceptible of explanation; it could be experienced, but not understood, and Plato and Aristotle were no more than the originators of ingenious explanations of which little would stand up to examination. This outlook, which in effect if not in intention was largely negative in its consequences, spread over the greater part of Europe. It was never wholly victorious, and never finally accepted, partly because man naturally desires to know more than Ockham allowed him to expect, partly because Plato and Aristotle and Augustine and Aquinas will always renew their appeal to individuals, and partly because the traditional conviction was preserved at the time by a celebrated religious order and was later asserted by the *magisterium* of the Church, but never again, in a society which grew more and more complex as the decades passed, was the tradition of a single comprehensive philosophy revived outside the schools of the Catholic Church. As an academic discipline philosophy survived in the last century of the Middle Ages only in a truncated and fossilized form, though individuals or even individual schools might be Platonizers or Averroists, and when the great revival came in the early seventeenth century a series of new systems arose, the creations of individual minds discovering or interpreting their own convictions rather than allowing the external world to deliver its message to their minds, already disposed to accept what the wise men of the ancient world had declared to be truth.

Epilogue

The history of medieval philosophy in Europe between the days of Lanfranc and those of William of Ockham is the history of the reception of Greek thought by the minds of an adolescent and rapidly maturing Latin Christian civilization. This simple statement, however, is far from expressing the complexity of the process that actually took place. The Greek thought that arrived in Western Europe was not the flood of a single pure stream, but a great river resulting from the confluence of tributaries, arriving one after another with waters heavily contaminated by the soil through which they had passed. These tributaries, if the metaphor may be extended, were of two main types, Platonic and Aristotelian, but whereas the Aristotelian waters were in the beginning reasonably pure, if scanty, and even when their volume increased were never wholly clouded, the Platonic streams were heavily laden with deposit that was never fully eliminated. Dropping the language of metaphor, we may say that the thought of Plato was never known to the schools in its fullness and in its purity; what came to Europe was Neoplatonism in three forms: that of Augustine, that of Dionysius and that of the Arabs. The thought of Aristotle, on the other hand, which came in three successive doses, was ultimately received in fullness and comparative purity. Therefore, although Platonism and Neoplatonism were of themselves more attractive than was Aristotle to Christian thinkers, they never established themselves as a system or systems in the schools. Aristotle had many great advantages: a complete system, a slow but comprehensive reception, and – what is perhaps most important of all – a control, from the beginning, of the methods and techniques of the medieval schools. The thinkers of the West had been nurtured from the beginning on Aristotelian logic and its technical terms; each successive addition to the system thus fitted naturally into a single great pattern.

The pattern that thus gradually evolved was near to being a re-creation of the Aristotelian line of ancient thought, and until the death of St Thomas, followed almost immediately by the condemnation of 1277, this could be regarded as the true and only answer to the riddle of the universe of Nature. Even St Thomas, though in effect he produced an essentially original system of metaphysics, regarded Aristotle as having provided once and for all the foundations and framework of true thought, while Bonaventure and Pecham, though they abandoned much of Aristotle, would have replaced him, not by a rival scheme of metaphysics, but by an outlook on the world that was theological rather than purely philosophical. In the process that ended in the thirteenth century, Boethius, the translators of Aristotle, the Arabs and the Jews added stone upon stone to the legacy of ancient thought, and all, in great or less degree, were of opinion that philosophy was a subject that could be taught and learned, and that the master of the wise was Aristotle. Upon and above this basis of philosophy stood theology, which used the same terms and methods in proving and elucidating its truths. In the eleventh and twelfth centuries this outlook was common to all thinkers of the West, save for a few aberrant 'heretics of dialectic'. From the middle of the thirteenth century the change came rapidly. First, philosophy became autonomous, with Aquinas as well as with Siger; and then Aristotle was in effect condemned. The theologians of Paris rebuffed philosophy at the moment when the European mind had reached a stature which enabled it to criticize and create with self-confidence in things of the mind. In Oxford in particular, where neither theologians nor artists had ever been integral Aristotelians, two peculiarly subtle minds were ready to re-think the very basis of logic and philosophy and to arrive at positions radically different from those of any ancient thinker. This, as we can see in retrospect, brought about a revolution in some ways as notable and as permanent in its effects as the theological revolution of the sixteenth century. Hitherto philosophy, like dogma, had been regarded by and large as a body of truths that could be elaborated and in effect developed, but which could not be challenged or changed in basic essentials. Now, this outlook was to vanish. In metaphysics, logic, epistemology, and indeed in every branch of speculative and practical philosophy, the field was open to demolition and reconstruction, and in the process the connecting links with theology were broken. This breakage was indeed never wholly complete within the Church, and the union was restored in great part by the Catholic philosophers and theologians of the Counter-Reformation, but in the wider field of European thought the *philosophia perennis* had ceased to exist. No doubt in the modern world and at the present day there are very many minds of the highest calibre who are rationally satisfied that the philosophy of Aristotle and Plato, as fused and extended by the scholastics and their successors, provides the only secure elements on which to build a system of thought, but for the most part those who think thus do so because they have come as Christians to a study of philosophy, and form the conviction that ancient thought, as re-interpreted by the medieval and modern 'scholastics', gives the firmest and most authentic rational basis for the superstructure of revelation.

Why, we may ask, did this new spirit arise in the very heart of the medieval world? Is it not a paradox that Western Europe should have broken with ancient thought as the vehicle of all sound thinking at the very moment when the epoch of what we call the Renaissance was about to open, in which an enthusiastic and even servile imitation of the ancients was to pervade every field of letters, of art and of taste? The historian cannot give cause for the deepest movements of the human mind, but it is possible to see some of the circumstances of the decline of scholastic philosophy. The erection of logic and dialectic as the sole training and method behind every intellectual discipline was a serious flaw in the education of the twelfth and thirteenth centuries. We have seen how logic ousted literature as the foundation of formal schooling towards the end of the eleventh century everywhere save in the cloister. Gradually this brought about a divorce between thought and life, and between dialectic and the muses. Life and the physical universe no longer continued to supply the philosopher with impetus for thought. Even the Bible and the traditions of the past had a smaller place in the theologian's interests. Thought divorced from life must always wither, and the philosopher of the fourteenth century withdrew more and more into his own world, in which definitions and conclusions were no longer controlled by all other kinds of human experience. Ideas and principles were strained to the limit, and ultimately thought preyed upon itself, and suffered fragmentation. In the process, no doubt, it revealed, if only by challenging established positions, many hitherto unsuspected fields in which to range, and turned to mathematical science and to the observation of physical forces, and in this way decay led to revival. It is hard to say how far the shift of interest from metaphysics and the search for abstract and general principles to the knowledge of the individual and direct intuition of reality can be linked with the new interest in human personality, and the characters and destinies of men, that becomes evident in theology (e.g., the salvation of pagans and unbaptized children) and in literature (e.g., Petrarch and Langland) at almost the same moment. We may perhaps notice that Dante has a foot in both camps. While he is the great medieval, theocentric poet of the divine order of things, who turns to a syllogism or an opinion of the schools to settle a point of conduct, he is at the same time, in his love of Beatrice and in his sympathy with the creatures of his imagination, the first poet of the Christian centuries to be conscious of personal emotion and the sadness of mortal things. When, therefore, we say that medieval philosophy, itself the 'production' of Greek philosophy, is on the wane at the middle of the fourteenth century, we do not suggest that this implies the death or decadence of all mental activities, or hinders the birth of other ways of thought. What we call the stream of history never ceases to move. We may, however, truly say that with the death of William of Ockham and his peers a great fabric of thought, and an ancient outlook on philosophy as a single, common way of viewing the universe gradually disappeared, and gave place, after two centuries in which pure philosophy was in eclipse, to the new outlook and varied ways of the modern world.

Suggestions for Further Reading

No attempt will be made here to supply a bibliography, even of the most summary kind, of the history of medieval thought. Several elaborate lists exist in the general works listed below; for the English reader marvellously rich bibliographical matter is given by E. Gilson in the notes to his *History of Christian Philosophy in the Middle Ages* (London, 1955). What follows is not even a 'reading list'; it is simply a short catalogue of works which might give an interested reader further help in appreciating particular philosophers or phases of thought. Some French titles are included, since an ability to read French is essential for serious study on most points, and specialized work demands also a knowledge of German.

GENERAL WORKS. The indispensable general outline is Gilson's work mentioned above. It is based on his classical *Histoire de la philosophie médiévale* (2nd edn, Paris, 1943), to which have been added valuable notes and discussions of the literature (pp. 552–804). For a discussion of medieval thought another well-known work of Gilson, his Gifford Lectures, *L'esprit de la philosophie médiévale* (2nd edn, Paris, 1944; Eng. trans., New York, 1948), should be consulted. Gilson's work, in common with that of all other scholars, is heavily indebted to the monumental volume by B. Geyer, *Die patristische und scholastische Philosophie*, in F. Ueberweg's *Grundriss der Geschichte der Philosophie* (Berlin, 1928; integrally reproduced Basel, 1951), and to M. Grabmann's unfinished *Die Geschichte der scholastische Methode* (Freiburg im Breisgau, 2 vols, 1909, 1911; repr. Darmstadt, 1961). Other general works are those of M. de Wulf, *Histoire de la philosophie médiévale*, 3 vols (Louvain & Paris, 6th edn, 1934–47; Eng. trans. of 6th edn) and F. Copleston,

History of Philosophy, vols II–III (London, 1952–3). See also *The Encyclopedia of Philosophy* (New York & London, 1967). Recent general surveys, with bibliographies, are F. Copleston, *A History of Medieval Philosophy* (London, 1972); *The Cambridge History of Later Greek and Early Medieval Philosophy*, ed. A. H. Armstrong (Cambridge, 1967; rev. edn, 1970); *The Cambridge History of Later Medieval Philosophy from the Rediscovery of Aristotle to the Disintegration of Scholasticism, 1100–1600*, ed. N. Kretzmann, A Kenny, and J. Pinborg (Cambridge, 1982); *A History of Twelfth-Century Western Philosophy*, ed. P. Dronke (Cambridge, 1988); J. Marenbon, *Early Medieval Philosophy (480–1150)* and *Later Medieval Philosophy (1150–1350)* (London, 1983–7); M. Haren, *Medieval Thought. The Western Intellectual Tradition from Antiquity to the Thirteenth Century.* New Studies in Medieval History, ed. M. Keen (London, 1985). See also J. le Goff, *Les intellectuels au Moyen Age* (Paris, rev. edn, 1985). A. C. Crombie, *Augustine to Galileo: the History of Science A.D. 400–1650*, 2 vols (2nd edn, London, 1952). For many individual figures the articles in the *Dictionary of Scientific Biography*, ed. C. C. Gillispie, 16 vols (New York 1970–80), are most useful, as are those in the *Dictionnaire d'histoire et de géographie ecclésiastiques*, ed. A. Baudrillart and others (Paris 1912–   ; in progress) and in *The Oxford Dictionary of the Christian Church*, 2nd edn, by F. L. Cross and E. A. Livingstone (Oxford University Press, 1974).

PLATO AND ARISTOTLE. For brief outlines of Greek philosophy, F. M. Cornford's *Before and After Socrates* (Cambridge, 1932) and W. K. C. Guthrie's *The Greek Philosophers* (London, 1950) may be recommended. The best introductions to Plato were written by Plato himself, whose *Dialogues* have often been published in English translations. Modern general studies are R. M. Hare, *Plato* (Oxford, 1982) as well as a fine essay by I. Murdoch, *The Fire and the Sun. Why Plato banished the Artists* (Oxford, 1977). More specialized but stimulating and influential are I. M. Crombie, *Plato. The Midwife's Apprentice* (London, 1964); R. Bambrough (ed.), *New Essays on Plato and Aristotle* (London & New York, 1965); G. Vlastos (ed.), *Plato* (New York, 1971); and Vlastos, *Platonic Studies* (Princeton, 1981). For Socrates see W. K. C. Guthrie, *Socrates* (Cambridge, 1971) or Guthrie's *History of Greek Philosophy*, vol. 3, part 2 (Cambridge, 1969), as well as *The Philosophy of Socrates. A Collection of Critical Essays*, ed. G. Vlastos (Notre Dame, Indiana, 1980; New York, 1971).

Excellent introductions to Aristotle are by A. E. Taylor, *Aristotle*

(London, 1943); D. J. Allan, *The Philosophy of Aristotle* (Oxford, 1952; 2nd edn, London 1970); G. E. R. Lloyd, *Aristotle: The Growth and Structure of His Thought* (Cambridge, 1968); J. L. Ackrill, *Aristotle the Philosopher* (Oxford, 1981); and J. Barnes, *Aristotle* (Oxford, 1982).

LATER PLATONISM AND NEOPLATONISM. For a short sketch see A. H. Armstrong, *An Introduction to Ancient Philosophy* (London, 1970), and for a detailed survey see P. Merlan, H. Chadwick, A. H. Armstrong and A. C. Lloyd in A. H. Armstrong (ed.), *The Cambridge History of Later Greek and Early Medieval Philosophy* (Cambridge, 1967, rev. edn, 1970). Recent studies which reflect a revival of interest in Neoplatonism are by R. T. Wallis, *Neo-Platonism* (London, 1972) and J. M. Rist, *Plotinus: the Road to Reality* (Cambridge, 1967). The fundamental earlier work of P. Henry, *Plotin et l'Occident* (Louvain, 1934) is not to be overlooked.

AUGUSTINE. Studies of Augustine include H. Chadwick, *Augustine* (Oxford, 1986); E. Gilson, *The Christian Philosophy of St. Augustine* (Eng. trans. L. E. M. Lynch, London, 1961; French version, 2nd edn, Paris, 1943); and H. I. Marrou, *Saint Augustine and His Influence through the Ages* (London, 1957). Historical and biographical accounts include those by P. Brown, *St. Augustine of Hippo: A Biography* (London, 1967) and G. Bonner, *St. Augustine of Hippo: Life and Controversies* (London, 1963). On Augustine and ancient culture H. I. Marrou, *Saint Augustin et la fin de la culture antique* (4th edn, Paris, 1958) is fundamental. The classic article by E. Portalié in J. M. A. Vacant's *Dictionnaire de théologie catholique*, vol. 2 (1903), has been translated by R. J. Bastian into English as *A Guide to the Thought of St. Augustine* (London, 1960). Outstanding too are recent studies by R. A. Markus, *Saeculum: History and Society in the Theology of St. Augustine* (Cambridge, 1970) and 'Marius Victorinus and Augustine' in *The Cambridge History of Later Greek and Early Medieval Philosophy*, ed. A. H. Armstrong (Cambridge, 1967, rev. edn, 1970), pp. 327–419.

English translations of Augustine's works include *The Confessions* by R. S. Pine-Coffin (Harmondsworth, 1961); *City of God* by H. Bettenson (Harmondsworth, 1972); and *On Christian Doctrine* by D. W. Robertson (Indianapolis & New York, 1958). Selected translations are given in *The Library of Christian Classics*, vols 6–8 (London, 1953, 1955).

ANCIENT EDUCATION. H. I. Marrou, *Histoire de l'éducation dans l'antiquité* (Paris, 1948) and, for Roman education, A. Gwynn, *Roman Education from Cicero to Quintilian* (Oxford, 1926).

BOETHIUS AND DIONYSIUS. *The Consolation of Philosophy* trans. V. E. Watts (Harmondsworth, 1969); H. Chadwick, *Boethius: The Consolations of Music, Logic, Theology and Philosophy* (Oxford, 1981); M. Gibson (ed.), *Boethius, His Life, Thought and Influence* (Oxford, 1981).

Perhaps the best beginning to the study of the thought of Dionysius is R. Roques, introduction to *Denys l'Aréopagite. La Hiérarchie céleste*. Sources chrétiennes (Paris, 1970). For his influence see D. E. Luscombe, 'Conceptions of hierarchy before the thirteenth century'. *Miscellanea Mediaevalia*, 12, ed. A. Zimmermann (Berlin & New York, 1979), pp. 1–19.

THE REBIRTH OF THE SCHOOLS. Cassiodorus' *Institutions* were trans. L. W. Jones, *An Introduction to Divine and Human Readings by Cassiodorus Senator* (New York, 1946). For a study see J. J. O'Donnell, *Cassiodorus* (Berkeley, 1979). The *Etymologiae* of Isidore of Seville were ed. W. M. Lindsay (Oxford, 1911). J. Fontaine comprehensively studied Isidore in his book, *Isidore de Séville et la culture classique dans l'Espagne wisigothique*, 2 vols (Paris, 1959). For surveys see M. L. W. Laistner, *Thought and Letters in Western Europe, A.D. 500–900*, 2nd edn (London, 1957); P. Riché, *Education and Culture in the Barbarian West. Sixth through Eighth Centuries*, trans. J. J. Contreni (Columbia, 1976); P. Riché, *Les écoles et l'enseignement dans l'occident chrétien de la fin du Ve siècle au milieu du XIe siècle* (Paris, 1979). Also, L. D. Reynolds and N. G. Wilson, *Scribes and Scholars. A Guide to the Transmission of Greek and Latin Literature* (2nd edn, Oxford, 1974). On monastic culture from the time of St Benedict to that of St Bernard see above all Jean Leclercq, *The Love of Letters and the Desire for God. A Study of Monastic Culture* (Eng. trans., New York, 1974, London, 1978, of the French edn, Paris 1957). John the Scot's masterpiece, *Periphyseon*, was partly edited and translated by I. P. Sheldon-Williams, *Periphyseon I–III* (Dublin, 1968–81). The approach to the study of John's writings, which is not easy, is now eased by the introductions of E. Jeauneau to his editions, *Homélie sur le Prologue de Jean* (Paris, 1969) and *Commentaire sur l'Evangile de Jean* (Paris, 1972). On the technical activities of Carolingian scholars, so important in establishing a tradition of study of the arts by way of gloss and commentary, see J. Marenbon, *From the Circle of Alcuin to the School of Auxerre. Logic, Theology and Philosophy in the Early Middle Ages* (Cambridge, 1981).

THE AWAKENING OF EUROPE. P. Wolff, *The Awakening of Europe* (Harmondsworth, 1968), offers an excellent survey of intellectual developments. On logic a study by A. van de Vyver remains fundamental, 'Les Etapes du développement philosophique du haut moyen âge', *Revue belge de philologie et d'histoire*, 7 (1929), pp. 425-52. M. Gibson, 'The Continuity of Learning circa 850-circa 1050', *Viator*, 6 (1975), 1-13. Further works on the schools are listed below under 'The New Universities'. A valuable study of the great abbey of Monte Cassino is that of H. E. J. Cowdrey, *The Age of Abbot Desiderius. Montecassino, the Papacy and the Normans in the Eleventh and Early Twelfth Centuries* (Oxford, 1983) – see especially pp. 19-26 and the references there cited.

THE REVIVAL OF DIALECTIC. R. W. Southern, *The Making of the Middle Ages* (London, 1953), is an exceptionally perceptive introduction to the period from the late tenth century to *c.* 1200. C. H. Haskins, *The Renaissance of the Twelfth Century* (Cambridge, Mass., 1927), remains stimulating as may be seen in the studies presented and edited by R. L. Benson and G. Constable with Carol D. Lanham, *Renaissance and Renewal in the Twelfth Century* (Cambridge, Mass. & Oxford, 1982). On the eucharistic controversies involving Berengar, Lanfranc and others see J. de Montclos, *Lanfranc et Bérenger. La Controverse eucharistique du XIe siècle* (Louvain, 1971) and G. Macy, *The Theologies of the Eucharist in the Early Scholastic Period* (Oxford, 1984). On Lanfranc see especially M. Gibson, *Lanfranc of Bec* (Oxford, 1978) and on Anselm see R. W. Southern, *St. Anselm and his Biographer*, Cambridge, 1962 – both are very valuable studies. See also G. R. Evans, *Anselm and Talking About God* and *Anselm and a New Generation* (Oxford, 1978, 1980). Anselm's writings were edited by F. S. Schmitt, *Opera omnia*, 6 vols (Edinburgh, 1946-61). Translations of some works exist in English, e.g. S. N. Deane, *Proslogium, Monologium* ... (Chicago, 1903), J. Hopkins and H. Richardson, *Anselm of Canterbury* ... (London, 1974-). Most useful is J. M. Hopkins, *A Companion to the Study of St. Anselm* (Minneapolis, 1972). There is ceaseless debate over Anselm's argument for God's existence; for bibliography see Hopkins or R. R. la Croix, *Proslogion II and III: A Third Interpretation of Anselm's Argument* (Leiden, 1972).

THE QUESTION OF UNIVERSALS AND PETER ABELARD. On the history of the text-books used in the study of logic see L. Minio-Paluello, *Opuscula: The Latin Aristotle* (Amsterdam, 1972). A masterly study of the question of universals and of its wider implications for the study of dialectic and theology is J. Jolivet, *Arts du langage et théologie chez Abélard*. Etudes de philosophie médiévale, 57 (Paris, 1969; 2nd edn, 1982). There is a growing literature on this and on other aspects of logic in the eleventh and twelfth centuries. An important treatise, the *Dialectica* of Master Garland (*fl.* 1080s) has been edited by L. M. de Rijk, *Garlandus Compotista. Dialectica* (Assen, 1959). De Rijk has published many other texts of logic and grammar in *Logica Modernorum*, vol. 1 and vol. 2 (parts 1 and 2) (Assen, 1962–7). For an up-to-date collection of studies see *A History of Twelfth-Century Western Philosophy*, ed. P. Dronke (Cambridge, 1988). R. W. Hunt's articles on *The History of Grammar in the Middle Ages* have been edited by G. L. Bursill-Hall (Amsterdam, 1980).

On Abelard see J. Verger and J. Jolivet, *Bernard-Abélard ou le cloître et l'école*. Douze hommes dans l'histoire de l'église, ed. J. -R. Armogathe (Paris, 1982). For a conspectus of recent studies of Abelard, see D. E. Luscombe, *Peter Abelard* (The Historical Association, London, 1979); on on recent criticism of the *Historia Calamitatum* and the other letters of Abelard and Héloise, *ibid.*, pp. 25–8; and 'The *Letters* of Héloise and Abelard since "Cluny 1972"'' in *Petrus Abaelardus*, ed. R. Thomas and others (Trier, 1980), pp. 19–29. For a recent expression of renewed disbelief in the genuineness of these documents see H. Silvestre, 'L'idylle d'Abélard et Héloïse; la part du roman', *Académie royale de Belgique. Bulletin de la Classe des Lettres . . .*, 5e série, t. LXXI (1985-6), pp. 157–200. See also C. Mews, 'On dating the works of Peter Abelard', *Archives d'histoire doctrinale et littéraire du moyen âge* (1985), pp. 73–134, and P. Dronke, *Abelard and Heloise in Medieval Testimonies*. W. P. Ker Lecture No. 26 (University of Glasgow Press, 1976). Editions and translations of Abelard's works are widely scattered. *The Letters of Abelard and Heloise* have been translated by Betty Radice (Harmondsworth, 1974); *The Ethics of Peter Abelard* have been edited and translated by D. E. Luscombe (Oxford Medieval Texts, 1971), and the *Dialogue between a Jew, a Christian and a Philosopher* has been translated by P. J. Payer (Toronto, 1979). For his influence see D. E. Luscombe, *The School of Peter Abelard* (Cambridge, 1969). Valuable essays are found in *Pierre Abélard. Pierre le Vénérable*. Colloques internationaux du centre national de la recherche scientifique, no. 546 (Paris, 1975); *Peter Abelard*, ed. E. M. Buytaert. Mediaevalia Lovanensia, Series 1, Studia II (Leuven, 1974); *Petrus Abaelardus*, ed. R. Thomas (as above) and *Abélard en son temps*. Actes du colloque international organisé à l'occasion du 9e centenaire de la naissance de Pierre Abélard (14–19 mai, 1979) (Les Belles Lettres, Paris, 1981).

THE 'SCHOOL' OF CHARTRES. R. W. Southern's influential revision, *Medieval Humanism and Other Studies* (Oxford, 1970), pp. 61–85, was answered by N. Haring, 'Chartres and Paris Revisited' in J. R. O'Donnell (ed.), *Essays in Honour of A. C. Pegis* (Toronto, 1974), pp. 268–329, and by P. Dronke, 'New Approaches to the School of Chartres', *Anuario de Estudios Medievales*, 6 (1969), pp. 117–40. Sir Richard Southern replied to his critics in 'The Schools of Paris and the School of Chartres' (in R. L. Benson and G. Constable, eds), *Renaissance and Renewal in the Twelfth Century* (Oxford, 1982), pp. 113–37) and in *Platonism, Scholastic Method and the School of Chartres* (The Stenton Lecture, 1978, University of Reading, 1979). Much of the stimulus prompting Southern arises from a newly broadened understanding of the writings of the 'Chartrains'. Valuable studies of several of these are provided in E. Jeauneau, *Lectio Philosophorum. Recherches sur l'Ecole de Chartres* (Amsterdam, 1973), and in *A History of Twelfth-Century Western Philosophy*, ed. P. Dronke (Cambridge, 1988), where full references to editions and to further studies will be found. Notably fine studies are those of Tullio Gregory, *Anima mundi. La filosofia di Guglielmo di Conches et la Scuola di Chartres* (Florence, 1955) and *Platonismo medievale, Studi e ricerche* (Rome, 1958).

JOHN OF SALISBURY. *The World of John of Salisbury*, ed. M. Wilks, Studies in Church History, Subsidia 3 (Oxford, 1984) now provides the best approach to John, including a full bibliography of recent studies. The *Policraticus* and *Metalogicon* were edited by C. C. J. Webb (Oxford, 1909, 1929); translations by J. Dickinson, *The Statesman's Book of John of Salisbury* (New York, 1927) (*Policraticus*, Books iv–vi, and parts of Books vii–viii); J. B. Pike *Frivolities of Courtiers and Footprints of Philosophers* (Minneapolis, 1938) (*Policraticus*, Books i–iii and parts of Books vii–viii); D. D. McGarry, *Metalogicon* (Berkeley, 1955). *The Historia Pontificalis* was edited and translated by M. Chibnall (Nelson's Medieval Texts, 1956; repr. Oxford Medieval Texts, 1986); the letters were edited and translated by W. J. Millor, H. E. Butler and C. N. L. Brooke (I,

Nelson's Medieval Texts, 1955, repr. Oxford Medieval Texts, 1986: II, Oxford Medieval Texts, 1979).

THE SCHOOL OF ST VICTOR AND ST BERNARD. A good beginning to the thought of Hugh of Saint Victor may be made with J. Taylor's introduction to and translation of *The Didascalicon of Hugh of St Victor*. Records of Civilization. Sources and Studies (New York & London, 1961). Hugh's *De Sacramentis* was translated into English by R. J. Deferrari (Medieval Academy of America Publication, 58, Cambridge, Mass., 1951). Guidance and material on the Victorines (and on many other medieval spiritual writers) is given in J. Leclercq, F. Vandenbroucke and L. Bouyer, *A History of Christian Spirituality*, 2. *The Spirituality of the Middle Ages* (Eng. trans. London, 1968, of the French edn, 1961). St Bernard's works were edited by J. Leclercq, C. H. Talbot and H. M. Rochais in *S. Bernardi Opera*, 8 vols (Rome, 1952–78); a translation, *The Works of Bernard of Clairvaux* (Cistercian Fathers series, Kalamazoo etc., 1970–), is in progress. See J. Verger and J. Jolivet, *Bernard-Abélard ou le cloître et l'école* (Paris, 1982) and E. Gilson, *The Mystical Theology of Saint Bernard* (Eng. trans. London, 1940, of the French edn, Paris, 1934). On Bernard's mastery of language (and much else besides) see J. Leclercq, *Recueil d'études sur saint Bernard et ses écrits*, 3 vols; and G. R. Evans, *The Mind of St. Bernard of Clairvaux* (Oxford, 1983).

THE NEW UNIVERSITIES. As a work of reference the edition by F. M. Powicke and A. B. Emden of H. Rashdall, *The Universities of Europe in the Middle Ages*, 3 vols (Oxford, 1936), has not been replaced; but it should be used in conjunction with more recent surveys which include: L. Thorndike, *University Records and Life in the Middle Ages* (New York, 1944; repr. 1971); A. B. Cobban, *The Medieval Universities, their Development and Organisation* (London, 1975); J. Verger, *Les Universités au Moyen Age* (Paris, 1973); *The Universities in the Late Middle Ages*, ed. J. IJsewijn and J. Paquet. Mediaevalia Lovanensia, Series 1, Studia VI (Leuven, 1978). On the organization of schools prior to the formation of universities see P. Delhaye, 'L'organisation scolaire au douzième siècle', *Traditio*, 5 (1947), pp. 211–68. On 'The Revival of Jurisprudence' see S. Kuttner in Benson and Constable, *Renaissance and Renewal in the Twelfth Century* (1982), pp. 299–323. On the academic study of Roman law in England see R. W. Southern, 'Master Vacarius and the Beginning of an English Academic Tradition' in *Medieval Learning and Literature. Essays presented to R. W. Hunt*, ed. J. J. G. Alexander and M. T.

Gibson (Oxford, 1976), pp. 257–86 and P. Stein, 'Vacarius and the Civil Law', *Church and Government in the Middle Ages. Essays presented to C. R. Cheney*, ed. C. Brooke, D. Luscombe and others (Cambridge, 1976), pp. 119–37. On the beginnings of Oxford University see J. I. Catto (ed.), vol. 1 of *The History of the University of Oxford* (Oxford, 1984). On Paris see S. C. Ferruolo, *The Origins of the University. The Schools of Paris and their Critics, 1100–1215* (Stanford, 1985) – more on the critics than on the schools – and J. Verger, 'A propos de la naissance de l'université de Paris: contexte social, enjeu politique, portée intellectuelle' in *Schulen und Studium im Sozialen Wandel des Hohen und Späten Mittelalters*, ed. J. Fried. Vorträge und Forschungen, 30, ed. Konstanzer Arbeitskreis für mittelalterliche Geschichte (Sigmaringen, 1986), pp. 69–96. On Salerno see P. O. Kristeller, 'The School of Salerno: Its Development and Its Contribution to the History of Learning', *Bulletin of the History of Medicine*, 17 (1945), pp. 138–94 (repr. in *Studies in Renaissance and Letters* (Rome, 1956), pp. 495–551). Kristeller has supported his view that Salerno's significance for the rise of scholastic method and of Aristotelian philosophy has tended to be underestimated in 'Bartholomaeus, Musandinus and Maurus of Salerno and other early commentators of the "Articella", with a tentative list of texts and manuscripts', *Italia Medioevale e Umanistica*, 19 (1976), pp. 57–87. For Montpellier (and we warmly thank C. O'Boyle for this information) see Louis Dulieu, *La Médecine à Montpellier*, 3 vols (Avignon, 1975).

THE REDISCOVERY OF ARISTOTLE. Syntheses of current knowledge are provided by M. T. d'Alverny, 'Translations and Translators' in Benson and Constable, *Renaissance and Renewal in the Twelfth Century* (1982), pp. 421–62 and B. G. Dod, 'Aristoteles latinus' in *The Cambridge History of Later Medieval Philosophy*, ed. N. Kretzmann, A. Kenny and J. Pinborg (Cambridge, 1982), pp. 45–79. Much of this knowledge derives from the brilliant work of L. Minio-Paluello, some of whose articles are collected in his *Opuscula. The Latin Aristotle* (Amsterdam, 1972).

ARABIAN AND JEWISH PHILOSOPHY. A beginning may be made with A. Hyman and J. J. Walsh, *Philosophy in the Middle Ages: the Christian, Islamic and Jewish Traditions* (New York, 1967). The following are important surveys of Islamic thought: Henry Corbin, *Histoire de la philosophie islamique*, vol. 1 (Editions Gallimard, 1964) – goes down to death of Averroës; M. Fakhry, *A History of*

Islamic Philosophy, 2nd edn (London & New York, 1983); W. Montgomery Watt, *Islamic Philosophy and Theology* (Edinburgh, 1962); F. E. Peters, *Aristotle and the Arabs*, (New York & London, 1968). For Jewish thought see Colette Sirat, *A History of Jewish Philosophy in the Middle Ages* (Cambridge & Paris, 1985). An edition of Averroës' *Commentarium Magnum in Aristotelis De Anima Libros* has been published by F. S. Crawford in *Corpus Commentariorum Averrois in Aristotelem*, No. 59 (Cambridge, Mass., 1953). Maimonides' *The Guide of the Perplexed* is translated by S. Pines (Chicago, 1963).

THE PHILOSOPHICAL REVOLUTION OF THE THIRTEENTH CENTURY. Since Knowles takes issue with some of van Steenberghen's conclusions it is all the more important to note van Steenberghen's continuing publications. They include *La Philosophie au XIIIe siècle* (Louvain & Paris, 1966; *Aristotle in the West. The Origins of Latin Aristotelianism*, 2nd edn (Louvain, 1970); *Introduction à l'Etude de la Philosophie Médiévale*. Philosophes médiévaux, 18 (Louvain & Paris, 1974); *La Bibliothèque du Philosophe Médiéviste*. Philosophes médiévaux, 19 (Louvain & Paris, 1974); *Maître Siger de Brabant*. Philosophes médiévaux, 21 (Louvain & Paris, 1977); and *Thomas Aquinas and Radical Aristotelianism* (Washington, DC, 1980). Van Steenberghen's views began to be formed and to be expressed in a series of books and other publications in the 1940s and 1950s.

ST BONAVENTURE. Bonaventure's *Opera omnia* were published in 10 vols at Quaracchi in Florence between 1882 and 1902. E. Longpré's article appeared in the *Dictionnaire d'histoire et de géographie ecclésiastiques*, 9 (1937), cols 741–88. The 1945 French edition of E. Gilson, *La Philosophie de saint Bonaventure*, appeared in an English translation, *The Philosophy of St Bonaventure* (New Jersey, 1965). J. G. Bougerol, *Introduction to the Works of Bonaventure* (Eng. trans., New Jersey, 1964) and J. F. Quinn, *The Historical Constitution of St Bonaventure's Philosophy* (Toronto, 1973) are also helpful.

ALBERT THE GREAT. Albert's *Opera omnia*, ed. A. Borgnet, 38 vols (Paris, 1890-9) are being re-edited by B. Geyer and others (Münster, 1951–   ). In the absence of a satisfactory single study of Albert's work see two collections of essays by various scholars: J. A. Weisheipl (ed.), *Albertus Magnus and the Sciences. Commemorative Essays 1980*

(Toronto, 1980) and A. Zimmermann (ed.), *Albert der Grosse, seine Zeit, sein Werk, seine Wirkung*. Miscellanea Mediaevalia, 14 (Berlin & New York, 1981).

ST THOMAS. The principal modern edition of Aquinas' works is the Leonine edition which is still in progress, *Opera omnia* (Rome, 1882–). The *Summa theologiae* has recently been published by the English Blackfriars in 60 vols (London, 1964–76) each with the Latin text and a facing English translation. E. Gilson, *The Christian Philosophy of St Thomas Aquinas* (New York, 1956), is outstanding on a subject which continues to inspire excellent studies including M. D. Chenu, *Towards Understanding St Thomas* (Chicago, 1964); J. Pieper, *Guide to Thomas Aquinas* (New York, 1962); and – this more useful as a work of reference than the foregoing – J. A. Weisheipl, *Friar Thomas d'Aquino, His Life, Thought and Work* (New York, 1974). On Aquinas as a philosopher see A. Kenny, *Aquinas* (Oxford, 1979).

SIGER OF BRABANT. F. van Steenberghen, *Maître Siger de Brabant*. Philosophes médiévaux, 21 (Louvain & Paris, 1977). Van Steenberghen lists in a *Table bibliographique* the titles of the earlier studies by Renan, Hauréau, Mandonnet, Baeumker and Grabmann to which Knowles alludes above on page 245. R. Hissette, *Enquête sur les 219 Articles Condamnés à Paris le 7 mars 1277*. Philosophes médiévaux, 22 (Louvain & Paris, 1977). F. van Steenberghen, *Thomas Aquinas and Radical Aristotelianism* (Washington, DC, 1980).

BOETHIUS OF DACIA. G. Fioravanti, 'Scientia, fides, theologia in Boezio di Dacia', *Atti della Accademia delle scienze di Torino. Classe di scienze morale* (1969–70), pp. 525–632; J. Pinborg, 'Zur Philosophie des Boethius de Dacia. Ein Ueberblick', *Studia Mediewistyczne*, 15 (1974), pp. 165–85.

THIRTEENTH-CENTURY ENGLAND. For Oxford university see *The History of the University of Oxford*, 1, ed. J. I. Catto (Oxford, 1984). For Robert Grosseteste see D. A. Callus (ed.), *Robert Grosseteste* (Oxford, 1953); J. McEvoy, *The Philosophy of Robert Grosseteste* (Oxford, 1982); and R. W. Southern, *Robert Grosseteste* (Oxford, 1986). D. A. Callus, 'The Introduction of Aristotelian Learning to Oxford', *Proceedings of the British Academy*, 29 (1943), pp. 229–81, remains valuable. On Bacon see S. C. Easton, *Roger Bacon and his*

Search for a Universal Science (Oxford, 1952) and D. C. Lindberg, *Roger Bacon's Philosophy of Nature* (Oxford, 1983).

THE AFTERMATH OF ARISTOTLE. R. Hissette, *Enquête sur les 219 Articles Condamnés à Paris le 7 mars 1277*. Philosophes médiévaux, 22 (Louvain & Paris, 1977). J. F. Wippel, 'The Condemnations of 1270 and 1277 at Paris', *Journal of Medieval and Renaissance Studies*, 7 (1977), pp. 169–210. D. A. Callus, 'The Condemnation of St Thomas at Oxford', The Aquinas Society of London, Aquinas Paper no. 5 (London, 1955).

HENRY OF GHENT AND DUNS SCOTUS. Henry of Ghent's *Opera omnia* are currently being edited by R. Macken and others (Leiden, 1979–   ); Duns Scotus' *Opera omnia* are being edited by C. Balić and others (Vatican 1950–   ). E. Gilson, *Jean Duns Scot* (Paris, 1952).

THE BREAKDOWN OF THE SYNTHESIS. Giles of Rome's philosophical works are currently being edited by F. del Punta and others at Pisa. For the writings of Eckhart the standard edition is the Stuttgart edition (1936–   ) with both Latin and German writings. There exist anthologies with English translations e.g., *Selected Treatises and Sermons . . .*, trans. J. M. Clark and J. V. Skinner (London, 1958); *Sermons and Treatises*, trans. M. O'C. Walshe, 2 vols (1979; repr. Shaftesbury, 1987). See also D. Knowles, *The English Mystical Tradition* (London, 1961).

WILLIAM OF OCKHAM. Ockham's *Opera philosophica et theologica* are currently being edited by G. Gál and others (Franciscan Institute, St Bonaventure's, New York, 1967–   ). L. Baudry, *Guillaume d'Occam: Sa vie, ses œuvres, ses idées sociales et politiques* (Paris, 1949). G. Leff, *William of Ockham: The Metamorphosis of Scholastic Discourse* (Manchester, 1975). J. Miethke, *Ockhams Weg zur Sozialphilosophie* (Berlin, 1969). W. J. Courtenay, *Adam Wodeham* (Leiden, 1978).

NOMINALISM AND REALISM. P. Vignaux, *Nominalisme au xive siècle* (Montreal, 1948); P. Vignaux, *Justification et prédestination au xive siècle* (Paris, 1934); G. Leff, *Bradwardine and the Pelagians* (Cambridge, 1957); G. Leff, *Gregory of Rimini* (Manchester, 1961); H. A. Oberman, *The Harvest of Medieval Theology: Gabriel Biel and Late Medieval Nominalism* (Cambridge, Mass., 1967); A. Kenny, *Wyclif* (Oxford, 1985) and A. Kenny (ed.), *Wyclif in his Times*

(Oxford, 1986). Wyclif's treatise on Universals has been edited by I. J. Mueller and translated by A. Kenny (Oxford, 1985). *From Ockham to Wyclif: Oxford Scholarship in the Fourteenth Century*, ed. A. Hudson and M. Wilks. Studies in Church History. Subsidia, 5 (Oxford & New York, 1987). E. D. Sylla, 'The Oxford Calculators' and J. E. Murdoch, 'Infinity and Continuity' in *The Cambridge History of Later Medieval Philosophy*, pp. 540-63 and 564-91. J. A. Weisheipl, 'Ockham and Some Mertonians', *Mediaeval Studies*, 30 (1968), pp. 163-213.

THE HISTORY OF THE STUDY OF MEDIEVAL THOUGHT. One of the merits of this book is Knowles' fine sense of the evolution of modern scholarship concerning medieval thought. In *History*, vol. LIV (February, 1969), pp. 1-12, Knowles published a perceptive and illuminating study of two of the most remarkable of the founding fathers of the critical study of medieval scholasticism: Heinrich Seuse Denifle (1844-1905) and Franz Ehrle (1845-1934).

Index

The figures in bold type refer to the principal passages in which a person or topic is discussed. Medieval persons will be found under their Christian names: e.g. William of Ockham. Peter *Abelard* and John *Duns* Scotus are exceptions.